Desire

'Provides a valuable overview of the history of sexuality in Europe since classical antiquity, synthesising as it does a mass of studies of specific regions and periods which have appeared during the past two decades.' Lesley Hall, *Wellcome Library, UK*

Desire: A History of European Sexuality is a survey of sexuality in Europe from the Greeks to the present. The book traces two concepts of sexual desire that have competed throughout European history: desire as dangerous, polluting, and disorderly, and desire as creative, transcendent, even revolutionary. Following these changing attitudes through the major turning points of European history, Anna Clark concludes by demonstrating that western European sexual culture is quite distinct from many other cultures, and asks whether the vision of sexual desire as revolutionary, even transcendent, has faded in the modern secular era.

While *Desire* builds on the work of dozens of historians, it also takes a fresh approach. Explaining how authorities tried to manage sexual desire and sometimes failed, the book introduces the concept of "twilight moments" to describe activities seen as shameful or dishonorable, but which were tolerated when concealed by shadows. Other topics addressed include:

- Sex in Greece and Rome
- Divine desire in Judaism and early Christianity
- New attitudes toward sexuality in the seventeenth and eighteenth centuries
- Victorian twilights.

Written in a lively and engaging style, this new survey contains many fascinating anecdotes, and draws on a rich array of sources including poetry, novels, pornography, and film as well as court records, autobiographies and personal letters. *Desire* integrates the history of heterosexuality with same-sex desire, focuses on the emotions of love as well as the passions of lust, and explores the politics of sex as well as personal experiences.

Anna Clark is the author of *Women's Silence, Men's Violence: Sexual Assault in England, 1770–1845* (1987), *The Struggle for the Breeches: Gender and the Making of the British Working Class* (1995), and *Scandal: The Sexual Politics of the British Constitution* (2003). She is a professor at the University of Minnesota, USA.

This book is dedicated to Anne Carter

Desire

A History of European Sexuality

Anna Clark

Routledge
Taylor & Francis Group

NEW YORK AND LONDON

First published 2008
by Routledge
711 Third Avenue, New York, NY 10017

Simultaneously published in UK
by Routledge
2 Park Square, Milton Park, Abingdon, Oxon OX14 4RN

Routledge is an imprint of the Taylor & Francis Group, an informa business

© 2008 Anna Clark

Typeset in Galliard by
Bookcraft Ltd, Stroud, Gloucestershire

Printed and bound in Great Britain by
CPI Antony Rowe, Chippenham, Wiltshire

British Library Cataloguing in Publication Data
A catalogue record for this book is available from the British Library

Library of Congress Cataloging in Publication Data
Clark, Anna.
Desire : a history of European sexuality / Anna Clark.
    p. cm.
    Includes bibliographical references. 1. Sex—Europe—History.
    2. Sex customs—Europe—History. 3. Desire—Social aspects.
    I. Title.
HQ18.E8C53 2008   306.77094—dc22

ISBN10: 0-415-77517-5 (hbk)
ISBN10: 0-415-77518-3 (pbk)

ISBN13: 978-0-415-77517-5(hbk)
ISBN13: 978-0-415-77518-2 (pbk)

Contents

Illustrations

Acknowledgments

First, I would like to express my thanks to all the authors whose books and articles I drew upon to write this book. Edward Ross Dickinson and Gail Bederman were particularly helpful in early discussions of the theme of sexual radicalism.

My family, friends, colleagues, and especially many colleagues at the University of Minnesota and elsewhere have contributed their expertise by reading and commenting on chapters, although responsibility for errors, of course, remains my own. Kevin Murphy read many chapters and was especially helpful for the introduction and the modern period. My parents, Sylvia Clark and David Clark, each also contributed their expertise on early Christianity. Christopher Nappa and Nita Krevans helped me revise the chapter on Greece and Rome with their knowledge of the ancient world. F.R.P. Akehurst illuminated the troubadours. Ruth Mazo Karras, an expert on medieval society, vetted the relevant chapters as well as helping me think through the introduction. Sarah Chambers, Jeani O'Brien, and Pat McNamara read and commented on the chapter on the age of exploration. Juliette Cherbuliez contributed her insight to the chapter on the Enlightenment. M.J. Maynes helped me rethink the nineteenth-century chapters. Eric Weitz made helpful suggestions for the interwar chapters. Laura Doan and Alison Oram read some of the modern chapters and made many insightful comments. My writing group, Lisa Disch, Jeani O'Brien, Kirsten Fischer, Gabriella Tsuritami, Jennifer Pierce, and Anne Carter, patiently helped me reshape many chapters. Members of the Comparative Women's History Workshop at the University of Minnesota also made useful comments, as did audiences at the University of Iowa and the University of Michigan. Thanks to Wendy Goldman and Elizabeth Wood for emailed help on Russian eugenics. I'm also grateful to the readers of this manuscript, especially Lesley Hall for her extensive and specific corrections, and to the anonymous readers of earlier rough drafts of the book, especially those with expertise in premodern history.

The College of Liberal Arts at the University of Minnesota and the anonymous donors of the Samuel Russell Chair in the Humanities greatly facilitated the research for this book by enabling me to hire research assistants. Megan Byrnes and Leslie Schumacher patiently tracked down hundreds of books, articles, and illustrations. Jennifer Illuzzi and Michelle Los enthusiastically translated German sources. My students at the University of Minnesota also helped shape the book as they listened to my lectures and participated in seminars, and Isaiah Jones was particularly helpful in commenting on chapters. Thanks to Rachel Neiwert for compiling the index. Also my appreciation to Ginny Gilmore and Matthew Brown for copy-editing and producing the book.

At Routledge, Vicky Peters was encouraging about the project, Eve Setch took over and provided much support and useful suggestions for rewriting, Emma Langley started the administrative process and Elizabeth Clifford handled illustrations, permissions, and production with aplomb.

Above all, Anne Carter copy-edited the entire manuscript but also helped me think through the ideas and shape of the chapters. Her patience, love, emotional support, and sense of humor got me through the writing process, as always.

Chapter 1

Introduction

Sexuality and the problem of western civilization

> If man were deprived of sexual distinction and the nobler enjoyments arising
> therefrom, all poetry and probably all moral tendencies would be eliminated
> from his life … [but] love unbridled is a volcano that burns down and lays waste
> all around it; it is an abyss that devours all – honor, substance, and health.
>
> Richard Krafft-Ebing, 1886[1]

This book will trace the competing concepts of sexual desire that run as a thread
through European history: sexual desire as polluting and dangerous, and sexual
desire as creative, transcendent, and transformative. The first has often been identified with Christianity. Since its inception, Christianity has regarded sexual desire
with deep ambivalence. Early Christians valued celibacy as superior to marriage
and feared that sexual desire would distract the believer from God. Over the
centuries, Christians eventually changed their attitudes to celebrate marital sex.
But the fear of sex as polluting has persisted.

Yet Christianity has valued desire in its wider forms of marital love and divine
love. Furthermore, both ancient Greek philosophers and medieval Christian
mystics used the language of erotic love to describe the ascent from earthly love to
spiritual love. The Greek philosopher Plato advised his students to desire a handsome youth as the first step on the path to knowledge. With discipline, they could
transcend the sexual desire for fleshly beauty to reach a higher spiritual desire for
the abstract ideal of truth. Medieval woman mystics rejected the love of man, but
they yearned for an ecstatic fusion with God.[2]

Other radicals, rebels, philosophers, and mystics have insisted that sexual desire
must be anchored in the body to be a source of creativity and transcendence. This
idea flowed into a recurrent underground tradition, usually secret and censored,
but sometimes emerging into the center of western intellectual traditions. Renegade Enlightenment philosophers claimed that women could learn to rely on the
evidence of their senses rather than authorities by exploring the body and its pleasures.[3] Bolshevik revolutionary Alexandra Kollontai envisioned sexual desire as the
"Winged Eros" that would energize people to transform society.[4]

This book, intended for students and the general reader, places sexuality in the
long sweep of western civilization. Western civilization has usually concentrated

on European history, with some attention to the United States, assuming a common culture. Indeed, Americans and Europeans share an inheritance in terms of the impact of Christian ideas about sexuality on the culture, but today Europeans understand sexuality in ways quite different than the dominant culture in the United States, and this book will concentrate on European history. The idea of "western civilization," furthermore, has come under attack by historians in recent years. Western civilization has been imagined as the triumph of rational values over barbarism and ignorance, but historians now see a more complicated story. Today, the history of western civilization is seen as dominated by conquest and imperialism. In the Middle Ages, Christian Spaniards expelled Jews and Muslims from Spain; later, Europeans invaded and colonized other lands. As we shall see, sexuality often becomes a flashpoint in these clashes of culture. During times of social crisis, such as medieval plagues or nationalist conflicts, anxiety about sexual disorder tended to erupt, and sex was seen as violating social boundaries. But during times when people began to think in new ways, such as the Enlightenment or the Russian Revolution, the idea of sexual desire as creative and transcendent also emerged.

But this is not a story of the victory of sexual liberation. Those who proclaimed that sexual desire was energizing and transcendent were not just freeing up natural sexuality, nor did they always want to free the oppressed. Some Nazis, for instance, celebrated aggressive sexual desire as creative. When radicals demanded sexual freedom, they usually wanted to manage and control sex in their own way; for instance Alexandra Kollontai wished to produce better workers for the Soviet Union. Radical calls for non-monogamy have been empowering for many women, but some other women have found non-monogamy to be humiliating and painful.

Most influentially, the French theorist Michel Foucault refuted the idea that the Victorians repressed sexuality and that the twentieth century liberated it.[5] When late nineteenth-century moralists fulminated about sexual pollution, he argued, they were not repressing sexuality. Instead, they were talking about it more and more. For instance, psychiatric doctors such as Richard Krafft-Ebing, with whose quote we began the chapter, published reams of work on sex, including a huge tome called *Psychopathia Sexualis* (1886).

Both those who feared sexual desire as polluting and disorderly, and those who celebrated it as liberating and transcendent, often assumed that sexual desire itself is a powerful, natural force, like rushing water, which must be contained lest it overflow and wreak havoc. Today, we are less likely to see sex as so powerful, but it is still assumed that sexual desire is based in biology, in hormones, and gender identity. A recent set of articles in the *New York Times* portrayed sexual desire in entirely physiological terms, looking at the mechanism of arousal as it differed in men and women, and how it could be stimulated pharmaceutically.[6] Today, people often speak of their "sexuality," as part of their personality – usually as heterosexual or homosexual. They often believe that humans are born with inherent attraction to someone of the opposite – or the same – sex, which leads to certain kinds of relationships, sex acts, and identities.

Sexuality is seen as something that is expressed or denied. But Foucault, as well as historians, sociologists, feminists, and queer theorists, has been demonstrating over the past 40 years that sexuality is not, in fact, such a natural force. Instead, sexual desire and behavior are constructed.

I define sexuality in its widest sense as the desires, relationships, acts, and identities concerned with sexual behavior. Desires, relationships, acts, and identities do not automatically flow from one to another; they must be considered separately, and they are often constructed separately. What we call sexual desire is actually made up of so many complicated emotions, not just the desire for genital contact: sexual desire can include the need for the sensuous touch of skin, for affection or passion, domination or humiliation, and all these desires can be fulfilled in many different ways. The emotions of sexual desire – love, lust, attraction – may be directed toward any object, not just men for women and vice versa, but also men for men or women for women, or for a fetish, such as shoes. Desire can even be conceived of as a form of emotional energy that is not necessarily focused on an object. While desire is often experienced through the body, it is created and stimulated through the mind and the imagination, through cultural representations.

In different eras, cultures have explained sexual desire in changing ways: for the Greeks, it was a force of nature, for the early Christians, a temptation of the devil, for Darwinian scientists, a biological urge to procreate and further evolution. Understandings of female bodies also shifted over the centuries. For instance, during the early modern period, many medical and popular sex manuals described the clitoris as the seat of female pleasure, and female orgasm as necessary for conception. But clerics and common people feared that women's strong sexual desires could be dangerous. By the late eighteenth and early nineteenth century, as Thomas Laqueur has shown, doctors discovered that the female orgasm was *not* necessary for conception, and the clitoris seemed to disappear from texts.[7] By the 1940s, some marriage counselors instructed wives that they should have vaginal, not clitoral orgasms, despite the anatomical evidence that the clitoris was the cause of female pleasure.[8]

The repertoire of more unusual sexual acts – and their meanings – has expanded and shrunk and expanded over the centuries. The ancient Romans developed an elaborate vocabulary differentiating between the penetrator and penetratee of different orifices; for instance, a man who liked to insert his penis into an anus was a *pedicator*.[9] But with Christianity, anal sex, whether committed on a man or woman, became a terrible sin. Today, sexologists hypothesize that some European heterosexual young people are increasingly willing to engage in anal sex because they are exposed to pornography.[10]

Learning about sex is not the same as following an instruction manual to assemble furniture – put tab A in slot B. As theorist Judith Butler has written, sexuality "can exceed regulation, take on new forms in response to regulation, even turn around and make it sexy.... This is not the same as saying that sexuality is, by nature, free and wild. On the contrary, it emerges precisely as an improvisational possibility within a field of constraints."[11]

In fact, most representations of sexual desire in western culture depict what people are *not* supposed to do – commit adultery – think of Lancelot and Guinevere, Tristan and Isolde. Such representations used the mode of fantasy to depict forbidden desires in highly alluring terms, and fantasy, of course, does not follow the logic of prescription. Such fantasies could present falling in love as natural and inescapable, felt by the body – the sensations of trembling, sleeplessness and anxiety. But these seemingly natural emotions were represented in highly stylized language which stemmed from an ancient literary construction. For instance, the sixth-century BCE poet Sappho wrote:

> my tongue is struck silent, a delicate fire
> suddenly races underneath my skin,
> my eyes see nothing, my ears whistle like
> the whirling of a top
> … and sweat pours down me and a trembling creeps over
> my whole body …[12]

Sappho was expressing what she felt as she saw her lover, another woman, sitting as a bride beside her new husband. However unconventional, the beauty of her lyrics inspired poets centuries later. When he fell in love with Mme de Houdetot, a married woman, eighteenth-century philosopher Jean-Jacques Rousseau declared: "I will not describe the agitation, the tremblings, the palpitations, the convulsive movements, or the faintings of the heart which I continually experienced." But he could only experience this emotion after he basically invented romantic love for his era in his novel *Julie, or the New Heloise*.[13]

We assume that sexual or romantic desire must have a physical expression. Historians sometimes try to discover whether individuals in the past "really" had sexual relationships or identities, for instance when Victorian married women wrote that they wanted to kiss and hold each other all night. Rather than investigate the "truth" of what these women actually did, it would be more productive to explore how people articulated their desires. Today, we often assume that people find their most intense, passionate relationships in sexual love that must have a genital expression. However, when romantic love and marriage were not so closely linked in the past, the most emotionally intense relationships may have been those of friendship or kinship. People often used what we think of as romantic language to express the emotions of intense friendship with a person of the same sex; these feelings could be seen as erotic, even if they were not genitally-based. What is interesting is that erotic language conveyed powerful emotions.

This book will look at the everyday regulation of sex as well as changing understandings of desire. Traditionally, parents, schools, religious institutions, and governments instructed young people to desire sex only in marriage. By celebrating marriage, they aimed to stimulate sexual desire within it. It was not grand passion, but the sexual economy which shaped most relationships in the past. The sexual economy includes the structures that determined who could afford to have sexual relationships, who could marry, and who had to exchange sexual services for survival. Marriage has usually been seen as the only legitimate sexual relationship, but throughout much of western history sexual desire has not been the main motivation for marriage. Of course, a young man and woman might fall in love, but their families would only allow the marriage if they were from the same class and had a farm or business, or a dowry. Love and companionship grew after marriage. People primarily married to establish a household as an economic unit, to produce children to work and to inherit the family's wealth, and to solidify alliances between families. They were obsessed with the fertility of people, crops and animals. In the eighteenth century, the expectation grew that romantic love should normally precede marriage, but young men still needed to be able to afford to marry.

Communities regulated marriage to preserve their boundaries. For instance, aristocratic elites did not want their dynasties "contaminated" by common blood. In colonial empires, authorities often legally forbade interracial sex and marriage to preserve the fiction of the purity of the "white race" and the credibility of colonial domination, as Ann Stoler writes.[14] Above all, institutions regulated sexual desires and behaviors to control the boundaries of gender. Following a double standard, families closely controlled daughters' and wives' sexuality to ensure that their property went to legitimate heirs, but they allowed husbands and sons to sow their wild oats. A man's sexual submission to another man was forbidden in part because it undermined the idea that men must always be dominant.

Different authorities and communities regulated sexual relationships in distinct ways, even in the same culture or era. Sexual mores sometimes differed dramatically by class and rank, between city and country, between different subcultures. For instance, medieval peasants often became pregnant after betrothal but before marriage.

In the first volume of his *History of Sexuality*, Foucault argued that the regulation of sex changed significantly from the premodern to the modern era. He asserted that in the premodern period, sodomy was seen as an act, not an identity. Authorities punished the act of sodomy, and they believed that men committed sodomy because they were led astray by evil desires which could infect anyone, not because they had a specific personality type. Only in the modern era did homosexuality become an identity, asserted Foucault, when psychologists and sexologists invented the idea of the homosexual. Psychiatrists, sexologists, criminologists, and other professionals began to use sexuality to tell people who they are, to explore their innermost selves. Modern regulation does not work just by telling people what not to do: instead, it shapes people's understanding of themselves through these discourses, and stimulates their desires.[15] By separating out acts from identities, Foucault made a great theoretical breakthrough in how we regard sexuality.

In terms of chronology, Foucault is often interpreted as insisting that sexual identities, especially same-sex desires, were fluid in the past, and that they became more rigid in the present. Foucault's own arguments, especially in his later works, were much more subtle. It is important to point out that premodern societies *did* have a concept of sexual identities, not just acts, as scholars David Halperin and Ruth Mazo Karras have demonstrated.[16] After all, the celibate priest, the procreative married couple, the prostitute, or the virgin spinster all had social identities defined by their sexual behavior or lack thereof. To be sure, in the premodern period identities generally derived more from external behavior and relationships with others than from the innermost essential self or personality. For instance, if an ancient Greek man dreamed that he had sex with a rich man, he did not wake up and think, "Ye gods, I'm a homosexual!" Instead, he might consult a dream book that told him he would soon acquire new possessions, since he dreamed of a social interaction with a rich man.[17] Dreams, therefore, did not reveal his innermost desires. However, if he took the passive, subordinate role in sex with another man, then he would acquire the stigmatized social identity of the *cineadus*, a man who was scorned as an effeminate male prostitute. In the Middle Ages, the prostitute may have been seen as a sinner who needed the help of God to defeat the evil desires which tormented her, but mostly she followed a recognized social role, wearing distinctive clothing, such as a yellow badge, to signify her profession in the municipal brothel. The notion of the "sodomite" also emerged in the early Middle Ages, contrary to Foucault's hypothesis.[18] This was not the same as the modern homosexual or the ancient *cineadus*, but the sodomite was categorized as a type of person, not just as someone who committed certain acts. The sodomite was regarded as beyond the boundaries of society – he was the abject, to be expelled by execution. The prostitute, however, was often regarded as a social necessity.

Relationships of inequality structured who had to perform sexual services. The women who ended up in medieval brothels often had few opportunities to make a living, and lacked friends or family to help. But men could fall victim to social inequality as well. For instance, male Roman slaves had to submit sexually to their masters. Rape is another form of sexual behavior that stems from relationships of inequality, since historically it has only been punished when a man's property and honor were at stake.[19]

Nonetheless, not all people who engaged in forbidden or unknown sexual acts became stigmatized with deviant identities. Men might frequent prostitutes, women sell sex, wives have affairs, husbands solicit rent boys.[20] To understand this phenomenon better, I will introduce the metaphor of "twilight moments" to describe those sexual activities or desires which people are not supposed to engage in, but they do.[21] The twilight fades into deepest darkness, and then the light returns at dawn, so twilight moments were those acts which people committed, or desires they felt, which could be temporary; they returned to their everyday lives, and evaded a stigmatized identity as deviant. Twilight moments were not "tolerated," in the modern sense of the word, which often implies openness and acknowledgment. Toleration implies a grudging acceptance, a recognition of unconventional acts and relationships.[22] Instead, regarding acts and desires as twilight moments was another form of regulation; these acts and desires were hidden because they were regarded as shameful and embarrassing. People who engaged in twilight moments may not have been burnt at the stake or exiled, or even labeled as deviant, but their neighbors gossiped about them or shunned them as not quite right, as promiscuous, odd, mysterious, or weird. However, after public repentance they could be returned to the fold.

Twilight moments include sexual acts and relationships which take place without ever being acknowledged or named – as if barely perceived in the murky twilight.[23] Desire between women has often occurred as twilight moments, perceived as if behind a veil. In the early modern period, passionate friendships between women were usually not seen as sexual and did not threaten traditional marriage. Chaste friendships might have been an "open secret," or an "impossible love," euphemisms which enabled women to carry out their desires without being fully recognized.[24]

Unconventional sexual behaviors or desires did not inevitably destabilize the conventional order. Interracial sex and prostitution could be seen as the shadow side of power, produced by structures of domination yet unacknowledged, an open secret which was not to be mentioned. When modern colonial empires prohibited interracial sex, white men still raped native women, visited them as prostitutes, and took them as concubines.

The double standard shaped moral judgments. Respectable Victorian middle-class men might be embarrassed if their friends discovered they visited prostitutes, secretly read pornography, or discreetly kept a native concubine, but they would still keep their position in society. If a respectable Victorian woman had sex outside of marriage, her family would reject her. But different cultures and classes would have different standards: a Victorian working-class family might scold an unmarried daughter, but not shun her.

Both prescriptive ideals and taboos ascribe fixed, permanent identities, either as the high status of a spouse or the denigrated shame of a deviant. Marriage was valued because sex created progeny, which ensured the continuity of the family line through time. Conversely, abject or marginalized identities – such as sodomite or prostitute – removed people from this cycle and permanently stigmatized them. But twilight moments were temporary, not creating a permanent identity, family, or subculture, which made them less threatening, yet still disturbing. For instance, an indigenous woman who was a concubine to a European man did not have the right to inherit his property, to take his name, or to pass them on to her children; she was cut off from the timeline of legitimate procreation. Thus the fiction of racial purity could be preserved.

At certain historical moments, twilight moments could become deviant identities. For instance, in fourteenth-century Florence, some young men commonly had sex with other men, although they would grow up to marry women. They were not "tolerated" – in fact the city set up an "Office of the Night" to prosecute them, but punishments were light. But when the plague broke, preachers and politicians would suddenly stigmatize men who had sex with men as sodomites and blame them for society's woes.[25]

Sources

How do we know about sexual desires, relationships, acts, and identities? A history of sexuality must take into account the lies, open secrets, and half-truths which pervade sexual desires and behavior. Very often, historians of sexuality have to read between the lines for obscure hints. However, it is not a matter of seeing through the murky twilight of the past to find the "truth" about sex; the hints, evasions, hidden messages, and ambiguity are precisely the most interesting aspects of sexuality.

Heterosexual intercourse often produces offspring, so records of births can give us some indication of sexual activity. Sometimes institutions such as church courts or foundling hospitals interviewed unmarried mothers, who told stories about how they got pregnant. Sex between men was often illegal, so arrests for sodomy produced court records, and even the testimony of witnesses, which reveals popular attitudes. Of course, we do not know whether such accounts revealed what actually happened between two men, or how a woman met the father of her child. The use of birth control also complicates these statistics, for people tried to control fertility through techniques such as withdrawal and abortion even before modern contraception was invented. We can count the number of prosecutions for sodomy, but we do not know if an increase meant that the police were more vigorous in their surveillance or whether behavior changed. But by analyzing the questions asked, and the patterns of response, historians can discern whether answers stem from an interviewer's bias, fit into a stereotype, or reveal a consistent pattern of behavior.

Foucault's *History of Sexuality* departed from histories of sexuality that concentrated on behavior. Instead, Foucault focused on "discourses," by which he usually meant the writings of clerics, doctors, psychiatrists and lawyers, who tried to produce a certain kind of knowledge about sex, defining and indeed inventing identities. Sexologists, psychiatrists, lawyers, and doctors all published many tracts about sex during the nineteenth century, and powerfully shaped ideas of sexual identities. They created a discourse that also influenced people who were not professionals – their understanding of sex pervaded society. But Foucault's theory does not really enable us to understand the full power dynamics of sexual language – who can speak it, when, and with what authority. In the nineteenth century, doctors of medical jurisprudence could pronounce in courtrooms that it was impossible to rape a child, and use explicit anatomical language; but if a woman testified using explicit words about sexual assault, her own knowledge would taint her reputation. Furthermore, in assessing the power of sexual discourses, we need to ask how widely discourses were circulated, who could read them, how much was censored.

Sexual information could be conveyed in a veiled fashion. For instance, popular sex manuals in the early modern period told women how to use herbal potions to solve the problem of blocked menstruation, which was supposed to cause terrible health problems. They warned women that such herbal potions could cause abortion, and should not be used by the pregnant. But a hidden message was that women could take these potions to get rid of an unwanted pregnancy.[26]

Erotica, pornography, and sexual humor are other genres of hidden sexual representations that often conveyed double messages. Although pornography certainly may have shaped behavior, since its primary purpose is to stimulate sexual desire and pleasure, pornography is also composed of fantasies, in which people could imagine all sorts of sexual activities in which they might never engage in real life. A character in a pornographic story might titillate the reader by describing in lurid detail a lusty priest seducing an amorous wife, or a sodomite seducing a youth, but then the character would disavow this pleasure by denouncing their actions as unnatural.

Religion

Religion is one of the most important ways in which sexuality is regulated. First, religious institutions establish rules for what people should and should not do. Foucault argued that by forbidding certain acts and desires, religious and other authorities could actually incite them. In the Middle Ages, the Church admonished its believers to confess their sexual sins to a priest, who would ask them very detailed questions about possible sex acts they might have committed. By asking these questions, priests might have stimulated believers to commit acts they had not heard of before, thus "constructing" their sexual desires, as Foucault suggests. But the priests might have learned about sex from their parishioners as well. A renegade priest from the sixteenth century claimed that friars "invented confession, so that they could investigate and discover whether there was any pleasure unknown to them that could be found among the laity."[27] Neighbors, families, and communities may have been just as or more important than religious authorities in shaping people's sexual behavior.[28]

Yet second, sexuality also plays an important role when people ask a higher power to intercede in their lives – to make something happen, through prayer or spells. In pre-Christian religions, such as the Greek or Roman cults, sexual images symbolized fertility, and believers used them to pray to the gods to ensure the fertility of humans, fields, and livestock. In Christianity, virginity was seen to have great power – the power of suppressed sexual desire. To grant human wishes, gods and goddesses had to be seen both as being like ordinary humans, and as more powerful than them – as anomalies. The Virgin Mary is an example of a sexual anomaly, an impossibility, for she was supposed to be a virgin and a mother.[29]

Third, sexual desire often becomes a metaphor for mystical experiences. Mystics used images of human love to express love for God – for example, worshippers as the bride of Jesus about to receive a mystical consummation. In mystical experiences, worshippers wished to transcend the limits of the ordinary human body and express an intense love for God, dissolving their individual identities into ecstatic fusion with the divine. The emotions of mysticism therefore resembled the emotions of sexual ecstasy, of losing one's sense of self in intense pleasure. This does not mean that mystics were sexually frustrated or perverted. They simply directed their desire toward God, rather than toward a sexual relationship with a human being.

Sex as metaphor

Above all, it is important to recognize that, in representations, sexual desire becomes a metaphor for other issues and other forms of desire, such as ambition. Sexual desire could symbolize transcendence – or pollution and disorder. Sexual desire and orgasm are linked with human fertility, of course, but they have often been connected with creative energy in general, for instance as the life force of the universe beyond procreation. In a strange way, Christian mystics resembled sexual utopians in their attitudes toward desire and ecstasy. Sexual utopians believed that in intense sex, lovers could experience losing themselves in a larger whole, and transcend the everyday through powerful pleasures. The energy of sex was not about individual relationships, but instead fueled revolution. Sexuality could also play an important role in artistic and philosophical explorations. Radical Enlightenment philosophers used pornography to criticize church and state.[30]

Sexual desire can also be seen as transgressing and dissolving conventional boundaries of society, as a metaphor for all that is destabilizing and polluting.[31] Why does sex in particular play such an important role as a metaphor of moral panic? Sex seems dangerous because it crosses the borders of our bodies. Anthropologist Mary Douglas argues that the whole, inviolate body often symbolized the sanctity of society. In sex, people's bodies are penetrated, they leak bodily fluids, and they might lose this sense of inviolability and wholeness. Sex therefore becomes a metaphor of people's fears of other kinds of boundary violation. Sex often seems to be pollution, which Douglas defines as "matter out of place," especially people, actions or substances which do not conform to the rigid categories set forth by society.[32] More recently, theorists such as Ann Stoler have shown that fears about sexual transgression concern wider fears about social and especially racial boundaries.[33]

The fear of sex tends to erupt when social boundaries are threatened, when plague threatens a city, when subaltern people demand their rights, when politicians need an enemy. For instance, when local uprisings or nationalist movements challenged imperial authorities, the fear of the "black rapist" emerged. This did not mean that there was an actual upsurge of indigenous men attacking white women; rather, the image of the black rapist became a metaphor for fear that colonized people would attack imperialism.[34]

These anxieties about sexual boundaries sometimes explode into "moral panics."[35] Moral panics happen when moralists, activists or journalists concoct hysterical popular stereotypes of those they consider sexually deviant, and blame them for a crisis in society. They stir up popular concern through sermons and speeches, and demand action, such as expulsion or even execution. For instance, when the Christians were trying to push Muslims out of Spain around 1400, preachers warned Christian men that Muslims were trying to rape their wives.[36] Moral panics are not a necessarily a response to changes in sexual behavior, but metaphors for these wider fears about social boundaries. Furthermore, moral panics do not instigate the repression of sex; sex is regulated in societies before moral panics, and when they subside, regulation continues.

Sexuality and the self

Sexual desires can also raise important questions about the integrity of the self and stable gender relations. Queer theorists have argued that same-sex desires destabilized the idea that male and female, heterosexual and homosexual, are fixed and stable hierarchies. Above all, Judith Butler argues that we are not simply born with our sexual and gender identities; instead, we must perform them over and over again, and we never get our roles exactly right. Drag shows reveal this artificiality in the most blatant way, but everyone performs their identity in everyday life. She also demonstrates that people incorporate the abject into their own "normal" identities.[37] To give a historical example, a medieval monk might define himself as celibate and morally superior, yet obsess continually about "loose women." Loose women became a foil which defined his idea of spiritual virtue in discourses and prayers, but he could not rid himself completely of their image. Because of these complexities, sexual norms are "opened to a displacement and subversion from within," Butler argues.[38]

Sexual desire poses problems for the self in many ways more interesting than the question of identity. Theorist Tim Dean looks at sexuality and psychic boundaries to suggest that "sexuality is understood in terms of what shatters the self." Even as they are socially constructed, sexual desires can feel overwhelming. Orgasm itself has been termed the "little death," a feeling of dissolving the boundaries of the self.[39] As Dean writes, "Homosexuality may remind us of how desire itself remains potentially antinormative, incompletely inassimilable to the ego."[40] At the same time, all representations of transgressive desire are socially constructed themselves, and they are often highly stylized.

Philosophers have used sexual desire to explore larger questions about the self. Did a man have a rational and coherent self if he could not control his own desires? Did he have free will if he had an erection when he did not want to, and was impotent when he desired sex? In the nineteenth century, social purity feminists advocated chastity as a way for women to discover their autonomy. By the turn of the nineteenth century, thinkers began to turn away from the idea of the unified self to regard sexual desire as a form of energy which could divide the self, as Freud portrayed the ego as tormented by the conflicting needs of id and superego. Especially in the twentieth century, artists and visionaries have often seen desire as a form of energy, almost as an abstract force separate from and uncontrolled by the rational self. The surrealists morphed genital shapes into oozing, distorted, even abstract forms.[41]

By the end of the twentieth century, the radical tradition went from celebrating sexual desire as a way of transcending the self – whether in a greater love for the divine, for nature, or revolution – to celebrating sexual desire as a way of knowing and expressing the innermost self. But the idea that sex is the truth about the self can be just as rigid and imprisoning as earlier restrictions, because it prescribes boundaries for the self in terms of identity.

Chronology and scope

Desire will trace how different societies have regulated sexual behavior, and how people have evaded, resisted, and accommodated this regulation. It will also highlight those moments when moral panics erupted about sexuality, and when sexual desire was celebrated as creative and transcendent. It is organized chronologically, following western civilization's landmarks. Given its page limits, the book cannot cover every aspect of sexuality in all European regions, religions, and eras; instead, it will concentrate on different cultures and times to illuminate major themes. It does not contrast European with non-western sexuality because there is no such thing as "non-western sexuality," rather, there are thousands of diverse sexual cultures. The book does address one example of a non-western sexual culture in detail, in Chapter 6 on the Spanish conquest of Mexico, and other chapters also touch on the important issues of imperialism and race.

It is important for those interested in modern sexuality to understand what came before, the subject of the first part of the book. The book begins with the Greeks and Romans because Plato's ideas on men's spiritual love for each other influenced concepts of same-sex desire for centuries. Furthermore, the classical world allows us to examine a culture whose understanding of sexual identity was radically different from our own. A Greek or Roman male citizen could have sex with a male slave, a youth, or a foreigner and still be regarded as masculine. Early Christianity, of course, had the most dominant influence on western ideas about sex, but it is important to understand how Christian notions of sex differed from those of the Jewish culture into which Jesus was born. While Jewish culture valued marital sex, for early Christians, marriage was second-best to celibacy. The earliest Christians believed the Second Coming was imminent, so human love and marriage distracted believers from the divine. Of course, as the Church became established and institutionalized, it established marriage as a sacrament, but it continued to regard sexual desire itself as evil. Unfortunately, given page limits, the period from about 400 to 1100 CE cannot be covered, but the medieval period is the subject of two chapters. Common people tended to regard sexual desire as natural, and as necessary for fertility; in their tales and stories they fantasized about sexual desire as powerful, frightening, and funny. During the Middle Ages, the Church denounced fornication, but municipal authorities believed desire was natural. So they set up official municipal brothels, where women who sold sex were supposed to work as prostitutes.

The Protestant Reformation inaugurated a new way of thinking about sex. Reformers such as Luther declared that celibacy was unnatural and celebrated sex in marriage instead. By the eighteenth century, radical Enlightenment thinkers went even further. The philosopher Diderot challenged the Church's denigration of sexual desire by claiming that Nature commanded humans to have pleasure and to procreate. But an underground tradition was far more subversive – arguing that sexual pleasure was an end in itself, and that exploring the body was a way of gaining knowledge of the material world which might contradict received authorities.

When European imperialism began, sex became a flashpoint in the clash of cultures. This book will illustrate this point with a chapter on the colonial Spanish empire in Mexico. The conquerors stigmatized the Aztecs and other peoples of central America as cannibals and sodomites. Following a common pattern, they at first took indigenous women as concubines and as translators and intermediaries, but soon prohibited intermarriage in order to preserve the boundaries of race.[42]

The great economic changes of modernity shaped sexual economies as well, as wage labor began to supplant the household as an economic unit. During the industrial revolution, new work opportunities drew young women and men away from the countryside to the cities, disrupting traditional courtship patterns of sex after a solemn promise of marriage. Men who had sex with men found each other in the burgeoning cities. Authorities tried new forms of sexual management to cope with what they saw as sexual disorder, part of the great carceral regime defined by Foucault – the growth of large institutions such as prisons, hospitals, schools and asylums, which identified, categorized, separated, and defined their subjects. Authorities forced unmarried mothers into work houses or reformatories, compelled prostitutes to register with the police and endure gynecological exams, and imprisoned men who had sex with other men. Although these new institutions made the lives of many women and men quite miserable, authorities could never totally succeed in controlling sexual behavior.[43]

The theories of Thomas Malthus and Charles Darwin influenced nineteenth-century thought on sexuality. Both respectable British gentlemen, they posited sex and death as motive forces in human nature.[44] Darwin built upon Malthus and others to argue that sexual selection, and the struggle for survival, impelled evolution. Sexual desire was therefore necessary for biological advancement. Darwin inspired some to see sexual desire as creative, while others feared that it would be polluting. Some moralists feared that Europeans could degenerate as well as evolve, that the boundaries of the European race would dissolve and decay at the very moment the great European empires were conquering and expanding. They wanted to cleanse society of illicit sexual desire – even excessive desire in marriage – and mounted an influential social purity campaign fighting against masturbation and prostitution. But radical thinkers used Darwin's idea of sexual selection to argue that desire was the source of all poetry and art. Sexual desire would also energize revolutionaries to transform society, they declared. Some socialists, for example, wanted to reshape sex as they reshaped society. The Nazis could also be seen as revolutionaries who wanted to manage sex for the purposes of the state, but in the service of their murderous vision of racial purity.

Consumer capitalism, however, was the most profound influence on the sexual culture of twentieth-century Europe. Movies attracted audiences with sexy stars, advertisements sold automobiles with pretty girls, make-up became a feminine necessity, and people could even advertise for sexual partners. By the 1960s, growing wages for young people helped create a popular culture in which they could use consumption to express their sexual selves – whether dancing to the

Rolling Stones or wearing a miniskirt. Sixties radicals then rejected consumerism and resurrected the revolutionary idea of sexual desire as a key to the imagination.

Today, Europe's sexual attitudes contrast with those of the United States. Europe's welfare systems support unmarried mothers and its laws allow gay and lesbian people to form civil unions or marriages. European schools teach teenagers about contraception, and their teenage pregnancy rates are much lower than in the United States.[45] In both Europe and the United States, popular culture is highly sexualized. But American politicians fulminate against gay marriage and pornography – until sexual scandals end their careers. In contrast, Europeans shrug off sexual scandals and tolerate pornography. American religious leaders influence what can be said about sex in public, but most Europeans pay little attention to religious admonitions against sex since so few of them go to church. But the vision that sexual desire could transcend the self and energize revolution has also vanished. Why is sexual desire sometimes seen as dangerous, and sometimes as transcendent? Why has the utopian vision of sexual desire disappeared? This book will attempt to answer these questions.

This work is based on hundreds of books and articles by historians who have opened up the field of the history of sexuality with detailed studies of different periods. Each chapter will end with a section of "Suggested reading" which lists some of the most useful works for that topic.

Suggested reading

Butler, Judith. *Undoing Gender*. New York, 2004.

Cocks, H. G., and Matt Houlbrook, eds. *Palgrave Advances in the Modern History of Sexuality*. Basingstoke, 2005.

Foucault, Michel. *The History of Sexuality: an Introduction*. Translated by Robert Hurley. New York, 1990.

Garton, Stephen. *Histories of Sexuality: Antiquity to Sexual Revolution*. London, 2004.

Halperin, David. *How To Do the History of Male Homosexuality*. Chicago, 2002.

Kuefler, Mathew, ed. *The History of Sexuality Sourcebook*. Guelph, 2007.

Laqueur, Thomas W. *Making Sex: Body and Gender from the Greeks to Freud*. Cambridge, MA, 1990.

Nye, Robert A., ed. *Sexuality (Oxford Reader)*. New York: 1999.

Chapter 2

Sex and the city

Greece and Rome

Timarchos' father left him a fortune, so he should have been well off. Yet he had such a good time drinking wine, gambling, hiring flute girls, and having sex with prostitutes that his fortune evaporated. To earn the money to keep up this extravagant lifestyle, he became the lover of several wealthy men. This shocked his fellow Athenians, who put him on trial for disgracing his status as a citizen. What may seem surprising to us is that his accuser, Aeschines, wrote poetry to beautiful male youths, and fought in the streets for their favors. The city even profited from the taxes paid by male prostitutes. Why was it acceptable for an adult man to love a male youth, but disgraceful for him to become another man's lover?

The answer lies in the place of sex in the Athenian city. The Greeks did not see sex in itself as either shameful or honorable. On one hand, sexual desire was closely tied to the energies of life. Of course, in this arid, stony land, sexual desire was often associated with fertility in the most positive way, but the Athenians did not think that sexual desire only flowed between men and women, nor did they conceive of the sexual identities of heterosexuality or homosexuality. Rather, they assumed sexual desire could be directed to, and satisfied by, either males or females. If harnessed, this aggressive sexual energy could be a positive force for fertility, culture, and spirituality. Greek myths about gods and goddesses did not instruct Greek citizens to feel guilty about sex; instead the gods and goddesses fell in love, tricked humans into having sex with them, quarreled, hurled thunderbolts, turned themselves into swans, bulls, or clouds to seduce beautiful human girls – or boys. In religious rites, obscene language, sexual images, and out-of-control behavior enabled humans to appeal to the gods.[1] For philosophers, the spiritual love of a beautiful boy could lead to a love of higher wisdom and truth; for politicians, the love between men helped bond together the city.

On the other hand, if out of control, sexual desire could pollute temples and endanger the city, just as the fertility of plants could bring lush harvests or choke the land with weeds.[2] The Greeks depicted desire as the god Eros, the winged boy who wounded his victims with a burning torch or arrows. Eros drove his victims into a state of madness.[3] Similarly, as James Davidson argues, the desire for luxuries, like prostitutes or fish, could overwhelm a man's rational control and leave him enslaved to his appetites – like Timarchos who sold himself to enjoy his pleasures.[4] Furthermore, a Greek man could only keep his masculinity if he was the dominant partner in sex – otherwise he would become like a woman. Sexual desire therefore potentially crossed the boundaries between man and woman, free and slave, even the gods and humans.

Sexual desire was like any other kind of pleasure: the honor or shame derived from how it fit within the boundaries of the social order. Athens was a small city-state that became a democracy by the fifth century BCE, but only about one half of its inhabitants were citizens; the others were slaves and foreigners. The order of Athenian society rested on two relationships: the household, or *oikos*, and the male bonding of citizens in the *polis*, or democracy. It was important for an Athenian man to be active and dominant, and to demonstrate his primary loyalty to his fellow male citizens. To prove their honor, men controlled their women in the household, debated in the forum, and fought against the Persians on the battlefield. The wealthy Athenian man had time to exercise at the gymnasium, to debate in the forum, and to carouse at parties because his wife and slaves took care of his daily needs. An Athenian male citizen was equal to his fellows because he was *not* a slave, a foreigner, or woman. By providing sexual services to other men, Timarchos acted like a slave, not a citizen.

Athenian society was based on a system of honor and shame, not internalized guilt. If a man failed to protect his own honor, if he violated the honor of the state, or raped someone else's women and slaves, he had committed the offense of *hubris*. Today, *hubris* is usually understood as overweening pride that offends the gods and leads to a fall. Actually, the ancient Greek definition was a little different. While arrogance, unwarranted superiority and pride motivated *hubris*, classicist Douglas Cairns defines the actual offense as "the serious assault on the honor of another, which is likely to cause shame, and lead to anger and attempts at revenge." Seducing another man's wife was one of the worst offenses of *hubris*, for it destroyed the *oikos*, or household, and endangered the legitimate citizenship of the husband's offspring. A citizen could also commit *hubris* against himself, like Timarchos did when he dishonored his own status by prostituting himself, and then dishonored Athens by attempting to speak in the forum.[5]

Outside the *oikos* and the *polis*, Greek men also enjoyed a rich world of leisure – the theatre, with the tragedies of Euripides and the comedies of Aristophanes, the brothels, where male and female prostitutes provided sexual services, and the symposia, or drinking parties, where men caroused and drank, were entertained by dancing girls, told stories, and discussed philosophy. Rules and regulations governed the sexual boundaries of the *polis* and *oikos*, but fantasy inspired sexual desire and representations of sex in the world of leisure. Laws and court cases mandated strict controls, especially over women, and disapproved of some kinds of male-male sex, yet plays and painted pottery depicted orgies, out-of-control women, and male-male eroticism. Sex was entertaining and titillating, but it was also good to think with. Playwrights, artists and philosophers experimented with representations of excessive sexual desire to explore the limits of the human experience. Often, they did not depict *how* people were *supposed* to behave, or even how they actually behaved sexually – instead they represented sexual desire as excess, as fantasy, frightening, or funny. The comic playwright Aristophanes satirically depicted politicians with gaping anuses who voraciously craved sex with other men. The tragic playwright Euripides told how sexual desire, fate and ambition destroyed families and dynasties.

The tension between the dangers of eros and the honor of the citizen was especially acute when it came to daughters and wives. To ensure the honor of the *oikos*, or household, Greek men idealized wives who were quiet, chaste, and confined in the women's quarters of the household. Yet in the plays that Athenians attended in their outdoor amphitheatres, female characters were anything but quiet and passive: Clytemnestra killed her husband for revenge and power, and Lysistrata led a women's strike against war where they took over the Acropolis and flourished dildos. Greek men seemed to have feared that their chaste wives would easily erupt in uncontrolled desires, and tried to tame this wildness. As art historian Andrew Stewart writes, this image of women as uncontrolled therefore legitimated their confinement.[6]

The primary purpose of marriage was to produce legitimate Athenian citizens, so men wished to ensure that their wives and daughters did not get a chance to bear illegitimate children. They attempted to seclude their young daughters in the household quarters, where they lived in a female world with their mothers, female relatives, and female servants, training in the household arts, and spinning and weaving to clothe the household.[7] Greek vases depicted men as suntanned and swarthy, and women as pale from their seclusion. To be tamed, young girls went through a religious ritual called the Brauronia, in which they dressed up like little bears, and possibly ran races nude, symbolizing their wild, animalistic nature. They worshipped Artemis, the virgin goddess of the moon, the forest, and the hunt. As they went through the initiation rite, they shed their wildness and prepared for their future roles as wives by donning saffron or "frog-green" gowns with embroidered and scalloped hems.

In slightly earlier Greek societies, girls spent some years before marriage singing in school choruses. Some poetic fragments suggest that erotic tensions between young women flourished there. In one lyric by Alcman, a girl praises her leader Hagesichora "of the fair ankles," golden hair, and silver face, complaining that she "wears me out with desire." She may have been singing of her crush on a teacher, or expressing her allegiance and attachment to her leader.[8] On the isle of Lesbos in the sixth century, the famous poet Sappho also expressed her desire for women, although only fragments remain of her poetry. This poem expresses some of the sorrow and erotic longing the bride's female lover might feel as she saw her sitting next to her new husband:

> He seems to me the equal of the gods,
> that man, who sits with you
> face to face, and near you, listens closely to your lilting voice,
> Your tempting laugh, which sets
> my heart a-flutter in my breast.[9]

In Athens, male citizens would arrange marriages for their daughters at the age of 16 to 18 years old, fearing the consequences if the daughters let their passions loose. A girl who took a lover might conceal her pregnancy and abandon the child to die, but if her father found out, he could sell her into slavery for dishonoring the household. Conversely, a man who seduced or raped an unmarried girl could be killed.[10]

Religious fertility rites also mediated the tension between female purity and wildness. For the Greeks, the story of Demeter and her daughter Persephone explained the seasons. One day, while the young Persephone wandered through the flowered fields, the god Hades abducted her down into his underworld of death, raped her, and married her. The loss of her daughter so grieved Demeter that she could not ensure the earth's fertility: the trees lost their leaves and the crops died – a mythical explanation for winter. However, Persephone could leave Hades to visit her mother for eight months every year. When she reappeared, Demeter was so overjoyed that the earth burst forth into blossom. The all-female festival Thesmophoria commemorated the abduction of Persephone. Women threw suckling pigs and cakes baked in the shapes of snakes and penises into pits; they later retrieved the decomposed remains and offered them on the altar of Demeter, praying for fertility. They also danced and shouted obscene jokes, celebrating Baubo, the old woman who raised her skirt and made her labia smile to amuse Demeter as she grieved for her daughter. These women abstained from sexual relations during the festival; they detached themselves from their earthly relations with their husbands to use their sexual power to reach the goddess. One scholar has suggested that despite the overt celebration of fertility, women also used herbs in the festival that enabled them to control their fertility, such as pennyroyal, pine branches, and pomegranate, which could be used for menstrual cleansing and might have induced abortions.[11]

Sexual pleasure between husbands and wives was important for fertility. Many Greek doctors advised husbands to please their wives sexually, assuming that the female orgasm was necessary for conception because women, like men, emitted seed. While Aristotle believed women could conceive without pleasure, his was the minority view.[12] But playwrights found female desire comic and even dangerous. The female characters in Aristophanes's *Lysistrata* "thrust back" when making love with their husbands, and brag of their skill at the "lioness on the cheesegrater" position. In this play, Athenian women take over the Acropolis and refuse to have sex with their husbands in a peace protest, but they smuggle in dildos because they are so sexually frustrated.[13]

The adultery of a wife violated the integrity of the *oikos*, or household, and dishonored her husband. Her husband had to divorce her, and she was also prohibited from participating in religious rituals for fear she would pollute the boundaries of the state. Interestingly, Athenian law punished a man who seduced a married woman more severely than a man who raped a woman. If he raped her, he damaged her and invaded the *oikos*, but if he seduced her, he won over her will and turned her into an enemy of her husband within the *oikos*. An adulterer could be fined, killed, or anally raped, for he had committed *hubris*, indulging his own desires while failing to respect the honor of another man.[14]

Athenians differentiated sharply between those women with honor and those without. Formal marriage required a dowry and produced legitimate citizens, but men could also take women as *pallakai*, or concubines, in less formal arrangements without a marriage contract. As Apollodorus proclaimed in a legal case, "Mistresses (*hetairai*) we keep for the sake of pleasure, concubines (*pallakai*) for the daily care of our persons, but wives to bear us legitimate children and to be faithful guardians of our households."[15] By mandating only marriage between citizens, politicians attempted to create bonds among all citizens as equal, but also distinguishing them from foreigners. In fifth-century Athens, citizenship was a privilege of the native-born, shutting out foreigners, who were one-third to one-half of the population.[16] Only formally married wives could participate in the religious and civic life of the city. The Athenians were very concerned that the purity of this citizenship could be polluted by illicit marriages or by concubines posing as wives.

Hetairai are sometimes thought of as high-class courtesans, in contrast with the lower-class *porne*, or common prostitutes, but the lines between them were hard to draw. *Porne*, or common prostitutes, worked in the streets or in factory-like brothels where they had to receive one man after another in small cubicles. In contrast, *hetairai* entertained Athenian men at symposia by singing, dancing, performing acrobatic tricks, and wittily conversing. Some, such as Aspasia, who became concubine of the politician Perikles, were renowned for their learning and wisdom, but we do not know how much this was myth and how much reality.[17] The most favored *hetairai* could choose their lovers, and could even become the semi-permanent mistresses of men as concubines, but they could easily lose this wealth and control. Most *hetairai* faced increased degradation as they grew older. One vase, for instance, depicts a man making love face-to-face with a young, smooth-skinned *hetaira*, gazing into her eyes; but the other side of the vase portrays a man penetrating from behind an older woman with sagging breasts, humiliating her in this dominant position, perhaps through anal sex.[18]

Neaera's career demonstrates the profits and perils of the *hetaira*'s life. When Neaera was a tiny girl, Nicarete, the wife of a cook, purchased her and several other young girls to train them up as prostitutes, and imported them to Corinth, a Greek city known for its brothels. When Neaera was still very young, probably prepubescent, Nicarete sold her sexual services to several men of the city. According to the orator Apollodorus, Neaera "plied her trade openly in Corinth and was quite a celebrity, having among other lovers Xenocleides the poet, and Hipparchus the actor," but she was still Nicarete's slave. So Neaera eventually collected money from all her lovers and purchased her freedom, and took a new lover, Phyrnion. Neaera hoped that Phyrnion would treat her well; since she was no longer a slave, she did not have to crop her hair, and she expected that he would bring her gifts of clothes and jewels. However, Phyrnion still was her master. He brought her to Athens, where "he treated her without decency or restraint, taking her everywhere with him to dinners where there was drinking and making her a partner in his revels; and he had intercourse with her openly whenever and wherever he wished, making his privilege a display to the onlookers." He even got her so drunk at parties that any man, even the servants, could have sex with her. Angry at this degradation, Neaera left Phyrnion, and took another lover, Stephanus. By age 50, she passed as Stephanus's legal spouse, and her daughter passed as a citizen wife. When her daughter performed religious rites in the city, the Athenians discovered that her mother had been a prostitute, and proclaimed their outrage that she polluted the purity of the polity.[19]

The provision of sex helped unify men in the *polis*, the city as a political and social community. As historian David Halperin notes, Solon, the great lawgiver of early Athens, legendarily established public brothels to give all men access to sexual services, just as he widened citizenship to give all citizens access to political participation.[20] Taxes paid by male and female prostitutes contributed to the city's treasury. By establishing public brothels, politicians could reduce the distinctions between aristocratic men, who could enjoy the luxuries of the city, such as fresh fish, silken clothing, wine, and music, and *hetairai*, and poor men, who had to spend most of their days laboring for their families. By going to prostitutes, poor men could also theoretically enjoy the sexual services aristocrats demanded from *hetairai* or their concubines, or *pallakai*. But, more often, a man would be titillated by the sexual acrobatics of the flute girls and boys at the symposia but, unable to afford their services, he would trudge home and demand sex from his wife.[21]

Greek men also faced the tensions and dangers of sexual desire: they needed to be dominant and in control, but they also had to respect the honor of other men, and keep their own honor by controlling their own desires. On one hand, masculine sexual desire was linked with aggression and the defense of the city. Statues of Priapus, with his huge, erect phallus, stood everywhere in Athens. They celebrated the democratic polity of Athens and the military victories won by Athenian citizens fighting together; in the festival of Dionysios, Athenians carried huge phalluses through the streets. Guarding the gates of the *oikos*, they also signified the status of each man as head of his household. Their aggressive masculine sexuality warned passers by not to violate the boundary of the household, and also warded off evil spirits.[22] Dominant male sexual aggression was also a way of humiliating foreigners. On the Eurymedon vase, for instance, produced when the Athenians had just defeated the Persians, a male youth with his hand on his penis runs toward a barbarian figure, who bends forward and raises his hands in surrender.[23]

Too much masculine sexual desire could be dangerous, uncontrollable, and lead to the transgression of boundaries. *Hubris* could be seen as deriving from excessive masculinity, an "excess of vigor, quickness and manliness."[24] As Aeschines argued, "unrestrained physical pleasures and a feeling that nothing is ever enough, these are what recruit to gangs of robbers, what fill the pirate ships, these are each man's Fury; these are what drive him to slaughter his fellow citizens, serve tyrants, conspire to overthrow democracy."[25] This excess desire could make men too much like animals. Greek culture, for instance, celebrated, feared, laughed at, and

Figure 2.1   *Hetaira* attacked by satyr. Greek *kylix* vessel from the Late Archaic Period, *c.* 500BC. Wider circle of: the Nikosthenes Painter. Ceramic, red figure, 11.1 x 32.6cm. Museum of Fine Arts, Boston. Gift of Edward Perry Warren, RES08.30a. Photograph © 2008 Museum of Fine Arts, Boston

mocked the satyr. On symposia drinking cups, these bestial, sometimes cloven-hoofed male creatures rampaged through forests to rape unwilling nymphs and penetrate and fellate each other. As art historian Andrew Stewart explains, they expressed "life's most basic ingredients – raw desire and manic energy," and embodied the masculine "fantasy of absolute sexual freedom, of totally uninhibited promiscuity, and thereby validate[d] the need for sexual self control."[26] Men could act like satyrs at the symposia, as in vase paintings which depict men beating older *hetairai* and forcing them to submit to oral and anal intercourse from two men at the same time, in an orgiastic outburst of domination and revelry. To such men, the satyrs were funny, but they also were hubristic, overturning proper boundaries. The city needed to regulate masculine desire in order to survive.[27]

Another male image, the *kinaidos*, was totally negative. This was the man who was represented as acting in an effeminate fashion, by implication taking the passive role in sex because he could not control his appetites. The male prostitute or *kinaidos* was very different from our modern notion of the homosexual. The male prostitute was not expelled from society because, like the female prostitute, he provided a sexual service, albeit a shameful one. A man was not seen as born a *kinaidos* or male prostitute – it was a role he acquired. Like Timarchos, if a man wasted the fortune his father left to him on prostitutes and the pleasures of the symposia – eating, drinking, gambling and sex – he was considered shameful because he was unable to control his desires, and might prostitute himself.[28] As Marilyn Skinner observes, however, the *kinaidos* could also function as a "scare figure," the antithesis of what a proper man was supposed to be: uncontrolled versus controlled, insatiable versus rational, submissive versus dominant.[29]

Orators would insult their enemies as *kinaidos* or as male prostitutes. For instance, Aeschines had a grudge against Timarchos and was trying to destroy his political career, so he accused him of being a male prostitute or male *hetaira*, although he did not explicitly describe him as a *kinaidos*.[30] An Athenian man who prostituted himself was stripped of his citizenship rights. Found guilty, Timarchos could not serve as an *archon*, act as a priest in civic religious rites, or speak or vote in the assembly. He had endangered the bonds of equal male citizens by entering into a relationship of dominance and submission, and by allowing his desires to overcome prudence and self control. Aeschines warned that any man who would sell himself for luxury would also sell out the interests of the city. Timarchos threatened the boundaries between slave and free, and between male and female. His body was "unclean" so the law forbade him from entering the "purified area of the agora."

Yet the Athenians did not punish sodomy with any physical penalty, death or imprisonment, just disgrace. Men such as Timarchos or the playwright Agathon could be accused of male prostitution or passive sex while still living free in the city. At the same time, these shameful images functioned to draw the boundaries of masculinity.[31] Aeschines proclaimed that "The acts that this man felt no shame to commit in practice are ones that I would rather die than describe clearly in words among you." But this shameful role was not just an attribute of performing certain acts; it stemmed from his inherent desires. Aeschines claimed that even when Timarch0s had lost his looks and could not attract more lovers, "his vile and unholy nature still longed for those same pleasures."[32]

At the same time, intense male bonding, even erotic bonding, bound Athenian men together into the city. Aeschines admitted that he himself had written poetry to young men, and he praised the legendary love of Athenian heroes Harmodias and Aristogiton. Harmodias and Aristogiton had assassinated the tyrant Hippias because he tried to seduce Harmodias. In doing so, they enabled the eventual restoration of democracy. In Plato's *Symposium*, Pausanias argues that "tyrants … cannot tolerate the free thinking of men bound by love."[33] Aeschines proclaimed that desire for beautiful boys, "those who are noble and decent, is characteristic of the generous and discerning spirit," and pointed out that the law did not prohibit relationships between free men and boys.

Athenian culture had to reconcile the intense value it placed on romantic bonds between males and its ambivalence about sex between men. The love between an adult man and a male youth had been ritualized into romance in an earlier aristo-cratic era, from the sixth and fifth centuries.

As the Greek poet Anacreon wrote:

Boy with the girlish glance
I pursue you, but you won't listen,
you don't know that you hold the reins
of my soul.[34]

From the point of view of many older male lovers, boys and girls were equally desirable, but elite girls were secluded at home, while boys went to school and exercised nude at the gymnasium. Teenage male youths were seen as the most beautiful objects of desire, muscular yet still hairless, smooth-skinned, with the small, delicate penises adult Greek men regarded as erotic. Since they were young they did not have the status of adult males and could be seen as somewhat femi-nine. When boys reached the age where they began to sprout beards and pubic hair, when their skin grew coarse, they seemed much less desirable; they acquired the status of citizens, and might pursue their own young male lovers before they married. The *erastes*, the adult male lover, would offer gifts, such as the apple (with its erotic significance) or a rooster, or more extravagantly, a horse or chariot to his young male beloved, the *eromenos*. In vessels probably intended for symposia, painters depicted sex between men and youths as "intercrural" intercourse, the man's penis inserted between the boy's thighs.[35] It would have been shameful for the boy to submit to anal sex. This behavior continued in classical fifth- and fourth-century Athens, but it had to be carefully modulated. A man gained honor by aggressively pursuing and conquering a boy, but if the boy surrendered for money, then he would lose honor. It was shameful for a father or guardian to pros-titute his own son, and if he did so, the boy had no obligation to support him in his old age. The violation of a free boy was *hubris*, or wanton disregard of the rights of another, and could lead to the death penalty.[36] Apparently fathers scolded and schoolmates teased boys who had lovers. But we do not know how often these relationships were sexual; they might have been twilight moments, frequently occurring yet rarely acknowledged. Seducing a boy might have been like seducing a girl in Regency England; high society would gossip about such libertine men but not shun them as unnatural pariahs.

In Plato's *Symposium*, several philosophers defended male-male love from teasing schoolmates and scolding fathers, but they also emphasized its spiritual nature. Like regular symposia, it was a supper party at the house of the playwright Agathon. The guests brag and lament over their headaches from heavy drinking the night before, so they decide to forgo flute-girls or dancing boys; instead, they discuss the philosophy of love. Pausanias, Agathon's lover, proclaims there were two kinds of love: first, that of the common "Aphrodite Pandemos," which was the bodily desire felt by "the meaner sort of men" who did not discriminate between women and youths, and second, that of the "heavenly Aphrodite Urania," the spiritual love felt by those who "turn to the male, and delight in him who is the more valiant and intelligent nature." Unlike depictions of the beloved boy as a young teenager, Pausanias believes the most desirable youth was on the brink of manhood, with his first beard, because then the boy can engage in an intelligent conversion. Pausanias defends love between a man and a youth as leading to higher truth; a youth should "yield" to his lover, but it is implied that this yielding is spiritual rather than physical. These attachments should be valued for their permanence and fidelity, argues Pausanias.[37]

Aristophanes, the playwright, then explains why some men yearn for other males, some women for other women, and some men for women. In the beginning, humans were "globular in shape ... with four arms and four legs, and two faces, and two lots of privates." Some had two sets of male genitals, some two sets of female, and some one of each. They could run so fast with their four legs that they tried to "scale the heights of heaven and set upon the gods." Affronted by their arrogance, Zeus "cut them all in half, just as you or I might ... slice an egg with a hair," leaving each half with one face and one set of genitals. To compensate for this wound, Zeus constructed the new humans to enable the male and female who clasped together to propagate, continuing the human race. Those originally all-male still sought out other men, all-female sought out other women, and the mixed sought the opposite sex. They were motivated by "a desperate yearning for one another," which explained sexual desire, which Aristophanes differentiates from the desire for procreation. Men and women who desire each other are like the adulterer and the unfaithful wife – showing how sexual desire could be seen to endanger marriage. But the desire of men for each other is based on "daring, fortitude and masculinity" and produces "the only men who show any real manliness in public life." They marry and procreate as a duty, but they would rather "spend their lives with one another." For Aristophanes, love is the search for one's lost self.[38]

Finally, the philosopher Socrates depicts the passion for a youth as the first step on a heavenly ladder to wisdom. The true philosopher, he argues, would begin by loving a youth who combined virtue, wisdom and beauty in his soul. Learning philosophy together, they would be "married by a far nearer tie and have a closer friendship than those who beget mortal children, for the children who are their common offspring are fairer and more immortal." But the wise man would abandon this human love first for the love of science, art, politics, and philosophy, and then the divine love of abstract beauty itself. At the end of the *Symposium*, the handsome yet unreliable hero Alcibiades recalls how he tried in vain to seduce Socrates. Alcibiades says that Socrates always appears so "fond he is of the fair," always associating with them and "always being smitten by them," but he is able to resist these passions. Indeed, Alcibiades recounts that one night he decided to yield himself physically to Socrates, and crept into bed with him. Socrates, however, spurned the blandishments of this most alluring man.[39]

Socrates also explains these ideas in *The Phaedrus*, where he compares the rational self to a charioteer, who takes the reins of the twin horses of the passions of honor and physical appetites. The erotic energy of the appetites could propel the self toward a higher spiritual goal, but only if it was strictly controlled. Like Sappho, Socrates describes the lover as trembling, sweating, and burning with fever, so tormented is he by erotic passion for the beautiful beloved male youth. But erotic love possesses the lover like a deity; if the lover is sufficiently wise, his soul grows wings and ascends toward the higher love of beauty and truth.[40] Critics have debated whether Plato, via Socrates, wants to draw a sharp line between fleshly and heavenly eros, or if he sees the former as a stepping stone for the latter.[41]

From the late fifth century, Greek culture began to focus more on romance between men and women. As democracy faded in Athens and citizens slowly lost the power to debate and vote on politics in the public arena, they retreated to their private lives and celebrated the world of marriage and the household. Male citizens may have enjoyed fewer freedoms under the new empires of Philip and Alexander, the Hellenistic Egyptians, and eventually, the Romans, but women began to appear more in cultural life. Comedies and novels now entertained audiences with the stories of young couples who had to overcome many obstacles to marry and start a family.[42]

Rome

Romans imagined their city's beginnings as a dramatic tale of rape and abduction. In the founding myth, the men who were Rome's first inhabitants needed to find wives. A neighboring tribe, the Sabines, refused to give their daughters in marriage to the Romans. In revenge, the Roman men attacked the Sabine city: they seized the struggling Sabine women, raped them, brought them back to Rome, and married them. By acquiring women, they created families and ensured the future of Roman civilization. Unlike the Athenians, who based their citizenship on descent from those of Athenian blood, Rome was based on the intermingling of peoples through conquest.[43] This myth also depicts sexual aggression as essential for Rome's foundation. As critic James Arieti observes, Romans viewed Mars (the god of war) and Venus (the goddess of love, equivalent of the Greek Aphrodite) as opposites who attracted. The cosmos was composed of these elements of destruction and creation, which together fueled the Roman state. An act of destruction, rape, could lead to new life and procreation.[44]

As Rome flourished as a republic, conquering new lands, Romans upheld the values of austerity.[45] The ideal Roman was the soldier citizen, who bravely fought in the wars to serve his country, soberly participated in the governance of the city, and managed his household prudently. The Roman citizen's highest quality was *virtus*, which connoted courage, aggression, masculinity, and dominance. Men were also expected to exhibit the virtue of *pudicitia*, or sexual virtue, which did not mean abstinence but the qualities of temperance, honor, self-control, and protection of the weak. It was allowed for citizen men to satisfy their lust by penetrating slaves or prostitutes, but their *pudicitia* would be violated if they allowed passion or anger to get the best of them and seduced a citizen's wife or sons. Similarly, if they took the passive role in sex, they would lose honor. The sexual virtue – *pudicitia* – of Roman wives and daughters was also extremely important as a symbol of the integrity of the city and the boundaries between slaves and free. Women were supposed to have the self-control to preserve their virtue from adulterous affairs, and to display their modest comportment in temples and other public places. This value is evident in another founding myth of Rome: the beautiful Lucretia kills herself after being raped by an Etruscan prince and inspires the Roman men to claim independence.

Roman manhood was also based on the idea of dominance and penetration. Roman politics were based on inequality, as the city was divided into patricians, the elite, and the plebeians, or commoners. But even plebeian men were Roman citizens, and their bodies were inviolate; their citizenship protected them from beating by state officials, and they could not be sexually penetrated. In contrast, male and female slaves had to submit to any sexual services from their masters. Even more so than Greece, masculine Roman sexuality was constructed as extremely aggressive.[46]

Luxury competed with austerity in Rome's history. Rome became wealthy through its conquests, and imports flooded into the country from the East – fine wines, gauzy silks, statues, and mosaics. Rome also imported slaves from its far-flung conquests, ranging from red-haired Celts to Spaniards to Africans, and their labor produced much of its wealth. These slaves, as well as free people, also serviced the Roman luxury and leisure industries by selling sex and entertaining the public with dancing, acting and fighting. Roman law regarded them as a social necessity, yet it also stigmatized slaves, gladiators, actors, and prostitutes with the status of *infamia:* they did not have rights in trials, they could not serve as priestesses or priests, and they could be beaten without recourse; their bodies could be violated in many ways. But slaves could become free, and freedman were often wealthy merchants; their children eventually acquired the status of Roman citizenship.[47]

Roman men feared that the desire for luxurious pleasures would overcome the virtues of dominance and austerity. A man who wanted to indulge in luxuries might be tempted to subordinate himself sexually to get ahead. Ordinary citizens had to curry favor with their patrons – wealthy, elite men who could grant them offices, contracts, and recognition. This social subordination could be represented metaphorically as sexual submission. The famous orator Cicero, for instance, accused many politicians of being *pathici*, or men who submitted to sexual domination out of ambition. Most notoriously, he alleged that Julius Caesar had sexually submitted to King Nicomedes and that Mark Antony prostituted himself as a youth before he became Cleopatra's lover.[48]

Roman laws enshrined the austere virtues of the citizen family, but they proved to be more flexible in practice. Officially, the Roman citizen had the power of life and death over his household, including his wife, children, and slaves; he could kill his wife if he found her with a lover, and he could order his offspring abandoned if he did not want to recognize the baby. Marriages among upper-class Roman citizens were generally arranged by parents or guardians for financial, social and dynastic reasons. Patricians sometimes sought marriages with wealthy commoners. Husbands married as adults and wives in their late teens. The chastity of Roman matrons was highly valued; they wore long robes that covered and protected their bodies, and they could be divorced if they committed adultery or failed to bear children.[49]

Roman women actually had much more freedom and power than Greek women. Despite these arrangements, many marriages were affectionate. They attended the theatre and banquets with their husbands. They could buy and sell property; some even acquired fortunes on their own, through real estate and money lending. They could also divorce their husbands for egregious misconduct, such as bringing a mistress into the house. Wealthy Roman woman could also acquire social power through patronizing tradesmen, artists, and writers, and their family connections also gave them some indirect influence over politics. Especially during the last century of the republic, rumors swirled that Roman wives took advantage of this freedom to commit adultery. The complexities of Roman women's lives can be illustrated by the story of the Emperor Augustus's daughter Julia. Julia was first married off to Agrippa, an older man who was her father's closest friend, and then forced to divorce him and marry Augustus's stepson. She supposedly enjoyed many lovers and avoided the possibility of bearing an illegitimate child by only having sex when she was pregnant. But she was eventually exiled for adultery.[50]

Romans used religion to control sexual behavior, but they also mediated and harnessed sexual desires for spiritual and civic ends. But Roman religion was not based on a sacred text that regulated the behavior of its citizens. Instead, Romans sacrificed to different gods in the hope that they would intercede in human affairs to guarantee the safety of the city, or success in love and business. As classicist Amy Richlin observes, sexual desire itself was not polluting; the "obscene" was that which polluted religious boundaries, for instance prostitutes stepping inside a temple, or Vestal Virgins taking lovers. Sexual images could be seen as imparting magical properties, especially when people prayed for fertility. Roman festivals celebrated sexuality, such as the Florales, where sexual mimes entertained the crowds, and exhibitions of naked prostitutes titillated them.[51]

Sacred anomalies – men or women who acted outside the boundaries of normal masculine or feminine roles – could be seen as having special powers in ritual contexts. For instance, the Vestal Virgins represented not the denial of sexuality, but its power when devoted to the gods. The Vestal Virgins were six women, of pure Roman citizenship, who served the empire for 30 years by guarding the sacred fire and carrying out other sacred civic rites. The purity of their virginity symbolized the inviolability of Rome; their sexuality was all the more potent because it was suppressed. If they were found to have been unchaste, they would be buried alive. In some ways, the Vestal Virgins were seen as a third sex, since they had much more legal freedom than ordinary women; unlike any other women, they bore emblems of civic power. But once their term ended, they could marry.[52]

The *galli* were also sacred anomalies. The worship of the mother goddess Cybele, a foreign import from Syria, inspired men to sacrifice themselves to the goddess by castrating themselves. Cybele's priests were known as the *galli*; these men wore yellow or multi-colored robes with a tiara, and "adorned [themselves] with ornaments," rings, and earrings; they wore white make-up and curled their long hair. On one hand, the *galli*'s feminine appearance and castrated genitals gave them a spiritual, hermaphroditic power: by sacrificing his genitalia to the goddess, "he assimilated himself to her so completely that he shared in her life-giving power," as Rabun Taylor observes. The common people gave the *galli* food, money, and gifts in return for rituals. But on the other hand, the *galli* were feared and scorned; Roman citizens were not allowed to become *galli*, because Roman men could not give up their manhood.[53]

Cults provided outlets for women. As historian Julia Staples writes, legend has it that "the festival of the Carmentalia ... was instituted because the Roman matrons, angered at being deprived of the privilege of riding in carriages, performed abortions on themselves in order to punish their husbands by denying them children. The senate restored to them the right to ride in carriages and instituted the rites to Carmenta on the ides of February to ensure birth of healthy babies."[54] In the ritual of the Bona Dea, matrons, Vestal Virgins and perhaps even freedwomen priestesses drank wine as female musicians entertained them. They sacrificed a pregnant sow, milk and honey to the goddess and took up myrtle and serpents to enter into states of ecstatic possession. Cicero believed that this cult, presided over by Roman matrons, upheld Rome's aristocratic ethos and civic unity, but the satirist Juvenal alleged that these mysteries degenerated into an orgy: "when the flute stirs the loins and the Maenads of Priapus sweep along, frenzied alike by the horn-blowing and the wine, whirling their locks and howling. What foul longings burn within their breasts! What cries they utter as the passion palpitates within!" He depicts wives indulging themselves with slave boys. This is not a description of what actually happened, of course, but the fear of what might happen when women were not under the control of male authorities.[55]

Dominance and self-control defined which acts were acceptable and which unacceptable in the rich and elaborate sexual culture enjoyed by Roman men. The stern moralist Cato thought that an occasional visit to a prostitute was better than pursuing a freeborn woman or squandering one's fortune on a mistress. He congratulated a young male friend he saw visiting a brothel, for he realized "that lust had to be curbed without crime." However, when Cato saw the young man there once too often, he declared, "I praised you because you came here, not because you lived here!" The young man risked becoming a denizen of the world of luxury himself, losing his status as a citizen.[56] The Latin sexual vocabulary had specific terms to describe each actor in different types of sexual intercourse. The man who liked to insert his penis into a vagina was a *fututor*, if he liked to insert his penis into an anus he was a *pedicator*, and if he inserted his penis into someone's mouth he was an *irrumator*. A *fello* was the person who was the recipient, and this was seen as highly humiliating. The word for having sex, *futuo*, was also related to the term to beat and to strike. To be the penetrated party was to be like a woman, but it was not particularly humiliating for women to enjoy penetration, since that was seen as appropriate. At the same time, Romans were fearful of and fascinated by those people who did not conform to the rule of dominance. Romans were well aware of women's sexual pleasure – the word clitoris appeared in their vocabulary – but they feared that this organ would be too large and make women aggressive.[57]

Roman sources concerning female–female desire depict such women as masculine and aggressive. In Lucian's *Dialogue of the Courtesans*, Megilla, a rich woman of Lesbos, hires a courtesan to have sex with her and her lover, Demonassa. She tells the courtesan, "I was born a woman like the rest of you, but I have the mind and desires and everything else of a man." However, she does not need a penis to penetrate her lover, but "something better" which is not specified. This may have been a dildo, or Lucian may have believed that such women had large clitorises.[58] In a poem by Martial, a woman named Philaenis works out at the gym, guzzles wine, gobbles steak, and finishes off her day by licking a girl's "juicy quim," in the words of one late Victorian translator; but the poet attacks her for transgressing her sex and wishing she would "learn to suck a penis," a vicious insult in Roman culture.[59]

Roman men also feared that men might enjoy being penetrated, which would make them into *cinaedi*. This word derived from the Greek *kinaidos*, and may have connoted a male prostitute or effeminate man, or *pathicus*, which meant a man who took the passive role in sex. While these terms were terrible insults, *cinaedi* were also familiar sights on Roman streets. One tavern wall painting shows them as wearing long hair in a bun, with long, highly colored gowns, crossing their legs in a feminine manner, clearly distinct from the short haired, muscular men in other paintings. At the same time, they were portrayed as regular customers in the tavern, demanding wine just like anyone else.[60]

Although the pious Romans believed in self-control and modesty, they did not always relegate sexual words and depictions to private realms, since public leisure was also highly sexualized. Poets such as Catullus and Martial, famed for the beauty of their lyrics, used extremely explicit sexual language, and sexual images appeared on wall paintings in living rooms in homes and on vases made for elites and common people alike. Roman luxury wares, ranging from wall paintings to ceramic or silver vessels, often represented sexual postures that were thought to be degrading, such as men performing oral sex on each other or on women, *cinaedi* being penetrated, or women mounting men. Art critic John Clarke suggests that Romans found such images to be grotesquely funny, and that laughing was also a way of warding off the evil eye. Similarly, depictions of hypersexual, phallic black men could function as charms to ward off evil spirits, especially in the baths.[61]

Sexual commerce was carried on throughout Rome, not segregated into certain zones. Roman men met in taverns, where they could drink, make deals, meet their

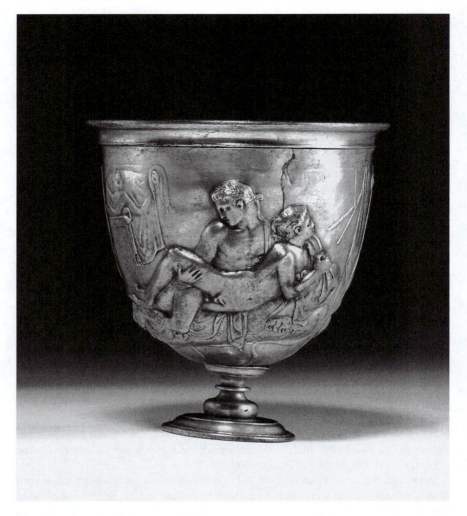

Figure 2.2 The Warren Cup, , Roman, mid-first century AD. © The Trustees of the British Museum

neighbors – or buy a prostitute's services.[62] These brothels supplied both male and female prostitutes: "Pretty boys were regarded as a luxurious import like fancy foodstuffs and furniture."[63] Female prostitutes were supposed to wear a man's toga, which implied that they were public women, not proper women, but in fact, they often displayed their bodies through filmy, colorful silk gauze garments.[64] Most prostitutes, both male and female, were often sold into slavery by their parents or brought back to Rome as booty from a conquest. But prostitutes were not entirely powerless. In the brothel, "the women themselves form some kind of community, as they share meals and intimacies, welcoming new arrivals with kisses and training them in the tricks of the trade."[65]

Furthermore, the relationships of customers to courtesans and concubines, both male and female, blurred the line between patronage and prostitution, between sexual commerce and emotion. A beautiful youth (or woman) could play off potential lovers as a means of advancing socially and financially.[66] If a man took a loan of money from a lady, people might think he was a gigolo who paid her back with sexual favors.[67] Conversely, some of the poet Catullus's mistresses may have been free women who sought out wealthy lovers, but did not seek customers on the street. These relationships could be based on love as well as money. For instance, in Lucian's *Dialogues of the Courtesans*, older women warn younger ones not to fall in love with men who do not pay them, because that would endanger their savings for retirement. But a clever courtesan made her lover feel like he was the only one, that she really was madly in love with him.[68]

The Roman wife was supposed to be known for her sober chastity, but Latin poets depicted elite Roman ladies as lustful and deceitful, manipulating desire to subvert the rigid Roman systems of gender, honor, and power. Most depictions of adultery, therefore, come from male poets, whose depictions of lusty women were based more on fantasy than reality. The works of only one female poet survive to express feminine desires outside marriage. Sulpicia, a well-bred and educated woman, made a show of modesty, fearing that her beloved Cerinthus might be an "ignoble lover" unworthy of her status. But after leaving him one night, "wanting to hide my heat," all she regretted was that she had failed to reveal her "blazing passion."[69] Of course, Sulpicia was writing within the conventions of the genre of transgressive love poetry as well.

In the genre of poetry, poets could flout Roman systems of law and honor by celebrating their depravity.[70] Young men pursued married women, whose inaccessibility made them all the more alluring. Horace, for instance, depicted such a wife "swathed in a long dress," "jewels glinting green and pearly white," whose defenses drive the lover "wild."[71] But all too often the poets felt conquered by their own desire, enslaved by the women and youths who should have submitted to their status.[72] As critic Ellen Oliensis writes, a lover trying to seduce a married woman in some ways resembled the client trying to curry favor with his patron, a constant activity for the Romans. The adulterous heterosexual relationship, therefore, could be seen as an inversion of conventional male dominance, as the mistress could playfully grant and then withhold her favors, and the lover had to beg for them by abasing himself. But while Roman poets such as Martial and Catullus played with the romantic inversion of conventional power relationships, they also used their verbal power to reestablish dominance over their mistresses, who were after all their poetic creations and not real women at all.[73] Catullus was passionately in love with his mistress Lesbia, but when she left him for another man, he accused her of standing at the "crossroads and alleyways" to "husk" Roman men.[74]

Catullus also desired the boy Juventius, who may have been a citizen of a noble family.[75] He asks Lesbia for a thousand kisses, but in a lyric to Juventius, he writes:

> If someone would let me keep on kissing
> your honeysweet eyes, Iuventius
> I'd keep kissing up to three hundred thousand times
> and never feel close to satiety.[76]

Unlike the Greeks, the Romans did not value the custom of courtship of free-born male youths. A citizen's son would also wear distinctive clothing to show his status, including a *bulla* (amulet) around his neck, to mark him as off limits for sexual predators. Nonetheless, adult men lusted after aristocratic Roman youths as they raced horses, swam in the Tiber, and preened themselves in the baths. Relationships between males were supposed to be based on dominance and submission, and the passive, youthful partner was not supposed to feel pleasure: Juventius, for instance, asserted his power over Catullus by resisting his kisses, appropriately for a citizen boy. But in other poetic and visual sources, beloved male youths sometimes feel desire and respond sexually.[77] Tibullus declares:

> he'll soften up for you, then you'll be able to take sweet
> kisses; he'll fight back, but will give you the ones you take.
> At first the ones you take, then, if you ask, *he'll* offer them,
> and then he'll want to wrap himself around your neck.[78]

These relationships were economic as well. For instance, beautiful male youths cruised the bathhouses or theatres, looking for men who might become permanent patrons.[79] A man might keep a slave as a beloved *concubinus* until he married.

During the last two centuries BCE, traditionalists worried that the luxuries brought by conquest, and by Greek influence, were effeminizing young Roman citizen men. Beautiful male slave youths were highly desired, and could inspire mad, shameful passions. Cato feared that young citizens were plucking their eyebrows, learning Greek dances, wearing fine clothing, and even submitting to sex themselves. The laws that forbade the seduction of freeborn youth seemed ineffective, and the emperor Augustus feared that luxury-loving male youth would fail to raise a future generation of Roman citizens. He passed a series of laws aimed at restoring traditional sexual morality to Rome: for instance, in 18BCE, the *lex Julia* required husbands to prosecute their wives for adultery, now seen as an offense against the state. He tried to strengthen the boundaries of status by forbidding marriages between those of the senatorial classes and freedmen, prostitutes, gladiators, and others subject to *infamia*. These laws mainly functioned as an ideological marker, however, legitimating Augustus's rule as a paternal figure by recalling a mythical golden age of Roman austerity, and they did little to stem the tide of luxury.[80] Chroniclers depicted later Roman emperors as lustful and decadent. The Emperor Commodus, for instance, allegedly had a harem with three hundred women and as many youths; the unwilling denizens of the harem would be raped if they resisted. On one hand, the chroniclers might have been implicitly comparing the emperors to gods who could seduce humans with impunity, but on the other, the chroniclers also symbolized excessive power as excessive lust.[81]

In contrast to this decadent world, the philosophical school known as the Stoics developed an alternative code of sexual morality. They believed that the wise man must focus on controlling his own desires in order to cultivate the autonomy of his own self. While Plato had believed that the rational self could harness erotic energy to a higher path, the Stoics believed that the rational self could totally suppress desire. For them, the ideal state was *apatheia*, or passionlessness, and that a man could attain this state using his reason. While earlier Greek Stoics such as Zeno had advocated the philosophical love of boys, the Roman Stoics scorned this love as unnatural. To have sex with a prostitute or a boy was even worse, for it harmed the self's honor. Like contemporary physicians, the Stoics prescribed that sexual desire must be indulged only in moderation, and ideally, only for the purposes of procreation in marriage. Musonius Rufus stressed marriage as companionship between men and women, and as the foundation of cities. Living up to these ideals could be difficult. After all, the Stoic Seneca was the Emperor Nero's philosopher and could not restrain his pupil's debauchery. Juvenal often satirized the Stoics as austere, disheveled, plainly dressed philosophers who advocated self-control but indulged in boys and drink behind the scenes. While this was probably just the usual invective, it may reflect the fact that, as several scholars have pointed out, the Stoics advocated a self-controlled ideal of masculinity quite different from the Roman celebration of violent, exploitative masculine sexual desire.[82]

In the first century, a new approach to spirituality and sexuality emerged – that of Christianity. Like the Stoics, Christians advocated abstinence and self-control. Like Plato's Diotima, they insisted that a heavenly desire for God was superior to the earthly desire for flesh.[83] Like the Stoics, Jesus presented a vision of masculinity different from that of Roman men, as Diana Swancutt and other scholars point out. While they prided themselves on domination, he was portrayed as gentle, submitting himself to the will of God to sacrifice himself for the good of all, humble and poor in contrast to the luxurious, overweening Roman empire.[84] However, Christianity was in many ways radically different from Stoicism. Christianity was a religion, not a philosophy. Stoics told men to use their reason to control their desires; Christians told men and women to rely on their intense faith in God to attain sexual purity.

Christians rejected the tie between sex and the city. They refused to sacrifice to the Roman gods, so the Romans refused to tolerate them as they had tolerated other foreign cults. To amuse the crowds at gladiator fights, Christians were thrown to wild animals. As Carlin Barton observes, watching a person being torn to pieces may have evoked the bacchanalian, spiritual power of ancient animal and human sacrifices for the Roman crowds.[85] But for the Christians, the sanctity of their virgin bodies, their refusal to submit to Roman law, represented the power of negative sexuality, the transcendence of the flesh reaching spiritual ecstasy through death.

Suggested reading

Bing, Peter, and Rip Cohen, eds. *Games of Venus: an Anthology of Greek and Roman Erotic Verse from Sappho to Ovid*. New York, 1991.

Clarke, John R. *Looking at Lovemaking in Roman Art*. Berkeley, 1998.

Cohen, David. *Law, Sexuality and Society*. Cambridge, 1994.

Davidson, James N. *Courtesans and Fishcakes: The Consuming Passions of Classical Athens*. New York, 1998.

Edwards, Catherine. *The Politics of Immorality in Ancient Rome*. Cambridge, 1993.

Foucault, Michel. *The Care of the Self*. Translated by Robert Hurley. 3 vols. Vol. 3, *The History of Sexuality*. New York, 1988.

——— *The Uses of Pleasure*. Translated by Robert Hurley. New York, 1990.

Hallett, Judith P., and Marilyn B. Skinner, eds. *Roman Sexualities*. Princeton, 1997.

Halperin, David M., John J. Winkler, and Froma I. Zeitlin, eds. *Before Sexuality: The Construction of Erotic Experience in the Ancient Greek World*. Princeton, 1990.

Keuls, Eva C. *The Reign of the Phallus: Sexual Politics in Ancient Athens*. Berkeley, 1985.

Langlands, Rebecca. *Sexual Morality in Ancient Rome*. Cambridge, 2006.

McClure, Laura. *Sexuality and Gender in the Classical World*. Oxford, 2002.

Nussbaum, Martha C., and Juha Sihvola, eds. *The Sleep of Reason: Erotic Experience and Sexual Ethics in Ancient Greece and Rome*. Chicago, 2002.

Richlin, Amy. *The Garden of Priapus: Sexuality and Aggression in Roman Humor*. Revised edn. New York, 1983.

Skinner, Marilyn B. *Sexuality in Greek and Roman Culture*. Malden, MA, 2005.

Chapter 3

Divine desire in Judaism and early Christianity

Kiss me, make me drunk with your kisses!
Your sweet loving
is better than wine ...
My lover, my king, has brought me into his chambers.
We will laugh, you and I, and count
each kiss,
Better than wine.

These verses from the Song of Songs celebrate erotic desire and fertility. They praise the breasts and belly of the lover, in a land full of pomegranates and deer, wheat and figs, cedars and myrrh. Originally love songs passed on in an oral tradition, they were eventually incorporated into both Jewish and Christian scriptures.[1] How could such a frank celebration of sexual love become part of holy traditions? The answer is easier for Judaism, which had always valued marital sex and fertility. The Hebrew scriptures used sexual desire – or infidelity – to symbolize God's love for his people and their betrayal of him. The Song of Songs became the Song of Solomon, a metaphor for the love of God and his chosen people in the land of Palestine. Christians also interpreted the Song of Songs as a metaphor for God's divine love, and the pleasure of a mystical union with him. But they insisted that this divine love was quite different from human erotic love, which was selfish and twisted. For them, celibacy was superior, and marriage second-best. This represented a marked departure from Jewish traditions.

Christian ambivalence about sexual desire posed several problems. First, the early Christians believed that sexual desire distracted the believer from union with God and that it was polluting. But how could they celebrate divine love and denigrate eros, or human love? Second, the Church fathers claimed that celibacy was superior to marriage. In response, some early Christian women rejected their husbands and claimed a holy virginity. How could the Church reconcile female virginity with the tradition that women should submit to marriage? Third, how could Christianity perpetuate itself if believers were celibate?

To trace the contrasting Jewish and Christian views of sexuality, it is important to treat the scriptures as historical documents and to place their attitudes toward sex in context. Most of the Hebrew Bible was written between the ninth and the fifth century BC, although it referred back to earlier events. The New Testament Gospels all present different stories about Jesus and were written decades after his death. Within the scriptures, different authors present different interpretations of morality, which try to reconcile the tensions between virginity and marriage, between purity and pollution, and between celibacy and fertility.

The Jewish heritage

For most of Jewish history, sexual desire in itself was not seen as evil; marital sex and procreation were celebrated. The ancient Israelites needed marriage to survive as a community, for they began as a small tribe in a harsh, infertile upland frontier country.[2] In early Israel, fertility was much more important than monogamous marriage. The Ten Commandments prohibited adultery, which was like stealing another man's goods, but they said nothing about sex before marriage or virginity. The patriarchs, such as Abraham, kept concubines who could bear children if their wives turned out to be barren. Sarah gives her handmaid Hagar to Abraham for this reason. As scholar David Biale points out, the story of Ruth and Naomi illustrates this concern with fertility above all else.[3] Naomi's husband, Elimelech, and her two sons died, leaving no sons to carry on the family name. But Naomi's daughter-in-law, Ruth, pledges to remain with her and help her. She declares, "Whither thou goest, I will go"; this beautiful verse, so often read in weddings, thus refers to the love and loyalty of two women for each other. Above all, Naomi wants a male heir, so they could perpetuate Elimelech's name – and retain his inheritance. So Naomi urges Ruth to go to Boaz, a distant kinsman of Elimelech. One night, when Boaz lies in a drunken stupor on the threshing floor, Ruth, perfumed and ornamented, surprises him; he covers her with the corner of his cloak and they sleep there all night. Ruth and Boaz then marry (Ruth 3:18).

Fertility was sacred, powerful, and dangerous. The ancient Israelites emerged from among the Canaanites, who worshipped fertility gods and goddesses. Although the Hebrews separated themselves off by their distinctive worship of Yahweh, archeological evidence reveals that women continued to pray to the fertility goddess Asherah in their household devotions.[4] But sex itself made Jews ritually unclean, and they were supposed to bathe afterwards. This did not mean that they saw marital sex itself as evil. Rather, the power of marital sex needed to be contained and purified through ritual. Pollution was matter of out place, so, if menstrual blood or semen were not contained, it was defiling. (The Hebrews believed that menstrual blood was a woman's seed, like male semen.) If a man masturbated, or spilled his seed on the ground, like Onan in the scriptures, he wasted his seed and committed a terrible sin.

By obeying their rules for sexual purity, the Hebrews expressed their monogamous relationship with Yahweh, the one God. As historian Kathy Gaca argues, the Hebrews believed that if they engaged in "rebellious sexual fornication," such as having sex while worshipping the pagan god Baal, or later, marrying pagan women, they violated this covenant with their God.[5] Prophets denounced their own people as harlots for turning away from God and worshipping pagan idols. Hosea warned unfaithful kings and irreligious men that they were like promiscuous women. Instead, they should become like faithful wives to God.[6]

After they had been exiled in a foreign land, the Hebrews became especially conscious of the need to regulate sex to preserve the boundaries of religion. Prophets began to denounce intermarriage, which the Hebrews had practiced in earlier years as a way of gaining wives. They pressured men to dismiss foreign wives they had brought back with them from exile, for they might introduce pagan religious practices into the household, the center of Jewish religious life (Ezra 10:19). Jubilees 30:7 proclaimed that a daughter who married a Gentile would be stoned to death, along with her father who authorized such a marriage. An adulterous wife threatened the transmission of the Jewish line through the male patriarchs. As historian Helena Zlotnick recounts, if a husband suspected his wife of adultery, he could take her to the temple, "where she would be bound, put on public display, and made to take bitter herbs; if they harmed her, she was guilty, if not set free." As Zlotnick observes, foreign women threatened "sanctified land and its power of procreation."[7]

Yet sexual desire could also become a metaphor for the love of God and his people. The famous Song of Songs may have been written in the period after the exile. The Shulamite – a dark, beautiful woman – and her lover king suffer from an intimate "fever of love" as they meet in hidden gardens where the vines bud, the blossoms open, and the "pomegranate is in flower." The couple also become metaphors for the land of Israel, the lover "Tall as Mount Lebanon, a man like a cedar!" and the woman's "hair like a flock of goats, bounding down Mount Gilead." The Song of Songs also praised King Solomon's Temple and the joyful day of his wedding, leading many subsequent commentators to regard the poem as a metaphor for God's marriage with his people.[8]

The book of Proverbs also celebrated ordinary marital sex, advising a young man to avoid:

> evil temptresses and instead,
> … rejoice with the wife of your youth.
> As a loving deer and a graceful doe,
> Let her breasts satisfy you at all times;
> And always be enraptured with her love.
>   Proverbs 5:18–19

A more ascetic tendency influenced Palestinian Judaism around the time of Jesus' birth. Plato's notion that the body must be transcended to attain a higher spiritual path influenced some Jewish thinkers, such as Philo. He was a Jewish mystic who believed that sexual desire led to spiritual and social disorder, distracting the soul from God. Reading the Stoics as well, Philo advocated sexual continence.

Some Jewish groups, such as the Essenes, also practiced celibacy so they could "open their hearts to God" and focus on their task as elite warriors defending Israel against the Roman empire.[9] An apocryphal scripture, the Wisdom of Solomon, blessed the "barren woman who is undefiled" and "eunuch whose hands have done no lawless deed." Happiness was to be found in the worship of divine wisdom Sophia, personified as Solomon's bride (Wisdom of Solomon: 3). However, none of these groups enjoined the rest of the Jews to become celibate: celibacy was the sign of prophecy and the spiritual elite. The rest were to follow Jewish marriage rules to preserve fragile Hebrew culture from dominant pagan influence.[10] Philo also believed that marital sexual desire was good because it bound couples together with affection *and* produced children.[11]

Jesus

Unlike the elegantly educated Philo, steeped in Greek culture, Jesus came from a poor village in Palestine. The earlier Gospels portray him as a wandering Jewish preacher and faith healer. Far from celebrating family values, he tells his followers to leave their families, give all they had to the poor, and follow him (Matt. 11:35). In fact, he declares he would turn families against each other. As theologian Halvor Moxnes observes, Jesus and his followers were somewhat like a cult movement who wanted to remove believers from their families and provide them with a new, spiritual family.[12]

In contrast to the conventional Jewish celebration of marital fertility, Jesus praises barren women and even those men "who made themselves eunuchs for the sake of the kingdom of heaven" (Matt. 19:12). What did he mean? Later Christian tradition interpreted this as a praise of celibacy. But Matthew had Jesus use the word "eunuch." Self-castrated *galli* who worshiped Cybele wandered around Palestine, and eunuchs served at Herod's court. As an unmarried man in his thirties without a business, wife, or children, it may have been that Jesus was insulted as a eunuch and, as he often does, turns these insults around to celebrate his status. He and his followers are not tied to the interests of their earthly families, but devote themselves to the spiritual world of God.[13]

Jesus also rejects the Pharisees' rules about polluted people, such as Samaritans, bleeding women, prostitutes, and moneylenders. He eats with sinners, praises the sinful woman who anoints his feet, and proclaims that prostitutes and sinners would attain the kingdom of God first, because they listened to the message of John the Baptist (Matt. 21:31), However, this does not mean that sin is unimportant to him. Jesus denounces fornication and adultery along with stealing, murder, lying, and so on. He focuses on the motivations of the inner heart, rather than outer observances of laws about ritual pollution. For instance, in Matthew he proclaims, "I say to you that everyone who looks at a woman with lust for her has already committed adultery with her in his heart" (Matt. 5: 28). However, his chief message concerns love, compassion, and forgiveness. The greater the sin, he preaches, the greater the power of God to forgive.

Paul and the apostles: first century CE

As Paul and other apostles began to spread the practice of Christianity in the middle of the first century, they developed a negative attitude toward sexual desire.[14] The early Christians were still part of Jewish culture, and, like Jewish synagogues at that time, they also attracted Gentiles. Paul traveled to synagogues and household-based congregations around the Roman world. He and his followers were often rather humble people: he was a tentmaker, some of his followers were slaves, and others were tradesmen and women, although some wealthy aristocratic Roman women and men patronized the cause.

The early Christians wanted to create a new kind of community united by worship, love and charity toward each other, but by emphasizing sexual purity, they also created boundaries between themselves and the surrounding Greco-Roman society, with its luxurious and violent sexual culture. They denounced the pagans for using their bodies in a "passion of lust." Paul proclaimed that "neither fornicators, nor idolaters, nor adulterers, nor the effeminate, nor men who have sex with men, nor thieves, nor the covetous, nor drunkards, nor revilers, nor swindlers" would go to heaven, and indeed God would punish them (1 Corinthians 6:9–10). There has been a great deal of debate over the meaning of Paul's references to effeminate men and men who had sex with other men. Did he mean just male prostitutes? Could he be referring to the *galli*, or sacred eunuchs?[15] Whatever the case may be, Paul was rejecting the conventional Roman tradition that men could take the dominant role in sex with males or females without incurring shame; for Paul, all extramarital sex was shameful.

For many members of early Christian congregations, this was a radical new idea of sexuality. In Roman culture, women and slaves had to provide sexual services to dominant men; they did not own their own bodies. Conversely, it was perfectly legitimate for a citizen male to demand such services, as long as he did not infringe on freeborn women and youths or other men's property. The early Christians clearly denounced this culture. Could it be argued that they were denouncing the violence and exploitation inherent in it? Christians were warned not to "take advantage of and defraud" each other in matters of sexual lust (1 Thessalonians 4:6). However, in general, the early Christians seem to have been more concerned with pollution than with exploitation. First, Paul declares that "he who unites himself with a prostitute is one with her in body. ... For it is said, 'The two will become one flesh'. ... All other sins a man commits are outside his body, but he who sins sexually sins against his own body." However, in telling women and slaves that they were free within the body of Christ, Paul does not tell them that they owned their own bodies: "Do you not know that your body is a temple of the Holy Spirit, who is in you, whom you have received from God? You are not your own; you were bought at a price. Therefore honor God with your body"(1 Corinthians 6:18-20). But in a radical reversal, he tells those male Roman citizens that to be Christian they must be slaves to God and should not demand control over their own bodies. To enter the community of the faithful, and to rid themselves of this pollution, they could renounce their previous sins, for belief in Christ would wash them clean of their sins.

Did Paul denigrate just adultery and fornication, or all sexual desire? First, Paul believed that celibacy was preferable; he himself did not have a wife. The cares of a spouse and household distracted the believer from a focus on God. Second, unlike the older Jewish tradition, he did not value marital sex as a good in itself, even for fertility. This was because he believed that the Second Coming of Jesus was at hand, so that there was no need to carry on procreation.[16] As Paul proclaims, "What I mean, brothers, is that the time is short. From now on those who have wives should live as if they had none" (1 Corinthians 6:29). It was better for a virgin to remain a virgin, or a man not to marry.

However, while couples should temporarily abstain from sex, "for a season, that you may devote yourselves to prayer," they should remain married and fulfill their "conjugal debt" by having sex with each other during other times. This was different from traditional Jewish rules about ritual purity. Paul never describes marital sex in a positive light; rather, it was just a way of avoiding the desires which Satan implanted toward fornication. It was "better to marry than to burn," he advises the unmarried who did not think they could remain celibate (1 Corinthians 7:1–40). Paul realizes that if all his followers became celibate, his congregations would lose their base in the devout households of Corinth. Furthermore, he recognizes that most of his followers were not blessed with the gift of celibacy. If the women refused to have sex with their husbands, their husbands might be tempted to go to prostitutes. Apparently, some women of the Corinthian congregation were interpreting the Christian message to mean that they should remain pure and refuse to sleep with their husbands so that they could focus on spiritual matters.[17] The Corinthian women were also praying and prophesizing in church, for in early Christianity women played an active leadership role, serving as missionaries, patrons of the church and even as deacons. Paul asserted that "there is neither Jew nor Greek, there is neither slave nor free man, there is neither male nor female; for you are all one in Christ Jesus" (Galatians 3:28). But this egalitarian promise conflicted with his insistence that wives must obey their husbands, and with the warning, thought by historians to have been inserted by later Christians, that women must not speak in church.

Paul and the other apostles recognized how difficult it is to control sexual desire. As Paul declares, "I have the desire to do what is right, but not the ability to carry it out. For I do not do the good I want, but the evil I do not want is what I keep on doing" (Romans 7:18–20). The author of Timothy has Paul blame this inability to control the will on desire, that "gives birth to sin, and sin, when it is full-grown, brings forth death" (1 Timothy 4). The only solution was to "crucify" the flesh and instead join the body of Christ (Galatians 5:24). Yet Paul did not reject the human body itself as the source of sin. Paul could not reject the body, because the point of Christianity was that God was made flesh in the person of Jesus, who suffered and died as a human being made divine. Paul thought the body should be respected and made holy, even the most lowly parts

(1 Corinthians 12:23). But to do so, the sexual passions had to be defied and these parts of the body kept pure from sex. As scholar Daniel Boyarin observes, for Paul, the body was linked to the body of Christ, while the flesh was identified with the unruly passions of sex.[18] Interestingly, Paul rarely singled out women or female characters as temptresses or evil harlots, unlike the Hebrew prophets or the later Church fathers. The apostles' admonitions against sexual immorality were addressed to men and women alike.

In opposition to the selfish desires of lust, which led to many other sins, such as lying, stealing, and idolatry, Paul celebrates love. Some scholars have argued that Paul thus differentiated between "eros" which was seen as selfish, aimed at fulfilling the ego's desires, and "agape," which was selfless, and aimed at serving the community.[19] As Paul declares, "Love (agape) is patient, love is kind and is not jealous; love does not brag and is not arrogant" (1 Corinthians 13:4). The most important commandment was always "love thy neighbor as thyself."

Virginity and celibacy in the second and third centuries

For Christians, divine love was more powerful than earthly ties, even more powerful than life itself. The Roman empire often persecuted the fledgling movement of the Christians because they refused to worship at the state temples; many were martyred, even sought martyrdom. The early Christians especially treasured virgin martyrs, who sought death rather than give up their chastity. Thirteen-year-old Agnes, for instance, was threatened with being sent to a brothel or death. She chose death, and met her fate in the arena, where a burly executioner stomped toward her slight frame, sword held high. As legend has it, Agnes proclaimed:

> I exult that such a man comes –
> crazy, savage, violent armed man,
> rather than a languid tender youth
> soft and scented with perfume
> who would destroy me by the death of my chastity.
> This lover, this one I want, I confess it.
> I shall meet his onrush half-way
> and not postpone his hot desires.
> I shall take the sword's length into my breasts
> and draw the force of the sword to my inmost heart.
> Thus wedded to Christ I shall leap up
> above the darkness of the sky.[20]

For Prudentius, the author of this tale, the languid youth would stimulate Agnes's own desires, polluting her body and soul. Instead, she turned her desire toward Christ; she could ardently manipulate the executioner's "hot desires" to obtain the divine union for which she yearned.

In legends, however, other virgins survived, and their tales represented a challenge to the nascent Church of Rome. Early Christianity was sharply divided between those who were trying to create institutions, building from household churches to large basilicas, and those in radical movements who advocated followers to leave their families, abandon their possessions, refuse marriage, and retreat to holy chastity. In the second and third centuries, a series of apocryphal scriptures – that is, scriptures that were eventually rejected from the official canon – denigrated sex in marriage and celebrated virginal, heroic women.

Some of these tales resembled the Greek stories of star-crossed lovers thwarted in their love by evildoers and misfortunes. The spiritual virgins have just as many adventures as the heroines of Greek romance, but instead of seeking the love of a man, they flee it. The heroines of these tales are often engaged, but they refuse to marry handsome, rich, and powerful men. If they are married, they will not have sex with their husbands. In these stories, men are portrayed as too prone to lust themselves, as ineffectual at best and, at worst, as tyrants. However, the virginal heroines can miraculously defy them, with the help of friendly animals and marvelous coincidences.[21]

The story of Thecla, for instance, was written down in the second century by a pious deacon who may have drawn on popular legends about virgins but admitted inventing quotations from Paul. Thecla is a daughter of one of the first families of Iconium, who are proud that their beautiful daughter is betrothed to the wealthy man Thamyris. One day the apostle Paul comes to preach at Onesiphorus's household of believers. As they bustle around preparing bread for communion, he preaches, "There can be no future resurrection, unless you continue in chastity and do not defile your flesh." This was, of course, different from Paul's preaching in his own letters. Thecla lives around the corner from Onesiphorus, and if she sits "like a spider's web fastened to the window" she can hear his preaching. "Captivated" by his message of chastity, Thecla tells her parents that she refuses to marry Thamyris. Thamyris is outraged at the loss of his beautiful bride. In fact, the whole town objects that Paul's preaching of chastity "deprives young men of their intended wives, and virgins of their intended husbands." Furthermore, the Christians refuse to sacrifice to the emperor-god of the Romans. The governor of the city, Castellius, responds to these complaints by throwing Paul into jail. Thecla faces punishment too. Her angry mother declares to the governor, "Let the unjust creature be burned... in the midst of the theatre for refusing Thamyris." Thecla is dragged to the amphitheatre and bound, naked, to the stake, and the young people of the city pile up wood and light it on fire. Her death is supposed to warn all women not to refuse husbands. But as Thecla prays, the ground bursts open in a quake, the sky pours down rain to extinguish the fire, and she flees the ampitheatre and leaves town. As Thecla wanders around the Middle East witnessing for Christianity, wicked men continually try to rape her, and Paul is not much help. For instance, the ruler of Antioch, Alexander, tries to molest her in the street, but Paul claims he does not know her. So Thecla tears Alexander's "coat, and took his crown off his head, and made him appear ridiculous before all the people." When Alexander throws her

Figure 3.1   *Saint Thecla with Wild Beasts and Angels,* Egyptian 5th century CE. Limestone, diameter 25.5 inches (64.8cm). The Nelson-Atkins Museum of Art, Kansas City, Missouri. Purchase: Nelson Trust 48:10. Photograph by Jamison Miller

to the beasts in the amphitheatre in revenge, the lions and bulls do not tear her to pieces; instead, they lay down asleep in front of her. Thecla then went about dressed as a man, converting and healing many women, who later worshipped at her shrine after her death.[22]

The emphasis on virginity allowed many female Christian believers to reject marriage and form communities of women devoted to each other and spiritual knowledge. Leaders of the early Church, such as Jerome, praised their sanctity and encouraged them to read. Christian virginity was lifelong and closely associated with the inviolability of the soul, which could escape the constraints of the body and concentrate on things of the spirit. By sanctifying their bodies, as theologian Teresa Shaw observes, "The individual virgin remove[d] herself or himself from procreation's cycle of birth and death;" her pure, shining, inviolate body seemed to promise the salvation of her soul, and therefore "the immunity to biological processes of decay, disease, and death, and anticipates the incorruptibility that will be restored in paradise."[23] For people in these early centuries, life was brief and fleeting; children broke their parents' hearts when they died as infants or children. Sex was therefore inexorably linked with the reproduction of mortal human bodies which would die. As historian Peter Brown writes, a spiritual transcendence through Christianity was a way to stop the terrible tragedy of time.[24]

Christianity was also very unusual in valuing virginity for both men and women. A few hardy men and women freed themselves of the encumbrances of the world and retreated to the desert to purify their bodies and souls. Both male and female virgins were advised to eat very small amounts of unappetizing food to suppress the desires of the flesh. Male hermits hoped this would help them avoid sexual dreams and polluting nocturnal emissions.[25] To prevent men from lusting after them, virgins were advised not to bathe so that their bodies would become dirty and malodorous, in contrast to the Roman matrons who luxuriated in the bath and perfumed their flesh.[26]

Among some Christians, the celibate male hermit had a higher status than the married householder, unlike in the Jewish world, where men had a holy duty to marry, and the pagan Roman world, where men expressed their dominance through sex. However, the Church fathers worried that some men had apparently taken Jesus' mysterious admonition about being a eunuch for the sake of heaven too literally, and castrated themselves so that they could live a pure life, even living with female ascetics without sexual temptation.[27] Holy men retreated to the desert to devote themselves to prayer, like St. Anthony, but visions of women tempted them.[28] Although Jerome's only companions in the desert were "scorpions and wild beasts," "I often found myself amid bevies of girls. My face was pale and my frame chilled with fasting, yet my mind was burning with desire, and the fire of lust kept bubbling up in me when my flesh was full as dead."[29]

By praising virginity, the early Christian fathers did not abandon their patriarchal assumptions. The Church fathers admired virgins because they renounced their sinful femininity, and became like men. Jerome wrote that "As long as woman is for birth and children, she is different from man as body is from soul. But when she wishes to serve Christ more than the world, then she will cease to be a woman and will be called man."[30] The spiritual power of virgins could also threaten the male leaders of the church. Virgins must submit to male leadership, they increasingly demanded.[31] At the mid-fourth-century Council of Gangra, bishops criticized women who left their spouses and neglected their children; they were horrified at women who wore men's clothing and cut their hair as a declaration that they were no longer subject to men.[32]

Some Church fathers increasingly portrayed femininity itself as extremely polluting. They blamed women for Eve's taking of the apple from the serpent, which led to the expulsion of humanity from Paradise, and the curse of original sin. Tertullian fulminated against women, "You are the devil's gateway: ... you are she who persuaded him [Adam] whom the devil was not valiant enough to

Figure 3.2 *La Tentation de Saint Antoine*, Lucas van Leyden (Lucas de Leyde [dit]) (1489/ 1494–1533) (C) Photo RMN © Michèle Bellot. Paris, Musée du Louvre, Rothschild collection

attack." Tertullian even blamed women for the death of Christ, since by the expulsion from Paradise, Adam and Eve had to face death instead of eternal life, and only the death of Jesus could restore immortality to humans through the resurrection.[33] In the fourth century, Church fathers often symbolized heretics as promiscuous women. As historian Virginia Burrus notes, "Just as she allows herself to be penetrated sexually by strange men, so too she listens indiscriminately and babbles forth new theological formulations carelessly and without restraint: all the gateways of her body are unguarded."[34] The Church fathers also denounced heretics as "effeminate men," and they tried to create a new masculinity based on religious authority and ascetic self-control, as historian Matthew Kuefler argues.[35]

The problem of marital sex

As part of a larger movement to withdraw from the world into celibacy and poverty, some early Christian groups even denigrated marital sex. In the second century, Marcion believed that a bad god, or demiurge, created the world, and that the God of Love sent Jesus to rescue humanity from it. Syrian Christians who followed him required followers to pledge to celibacy before they could be baptized.[36] Similar texts, such as the Acts of Thomas, reviled even marital intercourse. Thomas was supposedly the apostle sent by Jesus to evangelize India. When he arrived there, the king's daughter was about to be married in a lavish ceremony. Called upon to bless the perfumed marriage bed, Thomas told the newly wed couple that "if ye abstain from this foul intercourse, ye become holy temples, pure, being quit of impulses and pains, seen and unseen, and ye will acquire no cares of life or of children, whose end is destruction." Persuaded, they converted and lived a life of celibate holiness.[37]

The focus on celibacy was also linked with the Gnostics and Manichaeans, two closely related movements. The Manichaeans, who followed the Persian prophet Mani, were pale and tattooed and wore long robes. They believed that a bad god created the material world and flesh, and that the good god created the spirit and the heavenly world. Because they did not believe in an institutional church, they had no single dogma, but explored the self through gnosis, or spiritual knowledge, elaborate cosmologies, and mystic rituals.[38] The Gnostics urged the most committed believers to reject the corrupt material world entirely by abstaining from sex, marriage, and money. Other followers carried on their ordinary lives of family and work, but they believed that the spiritual world was much more important than these dull daily concerns.[39]

To combat this heresy, the Church fathers not only argued logically, they accused the Gnostics and Manichaeans of sexual crimes. Some alleged that the Gnostics thought that it was preferable to indulge in "unnatural" sex which would not lead to procreation; since semen perpetuated the flesh, the more semen that was discharged without creating new humans, the quicker the material world would evaporate. Some claimed to have witnessed orgies in which Gnostics turned out all the candles, grabbed the nearest woman, regardless of whether she was a sister or mother, and copulated with her. When babies were born nine months later, they were sacrificed and their blood drunk by the believers. Of course, the Romans had accused the first Christians of such practices, suspicious that their "love feasts" – when they drank the body and blood of Christ – were actually orgies of cannibalism.[40] Augustine denounced the Manichaeans for using birth control in order to avoid perpetuating the material world of human beings.[41]

The Christians who became dominant in the struggle against the Gnostics needed to refute these ideas, not only because marriages and households were necessary to build an institutional church, but also because theologically the Gnostic rejection of the body went against the Christian belief in Christ's incarnation. While the Gnostics rejected the body, the Christians affirmed the body in many ways; they insisted on the resurrection of the body, they described the church as the body of Christ, the body which united believers, and they insisted that Jesus was both divine and embodied as a human being. Since God created the material world of bodies and animals, which could only be perpetuated through fleshly generation, it had to be good. Yet the early Christians had a heritage of denigrating sexual desire as polluting.

The Church fathers, therefore, needed to reconcile their belief in the superiority of celibacy and virginity with the necessity of marriage. On one hand, they rejected those thinkers, such as Jovinian, who argued that sexual desire was not a bad thing. On the other, they needed to oppose the Gnostics and others who denigrated marriage and celebrated celibacy. Some Church fathers, such as Jerome, were quite hostile even to marital sex, arguing that, "In view of the purity of the body of Christ all sexual intercourse is unclean."[42] Jerome advised, "If we abstain from intercourse, we give honor to our wives: if we do not abstain, it is clear that insult is the opposite of honor." Although the organs of generation were God's creation, humans should focus on spiritual rather than earthly things. But other Church fathers believed that the irascible Jerome had gone much too far.[43]

By the fourth and fifth century, most Church fathers affirmed marriage. Clement declared that marriage was holy, since God made humans to procreate, and his Son was incarnated in the flesh.[44] According to Basil of Ancrya, writing in the fourth century, a merciful God gave humans sexual desire so people could procreate and continue the human race, compensating for the introduction of death.[45] For Augustine, only procreation could take the chaotic raw material, the fluids of semen and female ejaculations, and turn them into the order of God's creation.[46] After all, God created nature, including the bodies which needed to have sex to procreate, so procreation itself was good, because children may be born again and become "sons of God." Marriage was thus a good thing – although still second best to celibacy.[47]

Yet the acceptance of marriage and procreation was still grudging. The prophecy that the Second Coming would make procreation unnecessary remained an abstract, if now distant, hope. John Chrysostom accepted marriage as necessary for the perpetuation of the Church, but he argued that Christians should not celebrate marriages with great feasts and processions, as the Romans did, for with the Second Coming, Christians would no longer need such nuptials.[48] While Paul had admonished married people to give each other sex when necessary to avoid temptation, the Church fathers established that marital sex was only permissible for the purposes of procreation. This advice resembled that of the Stoics who taught the same message. However, while the Stoics advocated marital continence as an exercise in self-control and a way of improving health, Christians advocated abstinence except for procreation as part of their covenant with God.[49]

How could the good of procreation be reconciled with the pollution of desire? For Clement, couples should make love undistracted by the sinful power of sexual desire, which was "death bearing enslavement." Clement instructed couples to procreate calmly and without pleasure, avoiding sex in the daytime; "even at night, although in darkness, is it fitting to carry on immodestly or indecently?"[50] This restraint of desire was part of a much larger program of asceticism: believers should avoid drinking and eating too much, and refrain from wearing fine clothes, sparkling jewels, and fragrant ointments.

If sexual desire was so bad, where did it come from? Some Church fathers decided that marital procreation became necessary due to the fall of Adam and Eve from the garden of Paradise. In Paradise, Adam and Eve did not sexually desire each other, and they did not need to procreate because they had eternal life. But since Eve gave in to the serpent and tasted of the tree of knowledge, disobeying God's command, God expelled them from Paradise, and death came into the world. For John Chrysostom, marriage was God's "concession to the weakness of humanity, granted in the beginning in our inferior, childlike state after the fall." God implanted sexual desire in bodies "for a useful purpose."[51] For Augustine, the problem was that Adam wanted sex too soon, not that he wanted sex at all. Augustine even acknowledged that married couples sometimes had sex without needing to procreate, and he excused it as a venial sin, not a mortal sin if they did not try to prevent the birth of children. Lust was still sinful, but God had instituted marriage so that this sin could be turned to a good end and forgiven by his mercy.[52]

Writing at the end of the fourth century, Augustine himself struggled mightily with the problems of sexual desire and marriage. It was difficult to live the ascetic life that Clement commended, in the midst of Roman civilization, still flourishing in its luxury, where beautiful, pampered matrons ornamented themselves with gold ornaments, diadems, colorful silks, and fragrant perfumes, and laughed and drank, reclining, at their husband's dinner parties, where erotic pictures ornamented the walls. An ambitious young scholar in North Africa, Augustine knew that to get ahead he had to learn Roman verse, with its elegant indecencies (such as Martial and Catullus), argue ruthlessly against his opponents without regard to morality, and marry for social advantage. In his youth, he remembers, "I ran wild in the shadowy jungle of erotic adventures. ... Clouds of muddy carnal concupiscence filled the air."[53] Present-day Algeria, his home, was only partially Christianized, and many pagan remnants remained infused into Christian practice. In his late teens, he also began a long, loving, and monogamous relationship with a concubine, and had a child. He also had a close male friend with whom he lived for a while in a sort of intellectual commune. He later regretted that in his youth he "could not mind the bright path of friendship, but out of the dark concupiscence of the flesh and the effervescence of youth exhalations came forth which obscured and overcast my heart, so that I was unable to discern pure affection from unholy desire." Did this mean his affection for his male friend or his concubine? In any case, his mother Monica wanted him to marry to advance his career in the Roman bureaucracy, and picked out a very young girl from a good family for him. He obeyed his mother and sent his concubine back to north Africa, suffering great grief at this loss of her loving care. But his future wife was still too young to marry, so, unable to stay celibate, Augustine took another concubine.[54]

Augustine did not want to condemn the flesh as sinful in itself, as had the Gnostics. As a young man, he had been intrigued by Gnostic dualism, by the idea that the material world was evil and the spiritual world divine. Augustine finally renounced the things of the world, both sex and worldly ambition, to commit himself to the church and celibacy. As a bishop, he rejected Gnosticism and determined to vindicate marriage and procreation against the Gnostic belief that procreation just perpetuated the corrupt material world. Yet even as he abandoned his concubine and decided not to marry, in sleep the images of those pleasures he rejected came back to haunt him. How could he consent to sexual activities in his dreams which he had finally renounced in his daily life? For Augustine, sexual desire was emblematic of all the wicked desires – greed, ambition, selfishness – which distracted the soul and led it to "fornicate against God," one of his central metaphors. Augustine found it amazing that although a man could control every part of his body with his will, when it came to the sexual organs, they would "not obey the direction of the will, but lust has to be waited for to set these members in motion, as if it had legal right over them, and sometimes it refuses to act when the mind wills, while often it acts against its will!" In other words, the penis refused to become erect when a man wanted to procreate, but became aroused when he did not want it to.[55] Transgression also divided the self, which could only find unity in God.[56]

For Augustine, the body itself, including the sexual organs, was not the problem, but the unruly will. Augustine decided that his sexual dreams, and sexual desire itself, were one manifestation of the disobedient human will, of original sin. Referring to the expulsion of Adam and Eve from the Garden of Eden, he asserted, "When the first man transgressed the law of God, he began to have another law in his members which was repugnant to the law of his mind, and he felt the evil of his own disobedience when he experienced in the disobedience of his flesh a most righteous retribution recoiling on himself."[57] Humans were powerless to control sexual desire on their own. Instead, they had to rely on God's grace to forgive this original sin, to forgive all their sins, and to bestow the gift of celibacy. Unlike some of the other Church fathers who blamed women for tempting men's lust, Augustine focused on the male organ as emblematic of unruly sexual desire, as Joyce Salisbury points out.[58] At the same time, Augustine drew a parallel between the unruly male member and women by arguing "Your flesh is like your wife … It rebels against you, just as your wife does. Love it, rebuke it; let it be formed into one bond of concord between flesh and spirit." The flesh is not evil, therefore, "unless it is unmastered."[59] Yet Augustine was not an ascetic, who tortured his body in the desert; instead, he thought that a calm spiritual union with God provided eternal pleasures far superior to the temporary lusts and sorrows of the body.

While Augustine denigrated sexual desire as the disobedient will, he also celebrated love. The problem with eros, or fleshly love, is that it distracted the
believer from loving God. Eros was selfish, using others as objects, unlike God's
outpouring of love. As scholar David Tracy notes, Augustine tried to transform
eros through agape into the idea of caritas, or God's love.[60] Love, or caritas, was
based on caring and love for neighbors, as well as God's love, a selfless love that
could overcome original sin.[61]

Augustine lived just before the decline of the Roman empire, at a time when classical culture still flourished. In the early fourth century, the Emperor Constantine
declared the Roman empire to be Christian. He helped to establish Christianity as
an institution by expelling those who did not follow the Nicene Creed, and persecuted adultery, prostitution and sex between men. The western Christian church
resolved the tension between marriage and celibacy by upholding celibacy as the
highest spiritual status, while marriage was second best. Monasteries of chaste men
and women preserved the faith in chaotic times. The ideal of celibacy for priests
began to become important in the fourth century, but the practice was not widespread until the sixth century, and many priests continued to keep wives or concubines. Only five to ten percent of those within the Roman empire practiced the faith,
and the empire itself was slowly crumbling. In the next few centuries, after the
Roman empire collapsed, Christianity gradually spread through pagan Europe, but
the tensions between earthly love and heavenly love persisted.

Suggested reading

Biale, David. *Eros and the Jews*. New York, 1992.
Boyarin, Daniel. *Carnal Israel*. Berkeley, 1993.
Brown, Peter. *The Body and Society: Men, Women, and Sexual Renunciation in Early
    Christianity*. New York, 1988.
Burrus, Virginia, ed. *Toward a Theology of Eros*. New York, 2006.
Clark, Elizabeth A. *Reading Renunciation: Asceticism and Scripture in Early Chris-
    tianity*. Princeton, 1999.
Gaca, Kathy L. *The Making of Fornication: Eros, Ethics, and Political Reform in Greek
    Philosophy and Early Christianity*. Berkeley, 2003.
Kraemer, Ross Shepard. *Her Share of the Blessings: Women's Religions among Pagans,
    Jews and Christians in the Graeco-Roman World*. New York, 1992.
———, ed. *Maenads, Martyrs, Matrons, Monastics: a Sourcebook on Women's Religions
    in the Greco-Roman World*. Philadelphia, 1988.
Pagels, Elaine H. *Adam, Eve, and the Serpent*. 1st ed. New York, 1988.

Chapter 4

Medieval fantasies of desire, sacred and profane

Hadewijch, a lady of twelfth-century Brabant, dreamily imagined two lovers mystically fusing, "with what wonderful sweetness the one lover lives in the other and so permeates the other that they do not know themselves from each other. But they possess each other in mutual delight, mouth in mouth, heart in heart, body in body, soul in soul."[1] Guilhem of Languedoc wrote that the joy of romantic love was indescribable:

> No man has ever had the cunning to imagine
> What it is like, he will not find it in will or desire,
> In thought or meditation.
> Such joy cannot find its like;
> A man who tried to praise it justly
> Would not come to the end of his praise in a year.[2]

Both portrayed desire as an intense union, an overwhelming force. But Hadewijch was writing about the soul's union with God, and Guilhem about romantic, adulterous love. Neither could conceive of finding this kind of ecstasy within marriage.

The Church itself was profoundly ambivalent about sexual desire in marriage. As we have seen, the Church fathers had regarded marriage as holy, but second best to celibacy. Officially, the church permitted marital sex only for procreation, and denigrated the pleasure that accompanied it. Some church authorities regarded all sexual desire as inherently polluting, and only excused it within marriage as an unfortunate necessity for procreation. Others distinguished between sexual acts that could lead to procreation, and those that could not, basing their moral judgments on nature.[3] But it took centuries to impose monogamous marriage on the common people, a task not accomplished until the tenth century, and priests commonly married and took concubines until the Church cracked down on this practice in the eleventh and twelfth centuries.[4] But by the twelfth century, facing the Cathar heretics who denigrated marriage, church authorities proclaimed marriage to be a sacrament and a legitimate way of living a holy life.[5] Husbands and wives were supposed to love each other calmly, having sex to procreate and prevent fornication, but moralists differentiated this sober marital love from burning passion.[6] Yet desiring God had always been an important theme in Christianity, and mystics such as Hadewijch developed a romantic language of divine union. But the Church feared that if mystics focused on their own desire for God, they might transgress the boundaries of church authority.

During the chaotic earlier period of the ninth and tenth centuries, the Church had not been a strong and unified institution; in fact, few central authorities exerted control in Europe. Monarchs fought fierce battles over territory, but their offspring lost sovereignty in the next generation as rebellious nobles sought to rule their own fiefdoms. In the eighth century, Islamic dynasties had conquered much of Spain, and established sophisticated urban centers. Arab scholars preserved Greek and Roman knowledge and added to it. Over the next few centuries, Christian kings and Muslim rulers struggled for control of Spain, but Christians, Jews, and Muslims coexisted there, sometimes uneasily, sometimes harmoniously. By the eleventh and twelfth centuries, chaos and disorder diminished and medieval societies began to grow and flourish. Trade expanded, cities bustled behind their walls, monarchs gained greater authority, universities revived the pursuit of knowledge, and the Church consolidated its strength, reforming its own institutions and revitalizing spirituality among the common people.[7]

The culture of the early Middle Ages overflowed with descriptions of romantic desire transgressing the bonds of marriage. The Cathar heretics rejected the Church's insistence that marriage was a sacrament. Like the earlier Manichaeans, they believed that the world of the spirit was good and the world of the flesh evil, and that the Church sanctioned the evils of the flesh by celebrating marriage.[8] Troubadours celebrated adulterous love; female mystics fought against arranged marriages. Men such as monks and knights even wrote passionate letters and poetry to each other, celebrating their burning passion.

Some critics have argued that expressions of desire between two masculine personas could metaphorically destabilize the conventions of medieval culture, based on normative relationships between men and women.[9] As Karma Lochrie has pointed out, however, heterosexual desire was not seen as "normal" for medieval clerics, because they had no notion of the sexually normative. Heterosexual desire, in terms of a craving and yearning for sexual pleasure with a man or woman, was seen as resulting from the expulsion of Adam and Eve from Paradise. While marital sex for procreation was allowed, intense desire between men and women was seen as dangerous.[10] All sexual desire, therefore, could potentially transgress the social and religious order. Passionate love between men and women could disrupt careful marriage arrangements and disturb convents and monasteries.

Yet an efflorescence of desire infused the twelfth-century renaissance.[11] Poets and scholars invented new discourses of desire beyond the Christian fathers: in the new universities and in cities and monasteries, scholars studied Arabic poetry and science, troubadour lyrics, and revived classics such as Ovid and Horace along with ancient anatomy. With greater prosperity, noblemen established elegant courts where singers and jugglers entertained. The idea of romantic love began to be explored in poetry, tales and song. Popular tales presented sexual desire in a less elevated way, depicting sex as funny, yet also excessive, and dangerous. Both men and women faced the harsh realities of the body: dirt, fleas and lice, hunger, plague, death. But fantasies of desire, whether sacred or profane, promised to transcend the body's fragility.

Ideas of desire in Spain: Muslim and Jewish culture

In early medieval Spain, Christian, Jewish, and Islamic cultures mixed and collided. Islamic attitudes toward desire differed somewhat than those of Christianity. The Koran regarded sexual desire as a necessary drive which should be satisfied in marriage. The Prophet valued marriage not celibacy, and imams married. Marriage was supposed to satisfy both men and women sexually and thus keep them from temptation; contraception was also allowed.[12] The "all too brief delight" of sex "arous[ed] man's longing for the lasting [delight] in the world to come."[13] But the Koran and *hadith* (authenticated traditions about sayings of the Prophet not found in the Koran) denounced fornication between men and women, sodomy, and drinking alcohol. However, in the courts of Muslim Spain, men enjoyed wine, poetry, and dancing; they seduced beautiful slave girls, kept concubines, and even pursued handsome youths. According to scholar Khaled El-Rouayheb, men who took the passive role in sex were scorned as different. But, he notes, if a man took the active role in sex with another man, authorities would scold him for that vice just as they would rebuke him for drinking or gambling. This sort of sex with men was less serious, for instance, than seducing a married woman.[14]

The tenth-century Andalusian writer Ibn Hazm wrote that "Allah has implanted in every man two opposed natures." The first is rational and just; it "counsels only good; and incites to what is fair and seemly," and pleasing to Allah. But the second "advises solely the gratification of the lusts, and leads the way to all that is evil and vicious." But he admitted that lovers found it difficult to control their passions, "for who among us would be so bold as to claim the mastery of his soul, or who will engage to control its wayward impulses, save with Allah's strength and power assisting him?" Both the love for humans and the love for the divine shared "a natural admiration for lovely forms," following the Platonic tradition of desire as a path to knowledge of beauty.[15] For the mystic Sufis, celibacy would enable the believer to focus on God, rather than on marriage and household. Celibate Sufi dervishes would contemplate a beautiful youth as an emblem of God's "radiant beauty"; the cruelties the beautiful youth inflicted on them just tested the poet's faith.[16] The Andalucian Sufi poet Shushtari drew on vernacular erotic songs for his mystical verse, and wrote, "In that passion, I am the master of my time,/the lover of my beloved, and in the love of the beautiful one, my life and my art are extinguished."[17]

In diasporic Judaism, the rabbis emphasized marital sexual pleasure.[18] Jews had to preserve their religious heritage in their homes, so the family became the center of worship, and procreation necessary for survival. In the rabbinic Judaism that evolved during this period, rabbis developed the purity rituals about sex even further, but they emphasized that sexual pleasure in marriage must be affirmed as an "obligation" to "preserve the line of Jewish blood." And rabbis, of course, were married. As scholar David Biale observes, "The sexual laws were to turn the body into a sacred site, a substitute for the Temple."[19] The rabbis conceived of sexual desire as *yetzer*, a necessary force that could lead to good and evil, a "creative churning and chaos" that helped create matter and ensured the world's continuity. Yetzer drove men to marry and to study the Torah, but it could also distract them from spirituality. Yetzer drove men toward sin, but, without it, men would not be able to choose between good and evil behavior.[20] At the same time, the great Spanish Jewish theologian Maimonides established rules restricting marital sex even further, since because he thought sex tied humans to the material rather than the spiritual world. However, Maimonides still regarded sex an obligation between couples. The twelfth- and thirteenth-century mystics of the Kabbalah, sometimes influenced by Sufi Islam, developed a more exalted view of marital sexual union. As Biale notes, "in Kabbalistic terms intercourse is uniting of the male and female aspects of God, rather than a merely physical act."[21]

In Spain, Jewish poets also shared the language of secret romance with Muslims; some of them would write love poetry to women or youths, and then, repentant and older, transfer their desires to the divine.[22] A poem by Judah al-Harizi, a Jewish man, well-expressed the intense eroticism of this hidden desire for a male youth:

> My soul is under the sole of his foot like a dot
> And he is haughty and proud above me like an exclamation point
> I approached the garden of his face like a thief
> To gather the delights of his mouth and eat them,
> And the sun of his cheeks rose on me –
> It is my 'bloodguilt' and I will pay with my soul.[23]

Troubadours and courtly love

Borrowing from ancient classical tradition, some early medieval men wrote of their intense friendship and desire for each other in the language of burning desire, intimacy, and great passion, but this did not necessarily mean that they had a physical, erotic relationship. As critic Stephen Jaeger writes, love between men was seen as ennobling and exalting, but sex was polluting. Poets praised those who could subdue the physical desires of eros, but claim its language of desire for a higher spiritual love. The language of erotic love was also a way a knight could express his intense loyalty and gratitude to his patron. By the twelfth century, however, this language of ennobling love was increasingly used for love between men and women.[24]

Most notably, the troubadours wandered from castle to castle in southern France, singing tales of thwarted love in the flickering light as lords and ladies listened. They borrowed the theme of secret love from Arab and Jewish culture in Spain, for Muslim traders and slaves mingled with the inhabitants of Toulouse and other cities. Troubadours also encountered Arab culture when on crusades, or traveling in Catalonia, which was a center of *trobador* culture, as it was called there. The troubadours developed a highly stylized philosophy which they called *fin'amor*, which was all about restrained, elegant love, in which the lover waited patiently for his mistress, or worshipped her from afar. Troubadours counterposed idealized spiritual love to marriage, which was based on dynastic considerations rather than desire. Some troubadours believed that love – although motivated by sexual desire – must not be consummated. In false love, the lover ascends through the stages of desire for the lady, praying to her to attain his wishes, serving her valiantly, finally gaining a kiss – but if he gains more, Love dies. Far superior would be spiritual love. The troubadour honors his lady, but he also hides his love, and moderates his desires. He serves her well and waits patiently, thus preserving love. The troubadours sang of their intense suffering for love, their unfulfilled desire:

> I find the pain of love so pleasing that, though I know it intends to kill me, I neither wish nor dare to live without *Midons* [My Lady] nor to turn elsewhere; for she is such that I will derive honour simply from dying as her faithful lover or, if she should keep me, a hundred times greater honour; therefore I must not be slow to serve her.[25]

Sometimes troubadours worshipped Desire itself – the woman was just a sign for it. Geoffrey, Prince of Blay, wrote that his Lady is a creation of his mind, and she vanishes at dawn. Often troubadours addressed their lyrics to Desire itself – Mon Dezir. Desire could also be a male friend or patron. Desire, therefore, could transcend the limits of gender.[26] Troubadour songs, like the related genres of courtly love of Arthurian romances and *Le Roman de la Rose*, were also closely intertwined with royal and aristocratic court culture. The troubadour owed fealty to the lady of his dreams as he would to his seigneurial lord. Sometimes men might have praised the great lady of a court in order to flatter her husband and to seek favors from him.[27]

Northern courtly love, which flourished in royal courts as a literary genre, was much more stylized than the heartfelt, plaintive lyrics of the troubadours.[28] The poets of courtly love portrayed it as intense desire for union with the beloved, yet often impossible; the lover burned with desire and trembled at the sight of his beloved, he could not sleep and love becomes a torment for him – or her. Of course, it was often impossible because it was outside marriage. A favorite game at court was to debate the advantages of love in or outside marriage. Marie of France asserted that true love cannot exist inside marriage because husbands and wives are compelled to render each other love's services, whereas lovers are free, compelled only by desire.[29] In his dialogues on love, Andreas Capellanus, a chaplain in a northern court, claims that true love cannot be found in marriage, because marriage lacks the uncontrollable power

Figure 4.1 Miniature of a couple in bed making love, *c.* 1300–1310. A man embracing a woman in bed. Illustration from *Le Roman de la Rose*, by Jean de Meun and Guillaume de Lorris. © British Library Board. All rights reserved. Egerton 881 f. 126

of desire, the secret rendezvous, the passion and jealousy. This is not so different, as historian John Baldwin notes, from Jerome, who says that "a husband who is an ardent lover of his wife is an adulterer." But Capellanus rejected earthly love for spiritual desire in the last section of his book on courtly love. He argues that physical desire is unhealthy for men, in part because they lose sperm and strength, and in part because women were wicked. Lovers must concentrate on spiritual love – or even better, love of God.[30]

Divine desire

Just as the knight had praised his lady's beauty and virtue, and begged for her favors, the troubadours lauded the Virgin Mary and pleaded with her to mediate between the believer and Jesus for the forgiveness of sins. The verses of the troubadours, and the romances of courtly love, therefore, developed an idea of desire based on the renunciation of bodily pleasure for spiritual and romantic ecstasy.

Some female mystics drew upon the metaphors of courtly love to express their desires for God. They rejected the doomed adulterous passion of the knight for his lady, but borrowed this very language for their religious visions. Hadewijch of Brabant took on the persona of a knight pursuing a lady in her poetry, drawing upon the troubadour conventions of the birds singing in the spring, inspiring love in the heart of the knight, who falls for the beautiful Lady Love – who represents God. Above all, medieval female mystics turned their romantic desires in a spiritual direction. Female mystics used intense, even erotic language to express their desire for God. Mechtild of Magdeburg imagined how "the most Beloved goes toward the Most Beautiful in the hidden chambers of the invisible deity" where "she finds the couch and the pleasure of Love." God tells her that He will eternally satisfy "your noble desire and your insatiable hunger."[31] The intense eroticism of this vision raises questions about the nature of the desire of female mystics. Were they sublimating their sexual desires into spirituality or were they eroticizing God?[32]

Mystical desire seems even stranger when we consider the male mystics' relationship to God and Jesus. For instance, the Song of Songs was often interpreted as an allegory of God's love for the believer. But for the male believer to apply this poem about passionate, sensual love between a man and woman to himself, he also had to imagine himself as the bride of Christ, putting himself in the feminine position. As Bernard of Clairvaux declared:

> It is my belief that to a person so disposed, God will not refuse that most intimate kiss of all, a mystery of supreme generosity and ineffable sweetness. … And finally, when we shall have obtained these favors through many prayers and tears, we humbly dare to raise our eyes to his mouth, so divinely beautiful, not merely to gaze upon it, but I say it with fear and trembling – to receive its kiss … Christ the Lord is a Spirit before our face,

and "he who is joined to him in a holy kiss becomes through his good pleasure, one spirit with him."[33]

In the intense atmosphere of convents and monasteries, passionate love between two monks, or two nuns, could also flourish. During the twelfth century there was an increasing emphasis on spiritual friendships as a path to enlightenment. As John Boswell recounts, Aelred of Rievaulx believed that love between two monks "could be used as stepping-stones to a loftier relationship involving the two lovers and God." Just as Jesus loved the disciple John above all others, and allowed him to rest his head on his bosom (evoking the Song of Songs), so could two monks provide love and solace to each other, "united in the intimate embrace of the most sacred love" meeting in the "inner room of the soul" where "you can confer all alone, the more secretly, the more delightfully." Just as in courtly love, love must be secret, it must be controlled, and it leads to a higher spiritual unity. This philosophy justified many expressions of intense romantic love between men, expressing the pain and anguish of being parted, and the jealousy toward rivals in love. But Aelred always insisted this love must be chaste, for carnal love was selfish, simply using the friend for the purposes of pleasure.[34] One Bavarian nun wrote to another that, "your love/ was sweeter than milk and honey. ... You alone are my love and desire," and another grieved intensely when she recalled "the kisses you gave me, And how with tender words you caressed my little breasts."[35] However, while the great composer, mystic, and influential abbess Hildegarde of Bingen celebrated female friendship, she denounced sexual relationships between women.[36] Monastic authorities worried about "particular friendships" and warned against unruly desires.

By detaching desire so decidedly from the body, spiritual desire was also detached from the assumption that desire only flowed between human men and women. Hadewijch sought an ecstatic fusion of the self with Lady Love:

> Thus love touches the beloved.
> And with unifying will unites her to herself
> In one being, without revoking.
> The depth of desire draws from love continually.[37]

These expressions of desire could also be seen as transcending gender, not just as a fusion of two female personas.

Spiritual ecstasy had much in common with the ecstasy of romantic love: on one hand, a yearning for fusion with the beloved, for ecstasy and transcendence of the self, and on the other, the fear that this passion will never be filled, the sense that this exceptional love must be kept secret, and the physical feelings of trembling and sleeplessness. These emotions of desire could be attached to a person or to an abstraction such as God. Mechtild wrote:

> And God said to the soul:
> I desired you before the world began.
> I desire you now
> As you desire me.
> And where the desires of two come together
> Then love is perfected.[38]

These mystics expressed meditation as fusion with God – as with a lover – and as a sweet, overpowering ecstasy which drew on all the senses. For instance, Beatrijs of Nazareth, educated by the beguines, said that in union with God the soul "experiences a great proximity to God a spiritual radiance, a marvelous bliss, a noble freedom, an ecstatic sweetness, a great overpowering by the strength of love, and an overflowing abundance of immense delight."[39]

As we have seen from troubadour verse and courtly love, the language of erotic love in this period was not a spontaneous effusion of emotion, but highly stylized. Medieval religious writers needed to make their spiritual devotions understandable to the people around them. To express the love of God, which could seem rather abstract, they used familiar metaphors of human relationships. Very commonly, the Church or the believer – whether male or female – was also imagined as the Bride, and Jesus as the Bridegroom, to be united in a mystical marriage, as in the Song of Songs. Sometimes the female mystics expressed a very heterosexual desire for the "manhood" of Christ. Mechtild imagined Jesus as "my lover, My longing."[40] In the *Ancrene Wisse*, a guide for anchorite women from thirteenth-century England, women were told to:

> Stretch out your love to Jesus Christ, and you have won him. Reach for him with as much love as you sometimes have for a man. He is yours to do all that you want with. ... Is not God incomparably better than all that is in the world?[41]

Historian Carolyn Bynum has observed that the metaphor could be taken further: "Catherine of Siena saw herself as married with Christ's foreskin and the Viennese beguine Agnes Blannbekin received the foreskin in her mouth and found it to taste as sweet as honey." But as Bynum emphasizes, some of these metaphors concerned kinship, rather than erotic relationships. God, of course, was symbolized as father, the Virgin Mary as mother, and Christ could be imagined as a human, male baby, not a male lover.[42]

As in courtly love, renunciation was a higher virtue than satisfaction. Love was also suffering for Hadewijch, a "fierce fury" of passion; often she felt abandoned and alone. But she believed that, as in courtly love, this suffering was a necessary sacrifice for Love – for God's love.[43] But ascetic renunciation was not only about renouncing sex, it was also a hatred for the body as diseased, corrupt, putrid, and prone to death. Taming the body was also about inflicting suffering on oneself – in imitation of Jesus' sufferings – and forgoing food and other comforts.

Spiritual ecstasy was also *different* from romantic love in important ways.[44] While Jesus was conceived as incarnated in the flesh, God, or the Holy Spirit, could be conceived as utterly different from humans – as Bernard of Clairvaux explained, God does not have a body or fleshly form, but rather, is conceptualized as the Word and the Light. In his meditations on the Song of Songs, Bernard emphasized that Christ would kiss the believer with his mouth, but it was not a fleshly mouth; instead it was the Word, or Logos.[45] Furthermore, a kiss was not necessarily sexual in the Middle Ages; men greeted each other with a kiss. Spiritual, mystical unions had a different relationship to time than erotic physical unions. In the moment of orgasm, two lovers might experience a mystical sense of union, but it would quickly evaporate. When Augustine imagined a mystical union with God, he imagined fragrance and light which never ended, in infinite space. Lost in mystical ecstasy, the believer could try to gain a sense of the infinite through God.[46] Of course, mystical spiritual union was temporary too, taking immense concentration to attain; the soul could only hope for permanence when the body was given up in death. As Bernard of Clairvaux poetically observed, "Does the consummation of joy bring about the consuming of desire? Rather it is oil poured upon the flames. So it is. Joy will be fulfilled, but there will be no end to desire, and therefore no end to the search."[47]

Devout and mystical women rejected marriage in favor of spiritual desires, for they believed the physical body and its needs had to be transcended to obtain spiritual bliss. Christina of Markyate, for example, vowed as a child to devote her virginity to God. Her story, written by a later confessor, used the conventions of courtly romance to celebrate a chaste spiritual love as better than an earthly love, as Jaeger observes. Her family, provincial nobility, wanted her to make an advantageous marriage. They broke down her resistance and forced her to consent to the marriage – but she refused to have sex with her husband. On her wedding night, she sat beside her groom on the bed and spoke to him for hours about the shining virtue of chastity, and asked him to engage in a celibate marriage with her. He finally agreed, but when he told her relatives, they scorned him as a "spineless and useless fellow" and exhorted him to be a man and force her to submit. They sent him again into the wedding chamber, but she fled, miraculously jumping over a high spiked fence. But in the end, she only escaped sex by immuring herself in a cell in an isolated hermitage, deep in the woods, protected by a noble cleric. Yet Christina of Markyate found herself tormented by passion; indeed, tales of virgins and mystics at this time sometimes frankly depicted women as struggling with their own desires. She burned with the desire for the noble cleric, and he lusted after her so much that he crawled naked to her, begging for satisfaction. She refused, pretending to feel nothing, but she was so "inwardly inflamed that she thought the clothes which clung to her body might be set on fire." She could only conquer this lust by praying for long hours on her knees, eating raw herbs from the forest, and scourging herself. For Christina, her body was the enemy through which the devil could tempt her soul; the cleric appeared to her as a "wild, ugly, furry bear," his lust turning him into an animal. Only a vision of the infant Jesus quenched her sexual desires.[48]

The beguine movement, which began around 1200 in Northern Europe, provided a home for women who did not want to marry and instead wished to devote their lives to God. Like nuns, beguines wished to devote themselves to a spiritual life of chastity, poverty, and service to others, but they did not or could not join convents. Convents demanded a high dowry payment for entrance, which many poor women could not afford. The more informal communities of beguines also allowed women some autonomy from church hierarchies and allowed them to study, read, write, and even interpret the scriptures. The beguines allowed women who had been married to take on the new role of celibate. Like Christina, the beguine Marie of Oignes was pressured into marriage by her parents at age 14, but she "convinced her husband John to live in chastity shortly afterwards."[49]

By emphasizing a direct communion with the divine, mystics and beguines threatened the power of the priest as a mediator between the believer and God, challenging priestly monopolies of knowledge and the Pauline admonition against women preaching. By criticizing lustful clergymen, the beguines and mystics also undermined the credibility of the church. The enemies of the beguines portrayed them as disorderly, impudent, even unchaste women who concealed their antics under their holy, ascetic lifestyle. They also suspected them of heresy. In 1310,

Margaret Porete was actually burnt at the stake in Paris for her tract "The Mirror of Simple Souls," which advocated individual communion with God. The beguines' enemies also linked them with the Brotherhood of the Free Spirit. This group advocated an ascetic life and criticized the clergy, arguing the antinomian heresy that following the "law" or biblical admonitions could not save believers, but only God's grace. But the Inquisition accused them of engaging in free love, sodomy, and even infanticide, although confessions of such activities were probably extorted under torture. By attacking heretics, the Church also consolidated its institutional power.[50]

Profane desires

Secular attitudes toward sexual desire did not directly oppose the church, but they focused much more on fertility and pleasure as positive, if difficult outcomes. Most medical texts in the Middle Ages derived from Greek authorities such as Galen and Hippocrates, and often perpetuated the idea that desire for sexual intercourse between men and women was prompted by the humors of the body, much like an itch that needed to be scratched. They advised husbands to kiss their wives, toy with their breasts, and rub their vulvas to make them ready for sex. Some medical authorities believed that sexual pleasure was necessary for the health of both men and women, but there was no consensus on the question of whether women needed to have pleasure in order to conceive.[51] Occasionally, they also referred to methods of contraception and abortion, although they were recommended only for reasons of health. Overall, medical authorities believed sexual activities had to be carefully regulated to ensure the balance of the humors in the body and avoid disease.[52]

For common people, fertility was much more important than the control of lust, and to ensure it, they drew on Christian and non-Christian beliefs. They prayed to saints who could ensure the birth of healthy children, relief of illness, or a good harvest. But they also tried to ensure fertility with pagan rites. For instance, in Friuli, Italy:

> two groups of youths, respectively impersonating demons favorable to fertility and the maleficent ones of destruction, symbolically flayed their loins with stalks of fennel and sorghum to stimulate their own reproductive capacity, and by analogy, the fertility of the fields of the community.[53]

Conversely, women also used herbs, spells and magic potions to try to avoid conception.[54]

Common people also worried that spells could be used to block fertility. In Western France and Languedoc, couples worried that evil, jealous people would curse their marriages by tying a knot in a cord and surreptitiously throwing it in the bridal couple's path. The knot would cause infertility and impotence, blocking the natural fluids of intercourse and procreation. Languedoc people also feared that priests would hex their weddings and cause impotence. To avoid their curses, villagers would marry a few days before the official wedding in a distant village where the priest did not know them and would have no reason to harm them. Then, the couple could legitimately have sexual relations, and the curse of the knotted cord would not work on them. One elderly curé even charged his parishioners large sums to undo such a curse, thus buttressing popular belief in his magical powers. But the higher-up clerical authorities thundered against this belief. They claimed that only the church hierarchy could determine what was caused by demons and what was caused by evil magic.[55] Notoriously, the witchcraft manual the *Malleus Maleficarum* claimed that witches could curse men into impotence, causing their penises to become detached and disappear, only to reappear, perched like birds, in trees. However, the *Malleus* reflected fairly extreme clerical attitudes rather than popular beliefs, and the intense persecution of witches did not erupt until the sixteenth and seventeenth centuries.[56]

Like religious moralists, secular sources such as tales and poems depicted desire as excessive, outrageous, and fantastical. While courtly love poetry such as *Le Roman de la Rose* (late thirteenth, early fourteenth century) could be romantic and soulful, it could also be satirical and bitter, as wives connive with their lovers to deceive husbands, and supposedly chivalrous knights rape and abandon peasant girls. As theorist Mikhail Bakhtin observes of the writer Rabelais, popular tales depicted the body as "grotesque." But they also celebrated the physicality of the body with its sex, fertility, defecation, and death, and entertained audiences with wild, carnivalesque tales of out of control bodies and desires.[57]

The popular tales depicted characters who ridiculed the church as hypocritical for proclaiming that sexual desire in marriage was a sin. They often featured lusty priests who rebuked their parishioners by day and seduced their wives by night. Chaucer has his character the Wife of Bath declare that the "generative organs" were made for:

> both use and pleasure in
> Engendering, except in case of sin.
> Why else the proverb written down and set
> In books: "A man must yield his wife her debt?"
> What means of paying her can he invent
> Unless he use his silly instrument?
> In wifehood I will use my instrument
> As freely as my Maker me it sent.[58]

Chaucer was inspired by the *fabliaux*, the comic tales of the twelfth and thirteenth centuries. Jongleurs, who were entertainers much like troubadours, told these tales to entertain audiences including the nobility, but also clerks, merchants, and artisans. Peasants often featured as characters in the *fabliaux*, but mostly to be ridiculed as crude animals; women were depicted as sexually voracious, like the Wife of Bath. The jongleurs may have learned these stories from ordinary people who told them around a fireside, and then repeated them or wrote them in manuscripts to circulate among the literate.

The *fabliaux* represented sexual desire as comic excess; people did not control their desires – their genitals impelled them to have sex. In these tales, pleasure was more important than fertility. In one, as a peasant and his wife trudge home, tired, poor, and hungry, Saint Martin miraculously appears and promises them four wishes. Before the peasant can open his mouth to ask for abundant treasure, his wife, frustrated by his impotence, asks for sexual satisfaction: she wishes that her husband were "endowed, by God, with pricks in every place" all over his body, "and let not one be soft or limp, but stiffer than an iron bar: you'll then appear the prick you are!" And low and behold, penises sprout all over the peasant, his face, on both his knees, "while downward to his feet the hick's whole body was a mass of pricks." In retaliation, he wishes that "cunts" appear all over her body, and they immediately appear, "hairless cunts, cunts piled and plushy. The peasant's joy was now complete." In this tale, insatiable lust compels the peasants, especially the wife, to fantasize about a body totally devoted to sexual satisfaction. They imagine that sexual desire originates in the genitals, which acquire a life of their own. But a thinly veiled hostility also emerges in the story. The wife sees the husband as a prick, reduced to his own inadequate sexual organ. The husband wants to humiliate his wife sexually. But they realize in horror that they cannot make love with such a surfeit of genitals, so the couple wishes they would disappear. The saint immediately grants this third wish, and all their genitals vanish, leaving them sexless. The peasant and his wife have to use their last wish to regain their ordinary genitals, and realize they must be satisfied with the prosaic necessities of marital sex.[59]

This story presented a common medieval fantasy of utter abundance, of wild excess in sensual pleasures, not only sex but also food: the bringing of banquets when peasants drank vats of beer and consumed huge piles of tripe, but a few times a year, at harvest feast days. These fantasies of excess also indicate an economy of deprivation and scarcity. Medieval people were preoccupied with the precarious pleasures of the body and its ills – the pleasures of sex, eating, and defecating, the pains of sickness, aches and bruises, wounds, and hunger. In 1532, the great comic writer Rabelais imagined the mother of Gargantua hastening his conception by "rubbing" the father's "bacon."[60] Sexual desire was necessary, pleasurable, but, like other sensations of parts of the body, potentially harmful and dangerous.[61]

Popular literature fantasized that women would lose sexual control. The female genitals were often portrayed as rampaging beasts which would take over women's minds and bodies. The sexual desires of older women and widows were especially feared, for these women were perceived as being outside of the power of men. In one *fabliau*, a new widow immediately seeks new sexual partners after losing her husband: "a sweet sensation pricks her heart and lifts up her spirit, and arouses in the bearded counselor under her skirts an appetite for meat, neither peacock nor crane, but that dangling sausage for which so many are eager."[62]

Somewhat later, Rabelais claimed that "nature hath posited in a privy, secret and intestine place in [women's] bodies, a sort of member, by some not impertinently treated an animal," which engenders in them, "certain humours, so saltish, brackish, clammy, sharp, nipping, tearing, prickling, and most eagerly tickling, that ... their whole body is shaken and ebrangled, their senses totally ravished and transported, the operations of their judgment and understanding utterly confounded."[63]

But a fifteenth-century female Welsh poet presented a more positive view of the "cunt": "it is full of love, very proud forest, faultless gift, tender frieze, fur of a fine pair of testicles, a girl's thick grove, circle of precious greeting, lovely bush, God save it."[64]

Chaucer's Wife of Bath strongly asserted that women deserved sexual satisfaction – and mastery in marriage. Of course, this bawdy tale was making fun of her, confirming male fears about dominant, insatiable women. The Wife declared that her desire came from her physiognomy:

> And truth my husbands said to me
> I had the best quoniam that might be,
> ... Venus gave me desire and lecherousness
> And Mars my hardihood, or so I guess.
> I ever followed natural inclination
> Under the power of my constellation
> And was unable to deny, in truth,
> My Chamber of Venus to a likely youth.[65]

While women were seen as sexually insatiable, sex was still seen as something men did to women (or to other men), as Ruth Mazo Karras observes.[66] The *fabliaux* portrayed male sexual desire as virile and aggressive, using violent language to describe sex, such as piercing, charging, striking, whipping, assaulting, beating, or combating.[67] Perhaps men believed that they had to overcome women, whose insatiable sexuality made them worthy antagonists. However, men were very concerned about their reputation for sexual prowess, their ability to satisfy women and produce children. In another *fabliau*, a young husband complains to his older wife, "Lady, you have a greedy mouth in you that demands to be fed too often. It has tired my poor old war-horse out."[68] Female desire was seen as especially frightening, but excessive male lust was problematic as well, as we shall see in the next chapter.

Conclusion

Whether sacred and spiritual, or secular and fleshly, medieval people often regarded desire as an overwhelming force. Spiritual love was necessary for religious devotion, but mystical spirituality could challenge the authority of the Church. The Church denigrated sexual desire, except in tightly controlled situations in marriage, but secular people – and often clerics – defied these religious prohibitions. Religious and secular authorities tried to control sex outside of marriage, such as premarital sex, prostitution, and sodomy, but it was impossible to prevent them altogether. As we shall see in the next chapter, one way of reasserting the Church's authority was to shift the blame from ordinary men and women to specific people: heretics, those who had sex across religious lines, prostitutes, and sodomites. In recurrent waves, such people were stigmatized and scapegoated for the woes of society in vulnerable times. As the Church of the twelfth- century Renaissance triumphed, it was also, as historian R. I. Moore observes, forming a "persecuting society."[69]

Suggested reading

Baldwin, John W. *The Language of Sex: Five Voices from Northern France*. Chicago, 1994.

Boswell, John. *Christianity, Social Tolerance, and Homosexuality: Gay People in Western Europe from the Beginning of the Christian Era to the Fourteenth Century*. Chicago, 1980.

Brundage, James A. *Law, Sex and Society in Medieval Europe*. Chicago, 1987.

Burger, Glenn, and Steven F. Kruger, eds. *Queering the Middle Ages*. Minneapolis, 2001.

Dinsmore, Carolyn. *Getting Medieval: Sexualities and Communities, Pre- and Postmodern*. Durham, NC, 1999.

Elliott, Dyan. *Fallen Bodies: Pollution, Sexuality, and Demonology in the Middle Ages*. Philadelphia, 1999.

Fradenburg, Louise, and Carola Freccero, eds. *Premodern Sexualities*. New York, 1996.

Karras, Ruth Mazo. *Sexuality in Medieval Europe*. London, 2005.

McCarthy, Conor, ed. *Love, Sex and Marriage in the Middle Ages: A Sourcebook*. London, 2004.

Salih, Sarah. "Sexual Identities: A Medieval Perspective." In *Sodomy in Early Modern Europe*, edited by Tom Betteridge, 112–30. Manchester, 2002.

——— *Versions of Virginity in Late Medieval England*. Rochester, NY, 2001.

Chapter 5

From twilight moments to moral panics

The regulation of sex from the thirteenth to the sixteenth century

The subdeacon Arnaud de Verniolle enjoyed partying with young men in a field in Pamiers in southern France. They would bring "some wine, silver cups and food" and "spread out a robe, dance, and wrestle, and afterward commit sodomy with each other." Arnaud told the young men that:

> it was written that if a man lies with another, and because of the warmth of their bodies semen flows, it is not as grave a sin as if a man carnally knows a woman; because, so he said, nature demands this and a man is made healthier as a result.

Eventually, the Inquisition caught up with Arnaud, and under torture he confessed that he had not only committed sodomy, but he flirted with heresy. Arnaud had sex with many women, and he did not seem to think of himself as having what we would think of as a homosexual identity. But he told the inquisitors "his nature inclined him to commit sodomy." In 1324, the inquisitors condemned Arnaud to a lifetime in chains, fed only bread and water in a dismal cell.[1]

Arnaud only came to the attention of the authorities because he was involved in the Cathar heresy in an area where the inquisitors carefully scrutinized people's behavior. Despite the Church's strict prohibitions on all sex outside of marriage – and much sex within it – medieval people sometimes fornicated, engaged in premarital sex, bought or sold sex, or made love with someone of the same sex. How did authorities respond to what they perceived as this misbehavior?

Officially, the Church wished to maintain the sexual purity of its parishioners, but it had to be realistic about how people actually behaved. In the earlier Middle Ages, penitential manuals instructed priests on what questions to ask their parishioners in confessions, and what penances should be handed out. They forbade fornication, adultery, and sodomy, of course, but they even mandated long periods of abstinence in marriage to purify the body several days before communion, on holy days, during menstruation, and for forty days before Christmas, Easter, and Pentecost.[2] A priest told a married couple who had sex on Easter Sunday that they had to stand in sackcloth and ashes outside the church for a day and a night.[3]

However, people may not have confessed more than once a year, and it is unlikely that a local illiterate priest might know all the variations of possible sexual sins about which to interrogate his parishioners.[4] Some church authorities also denounced the penitentials for being too sexually explicit, too fevered in their denunciation of lust. By the twelfth and thirteenth centuries priests allowed marital sex on more days and excused having marital sex out of lust – not just for procreation – as venial sin, rather than a mortal sin.[5] Even those who had sex out of marriage could be forgiven and returned to the fold, sometimes with private penitence, by paying indulgences, and sometimes with a public humiliation.[6] The Church recognized that all were sinners, so sins were inevitable.

More effectively, villagers indulged in gossip to shame those who transgressed local customs. Municipal authorities were more interested in maintaining parental control over marriage and keeping good order in their towns than in ensuring everyone was perfectly chaste. They punished the sexual disorder of young men lightly, thinking they were just sowing their wild oats. Sexual misbehavior could be seen as a shameful twilight moment, but those who committed it were still part of the community. While city authorities labeled women who sold sex, they recognized that they performed a useful social function.

In times of upheaval, however, certain people could be stigmatized as the abject, to be expelled from society. During the great wave of persecutions that washed over Europe in the thirteenth and fourteenth centuries, Church and state together burnt heretics, condemned sodomites, expelled Jews from the lands, and stigmatized prostitutes. The Church, monarchs and great lords mounted the Crusades to retake the "Holy Land" from the Muslims. Especially during such times of crisis, sexual desire could symbolize social disintegration. If plague decimated the population of the town, as people anxiously checked their groins for the feared black buboes of disease, they would search for someone to blame. Authorities often alleged that their victims indulged in sexual vice to justify persecuting them. And sex between men or between peoples of different religions aroused great concern about the pollution of social purity and the transgression of boundaries.

Sex and religious boundaries in Spain

In medieval Spain, authorities regulated sex in an attempt to keep strict boundaries between communities. By 1031 the Christians had begun the long process of reconquering Andalusia from the Muslims and reestablished their rule, building fortified cities and raising families. Nonetheless, Jews often remained in the cities as merchants, tradesmen, and artisans, while many Muslims still labored as peasants in the countryside. Christians, Jews and Muslims lived side by side in *convivencia*, but this uneasy co-existence was not based on equality, but on violence, as historian David Nirenberg argues.[7] Christians ordered Jews and Muslims to wear distinctive clothing and hats, and forced them to live in segregated parts of the city.

Sex could erode the boundaries of belief and status which kept these communities distinct. Christians forbade marriage with Jews or Muslims because marriage joined property and created ties between kin groups; intermarriage would undermine Christian status as exclusive and superior. Sex between religious groups threatened the purity of Christianity, and was feared. Yet Christian, Jewish, and Muslim men worked and socialized together. After their hard labor as farmers and artisans, they met in taverns to drink, gamble, trade, and gossip. They could mingle together without eroding the intimate boundaries of religious hierarchy, because rules established who could have sex with whose women, as Nirenberg observes.[8] Christian dominance was reinforced by the rule that only Christians could have sex with Christian prostitutes. As Nirenberg writes, the prostitute was "a concrete representation of a community of men united to each other by a common sexual bond." Christian men occasionally had sex with Jewish women, but this was seen as especially polluting.

More often Christian men frequented Muslim prostitutes, who were usually slaves, so their offspring would be slaves and could not "contaminate" Christian families. As historian Mark Myerson argues, both Islamic and Christian authorities colluded in this practice. Islamic courts did not punish Muslim men for adultery, but they would convict a Muslim woman of fornication or adultery, and order her to be put to death – or to be whipped so severely she would die. A Christian cleric might step in and reduce her sentence from death to slavery – and then purchase her as his own slave. He could then have sex with her himself, and choose to profit from her prostitution. Even worse, a Christian cleric could seduce or rape a Muslim woman, denounce her to the authorities as a prostitute, and then buy her as a slave.[9] For Christian men, sex across religious lines could be a twilight moment, commonly practiced if forbidden. But if a Christian man pursued Muslim prostitutes too openly, he could lose his good character, and judges could strip him of certain privileges or even banish him.[10]

Muslim or Jewish men who had sex with Christian women became the abject, and could be put to death. A Christian woman also faced severe punishments for having sex with Jewish or Muslim men; in many towns, she could be burnt at the stake. In Sepulveda, "A Christian woman who lived among the minorities or gave birth to a child of mixed blood was branded a 'bad' woman who deserved to be flogged and expelled."[11]

By the thirteenth and fourteenth centuries, as Christian rulers pushed back the Muslims still further, hostility between Muslims and Christians intensified, and Christians used sexual insults to attack their political enemies. Christian polemicists had long alleged that Muslim monarchs lusted after Christian women, or even boys, and they had also feared that the lush sensuality of Arab poetry would contaminate Christian men. At the court of Alphonso X of Castile, satirical poets termed their enemies "Jew-lover" or "Arab-lover."[12]

In the early fifteenth century, St. Vincent stirred up a moral panic against Muslims to revive Spanish Christian piety. He warned, "Today the law is not obeyed. [Christian men] want to taste everything: Muslims and Jews, animals, men with men; there is no limit." In 1415, he told a Zaragozan audience that "many Christian men believe their wife's children to be their own, when they are actually by Muslim and Jewish [fathers]." As historian Nirenberg notes, Christian women symbolized the bride of Christ, the inviolable and holy Christian Spain. If the citizens did not stop this intergroup adultery, St. Vincent warned, God would punish them with the plague. His sermon provoked a sexual panic. Christian patrols searched the streets, on the lookout for predatory Jews or Muslims who seduced Christian women. Inspired by this zeal, Christians forced Jews to convert at the point of the sword.[13] The example of Spain shows that when societies feared that their religious or cultural boundaries would erode, they often exploded into moral panics about polluting sex. As much as moral panics, however, it was the everyday regulation of sex, the double standard of twilight moments for Christian men and prosecution for Muslim and Jewish men who crossed sexual and racial lines that perpetuated these hierarchies.

Fornication, concubinage and prostitution: women and men

Sex was supposed to happen only within marriage, yet authorities feared that young people would be tempted to fornicate since they had to endure many years between puberty and marriage. Especially from the fifteenth century onwards, northern European urban men and women tended to marry in their twenties, after they had saved money for a business or trade. In southern Europe, men did not marry until they had established themselves in business or inherited property, frequently waiting until their thirties; they took teenage girls as brides, often in arranged marriages. Respectable girls were supposed to be married or in a convent by their late teens, although women without dowries did not have the choice of either prospect. As a result, southern cities contained large populations of unmarried young men. And not everyone married: in fact, marriage was a privilege. In some areas, around 30 percent of women between the ages of 15 and 49 were unmarried. Some men and women decided to become priests, monks, or nuns even if they lacked spiritual commitment, because the clerical life was a good career.[14]

Among English common people, engaged couples would join hands, plight their troth to each other in front of witnesses, and then retreat to bed to have sex: this was the ritual of trothplight. They believed sex after this betrothal was just as moral as sex after the formal marriage ceremony. Villagers did not care if a bride was pregnant on her wedding day, but they did not want to support the children of women who gave birth out of wedlock. If an unmarried bondwoman (serf) became pregnant, English manorial courts imposed a fine, or leyrwrite, on her, because her child might become a burden on a village. By fining her rather than expelling her, the courts regarded her pregnancy as a twilight moment, and restored her to her former status in her community.[15] Church courts, however, imposed more public punishments, ordering women accused of fornication to stand in sackcloth and ashes in front of the church or to march in a procession of sinners.[16]

Unmarried women were vulnerable. They labored in a wide variety of trades, such as servant, embroiderer, or brewster, but they earned half the wages of men, so it was difficult to support themselves. And their jobs tended to disappear when commerce declined or guilds decided to push them out. If a woman lacked a trade or parents to provide a dowry, she might have to become a concubine. Sometimes employers or even parents "sold" young women to be the concubine of a priest or a foreign merchant. In fourteenth-century Bologna, university students took *amaxia* to provide domestic and sexual services and even to wash their heads – full bathing was not very common in the Middle Ages.[17] Before 1250, in Spain and elsewhere civil and canon law provided some recognition for concubines who would live with a man, work as his servant, and "provide sexual services," but these relationships were temporary, lacking the protections of marriage; if her lover left, the concubine had no financial guarantees. After that time, marriage laws were tightened as municipal authorities disapproved of concubines, but they persisted in practice as twilight moments. However, communities did not regard concubines as honorable women, and sometimes prosecuted them.[18]

The lines between women who occasionally sold sex, concubines, and prostitutes could be hard to draw, but authorities tried to label women as prostitutes to make them easier to control. Authorities saw prostitutes as necessary but contaminating. Like Jews, who lent money to Christians, prostitutes provided a service which went against Christian doctrine. Both Jews and prostitutes, as scholar Linda Paterson observes: "might be regarded as unclean: an Avignon statute of 1243 prohibited both from touching bread or fruit on the market, or buying what they touched."[19] City laws often ordered prostitutes to wear special cords, *aiguillettes*, or long trains, to distinguish them from "respectable" women.

During times of concern about social boundaries, cities might try to expel prostitutes. For instance, during the twelfth-century crusades against heretics and Islam, many cities in southern France pushed prostitutes beyond the city walls. Cleric Robert Courson argued that they should be "kept apart, like lepers." Finally, in the mid-thirteenth century, many cities in France and Italy tried to expel prostitutes altogether. King Louis IX of France, known as St. Louis, forbade them from plying their trade even in the fields bordering the towns. This moralizing monarch also tried to suppress gambling and usury. However, the suppression of prostitution soon failed.

Secular and religious authorities began to regard fornication with a prostitute as a minor sin. After all, better that a young man have sex with a prostitute, who was seen as already polluted, than seduce a virgin or a married woman – for that would disturb the property relations of the family. St. Thomas Aquinas even argued that banning prostitution "would result in the pullulation of sexual passion and abuses." Spanish moralists said that the brothel was like a latrine, "Where the filth and the ugliness of the flesh are gathered like the garbage and dung of the city."[20] So continental cities began to think that if they could not prevent prostitution, they could at least control, and even profit from it by setting up municipal brothels.[21]

Men could spend a pleasant evening in a brothel, eating and drinking by a warm fireplace, playing board games or boxing, then retreating with a prostitute to an upstairs bedroom overlooking a garden, or splashing with a woman in the baths. As Chaucer wrote:

> presently the dancing-girls
> Small pretty ones, come in and shake their curls
> With youngsters selling fruit, and ancient bawds,
> And girls with cakes and music, devil's gauds,
> To kindle and blow the fires of lechery
> That are so close annexed to gluttony.[22]

Secular people saw the desire for sex and the desire for food as natural appetites that could become excessive unless satisfied in a legitimate manner – quite a different attitude than that of the Church. Clerics and married men were officially not supposed to go to brothels, but this rule was often regarded only in the breach. Both city authorities and young men believed that "nature" urged young men to have sex. As one young men from Toulouse explained, "nature had moved me to go sport."[23] However, municipal brothels were not constructed because young men had a natural sex drive that would explode unless satisfied; rather, the brothels themselves established the expectation that certain women must provide sexual services to men. The city fathers also did not establish brothels because young men married late. Leah Otis points out that in southern France, municipal brothels were established before the age of marriage for young men began to rise. Instead, city officials were responding to the plague, which disproportionately killed women. With the shortage of females, women had more opportunity to marry or work at their trades. By establishing municipal brothels, therefore, authorities might have been trying to force women into prostitution. They succeeded – Otis estimates there was at least one official prostitute for every thousand inhabitants of medieval Languedoc towns.[24]

Some women were coerced into prostitution. If neighbors denounced a Florentine woman as a prostitute, she could be forced to work in the municipal brothel.[25] Servants or laundresses who had been seduced and abandoned, or raped, could be accused of being bad women and be compelled to go into the brothel. And some women coerced girls into prostitution. Alison Boston, for instance, was put in the pillory for selling her 13-year-old female apprentice to a barber for eight shillings fourpence. Elizabeth Moryng hired a young woman named Joan as an assistant embroidress, but expected her to "live in lechery ... with friars, chaplains" and then steal their money.[26] Brothelkeepers only allowed prostitutes to keep a pittance of their earnings. But some women found selling sex to be quite profitable, given the paucity of women's wages. For instance, some pious neighbors tried to persuade a Florentine prostitute to abandon her trade by giving her several loaves of bread each week, but she retorted that she earned two florins a week in the sex trade.[27]

Figure 5.1   Carpaccio, Vittore *c.* 1455/65–1526. *Two Courtesans*. Oil on wood, 94 × 64cm. Venice, Museo Civico Correr. Photo: akg-images, London, Erich Lessing

Cities passed countless regulations mandating that prostitutes only ply their trade in the municipal brothel, forbidding them from eating and drinking at taverns, or wandering through city streets. But women who sold sex often preferred to work clandestinely, or with pimps, outside of the municipal brothels. This sexual commerce occurred as twilight moments, out of the jurisdiction of authorities. In 1422, Venice city authorities threatened prostitutes who refused to join the municipal brothel with stripping them of their garments, shaving their heads, and expelling them from the city. They prohibited prostitutes from soliciting on the Rialto, but the prostitutes laughed at them. Higher-class courtesans established their own luxurious houses, which were not controlled by the authorities.[28] In Spain, corrupt officials extorted bribes and sexual favors from women who wished to sell sex outside of the official brothels.[29] While the institution of municipal prostitution was intended to label women as prostitutes, and determine which men could have sex with which women, it did not always succeed in both these goals.

Medieval men were supposed to be dominant and aggressive, but this stereotypical masculinity could also endanger the social order. City fathers hoped that municipal brothels would help them contain the unruly young unmarried men who drank in taverns, gambled, brawled, frequented prostitutes, and kept concubines.[30] Yet in Italy and southern France, young unmarried men continued to rape and riot after the establishment of municipal brothels provided plenty of female prostitutes for them. In fifteenth-century Toulouse, gangs of young men invaded the houses of men who were away on business and dragged out their virgin daughters. Historian Jacques Rossiaud estimates that up to half of the young men in the city participated. By raping their daughters, young men may have been expressing their resentment against the older city patriarchs who controlled the businesses and young wives. But the rapists also assaulted women to force them into prostitution.[31] In Venice, the city authorities strictly forbade men to have sex with maids, nurses, or slaves, but usually failed to punish them for doing so. Instead, the victims themselves were shamed and often had no alternative but prostitution. The existence of municipal brothels may have encouraged this aggressive attitude toward women; in Venice, gangs roamed the streets at night harassing and raping women.[32]

Same-sex desire

In Florence and Venice, some young men also had sex with each other as they caroused in the darkened streets. In southern Europe, municipal authorities punished sodomy as just another form of dangerous male vice, like excessive gambling, drinking, whoring, or rioting. Did this mean that there was no such thing as a homosexual identity in medieval Europe, that men could indulge themselves with women or boys?

The early Church punished sodomy much like other sins, with long penances. But what they understood as sodomy did not map onto our present-day division between heterosexual and homosexual. The definition of sodomy rested on the distinction between natural and unnatural acts. For clerics, the distinction was between sex for procreation within marriage, an unfortunate necessity, and sex that was not for procreation, which could include oral or anal sex between a man and a woman or a man and a man. They regarded rape as less culpable than anal sex between men and women because rape might lead to procreation.[33] However, these relatively minor punishments did not mean that early Christian clerics tolerated same-sex sex; they wanted believers to repent for sodomy just like they repented for other sins.[34]

Some historians, following Foucault, have suggested that the "sodomite" was not therefore a personality type or identity, unlike the modern homosexual.[35] Yet the category "sodomite" did emerge in the Middle Ages, especially when clerical authorities were trying to establish their authority. In his 1050 *Book of Gomorrah*, reformer Peter Damian savagely criticized those penitentials who gave mild penances for sex between men. Damian believed that sodomites were the abject – they must be expelled from society, cast into the outer darkness. He saw sodomy not as an occasional sin, one of many disorders of desire, but the worst of all possible sins, because it overran the boundaries of nature: "Indeed, this vice is the death of bodies, the destruction of souls ... This vice tries to overturn the walls of the heavenly homeland."[36] He also invented, as Mark Jordan points out, the category of the "sodomite" as a person, as a sinful, "effeminate" man who must be cast out from society, who could not be forgiven. In the great twelfth-century persecutions against heresy, heretics were often accused of being sodomites, and the word "bougre" or bugger probably derived from Bogomil, a word for Cathar heretics. By the late twelfth and early thirteenth century, clerical authorities began to single out sodomy as the worst of sins even when it was not linked to heresy. By the mid-thirteenth century, St. Thomas Aquinas declaimed that, "the sodomitic vice is not merely ridiculous and shameful in the way gluttony is, it is also disgusting and horrifying in the way that atrocities are."[37] These clerical discourses provided a language for secular authorities to condemn sodomy. In the second half of the thirteenth century, many secular authorities also adopted strict injunctions against sodomy in their customary laws, mandating punishments of burning, castration, or burying offenders alive. Legally, sodomy might include bestiality, oral and anal sex, or even mutual masturbation, but in practice the latter was not punished as harshly.[38] To some extent, sex between men, like other crimes such as rape, was seen as compelled by "diabolical desires" which might infect anyone. But unlike rape, authorities believed that God would call down vengeance on sodomy, because it violated the order of nature.[39]

At the same time, other discourses within medieval and Renaissance culture provided a rhetoric in which men expressed intense love toward each other in ways which would make people today think they were lovers. Plato inspired Renaissance philosophers such as Marsilio Ficino to argue that by loving a beautiful youth, a man could attain a higher spiritual love. Poets also emulated Virgil to celebrate the love of handsome shepherd boys. But the same philosophers denounced the *physical* expression of this love as detestable sodomy.[40]

Social relationships between men were also characterized by intense bonding. As Alan Bray and C. Stephen Jaeger have written, men needed to cultivate personal favors with their male superiors in order to advance through patronage at court or even in the Church. On a lower social level, apprentices and journeymen bonded as they drank and worked together. Sharing beds at night, they shared confidences in the dark. Men may have felt more strongly toward their friends, whom they chose, than toward their wives, whom they often married for reasons of property. Men kissed each other as a greeting, and exchanged very affectionate letters. Men also teased each other by addressing each other as "mistress," secure in their manliness. As Jaeger notes, men could exchange such intimacies because these relationships were not seen in the same terms as sodomy. If they had been, the social bonds which held together the community would be threatened, as Cynthia Herrup observes. In general, intense prosecutions of the generalized figure of the "sodomite" only emerged during moments of crisis, when the sodomite could be linked with other threats, such as heresy and treason.[41] During the intervening periods, intense relationships between men were celebrated but sex between men was not accepted or even tolerated. Rather, it was regarded as shameful and suspicious, as a twilight moment. But two different patterns emerged toward sex between men in northern Europe and in Italy.

In Italy, sex between men seems to have been fairly common, but authorities alternated between moral panics and ineffective regulation. In the early fourteenth century, secular authorities worked together with the Inquisition to stir up popular hostility against sodomites with public punishments. In Italian towns, confraternities, or groups of pious laymen organized by Dominican friars, were instructed to hunt out sodomites in their towns, and then turn them over to the Inquisition.[42] In Orvieto, Italy, in 1308, a man accused of sodomy was first tortured, banned from offices or honors, and then "paraded around the city with trumpets before him, holding a cord tied to his male member."[43] By persecuting sodomites as well as heretics, the Church strengthened its authority and credibility as a moral arbiter.

Despite such prosecutions, sex between men, especially young men and youths, remained fairly common in some Italian cities. So in 1424–5, preacher Bernardino of Siena blamed the plague, war, and floods on sodomites – as well as witches and Jews – and told Florentines that sodomy was "the reason you have lost half of your population over the last twenty-five years." The babies who should have been born to sodomites, he warned, were crying out for vengeance. Bernardino believed that sodomites were effeminate and refused to marry, although somewhat inconsistently, he also saw sex between men as a vice all young men were prone to, afflicted as they were by waves of uncontrollable lust. Bernardino vehemently urged his Florentine audiences to tear sodomites limb from limb and publicly burn them; at the very least, people should "spit" on sodomites they saw to "extinguish their fire."[44]

As a result, as historian Michael Rocke has found, the city fathers established the Office of the Night to repress sex between men, and Venice had a similar institution. But this office was fairly ineffective, only pursuing one quarter of the cases that came to its attention, and most of them were subject to minor fines. First-time offenders would not even be stripped of their right to hold civic offices – in contrast to Roman practice. City authorities were annoyed, but they did not expel offenders from the city. The records of these offices reveal a rich picture of homoerotic practices.

In Florence, gangs would roam the streets, accosting beautiful male youths with sexual come-ons during the twilight hours. Once a man had obtained his prey, they would retire to a narrow alley, a secluded garden, or a church door to have sex. Men seeking sex went to certain taverns, for instance in the Street of the Furriers, where they knew they would find boys eager to service them. Men and boys also had sex as they worked together in butchers' shops and groceries on the famed Ponte Vecchio, the bridge which crosses the Arno, where tourists now go to buy antiques. Rocke has found that the office accused about 400 men a year, out of a population of 40,000.[45]

Young men did not engage in sodomy because women were not available, for there were plenty of prostitutes and concubines in Florence. Rather, sex between males in Florence fit into the larger masculine culture of the city, which was based on hierarchal ties between older and younger men. Older men married, headed families, accumulated wealth, and ruled the city. They dispensed patronage and largesse to younger and poorer men through personal favors. Young men also formed bonds with each other, in schools, as journeymen and apprentices working together, in artisanal and religious organizations, and in the vigorous tavern life. An informer explained that the carpenter Piero di Bartolomeo had sex with the 15-year-old son of a grocer "out of great love and good brotherhood, because they are in a confraternity [religious organization] together"; in patronizing the boy, "he did as good neighbors do." In Venice, goldsmiths, furriers, and barbers were often accused, perhaps falsely, of sodomy, because the initiation rituals of their trades may have had sexual overtones. Sex between schoolteachers and pupils, or between pupils themselves, seems to have flourished in schools for music, dancing, and fencing.[46]

Men aggressively proved their masculine honor through fighting and sexual dominance. A man might snatch a boy's hat, then demand that he sexually "service" him. Very often older men would give small gifts of money or treasures, such as a crystal goblet, to the young men who sexually serviced them. For instance, Leonardo da Vinci, who had at least once been accused by the Office of the Night of having sex with a male youth, kept a beautiful youth named Salai in his household for decades, buying him 24 pairs of shoes a year, giving a dowry to his sister, assisting his father, and painting his lovely curls, despite Salai's impudence, lies, and thefts.[47] While this resembled prostitution, many social and romantic heterosexual relationships in the Renaissance were nurtured by gift giving. Some parents even prostituted their sons, benefiting from the patronage or even payments of their lovers. Youths were also vulnerable to rape when groups of men dragged them into bell towers or other secluded places.

Figure 5.2   Signorelli, Luca (1441–1523). Detail from the *Adoration of the Magi* (two youths). Florence, Galleria degli Uffizi. © 1990 Photo SCALA, Florence. Courtesy of the Ministero Beni e Att. Culturali

Many men seem to have indulged in this practice, as passive partners as teenagers, and as active partners in their twenties, then going on to marry. Witnesses in
cases of sodomy often testified that an older man used a youth as if he were a
woman; sex was defined in terms of active and passive roles. Unlike in ancient
times, however, the active party was punished much more severely than the passive
one; in Venice, the penetrator in sodomy was often burned alive, while the passive,
often younger party received a milder punishment.[48]

Florentine young men often wore their long hair curled and paraded around in
multi-colored stockings, such as young teenager Torrigiano di Tadeo with his
"fashionable hose, half purple and half checkered." But Rocke did not find that
they took on feminine roles or clothing; after all, during the fifteenth and sixteenth
centuries, stylish Italian and Spanish men wore lace ruffs, colorful brocades; puffy
short breeches and clinging tights exposed their fine legs, and elaborate codpieces
proved their virility.

For some men and youths, sex led to more long-term relationships and
networks; it was not just a phase. In Florence, groups of men met at each other's
houses for dinner, gathered at taverns, and traipsed forth to the cool country hills
on feast days, bringing their beautiful boys with them. Some men even took on
their young shop boys or apprentices as long-term lovers, sleeping with them
every night, expressing their romantic love – even exchanging rings. In Venice,
networks could also be found of adult men and youths who interchanged the
active and passive role.

Yet despite its prevalence, communities did not accept sodomy; rather, it was
regarded as a twilight moment, to be kept shameful and hidden, or repented for if
revealed. Neighbors often rebuked men accused of sodomizing male youths; they
hung lanterns in front of a shop where the master was closeted with his apprentice,
and forced him to come out and apologize and beg for forgiveness. They
denounced notorious sodomites to the authorities, who subjected repeat
offenders to public humiliations, such as being whipped naked through the
streets. Popular songs also denounced sodomy. Families often tried to keep information about their sons' sodomitical relationships out of public view, by settling
cases with cash payments and persuading errant sons to give up their lovers. Some
men denounced themselves to the Office of the Night, hoping that their repentance would lead to a lighter punishment.

During times of political and religious turmoil, sodomites became the abject. In
early fifteenth-century Venice, dozens of men, including 15 nobles, were accused
of sodomy. Fearing this scandal would discredit the nobility who ruled the city, the
oligarchic Council of Ten took over control of sodomy from the Office of the
Night and ordered that notorious sodomites be burned alive or decapitated. But
sodomy continued, and in 1511 these men were blamed for a terrible earthquake
– and for depriving prostitutes of customers. Patriarch Antonio Contarini
complained that "the prostitutes say that they can no more live, no one goes to see
them any more; they must work until old age, so much is sodomy diffused."[49] In
Florence, the monk Savonarola mounted a huge campaign against decadence and

for morality in 1496, whipping up the inhabitants into a pious frenzy, inciting them to burn books, paintings, luxuries, and fashions, attacking prostitution – and organizing male teenagers to refuse to engage in sodomy. He accused the Office of the Night of being too lenient, and demanded more severe punishments. However, as Rocke has found, by 1511 well-connected male youths protested against harsh punishments for sodomy, and the moral panic subsided. The tactic of silence seemed more appropriate than overt persecution and publicity.[50]

Men who felt erotic desire for other men sometimes expressed and discussed the meaning of their feelings. In the decade of the 1480s, members of Lorenzo di Medici's circle celebrated erotic desire for young men, and carnival songs alluded to sodomy with "playful obscenity." Somewhat later, Antonio Rocco took a more positive approach to homoerotic sex. Quoting Pausanias, the follower of Plato, he argued that men with a "philosophical spirit" should avoid entangling themselves with women, marriage, and family, and instead pursue the "Paradise" of anal sex with youths. Rocco and others celebrated the pleasure of being anally penetrated, unlike the Greeks and Romans who regarded this passivity as shameful.[51]

In 1525, the Sienese Antonio Vignali boldly justified homoerotic desire in a satirical pamphlet about the war of the Cocks, the Assholes, the Cunts, and the Balls. Vignali declares that Nature has "no regard for any laws, pacts, or creeds. Nor has she ever been afraid of risky situations; in fact she strives with all her might to follow her inclinations." Nature might be satisfied with a "cunt" or with an "asshole," but the narrator of this dialogue affirms that he prefer boys, and only has sex with women out of necessity, admitting that he has a "reputation as a buggerer who prefers boys and follows them around." He proclaims, "If Nature had not wanted men to bugger each other, she would not have made it such a pleasant thing." Vignali misogynisticly regards women as aggressive and insatiable and denigrated vaginas – curiously, not anuses – for smelling of excrement. The cocks (and assholes and cunts), are imagined as detached from bodies, loquaciously demanding their desires. However, excessive male desire can also be tyrannical and out of control, like the Big Cocks who warred against the rest.[52] Vignali's pamphlet circulated clandestinely, but it was reprinted several times and may have influenced other men with like desires. For instance, a friar named Francesco Calcagno told the Inquisition that Vignali's *Cazzaria* influenced him to believe that "he would rather worship a pretty little boy in the flesh than God," and another priest echoed Vignali's claim that nature (or God) made anal sex pleasurable; therefore it must be good. However, these defenses of sodomy could only circulate in private.[53]

As historian Helmut Puff argues, German people seem to have been much less aware of sodomy. Theologians wrote that sodomy was so "vile or revolting" that it should not be spoken of, because the mere mention of the word would pollute people's ears; it was the "mute sin."[54] Authorities warned priests not to enquire too explicitly about unnatural crimes during confession, to avoid passing on information to those innocent of that possibility. Secular authorities often tried to keep cases quiet, warning those who escaped death never to speak of their case in public. Any information about cases was heavily censored, with euphemisms, such as the "crime which cannot be named," used in indictments. In fact, sodomy was rarely prosecuted. However, authorities occasionally discovered urban networks of men from "vastly different social backgrounds" who had sex with each other. For instance, in Augsburg in the 1530s, a wealthy man, a priest, and a teacher had sex in "a public bath, several inns, ... a presbytery and a schoolhouse." Only then did ministers preach that this vice led to terrible social disorder. People attributed sodomy to foreigners; in fact, the verb "florenzen" (from Florence) meant to have anal sex.[55]

The sodomite was almost always seen as the other – the foreigner, the Catholic. In the early sixteenth century, the Reformation brought much greater awareness of sodomy, because Luther and other Protestants accused the Pope and Catholics of indulging in this vice. To undermine the Pope's sacred authority, Luther portrayed him as the Antichrist. Luther depicted the Curia of Cardinals as composed of "hermaphrodites, androgynes, catamites [*cynaedi*], buttfuckers [*pedicones*] and similar monsters of nature." German pamphleteers also claimed that their own lands were innocent of all knowledge of sodomy, which was a papist, Italian invention.[56] English writers also fulminated against sodomites for infecting England with heresy, witchcraft, and Catholicism. They satirized men of the court and theatre for consorting with ganymedes and catamites, insulting terms for beautiful youths who provided sexual services to adult men. The sodomite was portrayed as a demonic, frightening creature who disturbed the order of nature, almost mythical in the stature of his evil, as historian Alan Bray observes.[57]

Yet when a neighbor found a schoolmaster molesting a boy, or a master caressing his male servant, he would not immediately denounce him as a sodomite. The image of the demonic sodomite, in fact, was so extreme that these ordinary men were not recognizable as such larger-than-life villains, unless they also denounced God or plotted against the king. But the rarity of prosecution did not signify social tolerance or a widespread acceptance of sex between men. Rather, communities might have preferred to ignore sex between men in authority and their subordinates – such as masters and servants, teachers and pupils – refusing to recognize it as "sodomy" unless they spectacularly transgressed the responsibilities of patriarchal authority, as Cynthia Herrup suggests.[58] Yet this behavior might have been seen as odd, shameful, and annoying – in other words, as twilight moments. As with all behavior perceived as deviant, medieval and early modern people preferred to regulate their own communities without recourse to authorities. As in Florence, German villagers gossiped about men known to make passes at other men; they warned young men against them, and if the behavior persisted over the years, the village might turn a man in to the authorities.[59]

There is also little evidence that northern European men who had sex with each other conceived of themselves as sodomites; they denied to themselves and others that they were guilty of that demonic sin and, with a few exceptions, did not form networks or subcultures. When men made passes at each other, for instance when sharing a bed while traveling, they did not use the word "florenzen," but rather, expressed their desires in heterosexual terms, suggesting that their bed partner was substitute for a "beautiful girl" or, more crudely, "a big fat cunt." These twilight moments occurred in a much deeper darkness than the fairly transparent moments of Florentine men. Rather, these men do not seem to have had the language of desire for men. It is possible that many more men had sex with each other without articulating what they were doing, and keeping their actions intensely secret.

Sex between women was even more difficult but not impossible to perceive. For instance, "nuns and boarding school girls" in Venetian convents supposedly engaged in "love affairs." One confessor asked whether Suor Fiorenza was found "in the parlor with Suor Elena and Suor Chiara," and if they "had their skirts lifted and their hands in their undergarments, whether the nuns were kissing." They would have to confess and do penance to be absolved. The authorities were much more concerned about love affairs between nuns and secular men, priests, or monks.[60]

Authorities were most likely to punish women who tried to take on masculine prerogatives by having sex with other women with dildos: they would be stigmatized as abject and harshly punished.[61] In Nuremberg, Katherina Hetzeldorfer confessed that when she first had sex with women, "she did it at first with one finger, thereafter with two, and then with three, and at last with the piece of wood which she held between her legs," which she had covered with padding and red leather. Else, wife of Henck Michel, said that during carnival she "stood, whored like a man, and she grabbed her just like a man." The Nuremberg authorities drowned her in the river in 1477, and exiled her sexual partners, who could not prove they thought she was a man.[62] For the most part, however, passionate relationships between women, like passionate relationships between men, were hardly perceived and rarely suspicious, especially in a sexual economy where sex was perceived as something men did to women. Since no seed was "wasted" in sex between women, authorities rarely worried about it; it was a twilight moment.[63]

In 1580 several women were discovered in Aragon having sex with each other, but the Inquisition decided it did not have jurisdiction because they did not use phallic instruments.[64] However, the Church valued virginity above all else, which can be seen in the strange case of Catalina de Erauso. She was a Basque nun who escaped the convent, eager to fight and flirt with "pretty faces." She spent decades as a conquistador in Peru and other areas of New Spain disguised as a man. Finally, she got into so much trouble for dueling and stealing that the authorities imprisoned her. To escape punishment, she outed herself as a woman to a sympathetic bishop. When she was found to still be a virgin, the Church and even the Pope celebrated her virtue and allowed her to continue living dressed as a man.[65]

The Reformation

When Martin Luther wildly accused the Pope of sodomy, he attacked Catholic attitudes toward all sexual desire. For the Catholic Church, the priest's status as celibate marked superiority over ordinary people; by suppressing his sexual desires, he gained spiritual power unavailable to the sexually active believer. Luther and his followers wanted to establish an immediate relationship between the believer and God, instead of relying on the priest as an intermediary. Popular tales had long mocked priests and monks for seducing married women and frequenting prostitutes, but Luther refused to shrug off their sins as peccadillos. Instead, he undermined their status as intercessors with God. He depicted the Pope as the Whore of Babylon, seducing believers into corruption.[66] Luther declared that it was unnatural for priests, monks, and nuns to be celibate, for they were trying, in vain, to suppress their natural desires behind "iron bars." Luther repudiated his own vows and married a former nun, Katherine Bora, who had been smuggled out of a convent. When the Protestants came into power in European countries, they dissolved the convents and monasteries, driving out nuns from their cloisters and urging them to marry. Women lost the possibility of living outside of marriage in a community of other women.

Protestants celebrated marriage and denounced celibacy. John Calvin, the other major reformer, pointed out that it was hypocritical for the Church to celebrate marriage as a sacrament, which made copulation holy, but to deny its pleasures to priests, monks and nuns.[67] Instead, Luther thought it was impossible for people to suppress their "natural" desires. As he declared, "Nature never lets up ... we are all driven to the secret sin. To say it crudely but honestly, if it doesn't go into a woman, it goes into your shirt."[68] For Luther, sexual desire could not be split off from other parts of creation, it had to be integrated, and even celebrated in marriage. As Luther argued in *The Estate of Marriage*, procreation was like other functions, "More necessary than sleeping and waking, eating and drinking, emptying the bowels and bladder." More specifically, for Luther, sexual desire was also innately heterosexual, as we would term it. Sexual desire was not something that came in from outside the self; rather, God created men and women to desire each other, and this desire defined their identities: "Therefore, just as God does not command anyone to be a man or a woman but creates them the way they have to be, so he does not command them to multiply but creates them so that they have to multiply."[69]

In fact, by denouncing sodomy, Luther emphasized the naturalness of heterosexuality: the people of Sodom, he declared, "departed from the natural passion and longing of the male for the female, which was implanted into nature by God." Nonetheless, Luther still retained Augustine's notion that the uncontrollability of sexual desire was original sin. In fact, he saw sexual pleasure as "so hideous and frightful ... that physicians compare it with epilepsy or falling sickness." Couples should not indulge in the "disease and frenzy of lust" but have sex with moderation for procreation.[70] While the devil implanted this lust, God provided marriage so that humans could be purified. At the same time, believers must be constantly vigilant so that they would not be tempted into adultery – even lust in their hearts. Luther and his supporters denigrated the Catholic Church for promising indulgence of sins if believers contributed cash or treasure to the Church. People could simply pay off the Church and sin once more.

Instead, Protestants needed to search their own hearts and monitor the behavior of their neighbors to ensure that sexual sins were not being committed. Luther denounced the common belief that sex between two unmarried people was not a major sin. Unlike Catholics, Protestants did not believe that prostitution should be allowed as an outlet for unmarried men who could not control their desires. Instead, young men were to marry early; the holy household and the God-fearing city could strictly regulate sexual behavior. The Protestant city closed the municipal brothels and instituted Church courts to prosecute fornication. In fact, as Lyndal Roper argues, evangelical Protestants "denied there was a category of prostitutes as such. Rather, there were women who engaged in illicit sexual relations." Fornication and sex before marriage were punished more harshly in women, who were seen as tempting young men, but even young men were warned to remain chaste. Certain types of sinners – such as prostitutes and vagabonds – were seen as irredeemably polluted, as flawed personalities, while others were the pure Elect.[71]

In response to the Protestant challenge, the Catholic Church engaged in its own reformation. While Catholic moralists had emphasized the sanctity of marriage before the Reformation, they now began to encourage a pious holiness between husbands and wives. But they also celebrated both Mary and her husband Joseph as virgins. St. Joseph was symbolized by a staff that burst forth into white flowers when he was chosen to marry the Virgin. While this obvious symbol of potency and fertility may have appealed to the common people who still espoused many pre-Christian beliefs, for Church authorities, St. Joseph's staff signified his life-long virginity, as historian Charlene Black Villaseñor has discovered.[72] The Church also cracked down on priests who kept concubines.[73]

The Spanish Inquisition tried to punish and eradicate Protestantism, along with bigamy and sodomy. The Inquisition also tried to stamp out the heresy that fornication was not a serious sin. Because the common people did not have property or a noble name they did not worry as much about sexual purity. Illegitimacy rates were very high, up to one quarter of births in some districts of Spain. Juan Pérez, a farm worker, said that "to have a young girl as a lover was not a sin," for instance, and Maria Cabrera, "a woman in love," was prosecuted for saying "it was not a sin for a married woman or a single one to have a lover." One young man claimed that "it was better to have sex with a single woman than a female burro." The Inquisition demanded public repentance for these statements, but these people were not burnt at the stake like more serious heretics.[74]

The sixteenth- and early seventeenth-century Spanish Inquisition also fiercely prosecuted men for sodomy. The Aragonese Inquisition, for instance, dealt with 823 cases over a 60-year period, and the common people cooperated by turning men in. Alfonso Gil, a Portuguese laborer, said he thought it "not a sin to do it to a man," but his companions said it was "a sin and a grave concern for the Inquisition." Gil said "in my breeches, now that's an Inquisition." As a result, he was banished for one year. For local people, men who molested youths violated the community's honor. Local people often denounced clergymen, who they suspected of abusing young adolescents. Foreigners, converted Jews, and slaves also came under suspicion. For instance, in 1585 a black Spaniard, Mayuca, found clients for "handsome, painted, gallants," and as a result the Inquisition sent him to the scaffold wearing makeup and a "large lace ruff." When the Inquisition discovered networks of men who had sex with other men, they wanted spectacular punishments to serve as an example: for instance, in a single year, eight men were burned at the stake for having sex under the fig trees outside the city walls of Seville. More often, the Inquisition simply banished, sent to the galleys, whipped, or humiliated most men accused of sodomy, inflicting lighter punishments than secular authorities. After 1625, the Inquisition backed off from public punishments of sodomites, preferring the shame of silence and fearing that elite men would be accused of this offense.[75]

Like Protestants, Catholic cities also tried to repress prostitution and did away with municipal brothels in some areas. By the mid-seventeenth century, the Spanish Church campaigned to have legal sanction withdrawn from brothels.[76] Even earlier, in 1560, the French monarchy repudiated the tradition of municipal brothels and banned houses of prostitution. As historian James Farr writes, prostitution continued, of course, but authorities would tolerate it as long as it remained in the "shadows," quietly practiced without disturbing the neighbors or public order.[77] From the thirteenth century to the sixteenth century, therefore, prostitution had gone from the abject – to be expelled beyond the city walls – to an unfortunate but necessary part of the city in municipal brothels, to twilight moments, shameful and illegal, but rarely punished.

Conclusion

Authorities, both secular and spiritual, realized that for the most part they had to excuse sexual misbehavior, forgiving the perpetrators and returning them to society. Mothers of illegitimate children could be fined, prostitutes could be confined in the municipal brothel, even sodomites could be slapped on the wrist. But this was not toleration of illicit sexual practices, but a form of regulation. During times of crisis, prostitution and sodomy moved from the twilight to the darkness of abjection. During the thirteenth century and the fifteenth and sixteenth centuries, prostitutes and sodomites became scapegoats in times of political and religious turmoil. Prostitutes and sodomites could be seen, in these special circumstances, as defined by their sexual behavior, their natures permeated with sin.[78]

The Reformation led to more emphasis on heterosexual desire between men and women as natural and superior. The Catholic Church had divided humans into two categories: the supposedly pure and celibate priests, monks, and nuns; and ordinary people. To be sure, sodomy came to be seen as the worst of sexual sins, but even ordinary marital sex remained sinful. At the same time, the Church recognized that everyone was a potential sinner, and provided mechanisms for forgiveness. Protestants did away with the category of spiritual celibacy, and instead divided humans into male and female, who naturally desired each other, and sodomites, who were unnatural. Everyone was still a sinner, but people had to examine their hearts to purify themselves of lust, rather than relying on a priest as intermediary. By celebrating marriage, Protestants may have made other forms of intense emotional and erotic relationships less legitimate. During the sixteenth and especially the seventeenth century, suspicions grew about female friendships or sexual relationships as potential threats to marriage, as Alan Bray and Valerie Traub observe.[79] By the seventeenth century, the growing visibility of urban subcultures of men who had sex with other men also raised suspicions about some male relationships. For instance, one of the first and most elaborate sodomitical subcultures was discovered in Mexico City in 1657 – a network of more than a dozen mestizo men who met at each other's houses to dress and dance like women, giving each other feminine nicknames and meeting on religious feast days to worship the Virgin Mary and the saints.[80]

As Europeans were questioning their moral compass and undermining the foundations of the Catholic Church, ships set out from Lisbon and London to circumnavigate the world. They discovered new cultures, where people understood sexuality in entirely different ways.

Suggested reading

Boswell, John. *Christianity, Social Tolerance, and Homosexuality: Gay People in Western Europe from the Beginning of the Christian Era to the Fourteenth Century.* Chicago, 1980.

Brundage, James A. *Law, Sex and Society in Medieval Europe.* Chicago, 1987.

Crawford, Katherine B. *European Sexualities 1400–1800.* Cambridge, 2007.

Dinsmore, Carolyn. *Getting Medieval: Sexualities and Communities, Pre- and Postmodern.* Durham, NC, 1999.

Farr, James R. *Authority and Sexuality in Early Modern Burgundy.* New York, 1995.

Flandrin, Jean-Louis. *Sex in the Western World: The Development of Attitudes and Behavior.* Translated by Sue Collins. Chur, 1991.

Fradenburg, Louise, and Carola Freccero, eds. *Premodern Sexualities.* New York, 1996.

Karras, Ruth Mazo. *Sexuality in Medieval Europe: Doing unto Others.* London and New York, 2005.

Lewin, Eve. *Sex and Society in the World of the Orthodox Slavs.* Ithaca, 1989.

McCarthy, Conor, ed. *Love, Sex and Marriage in the Middle Ages: A Sourcebook.* London, 2004.

Perry, Mary Elizabeth. *Gender and Disorder in Early Modern Seville.* Princeton, 1990.

Richards, Jeffrey. *Sex, Dissidence and Damnation.* New York, 1991.

Roper, Lyndal. *Oedipus and the Devil: Witchcraft, Sexuality and Religion in Early Modern Europe.* London, 1994.

Salisbury, Joyce E., ed. *Sex in the Middle Ages: A Book of Essays.* New York, 1991.

Weisner, Merry. *Christianity and Sexuality in the Early Modern World.* London, 2000.

Chapter 6

The age of exploration
Sexual contact and culture clash in Spain and colonial Mesoamerica

In 1479, a Chalcan slave concubine sang of the joys and sorrows of her life at the Aztec court. Montezuma I had defeated her people, the Chalcans, so as a sign of submission, they presented her and other women to the victors. In her song, the Chalcan concubine seduces her master, singing, "My dear lover; you, little Axayac`atl. Let me play with the honorable corncob! Rounded! Only I can make your stick rise up. I can blow it like a horn. Hooo yee!" But she soon expresses sadness as a noble woman conquered by the Aztecs: "In my desperation, I say it. Oh, child! I wish I would die!" Yet by making love with the enemy, she hopes to bring peace. Evoking the lush landscape, she sings, "The precious popcorn flowers, now the roseate spoonbill, the red jasmine. Just there on your flowery blanketed mat, we are lying within. Y yyoyyo! No longer do we go to war. Aylili!"[1]

Several decades later, another young slave woman was gifted to the victors in a battle. This was Malintzin, who came from Coatzacoalcos, a town in what is now central Mexico. Although independent, her people shared the Nahua language with the mighty Aztecs. She claimed to be from a noble family, and indeed she could speak the elaborate rhetoric of the elite, but as a young girl, she was sold into slavery and ended up in the Mayan-speaking town of Putunchan, in the Yucatán penninsula. In 1519, the Spanish landed nearby and attacked the Maya with steel weapons and guns; they were mounted on horses, which the Mayans had never seen before. To acknowledge their defeat, the people of Putunchan gave Malintzin to the victors as a slave along with 18 other women. Recognizing her beauty, poise and intelligence, the Spanish commander Hernando Cortés passed her on to one of the conquistadors and then took her for himself. But Malintzin also had special skills: she knew two languages, Nahua and Maya, and quickly learned Spanish. Malintzin translated between Cortés and the Aztecs and the Maya, passing on Christian doctrine and negotiating treaties. The Mayan people and others who had been defeated by the aggressive Aztecs thought that the Spanish would help them fend off this fearsome empire. Little did they know that their independence was about to be lost, their population decimated, and their culture transformed. Malintzin exposed the Aztec plot to kill the Spanish, thus enabling Cortés to capture Montezuma and his successors, and to destroy Tenochtitlan, the capital of the Aztecs.[2]

Malintzin's story illustrates how sex becomes an intimate flashpoint in the process of conquest. By concentrating on Spain's conquest of the Nahua and Maya people, this chapter will illuminate themes of the relationship between sexuality and colonialism which can be found in many other imperial ventures.[3] At first contact, some women mediated between two cultures – but more likely, women became victims of sexual conquest. To justify their conquests, imperialists often portrayed colonized people as sexually barbaric. For instance, the Spanish depicted the Aztecs as bloodthirsty cannibals who committed human sacrifice and sodomy. They claimed that they would convert the Indians to Christianity. As in many other imperial ventures, the imperialists wanted to transform indigenous cultures, portraying their religious, sexual and family customs as immoral. Historians must therefore carefully assess portrayals of colonized people's sexuality to distinguish between insulting portrayals by imperialists and the cultural logic and morality of indigenous beliefs.[4] Sexual behavior could also prove to be one of many sites of resistance, as Indians evaded and manipulated Spanish Christian religion and persisted in their own cosmologies of spirituality and fertility. Finally, the Spanish prided themselves on the purity of their blood, but as the conquistadors encountered Maya and Mexica women and had sex with them, their blood was mixed in their offspring. How could the fiction of racial purity be preserved in the face of the reality of widespread interracial sex?

Spain on the brink of conquest

By examining Spanish society and religion in the sixteenth century, we can begin to understand why the Spanish depicted the Indians as sodomitical cannibals and became obsessed with racial purity. The key Iberian concept of honor was defined in racial and sexual terms. Only honorable men, with generations of legitimately married, noble, Christian ancestors, could serve the Crown.[5] The Spanish monarchs, as we have seen, had earlier uneasily tolerated Jewish and Muslim populations, using sexual prohibitions to draw the boundaries between groups. Just before the age of exploration, the Spanish crown had fully "reconquered" Spain from the Muslims and by 1502 the Church and Crown of Castile demanded that remaining Jews and Muslims convert to Christianity. But the state feared that they were not loyal subjects, and the Church suspected they were hanging on to their old religion. Those condemned as secret practitioners of their old ways were burnt at the stake in the *autos-da-fé* of the Inquisition. As historian Mary Elizabeth Perry notes, Christian authorities suspected that women who veiled themselves and bathed often were secretly practicing Islam. But they also "sexually stigmatized" Moriscas – converts from Islam – as "promiscuous and lewd," and accused Islam of sanctioning sodomy.[6] As we have seen in the last chapter, the Inquisition also fiercely prosecuted men accused of sodomy, especially those seen as foreign or Jewish, as part of the larger campaign to stamp out sexual heresies that accepted fornication and bigamy.[7]

Churchmen and secular men sometimes differed somewhat in their definitions of honor. The ideal Spanish nobleman displayed passionate bravado and declared he would sacrifice himself for country, church and family. He fiercely defended the honor of his own wife and daughters, whose sexual purity guaranteed the reputation of the family. The Spanish nobleman believed he was honorable when he swaggered around town or galloped through the countryside on his fiery steed, seducing women and fighting duels. Spanish nobles also scorned the common people as dishonorable, for they had to work with their hands; in contrast, nobles displayed their status with feathered hats, flamboyant brocaded and bejeweled clothing, and starched ruffs. But this virile, violent honor existed uneasily with the Christian duty to be self-controlled. The Church denigrated such flamboyance as effeminate, and advocated a different model of masculinity based on self-control.

The conquest

The typical Spanish conquistador was belligerently masculine and difficult to control. When Governor Velasquez in Cuba sent Hernando Cortés to Mexico, he ordered him to explore and convert the Indians in the Yucatán, not to conquer territory. But the great wealth he found among the Maya and Aztecs tempted Cortés to attack. When his men hesitated at this mission, he burnt his boats so that they could not retreat. He justified his actions by claiming he opened up this populated land to Christianity. When the Spanish landed, they read out a proclamation that instructed the Indians to submit to the Spanish monarchy and the pope. If you obey, the conquistadors proclaimed:

> We will leave to you your wives and children, free and without servitude, that you may do with them and yourselves whatever you wish and see fit, freely, as has been done by nearly all the inhabitants of other islands. If you don't, we shall take your wives and children and make them slaves, and shall sell them and dispose of them as his Majesty should command.[8]

Cortés's troops first encountered the intimidating Maya of the Yucatán, whose warriors had lips pierced with "stone disks … spotted with blue, and others with thin leaves of gold." They saw priests whose long black robes and hair were soaked in blood from sacrifices, and their ears cut from rituals of blood letting.[9] The Maya had formerly ruled much of Mexico, but now they lived in scattered city states. The Maya shared much of their cosmology and culture with the Aztecs and both were wealthy and sophisticated cultures, with hierarchies of nobles and commoners.[10] The Aztecs were part of the larger Mexica culture, often known as the Nahua for their language. But the Aztecs aggressively defeated the Maya and many surrounding Nahua territories. Their capital city of Tenochtitlan was much larger than Spanish cities, with its elaborately carved stone buildings ornamented with gold, bustling marketplaces where women traded woven and embroidered cloth – and towering pyramids where priests sacrificed humans captured in wars against other Nahua people. Not surprisingly, the victims of the Aztecs often appealed to the Spanish for help.

Sex was often a point of bitter misunderstanding between the Spanish and the native peoples. Mexica rulers had used women to cement alliances – and show domination. The people of Quihuitztlan, for instance, complained to the Spanish that the Aztec tax gatherers had abducted and ravished their wives and daughters. But Mexica rulers also sent out their daughters to marry subordinate chiefs, creating an alliance and ensuring that their sons would become the next rulers of these territories. Montezuma himself kept many daughters of chieftains as his mistresses in his great palace. Not surprisingly, Mexica and Maya rulers often offered the Spanish gifts of female slaves – and their daughters as wives. The rulers of Tlaxcala presented the Spanish with 300 female slaves and in addition formally declared, "We wish to give you our daughters, to be your wives, so that you may have children by them, for we wish to consider you as brothers as you are so good and so valiant."[11] For the Indians, giving their daughters was a great honor and a sign of their intent to create an alliance. Giving gifts was also a way of demonstrating their prestige and power, in an effort to create a hierarchical yet reciprocal relationship.

When women provided sexual services, they were not just seen as property, but as completing the complex circuit of reciprocal tasks performed by men and women. Elite women engaged in advantageous marriages, valiantly gave birth to children, and performed ritual functions. Commoner women raised children, grew food, wove cloth, and traded. Slave women performed household tasks or became concubines, but slaves were not a separate category based on race or a permanent status; the children of slave women were free.

Recognizing that the conquistadors needed to make alliances, the Spanish monarch had at first advised them to marry the daughters of native rulers. Women such as Malintzin could also help educate them about indigenous cultures. But the Spanish often saw these offerings of women as a sign of submission, and interpreted the women as permanent slaves to be despised and exploited. They often refused to marry the noble women offered to them as gifts, arrogantly fearing that such unions would damage their racial honor. As Dominican cleric Bartolomé de las Casas reported, "next to death they thought marriage [to indigenous women] the worst torment, the greatest dishonor and affront." He described many of the conquistadors as "upstarts of low breeding and lower caste who had achieved an appearance of status," while others were poor nobles. He concluded, "Both, with the same presumptuous madness and detestable arrogance, held in contempt a people with whom they could have lived most honorably, since many were the natural kings and noblemen of the land."[12] Eventually in the early sixteenth century, however, some Spanish men married Indian women in order to gain alliances and land. These women acquired the honorary status of Spanish wives. In one pueblo in 1534, fully a third of married Spanish men took Indian wives.[13] Malintzin, for instance,

Figure 6.1   An image of conquistadors killing natives, in *An Account of the First Voyages and Discoveries made by the Spaniards in America* (*Den vermeerdenden spieghel der Spaensche teirannije geschiet in Westiniden waerin te sien is de onmenschelijcke wreede feijten der Spanjarden me samen*), Bartolomé de las Casas (1699). Amsterdam, Cornelius Lodewijcksz. vander Plasse, 1621. Verso, Quire G. From the collection of the James Ford Bell Library, University of Minnesota

married a Spanish don after having a child with Cortés. For the most part, however, sexual relationships between Spanish men and indigenous women were exploitative and took place outside marriage.

Sex became a way of dominating and exploiting rather than creating alliances and communicating. The Spanish raped Indian women as part of the spoils of war. When the Spanish conquered the Maya in the Yucátan, they sexually mutilated captive women and suspended them, hanging their children by the feet. One young wife refused to submit to Captain Alonso Lopez de Avila because she had promised her husband she would be faithful. So the captain threw her to fierce mastiffs that tore her apart. Bernal Diaz del Castillo recounts that discontent among the soldiers erupted when Cortés took all the beautiful Indian women and left the ugly ones for the soldiers.[14]

The Spanish thought of slavery as a permanent, degraded status based on racial difference. They wanted to exploit the labor of the Indians, and worked Indian men to death in the mines of the New World. Women were enslaved for sexual purposes. Friar Serrano protested that slave traders raped girls as young as ten "in the sight of innumerable assemblies of barbarians without considering anything but their unbridled lust and brutal shamelessness and saying to those who buy them, with heathen impudence, now you can take her, now she is good."[15] Indian women working in households were routinely raped or turned into concubines by their masters. Killings in war, the exploitation of Indian men and women in labor, and above all the foreign diseases brought by the Spanish, ravaged the population of Indians, which declined dramatically during the sixteenth and seventeenth centuries.

Yet the Spanish conquistadors had to reconcile their ruthless violence with their Christian mission. The Franciscan friars espoused a different version of masculinity than that of the conquistadors they joined in the New World. Their order had originated in the Middle Ages with St. Francis of Assisi, who came from a wealthy family but literally divested himself of all his worldly goods, standing naked in the town square to symbolize his humility before God. They ministered to the poor in Italy, and seized the opportunity to convert the Indians. As historian Inga Clendinnen notes, while the Spanish had a "passion for title, personal honor and pride in family," the friars abandoned their families and titles to join an "egalitarian brotherhood of Christ."[16] The friars often criticized the conquistadors, but they also wanted to control and conquer the indigenous people.

Religious moralists had rejected the idea that empires could simply conquer pagans without a rationale. To provide it, apologists for the Spanish cited the Reconquest of Spain, which they justified by portraying the Muslims as barbaric and deviant. Similarly, the Spanish and Portuguese developed the claim that the Indians were barbaric, cannibalistic pagans who were sexually immoral and promiscuous, "intemperate in lust and violence," characterized by deviant sexual desires: in sum, "our enemies, prejudicial, loathsome and dangerous." Cannibalism and sodomy, they concluded, set the Indians outside the bounds of natural law and human communities. When some friars wanted to abolish slavery and forced labor in 1532, royal official Gonzalo Fernandez de Oviedo y Valdés deposed before the royal Council of the Indies that "some Indians were sodomites, many ate human flesh, were idolatrous, sacrificed human beings, and were vicious people without pity who treated even their friends and relatives like inhuman beasts."[17]

Some friars refuted the notion that Indians were natural slaves and tried to explain away the customs of human sacrifice and the allegations of sodomy. Father Bartolomé de las Casas even pointed out that Mexica human sacrifice, while obviously repugnant, did have a function in their religion. After all, Christianity began with Abraham's willingness to sacrifice his son for God, and God sacrificed his own son to redeem mankind. De las Casas also stoutly repudiated rumors of sodomy as sailors' tall tales.[18] The missionary Francisco de Vitoria said that if sodomy gave the right to conquer, "the French king could make war on the Italians because they commit sins against nature."[19]

The Franciscan friars – and other religious orders – saw their mission as converting the Indians to Christianity. But they saw the Indians as children who should be treated with love and strictness. While the friars often criticized the conquistadors for their sexual indulgences and their abuse of the Indians, they helped in the mission of pacifying the Indians and transforming their culture to serve Spanish needs for labor. Indeed, in the 1530s, some friars in the Yucátan, frustrated at the persistence of Maya religion, tortured recalcitrant Indians, whipping them and hanging them up on hooks when they found them worshipping their own gods.[20]

The Inquisition was brought to Mexico, and at first its wrath was turned against Mexicans who refused to convert, but that tactic was soon abandoned. Instead, the friars thought persuasion would be more effective. To aid in this task, they needed to understand why the Indians carried out human sacrifice and other customs that seemed strange to the Spanish, so the friars gathered as much information as they could on Maya and Aztec religion and culture. For instance, in the mid-sixteenth century the friar Sahagún drew on a team of Nahua informants in his Florentine Codex, which recounts Nahua myths and customs, illustrated in the Mexica style. Sahagún sometimes subtly distorted accounts of Nahua mores to fit the Catholic worldview. But historians have found that some of the mythology in this codex closely resembles that from archeological finds and from pre-conquest codices, since the Nahua had a written pictorial language.[21] By reading against the grain and correlating these different texts, historians have put together a picture of Maya and Nahua belief systems that can help us understand the cultural logic of customs such as blood sacrifice and gender transgression.

In central Mexico, the monks thought that the Nahua-speaking people – the Aztec Mexica and their subordinates – followed a religion that had certain resemblances to Christianity. At times they fasted, mortified the flesh, and abstained, and they adorned their temples with images, much like devout Spanish Christians. But as Louise Burckhart notes, the friars did not really understand that the Nahua culture was based on quite different premises than those of Christianity – while the friars opposed sin with salvation, the Nahua were concerned with fertility above all, and, in their cosmology, the male and female principles were powerful – and fluid.[22] While the Mexican soil was very fertile, drought or hurricanes could ruin crops, so gods and goddesses needed to be placated. Sex was associated with earth, darkness, moisture, fertility, reproduction, but also death, so it was sacred, desired and feared.[23] For the Nahua, the forces of creation and destruction, order and harmony, were all part of the same system and necessary for life and death, for fertility and war.

Human sacrifice was very important for the fertility of people and crops, for they believed that the earth needed to be watered with blood. Further, the Aztecs believed that sexual desire between gods was necessary for the creation of the human race and the continuance of human, animal, and vegetable fertility. Creation and destruction were part of the same cosmic force. In the creation myth, the gods Quetzalcoatl and Tezcatlipoca came down and seized the female earth monster and tore her apart, creating earth and sky out of her body. Wrenched into pieces, she declared she would not bring forth crops unless they fertilized her with blood. In another myth, the human race was created when

Cihuacoatl, Woman Snake, ground up the bones of earlier creatures as if she were grinding maize, and then male gods, led by Quetzalcoatl, drew blood from penises to "moisten the ground bones." A man and woman took form from the dough.[24]

The female principle had an awesome if bloody spiritual power, celebrated in the festival for Toci, the grandmother and "earth power." As the inhabitants of Tenochtitlan prepared for the sacrifice of a maiden, warriors marched with "flowering branches" and midwives and healers played a game in honor of Teteo Innan, "Mother of the Sacred Ones," and Chicomecoatl, "Sustenance Woman." The sacrificial victim became "*teotl ixipltla,* the living receptacle of the heart of the goddess," and her blood would enable maize to grow and feed the people. Her face would be painted yellow, her ears pierced with gold, and she would be adorned with gold bells, a green cap with feathers, and robes painted with the lily, another fertility symbol. Some authorities even have it that the ruler Montezuma would deflower her in a secret ritual before her death.[25] As Inga Clendinnen describes it, the maiden would be ceremonially beheaded by a priest, and then her skin would be flayed. A "naked priest" would then don the skin, and become the embodiment of the goddess Toci, the skin giving him female power. She would be accompanied by four young "near-naked men," who processed through the city, phalluses erect, representing the Huaxtecs, a people of "legendary eroticism." Toci's festival celebrated the "Young Lord Maize Cob," the son she made with Huitzilopochtitli, the fearsome god of the Aztecs. This festival initiated the warriors, who could then prove themselves in battle.[26]

The Maya apparently only engaged in human sacrifice occasionally, during times of crisis, but blood also symbolized fertility in their cosmology. In ancient times, rulers of the classical Maya shed their blood in mystical rituals. Male rulers would pierce their penises with sting-ray spines and collect the blood on paper. Stone carvings represented female rulers piercing their tongues with long, knotted cords. By shedding blood and communing with holy serpents, these nobles believed they could communicate with the gods, ensuring the fertility of their lands. By mixing feminine and masculine images, these rulers could transcend the everyday in their bloodshedding rituals to attain a higher spiritual state.[27] As historian Pete Sigal speculates, "Maya rulers who embodied the power of gods may have seen themselves as analogous to the corn plant, alternately able to fertilize and give birth." During the penis-piercing ritual, the king or nobleman might wear female clothes so that he could access "'masculine and feminine realms of ritual power." By piercing his penis, he symbolically shed menstrual blood. By the time of the conquest, only men engaged in these rituals. Mystical rites gave noblemen access to the divine powers of blood and semen which empowered their lineages; in initiation rites, they passed on this knowledge to young men.[28] Diego de Landa observed men:

> gathering together in a line in the temple, where each person pierced a hole all the way through the virile member. They passed through as great a quantity of the cord as they could stand. And thus fastened and strung together, they anointed the statue of the *demon* of these parts with all of the blood.[29]

By shedding blood, they atoned for sins, they ensured fertility, they proved their masculinity and their lineage, and the trance state induced by pain gave them access to the spirit world.

Myths and rituals also enabled the people to "fantasize about sexual intercourse with and/or between the leaders, ancestors and gods," as Pete Sigal explains. In these myths, the moon goddess might acquire a phallus, and a male god change gender and give birth. These myths and rituals incited the people's desire for their rulers, and gave their rulers access to the creative and destructive power of both sexual energy and death. In a healing ritual, a male shaman would "cast a spell to forcibly cut and pound the lust of creation and the lust of the night." He told the god, "I am submerging/penetrating you with the genitals of your mother and the genitals of your father. You are the lust of the women's children, the lust of the men's children." The Maya did not conceive of masculine and feminine sexual desire as firmly anchored in male and female bodies. Instead, the power of the male and female genitals could be detached and harnessed by shamans, or by gods who constantly shifted shape and changed genders, as part of their divine power, which transcended human bodies.[30]

Among the Nahua as well, there are hints that there may have been a sacramental role for male-male sex or at least for cross-dressed men within Nahua culture. According to the Florentine Codex, the masculine god Tezcalipoca "enriched one, and thus could inflict one with pain and affliction." In despair, the victim of his affliction might mock the god's effeminate alter ego, Titlacauan, as a "great cuiloni," who is "sodomized, sacrificed and eaten." But as Pete Sigal notes, Sahagún translated *cuiloni* as *puto* or male prostitute, or sodomite, transforming the sacramental character of the god into a Christian sin.[31]

The friars did not understand that Nahua religious faith was very different than that of Christians in its understanding of sin and sexual morality. As Louise Burckhart explains, the Christians thought in terms of moral absolutes: sin was the ultimate evil, disobedience of the Ten Commandments and indulgence in the seven deadly sins, whereas God was the ultimate good. The Nahua concept of pollution was quite different than the Christian notion of sin. Sexual desire did not pollute the soul, rather inappropriate sexual behavior physically polluted the whole household. For them, sexual transgressions were akin to accidents or other disruptions of human and cosmic harmony; a mistake in weaving or a dirty house was caused by the unhappiness or manipulation of a god rather than the result of the free will of an individual. Sexual transgressions could cause illness in a spouse or child, much like physical pollution.[32]

Tlazolteotl was the "Filth goddess," the patroness of adulterous and promiscuous women, who caused pollution but then swept it away with her broom. Nahua misdeeds could be repaired with penance, appeasing the god. Tlazolteotl induced people to sin sexually, but she also symbolically "ate" the sins when they confessed to her, thus allowing a restoration of "sexual equilibrium," as Carrasco explains.[33] Sahagún, however, interpreted her as Eve, as the source of sin, ignoring the way in which the Nahua believed that she both created and cleansed filth and

VII. Tlaçolteotl, die Göttin des Unraths, die Erdgöttin

Figure 6.2   "Tlacolteotl," in Eduard Seler, *Codex Borgia* (Berlin 1904–9) vol.1, Section 3, 14, Number 7. (Wilson Library Rare Books 972A fC642). From the collection of the Special Collections & Rare Books unit, University of Minnesota

sexual excess.[34] Promiscuous women, for example – especially prostitutes and adulterers, as well as sodomites – were typically characterized in terms of bodily waste. Their carnal vices were all referred to as *tlaello* or *tlazolli*, meaning filth, garbage, refuse, or ordure, but also connoting excrement.[35] For the Aztecs, excess was the problem, not sex itself, for excrement also became fertilizing manure.[36]

The friars admired the Nahua for seeming to value female virginity – and occasional male abstinence. Their young women were instructed to keep their virtue intact, like a beautiful piece of green jade. Those boys and girls who learned religious dances in the song houses attached to temples were punished if they engaged in relationships: female officials could confiscate a youth's possessions, beat him, and expel him, and a girl would be punished by being forbidden to sing or dance with other women, as well as being expelled.[37] As Burckhart notes, "If a girl in temple service indulged in sexual acts, bats would fly into the temple chambers and mice would gnaw the ritual vestments."[38]

In understanding Aztec morality, it is also important to consider the social context of an expanding, aggressive empire in which nobles and warriors did not follow the same rules as commoners. Elite Aztec women painted their faces, twisted their hair into horns, and wore beautiful embroidered skirts and gold jewels, while common women were supposed to be modest. Nobles could keep many concubines, while commoners were expected to live in monogamous marriages. Aggression was an important aspect of Aztec masculinity. The Aztecs expected their priests to abstain periodically from sex but they encouraged their warriors to indulge sexually by providing them with beautiful girls. As Burckhart notes, "Immoral behavior gave one a certain power for activities like war and gaming."[39]

Among the wider Mexica and Nahua people, to be forced to wear women's clothes was to be ritually humiliated as the losers in battle. Soon after the conquest, Maya texts blamed the Itza, who were heavily influenced by Aztec/Mexica culture, for being cowardly, effeminate warriors, who allowed the Spanish to defeat them and at least symbolically penetrate them.[40] Similarly, the common people seem to have resented the Aztec nobles who claimed the privileges of taking many concubines, while commoners were expected to be monogamous; they later mocked their own nobles for committing sodomy and other indulgences, in part to blame them for the conquest.[41] According to the codices, the Maya and Nahua severely punished men who had sex with other men. As Sigal notes, they had been influenced by Spanish Catholicism's denigration of sodomy, but given their culture's emphasis on aggressive masculinity, it is unlikely that they "accepted" or "tolerated" male-male sex.[42] But their attitude was subtly different than the Spanish understanding of sodomy as the worst sin against nature.

Sigal finds that there may have been men among the Aztecs who performed an "institutionalized, if degraded role," wearing feminine attire, and kept by high level nobles "to perform household chores, to clean the temples, and to accompany warriors to war."[43] For instance, a Chichimeca man dressed as a woman fought the Spanish to defend a city near Tenochtitlan, and the Spanish were surprised that he was so brave. He told them that he had long dressed as a woman and made his living in that way. There was another report that some priests kept boys for sexual purposes.[44] Among the related Indian cultures in North America, such men have been interpreted as "berdache" or more recently, as "two-spirited." Some historians regard them as playing a valued role as a third gender in their culture, but other historians assert that in central Mexico they were denigrated and exploited.[45] We must also remember that authorities may revile and forbid certain behaviors, such as adultery, prostitution, and sodomy, which are nonetheless commonly practiced in their societies. After all, despite the intense persecution of the Spanish Inquisition, men formed networks seeking sex with each other. It would not be surprising in the large urban area of Tenochtitlan to find men who exchanged or sold sex.

The friars wanted to impose monogamous marriage on the Maya and Nahua people. Prior to the conquest, parents usually arranged marriages, approved by local officials, for these unions involved exchanges of property. A bride who was not a virgin would be shamed by a wedding banquet in which "food would be served in broken or perforated dishes."[46] The Maya expected both men and women guilty of adultery to confess to their priests or their spouses. But they did not believe in lifelong monogamy. Not knowing each other well, young couples often divorced. Widows and widowers married each other without ceremony and separated easily.[47] Some of the friars worried that when indigenous religious and noble authorities lost their influence after the conquest, sexual morality deteriorated and promiscuity increased.[48] The friars were appalled at the practice of easy divorce.[49] The Church prosecuted Indian villagers for living together outside of marriage, and rebuked the Maya elites, or *caciques*, for keeping commoners as concubines. As a result of Church pressure, government efforts to force Indians to live in villages, and deprivation of property, the old multifamily households and elite polygamous households disappeared, and Indian families were more likely to live in small nuclear families.[50] Without their kin living in the household to preserve Maya or Mexica traditions, the Church hoped that married couples would be more vulnerable to Catholic influence.

Although the Indians overall did convert to Christianity, they combined Christian beliefs with their own older religions to form a hybrid or syncretic religious culture. The friars built churches in place of the Mayan and Nahua temples which sat at the center of each settlement or village, and the image of the Virgin Mary blended in with female fertility goddesses of the Nahua tradition.[51] After the conquest, Maya noblemen wrote the secret shamanistic Ritual of the Bacabs to perpetuate their old ways. As historian Pete Sigal has found, the Christian figures of Jesus and Mary appear in these rituals, but their spiritual power was used to harness more traditional powers of fertility. For instance, one incantation that aims to heal an illness begins by appealing to Jesus and Mary, but then goes on to ask,

> Has the semen of creation, the semen of birth spread forcefully? I have not moved it. It is captured in the Chuen; it is captured in the clouds, it is captured in the land, it is captured in the wind; it is captured in the day; it is captured in the night; it is captured in front of men; it is captured behind me; it is captured in the virgin. Oh! its capture. The end.

The moon goddess became the Virgin Mary, who exemplified the power of virginity, but also more traditional powers of fertility: a chant to her praised the "virgin fire of the moon, and the beautiful lady of the maize." Sigal speculates that Maya communities praised the virginity of their maidens as a sign of their community's integrity, but also celebrated their sexual maturity.[52]

To ensure religious orthodoxy in the face of these beliefs, the friars tried to impose the new practice of confession to a detailed list of sins. Although they devoted more pages in confession manuals to making sure that the Indians submitted themselves to Spanish ideas about property and demands for labor, their second highest priority seems to have been imposing Catholic notions of sexual guilt. One 1611 confession manual, for instance, instructed priests to ask parishioners if they had engaged in anal sex, masturbation, if they had touched or kissed each other's private parts, or even if young girls had played with each other "like man and woman." The friars also proclaimed against efforts to limit conception and the practice of abortion, which seems to have been quite common, especially when Indian women were raped by Spanish masters or soldiers. Since Indian populations declined rapidly, abortion threatened the supply of available labor as well.[53]

The priests did not always follow the principles they preached. Christianized Maya and Nahua people resented the hypocrisy of exploitative priests who kept mestiza or Indian concubines or refused to hear women's confessions unless they had sex with them. One Maya informer complained:

> Only the Priests are allowed to fornicate without so much as a word about it. If a good commoner does that, the priest always punishes him immediately. But look at the priests' excessive fornication, putting their hands on these whores' vaginas, even saying mass like this.[54]

Maya and Nahua people also objected when priests molested young men, or kept them as lovers.[55] But the power of honor and respectability often meant that priests and other elites could get away with such behavior. As historian John Chuchiak observes, the Maya usually did not complain about priests who kept concubines unless they also violated the sanctity of the confessional or mass by having sex there. Using such complaints, the Maya also manipulated the contrast between Catholic ideals and Spanish behavior to their own advantage.[56]

The Church found it very difficult to control the sexual behavior of elite Spanish men. For instance, in Guadalajara in 1686, a bishop tried to have don Luis Hurtado thrown in prison, because he had a wife in one town but kept dona Francisca Chumazero as his concubine in another. However, higher authorities commanded the bishop to refrain, in order to protect the "reputation of virginity" of dona Francisca. Elite men sometimes flaunted their concubines, such as the official don Tomas Pisarro who took his lover, a married woman, to church and got her a box at the public bullfights, despite the fact that the Church had excommunicated him.[57]

Sexual mixing and the myth of racial purity

For descendants of the Spanish conquerors, their honor depended on a myth of racial purity. To guard this honor, they insisted on marrying virgins of pure Spanish descent. However, this racial purity was based on a fiction, of course, since very few people could claim "pure" Spanish blood – so many of the early conquistadors married or had children with Indian women. The Church was utterly unable to prevent the sexual mixing of Africans, Indians and Europeans in New World societies. However, religious and secular laws and customs functioned to create a racial hierarchy. Unlike in North American society, which relied on a strict black–white distinction in which any drop of African blood made a person black, the racial hierarchy of Central and South America was much more complex, based on a graduated hierarchy of color and culture – at the top the

Spanish, then the mestizos, or mixed race, then the Indians and Africans. While most mestizos were poor, some learned trades and engaged in businesses, and began asserting their own respectability and wealth. Spanish women in Mexico City, for instance, sometimes had liaisons with or married mestizo men. To keep up the myth of racial and sexual honor, interracial sex functioned as twilight moments, widely practiced but not acknowledged. In the late seventeenth century, the honor of Hispanic women was largely a matter of public reputation, and not always of private practice. If a woman had a secret love affair and concealed the birth of her infant and lived a chaste, pious, and penitent life there-after, her family might conceal her shame. The church might compel a man to marry a woman he had impregnated, even if she was of slightly lower status.[58]

Church and secular authorities also used marriage as a marker of racial honor, encouraging it for some and denying it to others based on race. To be sure, the Church insisted that rural indigenous people marry, and the state exempted them from nuptial fees. But mestizos and blacks had to obtain official permission to marry and pay high fees, which served as a deterrent. As a result, illegitimacy rates were quite high among urban Spanish people, mestizos, Indians, and blacks, although they were low for some rural Spanish and Indian people.[59] Mestizo, black and Indian single women were vulnerable to abduction by Spanish or mestizo men who wished to take them as concubines, or simply rape them. The Spanish colonists stigmatized these women as lacking honor, as already immoral. As historian Susan M. Deeds observes, "Persuading Spanish men that Indian and mixed-race women were lacking in morality and worthiness was crucial to main-taining a race-based hierarchy."[60] These affairs were always seen as "twilight moments," rather than creating a permanent lineage. Sometimes Spanish men passed on property to their illegitimate offspring, but they could not acquire elite status and, far more often, they were abandoned. Although women thus faced violence and exploitation, they also could resort to love magic and spells, for instance potions containing menstrual blood, to bewitch, entice or punish their male lovers. The Church and secular Spanish men therefore feared women as potentially disorderly witches unless they were quiet, confined and respectable.[61]

At the same time, Indian, mestizo, and African people had their own notions of honor which differed from those of the Spanish elite. African slaves often came from polygamous societies, and masters did not want them to marry, because they broke up families to sell slaves. For instance, in 1610 Geronima Negra asserted her right to live with her husband although her master did not want her to.[62] For poor women, engaging in sexual relationships could be a way of making a living, going from one man to another. They could also avoid marriage and live in households with other women.

By the eighteenth century, mestizo people became more interested in marriage and slightly less likely to have illegitimate children. Some black people even demanded the right to marry, suing their masters for preventing them. If black and mestizo people insisted on marrying, and the descendants of the Spanish had so many illegitimate children, how could the Spanish regard themselves as racially superior? In response to this conundrum, the Church became more interested in ensuring that marriages preserved racial hierarchies and was less likely to enforce men's promises of marriage, especially for those cases in which the woman was of a lower social status.[63] The harm incurred to his social status by marrying a lower-status or mestizo woman outweighed the damage to her reputation. A man's honor was not damaged by his refusal to marry a woman; it was a matter of his private conscience.[64] By 1776, the Spanish crown mandated parental consent for "unequal" matches, that is between people of different racial gradations.[65] Sexual controls, therefore, strengthened racial boundaries.

Conclusion

Sexual contact between the Spanish and the various Indian peoples of the New World marked an intimate, vulnerable connection characterized by dominance and exploitation. The Spanish experience in Mexico illustrates some common patterns of sexual conquest in the process of colonization. In the first stages, when a few European colonizers would land on alien shores, they sought out indigenous women – such as Malintzin – to act as cultural mediators, to understand the new peoples they were encountering, and to gain access to food, knowledge, and alliances. When indigenous people presented women to them as gifts, seeking honorable alliances, conquerors often exploited the women through rape, slavery and concubinage, using ideas of racial difference to justify their violent actions.

To justify imperial conquest, colonizers portrayed their victims as racially different, barbaric, and sexually immoral – in this case, as sodomitic cannibals. They often failed to understand the internal cultural logic of the religions they encountered, misinterpreting complex fertility rituals as signs of promiscuity. Similarly, the English would eventually denigrate Hindus and Muslims in India for the practices of early marriage, purdah and concubinage, and attack polygyny in many African cultures. Colonizers often tried to impose their own ideas of sexual morality, but even when indigenous people were converted to Christianity, they produced hybrid religions and cultures, retaining some of their own morality. As the colonizers became more established through the generations, interracial sex continued and produced racial mixing. In areas with chattel slavery, masters could demand sexual services from enslaved women and sell off their children. On a more subtle level of exploitation, French and British colonizers, for instance, often kept native mistresses.[66] The Latin American racial situation was somewhat distinct in its gradation of racial mixtures; in many other imperial situations, the distinction between "white" and "black" was much more stark. But interracial sex was often seen as a twilight moment, commonly practiced yet not acknowledged officially.

Yet for some Europeans, as we will see in the next chapter, encounters with non-European peoples also opened up the possibility that sexual morality could be constructed on an entirely different basis than traditional Christianity.[67] They began to explore new ideals about the sexual body and the sexual self, often fantasizing about native practices in an imperialist, orientalizing fashion, but at the same time, they challenged centuries-old presumptions about sexual desire.

Suggested reading

Burckhart, Louise. *The Slippery Earth: Nahua-Christian Moral Dialogue in Sixteenth-Century Mexico*. Tucson, 1989.

Clendinnen, Inga. *Aztecs: an Interpretation*. Cambridge, 1991.

Krippner-Martínez, James. *Rereading the Conquest: Power, Politics, and the History of Early Colonial Michoacán, Mexico, 1521–1565*. University Park, PA, 2001.

Lockhart, James. *The Nahuas after the Conquest: a Social and Cultural History of the Indians of Central Mexico, Sixteenth through Eighteenth Centuries*. Stanford, CA, 1992.

Seed, Patricia. *To Love, Honor, and Obey in Colonial Mexico: Conflicts over Marriage Choice, 1574–1821*. Stanford, 1988.

Sigal, Pete. *From Moon Goddesses to Virgins: The Colonization of Yucatecan Maya Sexual Desire*. Austin, 2000.

Socolow, Susan. *The Women of Colonial Latin America*. Cambridge, 2000.

Trexler, Richard C. *Sex and Conquest: Gender Violence, Political Order, and the European Conquest of the Americas*. Ithaca, 1995.

Chapter 7

Enlightening desire
New attitudes toward sexuality in the
seventeenth and eighteenth centuries

Thérèse, usually a beautiful young woman, suffers from a mysterious ailment. She complains, "I was listless, my complexion jaundiced, my lips inflamed ... I resembled a living skeleton." She consults a doctor, who surprisingly diagnoses a lack of sex, that "divine liquid which affords us the one physical pleasure." Thérèse regains her health with a remarkable discovery: while bathing her private parts, inflamed from abstinence, she finds "a little protuberance which caused me to shiver." Rubbing it, she "soon gained the heights of pleasure!" This happy woman is the heroine of a radical pornographic novel called *Thérèse Philosophe*, and her creator challenged the Church's antagonism toward sexual desire.[1]

Female sexual desire became a central theme of the new debates about sex in the Enlightenment period. It was nothing new to portray women with strong sexual urges; Church fathers had denounced female desire as the taint of Eve, and medieval popular culture had fearfully mocked female insatiability. By the eighteenth century, however, radicals celebrated female sexual desire because it was central to their philosophies. In both popular medical literature and philosophical pornography, the clitoris illustrated the necessity of female desire and its possibilities for excess.

Sexual desire became a way of thinking about nature, morality, the body, the relationship between the sexes, the self, and politics. Austere religious thinkers of the seventeenth century admitted that Nature was God's handiwork, and claimed that the Church's moral precepts were defined by Natural Law. But they regarded nature as part of the fallen world; natural instincts had to be strictly controlled to attain the higher plane of spiritual bliss. Eighteenth-century Enlightenment philosophers argued for the authority of science and philosophy to interpret Nature, the material rather than the metaphysical world. They popularized the new scientific and medical knowledge of the previous century, which was based on the empirical evidence obtained through dissecting bodies and peering at bodily fluids through the microscope.

Mainstream Enlightenment discourses – philosophical and medical – tended to celebrate only marital, procreative sexual pleasure. As historian Jonathan Israel points out, the mainstream Enlightenment thinkers tried to reconcile the new scientific and philosophical knowledge with theology and the established order, advocating reform rather than revolution. In contrast, many radical

Enlightenment thinkers advocated "toleration, personal freedom, democracy, equality, freedom of expression, and sexual emancipation."[2] By celebrating sexual desire and the body's own knowledge, they challenged the authority of the church and denied the concept of original sin. Some even proclaimed that sexual desire motivated human happiness.

In the eighteenth century, many Enlightenment philosophical and fictional works were distributed openly, and its ideas spread through plays, pamphlets and fiction. But even they faced challenges from censors. To evade it, some radical Enlightenment thinkers published abroad in clandestine editions, or circulated works in manuscript. Another way of getting around censorship was to combine philosophy and pornography, that is, explicit discourses that were primarily intended to stimulate the sexual desires of their consumers. The booksellers had to smuggle both in across the border, and erotic literature was more likely to sell. As historian Robert Darnton discovered, *Thérèse Philosophe* became an underground bestseller by folding radical ideas into a titillating plot.[3] Cheap medical tracts and sex manuals celebrated female desire in ways different from that of the new scientists. They sought to bring sexual information to the populace – and to make a profit. This chapter will concentrate on such sources from France, and to some extent Britain, because these countries produced most of this literature.[4]

All of these genres, but especially the popular and underground ones, tended to work on two levels. Despite challenging established authorities, philosophers and pornographers often veiled their meanings; they simultaneously denounced non-procreative desires in rational dialogues but titillated the reader with fantasies of transgression. Similarly, the popular medical works could declare that they aimed only to instruct their readers in how to conceive, but their anatomical detail about the sexual organs could be exciting enough to attract readers with no interest in making babies.

The anatomy of sex and reproduction

Medical experts had long debated whether female sexual pleasure – especially orgasm – was necessary for conception. For centuries, doctors had relied on ancient models of reproduction from Greek texts, but they contradicted each other.[5] On one hand, Aristotle believed that women were lesser beings, inferior to men. He thought the sperm contained a homunculus, or germ of the human being, and the mother merely incubated the fetus. While he acknowledged the existence of the clitoris and female sexual pleasure, it wasn't important to him, for he did not think that female sexual desire or orgasm contributed to conception. Men and women, therefore, were very different sexually. His rival Galen asserted that both males and females contributed "seed" to conception. When women gushed forth moisture during orgasm, their "seed" was fertilized by the male semen. No orgasm, no conception. Anatomists who followed Galen believed that the sexual desires and genitals of males and females were similar. They depicted the vagina as a penis turned inside out, and the ovaries as the equivalent of the testicles.

The new anatomical discoveries from the sixteenth century onwards intensified this debate. As anatomists dissected male and female bodies, some asserted that the ovaries and testicles were not comparable. The discovery of the clitoris in 1559 – by Renato Columbus – would also seem to make it difficult to argue that the penis and vagina were the same organ turned inside out or outside in. Anatomists debated whether males or females, or both, provided the "seed" that formed the human embryo. They began to insist that men and women's bodies differed from each other in every way. As a result, some medical men began to downplay the necessity of female pleasure. Dr. Roussel, for instance, argued that "the exterior parts of men carry a character of sensible utility; those of women seem to be nothing other than simple organs of pleasure."[6] By the late eighteenth century, experiments had shown that the female orgasm was not necessary for conception. Although this knowledge derived from experiments, this did not mean that it was objective – as Thomas Laqueur points out, it was shaped by cultural presumptions, especially that female desire was unimportant.[7]

During the seventeenth century, however, these medical works were often published in Latin, which few people could read; if they were in the vernacular of English or French, they were still very expensive. Slowly, medical literature began to circulate in more popular forms. In London in 1658, Levinas Lemnius published *The Secret Miracles of Nature*, a large, leatherbound compendium of advice on sex, generation, science, nature, health, and bizarre natural phenomena. Entrepreneurial authors soon plagiarized Lemnius and other sources to produce inexpensive pamphlets and small books more focused on sex and reproduction. They included the dozens of versions of *Aristotle's Masterpiece* (which had nothing to do with Aristotle), Jane Sharp's midwifery manual, and the French doctor Nicholas de Venette's *Conjugal Love*. These were often printed on rough paper and crudely stitched together as pamphlets, with a few plain woodcuts, and sold by peddlers around the countryside. They appealed to middle-class, laboring, and peasant audiences. The pamphlets might be given as a wedding present, but kept locked in a chest, or surreptitiously passed between adolescent apprentices.[8] *Aristotle's Masterpiece*, de Venette's *Conjugal Love*, and Jane Sharp's manual, of course, did not necessarily express popular attitudes, although they may have shaped them.

Sex manuals such as *Aristotle's Masterpiece* popularized the ancient idea that men and women were the same sexually at the same time as medical researchers began to disprove this idea. One typical version declared, "For those that have the strictest Searchers been/Find Women are but Men turn'd Out side in;/And Men, if they but cast their Eyes about,/May find they're Women, with their In-side out."[9] These texts reconciled the clitoris with the Galenic model by depicting the penis as the equivalent both of the clitoris and the vagina. They celebrated and emphasized female desire as necessary for conception. Lemnius, the early compiler of *The Secret Miracles of Nature*, vigorously refuted the Aristotelian idea that women's seed contributed nothing to conception. Jane Sharp, the midwife, dismissed this theory as the thoughts of "idle coxcombs."

Like *Aristotle's Masterpiece*, the popular sex manual, she argued that women were "lustfull and take delight in Copulation, and were it not for this they would have no desire nor delight, nor would they ever conceive."[10]

These popular manuals emphasized the clitoris as the seat of women's pleasure. Versions of *Aristotle's Masterpiece* from the 1690s to the 1790s described "the clitoris" as:

> a sinewy and hard part of the womb, replete with spungy and black matter within, in the same manner as the side ligaments of the Yard; and indeed resemble it in form, suffering erection and falling in the same manner, and it both stirs up lust, and gives delight in copulation: for without this the fair sex neither desire mutual embraces, nor have pleasure in them, nor conceive by them.[11]

Even though de Venette found the Galenic model unlikely, he also stressed the importance of the clitoris.[12]

Popular culture had always resisted the church's claim that sex was sinful; but it always had an ambivalent attitude; the medieval *fabliaux*, for instance, fantasized about excess desire but depicted it as grotesque and funny, often denouncing it at the end. Now some popular literature lauded sexual desire as natural and necessary, indeed holy. Lemnius argued that "it is most natural to procreate one like himself, and men ought to use it reverently as a divine gift, and Ordinance of God."[13] This attitude was congruent with the Protestant celebration of sexual desire in marriage in more mainstream texts. But the cheaper popular works celebrated sexual desire even more vigorously, tending to equate God and nature. They presented sexual desire as essential for the existence of human beings, "part of the plastick Power of Nature," which is the "only Energy of the Special Blessing, which to this Day, upholds the Species of Mankind in the World."[14] Similarly, the French doctor de Venette argued that nature made human beings with passion and the need to procreate; Nature, Providence, and God were all different words for the same divinity; therefore, sexual passion was not sinful.[15] Of course, the Church had always equated God with Nature, but asserted its own authority to define Nature. Now, Nature became an authority that could take precedence over the Church.

Most versions of *Aristotle's Masterpiece* regarded sex as one element in a loving, companionate marriage. Just as nature made male and female genitals to fit together, argued the anonymous author of *Aristotle's Masterpiece*, so she intended husbands and wives to become one flesh, to nurture and support each other. A good wife was "the best companion in prosperity, and in adversity the surest friend; the greatest assistance in business, the only lawful and comfortable means by which we can have issue, and the great remedy against incontinence."[16] These manuals instructed couples, albeit rather vaguely, in foreplay, which they justified for procreation but which obviously served the purpose of pleasure as well. De Venette also advised husbands to initiate new brides gently, and to kiss and caress their wives. He reported that philosophers permitted husbands to caress their wives in any manner, as long as they did not indulge in non-procreative, unhealthy, or exceptionally voluptuous sex. *Aristotle's Masterpiece* advised couples to "invigorate their mutual Desires, and make their Flames burn with a fiercer Ardor by those endearing ways that Love can better teach, than I can write." In a 1733 version, a husband tells his wife:

My rudder, with thy bold hand, like a try'd
And skilful pilot, thou shalt steer; and guide
My bark in love's dark channel, where it shall
Dance,
as the bounding waves do rise and fall.

Furthermore, while *Aristotle's Masterpiece* celebrated procreation, some versions gave information on how herbs could be used to release blocked menstrual periods – in other words, bring on an abortion. In several versions, it advised women how to cure the problem of missed periods, or retained menstruation which it said causes sluggishness, pain, and a slow pulse. The cure was to take "prepared Steel, savin, Fenugreek, Camomile, Melilote Dill, Marjoram, Pennyroyal, Feverfew, Juniperberries, or Calamint."[17] While some of these are known abortifacients, others were just herbs which would not have induced abortion.

By focusing on pleasure and procreation, the sex manuals represented a fantasy world of knowledge and delight. They claimed that sex was necessary for women's health. If not married early, the authors warned, adolescent girls would succumb to green sickness, becoming pale and mopish.[18] *Thérèse Philosophe*'s listless, skeletal state reflected this popular understanding of abstinence's dire effects on young women.

Despite their celebration of female desire, these writers expressed some anxiety about the clitoris because it raised the possibility that women could enjoy sex without men. Exotic foreign women were often thought of as abusing the clitoris for their own pleasure; indeed, before the anatomists, the clitoris was chiefly known among early modern Europeans through the work of Leo Africanus, who alleged that Egyptians excised the nymphae or clitoris because they grew too long. The 1693 *Aristotle's Masterpiece* said "the Jewish Women did abuse this part to their own mutual Lust, as St Paul speaks, Rom 1. 26."[19] Picking up on this theme, Jane Sharp recounted that:

some lewd women have endeavoured to use [the clitoris] as men do theirs. In the Indies, and Egypt they are frequent, but I never heard but of one in this Country, if there be any they will do what they can for shame to keep it close.[20]

For all Sharp's focus on pleasure, she was puzzled by the possibility that women could use the clitoris to have sex with each other – or indeed for non-procreative purposes. The French doctor de Venette was typically more open and explicit about lesbianism. In great detail, he claimed that women with excessively long clitorises could give other women nearly as much pleasure as men could with the penis. Convents were greatly troubled by such women, he alleged.[21]

While it is very rare to know how women who desired other women responded to this material, we do have one example. In her secret coded diary, early nineteenth-century gentlewoman Anne Lister seemed fascinated by the depiction in *Aristotle's Masterpiece* of the female genitals as being like the male's turned outside in, such that the penis was analogous to the vagina, and the testicles resembling the ovaries.[22] She seemed to think that since males and females were not that physically different, she could express her unique nature as she wished, and that this explained why her desires focused exclusively on women.

Although all these popular sources based their accounts of sexual desire on understandings of the body, they also agreed that the imagination stimulated sexual desire – it was not just a biological function. Jane Sharp asserted that the imagination stirred the clitoris to cast out the seed, and swelled the "yard."[23] But the female imagination was also seen as dangerous. The pornographic *L'Ecole des Filles* sardonically noted that the source of women's spiritual, beautifully elevated thoughts and fantasies about love was really the fire of lust, coming from their genitals.[24] De Venette, always concerned that wives might exhaust their husbands sexually, wrote of women, it is "the inconstancy of their Imagination, or rather to the providence of Nature, that has made them to serve us for Playtoys after our more serious Occupations."[25] As Laura Gowing observes, early modern people still believed that sex was something men did to women. Although they believed women had a voracious sexual desire, they also thought that women should be passive. Unmarried or adulterous women who displayed open, aggressive sexual desire were seen as "shameful and wanton."[26]

The imagination also meant that masturbation could be a problem. Religious authorities had long condemned masturbation on moral grounds, but by the eighteenth century it was increasingly seen as a medical problem. Although *Aristotle's Masterpiece*, de Venette, and Sharp do not seem concerned with masturbation, the popular pamphlets such as John Marten's *Onania* in 1712 and Samuel Tissot's *Onanisme* in 1760 presented masturbation as a terrible danger. Of course, even as these popular tracts denounced masturbation, they titillated their readers with bizarre sexual stories and explicit illustrations. These pamphlets were intended to sell as part of the burgeoning popular market in erotic literature. More seriously, doctors feared that masturbation would encourage sodomy between boys and tribadism between girls, harming their procreative mission. It was not only the waste of semen, but as Thomas Laqueur argues, too much imagination indulged in solitude which caused the harm of masturbation; Enlightenment thinkers valued sociability, which was the basis for the family, society, citizenship, and even the market – all of which masturbation endangered.[27]

Philosophy in the bedroom

In Diderot's *D'Alembert's Dream*, Dr. Bordeu asserts that there is nothing wrong with solitary sex; indeed, by getting rid of excess fluid and restoring health to frustrated virginal girls it could remedy the ills caused by continence. But as narrator, Diderot then repudiated this argument, reassuring readers that "to spread these principles abroad would be to trample all decency underfoot, draw the most odious suspicions upon oneself, and commit a crime against society."[28] This ambivalent dialogue was characteristic of Enlightenment texts. *D'Alembert's Dream*, which Diderot never published in his lifetime, was a dialogue in the form of a dream: the author could thus have different characters explore outrageous ideas without endorsing them himself.

In his youth, Diderot rejected his parents' plans for his professional career and advantageous marriage to strike out on his own, choosing his own wife – and then his mistresses. He also moved from the mainstream to the radical Enlightenment, from deism to radical materialism, but in his published writings he still remained on the moderate end of the radicals. Diderot celebrated sexual desire as part of nature's fecundity and human procreation. In his great *Encyclopédie*, he wrote an entry on "jouissance" (orgasm, pleasure) which claimed that God gave sexual pleasure for the purpose of procreation, but – and here he differed from the Church – not only for procreation. It was a divine pleasure, a delirium drawing the two sexes together. He declared "To enjoy is to know, to experience" and his *Encyclopédie* provided copious information about the anatomy of sexual pleasure, including the clitoris.[29]

By exploring "primitive" societies where sexual customs were very different, Diderot declared that morality was relative. He popularized many of these ideas in his work, *Supplement to the Voyage of Bougainville to Tahiti*, published in 1772. Parisians were delighted to learn about Bougainville's recent explorations of Tahiti, where beautiful half-clad girls offered themselves to sailors. Unencumbered by the fierce emotions of jealousy or the constraints of convention, the Tahitians seemed to enjoy a paradise of sexual freedom. As Diderot imagined it, the Tahitians simply obeyed nature's call to indulge in the "sweetest pleasure there is." For Diderot, procreation was the proper aim of sex. In his tale, when a chaplain refuses the sexual services of a daughter of a Tahitian family, protesting that his religion forbids him to enjoy her, the Tahitian father declares:

> "I don't know what you mean by 'religion,' but I can only think ill of it, since it prevents you from enjoying an innocent pleasure to which Nature, that sovereign mistress, invites every person; that is, of bringing into the world one of your own kind."[30]

Diderot used sexual desire to challenge the Church's authority over nature. He believed that "nature was creative, dynamic, organic, and self-developing," a benevolent principle of order rather than a dangerous chaos.[31] Diderot attacked the Church for irrationally suppressing a natural sexual desire that did not hurt anyone; he proclaimed, "there is nothing so puerile, ridiculous, absurd, harmful, contemptible and bad" as chastity and continence, which brought no benefits to the celibate individual, or to society as a whole. In fact, for Diderot, pleasure was the "principle of life and energy" that drove human beings to action and impelled humans toward each other; it spurred not only love, but sociability, commerce, and society itself.[32]

Diderot was intrigued by the sensationalist and materialist philosophers who argued that humans could only know the world through physical sensations, and their own judgments, rather than relying on received authorities. Sex was extremely important to the materialists because it revealed most sharply the discrepancy between the Church's morality – its condemnation of sex – and the body's knowledge – that sex was pleasurable. But these ideas were dangerous – Diderot was imprisoned for exploring them in print, which is why he never published *D'Alembert's Dream*.[33] The material philosophers were men like the notorious Marquis de Sade or the physician Julien Offay de La Mettrie who existed on the fringes of society – de Sade imprisoned by his relatives for sexual cruelties, and La Mettrie exiled to Berlin.

The materialists radically dissociated sexual desire from the Church by repudiating all metaphysics, not just religion. They began to think of all life as solely composed of matter, with its own innate impulses toward motion. Sexual desire could be considered as a form of energy, as matter moving toward other matter. As de Sade argued, "motion being inherent in matter, the prime mover exist[s] only as an illusion."[34] La Mettrie even declared that humans were just machines, "only an animal or a construction made of strings" motivated by his natural impulses, stimulated by what he perceived. The idea of the man-machine justified sexual pleasure, and La Mettrie refuted the notion that the sexual organs were "shameful," because they give us "our existence and our happiness." At the same time, he emphasized the imagination, which was the intermediary between the body's sensations and the mind, the force which impelled the body into action. La Mettrie thought that blind nature followed its own dictates, that there was no natural morality.[35] But Diderot believed that universal laws mandated morality, and the atheist Baron d'Holbach warned that "excess at all times relaxes the springs of thy machine." Voluptuousness and intemperance "will ultimately destroy thy being, and render thee hateful to thyself, contemptible to others."[36]

By writing about sex, thinkers could challenge established authority. The satirist Aretino began this tradition in the sixteenth century by mocking the church and celebrating elaborate sexual positions. But his works were difficult to obtain. Some of the most influential pornographic tracts, such as Nicholas Chorier's *Satyrica Sodica*, were written in Latin, unavailable to the populace. Elite men kept obscene etchings and handwritten bawdy verses in their private closets, sharing them only with close friends.[37] But in the eighteenth century, pornographic writings began to be circulated in the vernacular, and their authors took the opportunity to insert philosophical discussions into the action. For instance, in the

Figure 7.1   *Thérèse Philosophe* (c. 1780). Plate opposite p.171. © British Library Board.
All rights reserved. P.C.30.e.22

Marquis de Sade's *Philosophy in the Bedroom*, participants in an orgy suddenly notice a revolutionary pamphlet, untangle themselves, and read aloud its subversive message to each other.

Thérèse Philosophe was a best-seller in this genre. Its probable author, Jean-Baptiste d'Argens, was a nobleman and influential radical deist philosopher, known for his many mistresses.[38] He used materialist philosophy to challenge the authority of the Church with the authority of the body. Thérèse learns by experience that monks are hypocritical in criticizing sex. Father Dirrag tells her friend Eradice that the penis is a serpent, and the genitals tools of the devil. "Only by forgetting the body can we find unity with God," he warns her, and to drive the lesson home, he flagellates her as she kneels on a pre-dieu. As the young woman fervently prays, she thinks she is attaining spiritual ecstasy through pain, but in fact, the wicked father is penetrating her from behind with his grossly swollen member, which he pretends is a holy relic.[39] D'Argens thus mocks the long tradition of spiritual ecstasy through sexual renunciation. (Indeed, the Catholic Church constantly contended with priests who sexually abused young women in the confessional.)[40] In contrast to the false knowledge of the priests, Thérèse relies on the true knowledge of her body and learns that sex is pleasurable, not evil. By examining the contrast between the monk's message and her own bodily experiences, she is able to use her reason to challenge received wisdom.[41]

Radical philosophical pornographers began to disassociate sex and procreation, often arguing that nature creates more seed than was needed to conceive.[42] In *Thérèse Philosophe*, Abbé T proclaims, "there is no law, either human or divine, which urges – much less requires – us to work for the multiplication of the species."[43] Thérèse hesitates to consummate her relationship with her lover, the Count, because she fears the pain and danger of childbirth. To assuage her concerns, the Count instructs her in coitus interruptus, or the withdrawal method. Indeed, pornography may have been an important means by which French people learned the techniques of withdrawal, which, although notoriously unreliable, is thought to have contributed to the dramatic slowdown in the French birth rate in the eighteenth century.[44] In contrast, such techniques do not often appear in English manuals or pornography. However, by warning against abortion and contraception, they also spread information that control of births was possible. The *Present State of Betty-land*, for instance, denounced physicians who "destroy the Fertility of Betty-land, by teaching the shepherdesses how to shun the pains of Harvest, and yet enjoy all the full content of the Pleasure of Tillage."[45]

Focusing on the clitoris also helped some Enlightenment erotica to celebrate sex for pleasure, not procreation. For instance, in *Thérèse Philosophe*, the Abbé pleasures a woman without penetrating her, bringing her to orgasm. In seventeenth- and eighteenth-century England, as we have seen, the popular sex manuals mentioned the clitoris, as did the 1684 erotic poem, "A New Description of Merryland," which described it as the "pleasure seat" for women. And it appeared in *A Dialogue between Married Lady and a Maid* in 1740.[46] But it tended to disappear in some translations, for instance in the French translation of

·PL·M·

Figure 7.2   *Thérèse Philosophe* (*c.* 1780). Plate opposite p.182. © British Library Board.
All rights reserved. P.C.30.e.22

Chorier's *Satyrica Sodica*. It also was not emphasized in the most famous work of English pornography, *Fanny Hill*.[47] When it was mentioned in these texts, the clitoris raised the possibility that women could find sexual pleasure without men.

In eighteenth-century pornography, sex between two women – or two men – often appeared in the context of a dialogue. The pornographic text allows the rational mind to disapprove while the fantasy stimulates the emotions to enjoy. The dialogue form also allowed authors to consider outré opinions without endorsing them, by putting them in the mouth of a character and allowing another character to denounce the outrageous thoughts. With her words, a character could repudiate something – such as anal sex – but enjoy it in the action. In a characteristic scene, an experienced woman teaches an ingénue about sexual anatomy and the pleasures of sex with men, and as the words become more explicit and erotic, talk turns into action, and the two women explore each other's bodies. Because lesbian sex could be seen as a prelude to sex with men, it was not seen as terribly threatening. These dialogues represented lesbian sex as an impossibility which becomes possible, which is enjoyed and disavowed – in other words, as a twilight moment. *The Present State of Betty-land* imagines that in boarding schools, "the young Shepherdesses first learn the Art of Horsemanship and Horseplay, first riding one another, and then in a short time after, riding quite away with some Shepherds or other."[48]

In Nicholas Chorier's *Dialogues of Luisa Sigea*, Tullia is passionately attracted to Ottavia. To get her into bed, she proposes that they make love to help her learn how to enjoy sex with her new husband. Ottavia demurs; she doesn't think any pleasure can be gained from a maiden, even if she really is "a marvellous garden of all delicacies and attractions." Soon, she is singing a different tune, moaning, "thy garden is setting mine on fire." Tullia responds, "O – would to God thou wert my husband! what a loving wife thou wouldst have!" But then she repudiates this desire, adding "I really think, when men sleep with us, it is only in their embraces we can obtain a true and solid voluptuousness."[49] Ottavia then goes on to enjoy being deflowered by her new husband, and Tullia insatiably pursues many male lovers.

For philosophical pornographers, only heterosexual sex could bring true enlightenment. As Thérèse continues experimenting on herself, and gains the advice of a wise confessor, she reports that "the cobwebs in my mind were dissipating little by little, and I was growing accustomed to think and combine things in my reason." But lesbian sex was seen as a frivolous distraction: when Thérèse ends up in bed with the courtesan Bois-Laurier, stimulated by her tales of erotic adventures, "our follies took the place of reason."[50] Only a man could bring a woman to reason. After she is deflowered, Ottavia realizes, "Virginity resides with us, as it were, in the same abode as our reason, the two most precious objects of our life. The virile spear that opens our vulva also opens our reason concealed therein."[51] Lesbian scenes were a way of portraying women as secretly sexually voracious, even if they presented themselves publicly as chaste and virtuous. Strong female characters were often mouthpieces for male fantasies.

De Sade portrayed libertine women who use other women and men as instruments for their own sexual gratification, but they remained his own fantasies.

Most radical pornographers were much more ambivalent about sex between men. They questioned the prohibitions against unnatural sex, but concluded by condemning sodomy. In the *Dialogues of Luisa Sigea*, Chorier has his character Tullia discuss at length the historical precedents and philosophical justifications for sex between men, including the idea that nature produced so much seed it did not matter if it was wasted in unprocreative sex, but she concludes that nature intended men and women to be attracted toward each other.[52] In *Thérèse Philosophe*, the courtesan Bois-Laurier, who seduces the heroine, recounts the arguments of the "anti-physiques" who declare that nature gave them the taste for men, and that nature did not need procreation. However, she declares that these men are enemies of women and heretics against nature.[53]

The focus on the sensations of pleasure also produced the phenomenon of libertinism, which took materialist philosophy to its furthest extent, focusing purely on physical sensations and the pleasures of the moment. By the end of the eighteenth century, a pansexual pornography began to appear in which male libertines would take their pleasure with men or with women in complicated orgies, overthrowing all taboos including incest. If sexual desire was a sixth sense, a strong overwhelming passion that did not respect any taboos, then the libertine could engage in any kind of sexual pleasure in any orifice. The Marquis de Sade took this idea to its furthest extremes. In *Philosophy in the Bedroom*, he argued that nature did not require reproduction: "had Nature condemned sodomy's pleasures, incestuous correspondences, pollutions, and so forth, would she have allowed us to find so much delight in them?"[54]

Philosophers were also ambivalent about "unnatural" sex. In his unpublished *D'Alembert's Dream*, Diderot had Dr. Bordeu proclaim, "Nothing that exists can be against nature or outside nature, and I don't even exclude chastity and voluntary continence." Dr. Bordeu then goes on to consider the problem of humans cross-breeding with animals, implicitly equating sodomy with this outlandish possibility.[55] Some Enlightenment thinkers denigrated men who had sex with men for neglecting the biological sexual drive for sex with women; they were seen as "women-haters," rejecting the physical world of the flesh. "Sodomites" began to be called "anti-physiques." At the same time, Enlightenment philosophers argued that the Church had no business interfering in such matters, for "Nature" would solve the problem of those who went against her wishes by "defending her rights."[56] Some thinkers cited the classical toleration of sex between men to prove that morality was culturally constructed rather than divinely ordained. Helvetius noted that proud Greek republicans "never betrayed the interests of their country," even though they engaged in "acts of indecency" with other men. La Mettrie claimed that "Aristotle was in favour of sodomy in order to prevent too great a number of citizens, without worrying about the precept 'go forth and multiply.'" But the *Encyclopédie* denounced sodomy in conventional terms as a crime against nature and scriptures.[57]

Some Enlightenment thinkers began to suggest that people were born with individual sexual tastes, which defined their selves, and therefore could not be condemned. La Mettrie thought that "those with certain physical organizations" could be punished, but their actions could not be prevented. He argued that sexual desire could not be controlled because it was a natural manifestation of the body, of nature's needs: "We shall not try to control what rules us; we shall not give orders to our sensations. We shall recognize their dominion and our slavery and try to make it pleasant for us, convinced as we are that happiness in life lies there." Every person's desires, however unconventional, were natural, since they were created by the body. La Mettrie was so radical that he was "outside the pale of respectability."[58] The Marquis de Sade took this idea even further, arguing:

> Will it never be understood that there is no variety of taste, however bizarre, however outlandish, however criminal it may be supposed, which does not derive directly from and depend upon the kind of organization which we have individually received from Nature? ... Even were one to desire to change those tastes could one do so? Have we the power to remake ourselves? Can we become other than what we are?

Chillingly, in this context de Sade was arguing for the taste of torturing women.[59]

This idea of inmost sexual desires could also appeal to ordinary people who desired the same sex. For instance, an eighteenth-century Dutch vicar, Andreas Klink supposedly claimed that sexual desire for men was "proper to his nature," because when his mother was pregnant with him, her strong desire for her husband" had imprinted on him in the womb. Gerrit van Amerongen stated at his trial for sodomy in 1776 that men who committed sodomy were "born with it and they can be as amorous to each other as man and wife can be."[60] Early nineteenth-century gentlewoman Anne Lister told her female lover that "my conduct & feelings being surely natural to me inasmuch as they were not taught, not fictitious but instinctive."[61]

Most influentially, the philosopher Jean-Jacques Rousseau developed the idea of the singular self. He defined sexual desire less in terms of an irresistible impulse of the body-machine, and more as a powerful emotional force of the imagination which defined the self yet troubled the soul. The orphaned son of a watchmaker, Rousseau made it as a writer through sheer force of talent. He regarded himself as an alienated outsider, but his works became bestsellers that profoundly shaped understandings of sex and politics.

Rousseau regarded himself as unique and original, proclaiming at the beginning of his *Confessions*, "I am made unlike any one I have ever met; I will even venture to say that I am like no one in the whole world." Sexual desires were signs of the inward self, which was the voice of nature within. And to learn about oneself, to listen to this voice, one had to recognize one's own sexual desires, no matter how strange and unusual. As a young man, he felt himself wracked by desires he did not know how to satisfy, so he had recourse to his imagination. This could lead him to all sorts of bizarre fantasies and supposedly dangerous practices, such as masturbation. He confessed that his deepest desire was to be dominated by an older woman, remembering when his cousin beat him when he was a boy:

> To fall on my knees before a masterful mistress, to obey her commands, to have to beg for her forgiveness, have been to me the most delicate of pleasures, and the more my vivid imagination heated my blood the more like a spellbound lover I looked.[62]

In both his life and philosophy, Rousseau struggled to understand sexual desire as both natural, welling up from the unique self, and as social, a construction of society. As did the materialists, Rousseau believed that, in a state of nature, sexual desire was a natural instinct for self-preservation, a physical appetite, which could be pacified by satisfaction.[63] In a state of society, sexual desire became much more complex and emotional, an "extremely ardent and impetuous ... terrible passion that braves danger, surmounts all obstacles," and even "seems calculated to bring destruction on the human race which it is really destined to preserve." This was because the laws of honor but also the imagination inflamed the passions and led to violence.[64]

Rousseau had moved from an early sympathy with Diderot and the radical Enlightenment to a moderate view which stressed that nature provided laws of morality. Unlike the materialists, Rousseau believed that the soul provided an inner moral compass which would enable it to overcome these dangerous passions.[65] Rousseau argued that men had to examine their imaginations and deeply know themselves so that the positive aspects of the passions could be developed, and the negative ones understood.[66] Rousseau worked out the paradoxes between his idealization of the natural self and the necessity to harness the passions for society by advocating naturalness for men and control of the passions for women. In an ideal society, Rousseau believed that romantic love and sexual desire were essential forces in tying together a community. In Rousseau, individuals had to form intimate attachments in order to love their countries and participate as citizens.[67] But he believed that women must be pure, virtuous, passive, and domesticated wives.

Rousseau became extremely popular because his readers could vicariously experience intensive, forbidden, even transgressive passions through his novel and autobiography, yet take away the moral lesson that they – especially women – must control these passions in order to allow for a harmonious society. His novel *Julie, or La Nouvelle Heloise* invoked Abelard and Heloise, the doomed lovers of the Middle Ages. Julie's father wants her to marry his friend, a respectable older man. But she and her handsome young tutor, St Preux, fall madly in love. Overcome by desire, they consummate their love. Nonetheless, she obeys her father and marries his choice. Julie repudiates her love for her tutor and vows to make up for her sin by dutifully loving her husband. However, she is unable to live with the passion still burning inside her, and eventually dies, drowning herself by rescuing her son.

In the *Discourse on Inequality* Rousseau describes "romantic love as an artificial emotion invented by [women] to dominate the sex that nature intended them to obey."[68] The imagination could make men vulnerable to women, for it was women's domain. Libertine men complained that their all-too-human female lovers were prone to wallow in the imagination of romance rather than stringently focusing on the pleasures of the body.[69]

As Choderlos de Laclos wrote, once women realized that "imagination went farther than nature," they:

> learned first to veil their charms in order to awaken curiosity; they practiced the difficult art of refusing even as they wished to consent; from that moment on, they knew how to set men's imagination afire, they knew how to arouse and direct desires as they pleased.[70]

When men succumb to romantic love in libertine novels, such as *Liaisons Dangereuses*, they lose their power over women and fall from grace.

Female libertines?

Unlike pornographic fantasies, novels explored the complications of emotions and the tensions of social constraints. Although novels, again unlike pornography, were openly circulated and read in the mainstream of print culture, they also explored the allure of forbidden passion. In French novels, female adultery becomes a twilight moment, secretly practiced but never openly acknowledged. For instance, in *Liaisons Dangereuses*, the wicked character the Marquise de Merteuil writes that she had to construct a reputation for virtue carefully in order to hide her lovers. As the evening fell, her trusted servant would admit a handsome chevalier to a secret entrance, and she would take pleasure with him. But in public, she pretended to be pious and repelled the men who were attracted by her charms. As she hoped, they spread the word that she was a prude. Religious women then defended her virtue, allowing her to keep a stainless reputation while indulging herself in private. She never wrote letters to her lovers to avoid leaving an incriminating trace.[71]

In social practice, most marriages were still arranged among the upper classes, and adultery was common. Men could have their *maitresse en titre*, their official mistress, but married women had to be extremely discreet. A woman could be ruined, ostracized by all her friends, if she lost her reputation for virtue. In France, fathers or husbands could petition the king for a "lettre de cachet," which would authorize them to have their errant women locked up for having affairs. In England, families could not resort to such draconian measures; among the highest aristocracy, extramarital affairs were fairly common. But women still faced social disapproval; aristocratic married women bearing children by their lovers would discreetly disappear to the Continent for a year, but among the lesser provincial gentry they would probably be rejected by society. Affairs by married women were twilight moments; everyone knew aristocratic women indulged in them, but they had to be kept a strict secret.

For real women, the problem was not that female sexual pleasure exceeded the limits of a philosophical discourse, but that it threatened the realities of their lives. The correspondence of Isabelle de Charrière – originally known as Belle de Zuylen – a well-educated and well-born Dutch woman, illustrates this tension. Feeling herself to be a sensual being, she found celibacy to be rather difficult, but she had to wait to marry for years while her wealthy family negotiated with potential suitors. Meanwhile, she carried on a long, flirtatious correspondence with Constant d'Hermenches, a notorious libertine, but refused to meet him, fearing that she might approach him "provocatively, caressingly," and that his kisses would break down her resistance.[72] As she wrote to him, "If the inclinations of my heart are not pure, at least the maxims of my reason should be." But she feared marrying him, or any other libertine, because of the danger of venereal disease. She knew of a tragic case in her social circle in which a syphilitic woman passed on the disease to her husband and children. Once Isabelle married, she seems to have taken the opportunity to have an affair, although it ended badly. But she socially rejected a woman who scorned public opinion by taking a lover: Madame de Nassau had pretended to be a "veritable Lucretia," famous for her chastity, but she then "disgraced herself to such a point that it is no longer possible to see her." For his part, Constant d'Hermenches repudiated a female relative who he had loved "like a sister"; he disapproved of her marriage to her lover, a young man with no position.[73]

Constant d'Hermenches wanted to be known as a libertine with a conscience, but he regarded the seduction of women as a hunt. He admitted to Isabelle de Charrière that "with regard to women, my heart and my mind are what a hound is with regard to his game in the field; he pursues and devours it." But if the game – that is the woman, exhibits "reason" or expressed "fear or chagrin," he would not "devour" her – unless the hound were overcome with hunger at such an appetizing morsel. But Isabelle found this to be a chilling metaphor, for she, of course, identified with the hare. Hares – women – had to pretend "always to want the opposite of what it wants," and run from men even if they wanted to have sex, for fear of losing their reputations. If a man pursued a woman so vigorously that she was terrified and exhausted, and then did not penetrate her, he still forced her to recognize her weakness and his power.[74]

There were plenty of real women who engaged in sexual adventures and no doubt experienced sexual pleasure, but they also seem to have regarded their sexuality as a tool for political or economic advancement; women were simply too economically disadvantaged to do otherwise. The exception appears to be the actresses or wealthy women who took other women as lovers. Elizabeth de Fleury dressed as a man, rode horses, went to gambling houses, balls and even kept, like noblemen, a young official mistress. To be sure, conventional aristocrats scorned her, but intellectuals liked her "spirit, talent and courage." Yet her family locked her up in a convent.[75]

Sexual politics

It was not only the double standard that made female libertines so problematic. Many radicals depicted libertine women as sexually powerful aristocrats who abused their power. They counterposed the idealized natural domesticity and self-sacrifice of women such as Rousseau's Julie to the artificial desires of power-hungry aristocratic women. Like other radical philosophers, Rousseau regarded artificial desire as manipulative rather than genuine, as using sexual desire as a tool in the game of power rather than in the service of love. Rousseau's vision of a natural, egalitarian society contrasted with the hierarchies and corruption of the power of *ancien régime* aristocracy, church, and state. All of these institutions depended on control of their subjects' personal lives: the Church, of course, celebrating celibacy, the monarchy and the aristocracy together trying to control marriages in order to ensure the continuity of elite family titles and property. Artificial lust became a metaphor for the lust for unjust power.

Rousseau feared and hated the ladies who shaped French high society, and who had helped him in his career. Women who deployed their sexual charms for material or political ends, he believed, corrupted society. He built on the ideas of the philosopher Montesquieu, who alleged that female courtiers exercised too much power in monarchies. Montesquieu developed the theory that monarchical systems were flawed because they were based on the personality of the king, who could distribute power – such as patronage, offices, and so on – through his personal whims, rather than on the basis of merit. A woman did not become the "mistress of a minister in order to sleep with him – what an idea! It is so as to present half a dozen requests to him every morning."[76] This political philosophy began to give a dangerous charge to the rumors about the king's mistresses, such as the powerful Madame Pompadour.

Radicals also criticized the sexual adventures of male priests, aristocrats and monarchs, equating a lust for sex with a lust for power. In England, novels contrasted the pure, genuine love of middle-class people with the artificial, manipulative sexual desires of aristocrats; the male libertine could become a symbol of aristocratic power – self-indulgent, careless, and violent. Politicians could also use the image of the sodomite to criticize the monarchy and aristocracy. During the 1760s and 1770s, supporters of radical politician John Wilkes claimed that the court of George III was riddled with "sodomites," whom they depicted as effeminate, cowardly, and corrupt, sexually interested only in men, all too ready to bend over and submit. Wilkes himself celebrated his own "natural" pleasures with women as opposed to the "unnatural" lust for sodomy – and unconstitutional power – of the court. He denigrated the corrupt sexual power of highborn ladies, alleging that the prime minister obtained his position by having an affair with the king's mother.[77]

After the French Revolution erupted, a flood of obscene cheap pamphlets began to aim their sexual satires at Marie Antoinette, the Queen of France. Always unpopular because of her Austrian birth, she increasingly represented the decadence and self-indulgence of the court. The pamphlet "The Private Life of Marie Antoinette" claimed that since the dauphine, her husband, was impotent, she needed male lovers to produce an heir. But she always had a "natural inclination" for women, and acquired a series of special mistresses. Men at the court schemed to gain the eye of these women, who "cost the state vast sums, ... and sold bishoprics, benefices, offices, positions."[78] Caricatures depicted Marie Antoinette engaging in complicated orgies with clergymen, men and women, her own son, and even animals. By accusing Marie Antoinette of incest, the revolutionaries portrayed the royal blood as poisoned and unnatural, destroying the principle of dynastic inheritance. The bodies of clerics, aristocrats, and monarchs were all thought to have a certain kind of sexual power due to their status. Clerics were supposed to be chaste, their suppressed sexuality giving them spiritual power. Aristocrats and monarchs supposedly passed on their blue blood through advantageous marriages; they ornamented their bodies with powdered wigs, jewels, brocades, lace revealing décolletage, and kept their skin perfumed and soft, unlike the dirty, callused bodies of laborers who wore rags. By depicting clerics and aristocrats as naked bodies writhing in orgies, spewing bodily fluids, radicals reduced them to ordinary bodies, but also stigmatized them as perverse; their enormous sexual appetites became metaphors for their use of illicit power, especially personal power. They desacralized the royal body and made Marie Antoinette's execution possible.[79]

In contrast, the French revolutionaries wanted to reshape social, sexual, and family life to be what they saw as more "natural." Even before the revolution, French scholars had been particularly concerned that sexual restraint in marriage would diminish the population, and indeed the French population stagnated by the late eighteenth century. These thinkers criticized masturbation, abortion, concubinage, and prostitution for wasting the natural resource of children.[80] Some revolutionaries advocated reforming the family; one proposed contraception, feminists called for equal rights, and divorce was actually implemented. But in the end, the revolutionaries wanted to strengthen marriage and the family as the basis for the state. They believed that good women stayed in the home, chaste and virtuous, unlike the aristocratic women who had exerted too much power at court.[81] Similarly, in the German states, many thinkers believed that, carefully directed, sexual desire impelled men to work hard to be able to marry, to provide a well-furnished home for their families, to produce a large number of cherished offspring, and thus to serve the ends of the state. They saw bourgeois men – not women — as the "sexually potent, desiring, self-determining individual fit for active citizenship."[82]

Conclusion

The radical Enlightenment's vision of toleration, equality, democracy, and sexual freedom proved to be highly problematic by the end of the eighteenth century. First, their vision of sexual freedom failed to take into account the different situations of men and women. If sex was a natural pleasure to be indulged in like food, women were just objects to be consumed. Mary Wollstonecraft, the British feminist, struggled with these dilemmas in her life and writings. A self-made intellectual, she agreed with Rousseau's critique of aristocratic women who manipulated their sexual charms for power, but she advocated women's rights instead of domesticity. Then she herself succumbed to intense sexual passion. First she fell madly in love with an American entrepreneur; they scorned the conventions of marriage and idealistically sailed across the channel to observe the French Revolution. But when she became pregnant; he abandoned her, and she attempted suicide. So she wrote that while women had the common "passions and appetites" of humanity, they must control their sexual desire lest they endanger their personal integrity.[83] But then she fell in love again, with the austere philosopher William Godwin. Falling pregnant once again, they decided to marry, but she tragically died giving birth to her daughter. After her death, conservatives attacked Mary Wollstonecraft as a crazed feminist prostitute. The mainstream Enlightenment view of women as sentimental, sexually passive and domestic triumphed over the radical Enlightenment exploration of female sexual pleasure.

Second, the Terror dashed hopes for democratic social transformation, and in its aftermath Napoleon eventually imposed even more severe restrictions on women's sexual rights. As the guillotine worked away in Paris, the Marquis de Sade scribbled in prison, taking the radical materialist ideas of sex to their most negative conclusions. He believed that death and destruction were part of nature, in an endless cycle. For Sade, dead bodies simply provided material for nature to renew itself; sexual desire was a matter of stimulating the orgasm, and pain was stimulating; by torturing others, the ego gained gratification. Sodomy was a rational way of solving the problem of procreation.[84]

In mainstream thought, a new vision of nature – and procreative sexual desire – as destructive also emerged. Deep in the English countryside, an English clergyman named Thomas Malthus began to think about the dangers of too much procreation. Like the Enlightenment philosophers, he thought sexual desire was an inexorable natural force: "the passion between the sexes has appeared in every age to be so nearly the same that it may always be considered, in algebraic language, as a given quantity."[85] Sexual desire impelled men to form attachments and created the sweetest moments in their young lives, motivating them to labor for their families. But this natural desire would inevitably cause overpopulation, leading to famine and death. Malthus therefore exposed the dangers even in the seemingly benign vision of the procreative heterosexual family. Malthus, the French thinkers who preceded him, and even the Marquis de Sade opposed giving charity or welfare to poor people because it deterred them from working. The Enlightenment dream of sexual desire as a positive force seemed to be over. Instead, sexual desire needed to be managed carefully if personal and social disaster were to be averted.

At the same time, working men and women were undergoing their own transformation. As the power of the church and state over private lives eroded, what

Malthus most feared was happening. In many countries beyond France, the birth rate skyrocketed from the 1750s onwards, and births outside of marriage rose in tandem with those in wedlock. Had they been studying *Aristotle's Masterpiece* too carefully? Were men and women simply having more intercourse with each other? Or were their sexual relations transformed by a great upheaval in the economy?

Suggested reading

Cheek, Pamela. *Sexual Antipodes: Enlightenment Globalization and the Placing of Sex.* Stanford, 2003.

Cusser, Catherine. *No Tomorrow: The Ethics of Pleasure in the French Enlightenment.* Charlottesville, 1999.

Darnton, Robert. *The Forbidden Best-Sellers of Pre-Revolutionary France.* New York, 1995.

De Jean, Joan. *The Reinvention of Obscenity: Sex, Lies and Tabloids in Early Modern France.* Chicago, 2002.

Feher, Michel, ed. *The Libertine Reader: Eroticism and Enlightenment in Eighteenth-Century France.* New York, 1997.

Gowing, Laura. *Common Bodies: Women, Touch, and Power in the Seventeenth Century.* New Haven, 2003.

Hunt, Lynn, ed. *The Invention of Pornography.* Cambridge, MA, 1993.

Israel, Jonathan Irvine. *Enlightenment Contested: Philosophy, Modernity, and the Emancipation of Man, 1670–1752.* Oxford, 2006.

Laqueur, Thomas W. *Making Sex: Body and Gender from the Greeks to Freud.* Cambridge, MA, 1990.

Turner, James Grantham. *Schooling Sex: Libertine Literature and Erotic Education in Italy, France, and England 1534–1685.* New York, 2003.

Chapter 8

In the Victorian twilight

Sex out-of-wedlock, sexual commerce, and same-sex desire, 1750–1870

In 1815, Ann Chapman left her home in Lowestoft to work as a housemaid in Gower Street, London, near the British Museum. As she dusted the parlor, the footman flirted with her and even promised to marry her. In a quiet moment, they found a secluded part of the house and had sex. But when she became pregnant, he disappeared, and she gave birth to twins. In despair, she applied to the nearby Foundling Hospital to see if they would take the infants. Her mother had not told any of the neighbors about her new grandchildren, fearing gossip. She admonished her daughter to "pray with a fervent desire and endeavor to repair what we do amiss." But she could not stand the thought of sending the "blessed babes" to be brought up by strangers, so she promised to sell her watch and find a job as a cook so she could help take care of the two infants. Ann Chapman did not have to give away her babies after all.[1]

A few years earlier, official Patrick Colquhoun alarmingly claimed that 50,000 "unfortunate females" supported themselves "chiefly or wholly by prostitution" in London. On closer examination, it turns out that Colquhoun did not really think there were 50,000 common streetwalkers in London; he included in this number women who cohabited with men, had affairs, and bore children out-of-wedlock – women like Ann Chapman. When he looked at London, he saw streets full of thieves, beggars, forgers, and prostitutes, pubs full of married women drinking – and people who seemed too lazy to work. Around the same time, in 1813, London constables discovered something even more shocking – a pub in Vere Street where men met to have sex with each other.[2]

Colquhoun wanted London to establish a police force to monitor the inhabitants of London, and to build institutions where beggars and unmarried mothers could be trained to labor.[3] By the early nineteenth century, governments feared that unless they regulated the lives of working people, populations would explode, revolutions would erupt, crime would run rampant, and economies would collapse. As states became stronger and more complex in the late eighteenth and early nineteenth centuries, they established new institutions, such as the police, the workhouse, and the prison. As Michel Foucault has written, doctors and officials labeled and defined certain types of people who should be regulated, such as the prostitute or the sodomite.[4] But Ann Chapman and her mother certainly did not consider her to be a prostitute. How did working people respond to these efforts at regulation and control? Did they accept the definitions imposed on them by the authorities? While Ann Chapman's mother helped her daughter, would she have accepted a son who was arrested for sodomy, or a daughter who became a streetwalker?

Sexual regulation and the state

From about the middle of the eighteenth century, the number of women who gave birth out-of-wedlock exploded. Historians first blamed rising illegitimacy on a "bastardy-prone subculture."[5] But closer investigation soon proved that legitimate fertility rose at the same time as illegitimate fertility, for the size of Europe's population doubled between 1700 and 1835. Clearly, more people were having more procreative intercourse; they had sex before marriage, in some areas they married at younger ages, they had more children, and many of them gave birth out-of-wedlock.[6]

Governments were alarmed by the rise in population and the rise in illegitimacy. Influenced by Malthus, they thought that a huge and growing population would strain the food supply and overstock the labor market. Some early nineteenth-century German and Austrian states resurrected earlier laws that required peasants and working people to prove their respectability and their ability to support a family in order to marry. In Bavaria, police officials were supposed to hand out marriage certificates only to the healthy and industrious. To some extent, these laws made marriage so expensive and difficult that they may have inadvertently caused people to live together and have children out-of-wedlock. Moralists and policy makers were even more concerned about illegitimate children who might become a burden on the state. They often blamed unmarried mothers for leading men astray. Officials in the German state of Baden decided to make unmarried mothers, instead of fathers, totally responsible for their children. They hoped that if women knew they had to bring up a child without support, they would avoid sex. However, the plan did not work; women still had illegitimate children they could not afford to raise, so the taxpayers had to support the children.[7] In France, the Napoleonic code of 1804 prevented unmarried mothers from trying to gain any financial support from the fathers of their children. The law aimed to protect the male citizen's privacy and the interests of his legitimate family. Especially by the 1830s, French social economists declared that the state must not help unmarried mothers, because immorality caused poverty and political disorder.[8]

In 1834, the infamous Bastardy clause of the English New Poor Law also shielded men from any responsibility for their illegitimate children. Moralists had been outraged when parish authorities forced men to marry the women they impregnated; this just encouraged women to seduce men, they surmised. Lawmakers alleged that pregnant servants blackmailed their masters, or that village girls accused the local squire of fathering their children. The new law, they hoped, would force women to think before they had sex, because unmarried mothers could only get help in prison-like workhouses. The New Poor Law also aimed to deter even married people from procreating. If a man became unemployed and could not support his family, they would all have to enter the workhouse, where husbands and wives would be separated, and children torn from their mothers' arms. Working-class radicals declared that the bastardy clauses insulted the chastity of poor girls. By separating husbands and wives so they could not procreate, poor law officials treated laboring people like animals, who could be gelded to make them more tractable. Going even further, some early socialists advocated an alternative morality. They claimed that marriage was just a capitalist invention which treated women like property. These activists, known as Owenites in Britain and Saint Simonians or Fourierists in France, envisioned a new society based on small-scale cooperation rather than capitalism, and on freely-chosen love relationships rather than the shackles of conventional marriage. However, they tended to be on the fringes even of working-class movements.[9]

Working-class people did not start having children out-of-wedlock in such great numbers because they were promiscuous or because they followed an alternative morality. Instead, their old courtship customs no longer fit changing times. In the eighteenth century, sex after a solemn promise of marriage was considered acceptable, especially among lower-class people. Even before betrothal, young people sexually flirted without going all the way. During the late eighteenth century, in the German farming areas around Trier, girls would meet in each other's houses to spin together on long winter nights; young men would sneak in and flirt with the girls as they spun by candlelight and told stories. If a young man took a liking to a young woman in rural nineteenth-century Norway, he would call on her parents' house at night; they would lie together, fully clothed, in a separate room, or the dark corners of the cottage not illuminated by the flickering light of the fire. We do not know exactly what peasants did in these dark corners, but in rural France, they probably kissed, caressed, and stimulated each other with their hands.[10]

In the early eighteenth century, the fear of public humiliation deterred many from "going all the way." In Catholic areas, priests forgave petting with a few Hail Marys at yearly confession, but they thundered against fornication as a shameful, evil sin. In Scotland, church courts sentenced pregnant unmarried women to stand shivering in front of the chapel wearing sackcloth and ashes. In Lutheran Strasbourg, city fathers locked up unmarried mothers in jail. French midwives threatened to withhold help from unmarried women in the agony of labor unless they revealed the name of the father, who could be charged with the child's maintenance. In England, parish officers dragged young men to the altar and forced them to marry and support their pregnant sweethearts. These enforcement mechanisms meant that if couples had sex before marriage, they would probably marry.[11]

But during the eighteenth century, more young people had intercourse before marrying, instead of just kissing or cuddling. In the late eighteenth and early nineteenth centuries, as many as a third to a half of brides were pregnant when they walked to the altar in parts of England, Sweden, Vienna and the Netherlands.[12] But the enforcement mechanisms which had guaranteed that young men lived up to their promises began to break down. By the late eighteenth century, in many areas churches lost their ability to deter unmarried motherhood. In 1765 Frederick the Great declared unmarried mothers would no longer have to submit to shaming punishments, because he saw them as victims of seduction and abandonment.[13] After 1741, ministers allowed Swedish pregnant girls to prove their repentance in the privacy of their studies, instead of experiencing the humiliation of public purification.[14] In the Netherlands, the early nineteenth-century rise in illegitimacy was attributed to the decline in religious influence.[15] Similarly, the Church lost its hold on working people in Bologna, Italy, who commonly engaged in premarital sex or cohabited.[16]

In families and neighborhoods, some religious people would follow strict moral codes, while others would tolerate cohabitation and illegitimacy. Methodists shunned their neighbors' relaxed morality and tried to differentiate themselves by strict standards of chastity. They expelled members who went to masquerades or danced, let alone had sex before marriage. But other working people sought out alternative religious beliefs more forgiving of the realities of their lives. In early nineteenth-century London, the preacher John Church told his poor congregation that God would forgive all sins, even prostitution and sodomy.[17] In the rue Quincampoix in late eighteenth-century Paris, the police found a small community of working people whose leader argued they had no need for a priest to change sexual partners.[18]

Many working people would have liked to marry but could not afford a wedding. In nineteenth-century Paris, one of every five couples was living together without a marriage license, and almost a third of births took place outside marriage. To gain a wedding license in mid-nineteenth-century Paris, couples had to travel home – often far away in the provinces – to get their parents' written permission and a reference from the local mayor, and upon their return, pay a large fee.[19] In Vienna, up to a third of working class people could never hope to earn enough to marry and support a family. Some cohabited instead, while others, unable to even afford a room together, had to be content with brief visits in rooms rented by the hour. What seemed to be promiscuity was often stable cohabitation.[20]

Many other couples planned on marrying or cohabiting, but the woman was left to raise the baby on her own. The new capitalist economy could bring high wages and flush times. But a boom might suddenly end, throwing whole factories and towns out of work. Men might have planned to marry their sweethearts, then found themselves unemployed and forced to wander far from home in search of work. Hard times often produced a spike in illegitimacy. For instance, in the Netherlands, couples usually had sex before marriage, but illegitimacy was generally low, except in the poor economy of the early nineteenth century, which often made marriage impossible. Interestingly, except in France, illegitimacy rates were not highest in industrial towns, for women there often earned relatively high wages, for instance, by tending power looms in factories.[21]

In earlier times, communities regulated the morality of villagers. Neighbors observed who was courting who, and peered out of their windows to see a young man sneaking into a woman's bedroom. If her belly swelled and he balked at marrying her, her father and the neighbors knew how to pressure him to live up to his obligations. But in the new industrialized, urban economies, a young man could easily leave town and find work elsewhere, and his pregnant sweetheart would have no recourse. Female farm laborers and urban servants were most vulnerable to abandonment if they became pregnant, because they left home in search of work. London maids often encountered men on the street or in shops as they did errands for their mistresses. Even more often, fellow servants seduced maids and left them pregnant. When a city servant became pregnant, the father of her unborn child could disappear into the vast wilderness of streets, never to be seen again. No neighbors or parents would chase down her sweetheart and force him into marriage. While some mistresses were sympathetic, they certainly did not want to keep a pregnant servant, and most would immediately expel a maid from the house.[22]

In some farming areas, unmarried mothers and their children became part of an underclass. Areas of Austria where large capitalist farms prevailed had extremely high illegitimacy rates, up to 27.8 percent in 1870. Large farmers would foster the illegitimate children of their female laborers, hoping that the children would grow up to be "cheap and devoted" servants. These illegitimate children tended to stay on the lower rungs of agricultural society as herders and unskilled laborers. In one rural Swedish town, the timber industry began to buy up farms, making it difficult for young men to afford to buy a new farm when they married. As a result, they continued to engage in premarital sex with their sweethearts, but delayed marrying them until they had given birth to several children. On Scottish farms, male and female laborers would sleep together in huts, or "bothies," and if a woman became pregnant, her lover was probably working on another farm already – or had emigrated to America. However, peasants with their own farms tended to monitor their children's behavior strictly to prevent illegitimacy, and some rural areas had low illegitimacy rates. Local cultures could be more important than economic structure in determining illegitimacy rates.[23]

Working-class parents regarded their unmarried pregnant daughters with ambivalence. They sometimes thought of unmarried motherhood as "a twilight moment," accepted if it was a momentary lapse but not a way of life. In rural Banffshire, Scotland, the birth of an illegitimate child was considered a "misfortune" but not a tragedy; "at least she didna steal," grandmothers would ruefully sigh.[24] In Paris, parents would help out a girl who had one illegitimate child, but if she had a second child by a different father, they would reject her. But in Sweden and Bavaria, lack of support from kin probably explains why illegitimate infants and young children were more likely than their legitimate cousins to die, especially in the first half of the nineteenth century.[25]

Sometimes unmarried mothers had been forced into sex. In the records of the London Foundling Hospital, which took in the infants of unmarried mothers, 15 percent of the women interviewed claimed that they had been "seduced against their consent," "forced," or raped.[26] Few women claimed that a stranger surprised them in the dark. Far more often, men they knew or worked with raped them, as when the groom cornered the maid in the kitchen when no one was around and forced himself on her. In many of these cases, women were raped by men who were courting them. While many working-class men advocated a respectable, responsible masculinity, others unfortunately celebrated misogynist, even violent attitudes toward women.[27] In rural areas, some migrant laborers, unable to marry or afford a ribbon to allure a pretty girl, preyed upon women laborers working in isolated fields.[28] As one rapist told a shepherdess on Whitby Bay, "None but the ships will hear your screams."[29] However, many other men rejected this attitude. For instance, one night, after a bout of drinking, Glasgow weaver Richard Bates persuaded his friend William Wood to visit Mary Martin, a young laundress who lived alone. When Bates began molesting her, Wood told him, "It was a great shame to abuse a decent woman in her own house."[30]

Women found it difficult to articulate what happened to them, often telling officials they had been "seduced by force," or "seduced against their consent." For modern women, this language seems quite contradictory. Seduction implies a pleasurable experience of being allured and persuaded with sensual blandishments, while force is quite the opposite, just brute violence. Why did Victorian women use such confusing language? In part, this was because, like today, "rape" was considered to be a crime committed by a stranger on a virgin, and very difficult to prove. Victorian women had no words for "date rape" – it was a twilight moment, which could not be fully perceived or articulated. Above all, in the end, it did not matter to society whether these women had been raped or seduced – they were damaged property in any case. One might suspect that women applying to the Foundling Hospital would claim they had been raped to gain more sympathy. However, its officials rarely believed women who claimed they had been raped by strangers. They wanted to take in "respectable" women, usually meaning they had been seduced after a promise of marriage. It did not really matter to officials whether they had been seduced by force – although it mattered a great deal to the women.[31]

Some working women might also exchange sex for a little cash or a treat, highlights of their lives in their grim, low-paid work as servants or needlewomen. For instance, a Portuguese officer seduced Maria Stephens, a dressmaker, by discussing marriage and then buying her pastry.[32] Some working women even had to sell sex in order to survive, because female wages were so low. In St. Petersburg, peasant women coming to look for work in the city often had to give sex to men who provided lodging, or to bosses for jobs. In urban Germany, women from immigrant artisan families in declining trades tried to find work in needlework, as servants, serving in cafés – anything to help the family. But when they lost their jobs, they had to sell sex for food.[33] Later, if times improved, they might marry. For some women, commercial sex could be a twilight moment, rather than a full-time occupation. Paris police records reveal that women from the luxury trades who sold sex often refused to define themselves as prostitutes. Rather, they would proudly define themselves in terms of their own craft as a milliner or dressmaker.[34] Similarly, in eighteenth-century London, one laundress declared, "I wash and iron, and go to gentlemen's houses sometimes," but her neighbor "had no right to charge me with being a common woman of the town."[35]

Prostitution

The lives of women identified as full-time prostitutes tended to follow a different path from other working women, such as unmarried mothers. When they were incarcerated in police cells, venereal hospitals or reformatories, they told their stories to charity workers, investigators, or officials. Although they may have invented romantic tales, one factor was quite consistent: from Poland, to Paris, to Portsmouth, most prostitutes had lost one or both parents. Orphans brought up in workhouses, foster care, or orphanages, were often sent out to earn their own living by age 12. Unskilled and friendless, their masters or fellow servants could easily sexually exploit them. Emotionally and economically vulnerable, they turned to prostitution. Prostitutes reported that they first had sex at the average age of 16, around puberty, and one Polish study found that 40 percent had sex even before the age of 16. This was much earlier than unmarried mothers. However, although very young girls were prostituted all over Europe, they represented a tiny number among prostitutes as a whole.[36]

Most of these women did not enter into prostitution right away, but failed at finding steady work in the unstable, uncertain economies of industrializing Europe. Although moralists often stigmatized factory girls as promiscuous, few became prostitutes. Factory girls usually had higher wages, more steady work, and lodgings with their families or friends. Rather, women in the traditional, over-crowded fields of domestic service and needlework were most likely to become prostitutes. Domestic servants were particularly vulnerable because if they lost their positions, which could be due to a mistress's whims or a family's move, they also lost their homes, and, as orphans, had no families to shelter them. For impoverished seamstresses, working their fingers to the bone late into the night, prostitution might have been an attractive option. At a time when a lucky ordinary woman might earn wages of 10 to 15 shillings a week, a young healthy prostitute could earn several shillings for each encounter, although a "bunter" – who might have sex with a man under a bush – would only earn tuppence.[37]

Most men who went to prostitutes were middle-class and working-class. In eighteenth-century Paris, for instance, 53 per cent of patients at a venereal hospital – presumed to be infected by prostitutes – were artisans.[38] In London, out of nearly 500 men who prosecuted prostitutes for theft or robbery, 18.9 percent were gentlemen, middle-class men, and shopkeepers, 38.4 percent were artisans and tradesmen, and 42.7 percent laborers, soldiers, sailors, and servants.[39] In Russia, working-class urban men apparently spent "a considerable portion of their wages" on prostitutes. Often young and unmarried, migrating to cities in search of work, they could not afford to marry or cohabit. However, while going to prostitutes was a common activity among men, it was still something secretive or even shameful, a twilight moment never to be spoken of in polite company.[40]

Authorities preferred to regulate prostitutes, rather than their customers. Constables often harassed and arrested streetwalkers; they demanded bribes to release them from gaol. Policing, therefore, failed to diminish the numbers of streetwalkers. In despair, governments and philanthropists often set up institutions where "fallen" women were supposed to repent of their sins and reform. They often defined unmarried mothers, seduced women and prostitutes together as fallen women. When Catholic nuns and Protestant philanthropists established these institutions in France and England, they frequently named them for Mary Magdalene, the character from the New Testament who was traditionally thought to have been a penitent prostitute. The magdalenes had to cut their hair, abandon their finery, and wear plain grey dresses. The Magdalen institution trained these women in laundry, domestic service and needlework – the very overcrowded trades with low wages that drove these women into prostitution in the first place. These philanthropists genuinely believed that prostitutes – and seduced daughters – were victims of wicked seducers, and could be reformed with prayers and strict discipline. This discipline was only partially effective. Thirty-seven to 40 percent of the women in the Magdalen Hospital and the similar Lock Asylum could not stand the fierce discipline and fled, often returning to prostitution.[41]

Other authorities thought it was futile to try to reclaim prostitutes; instead, some governments began to regulate sexual commerce. By the early nineteenth century, the French authorities initiated the first system of state regulation of prostitution, which became influential in continental Europe by mid-century, and in Britain by 1864. The French feared the ravages of venereal disease, which spread virulently as troops rampaged all across Europe during the Napoleonic Wars. In turn, prostitutes infected respectable men with the pox, who then spread it to their wives. Under the regulatory system, the police would force women suspected of selling sex to register themselves as prostitutes and submit to medical exams. If they were found to be infected with venereal disease, they were sent to grim lock hospitals for medical treatment. The pelvic examinations for disease were painful and humiliating, described as "instrumental rape" by opponents of the system, as police surgeons would thrust cold, unsanitary speculums into resisting women. And the treatments for venereal disease – such as mercury ointments – were ineffective. Of course, since authorities only inspected and treated women, male customers could continue to transmit the disease to their wives and other women.

To find suspected prostitutes and to ensure they were registered, the police had to become very closely involved with the world of sexual commerce; they spied on streetwalkers and inspected brothels. In fact, the French police preferred that prostitutes work in brothels rather than walk the streets, because then they would be easier to monitor, register and regulate. The law mandated that the police "protect" prostitutes, but they sometimes forced girls to return to the brothels they had fled, and they protected brothel keepers from harassment. In France, however, brothel keeping and prostitution itself were still illegal, and brothel keepers could not obtain mortgages or claim any other kind of legal existence.[42]

By defining and labeling prostitutes, the regulatory system increased neighbors' hostility toward them. Earlier, some working people had regarded sexual commerce as a twilight moment; they did not always reject women who sold sex, but they may have regarded them with suspicion, pity, or disapproval. For instance, Mary Ann Sleeford "remonstrated" with her neighbor Bet Evans on the "impropriety of her conduct" in picking up men in Petticoat Lane, East London, but she still helped her and did not keep Bet away from her children.[43] Randolph Trumbach finds that over the course of the eighteenth century, family members became less likely to stand bail for imprisoned prostitutes, suggesting that prostitution was becoming a subculture more removed from plebeian neighborhoods. But in nineteenth-century Italian towns, ordinary working people stood surety for girls accused of prostitution and promised to return them to honest livelihoods. But as the regulatory system spread, neighbors may have responded to prostitutes with more hostility. When the police registered prostitutes, they humiliated them in front of their neighbors. The police would march through crowded slums to knock on the door of a supposed "known prostitute," and haul her, often kicking and screaming, past curious onlookers into the police station. Women who may have engaged in sexual commerce only occasionally, or lived with several men in turn, thus found themselves stigmatized as prostitutes. The system of state regulation gave quarreling neighbors a weapon against them. For instance, in St. Petersburg, neighbors could harass prostitutes by threatening to turn them into the police and register them. In French towns, neighbors, other prostitutes, or even their customers could denounce women to the police and force them to register.[44]

In trying to label and control prostitution, the police also restricted the freedom of women who did not sell sex. In Germany and France, the police forbade prostitutes from promenading at the zoo, the public gardens, or leafy boulevards. Ordinary working women could be arrested by the police simply for flirting with a man in the street, or walking from work through darkened lanes. In small French towns, the police would arrest and register any woman "caught in the company of a man who did not know her and would not answer for her."[45] In Italy, any woman without a job found on the streets at night or in a dancehall could be arrested, charged with being a clandestine prostitute, and forced to submit to a medical exam, or sent back to her family. In Warsaw in the 1880s, the police detained and examined 4,000 to 5,000 women every year, but only registered 700 to 1,200 as prostitutes; the rest were working women, such as maidservants out on the street at night. Having been arrested, these women often lost their jobs. In St. Petersburg the police used prostitution regulations to harass soldiers' wives or peasant migrants to the city who were not under the control of a patriarch.[46]

Prostitutes resisted these efforts at regulation and tried to manage their own lives. In Russian and French reformatories, women confined in venereal hospitals rioted and destroyed property in wild outbursts. As Alain Corbin observes, "In the police cells at Marseilles and Paris, amid all the shouting and laughter, the women lived without any rules whatsoever, playing cards, sharing their food, writing obscene graffiti on the walls, and practicing homosexuality."[47] Most prostitutes

THE GREAT SOCIAL EVIL.

TIME:—Midnight. A Sketch not a Hundred Miles from the Haymarket.

Bella. "AH! FANNY! HOW LONG HAVE YOU BEEN *GAY?*"

Figure 8.1   "The Great Social Evil," *Punch* 33 (12 September 1857): 114. Reproduced with permission of Punch Ltd., www.punch.co.uk

evaded the system of registration altogether, selling sex in a series of twilight moments, refusing to be labeled and marginalized. They knew that the police controlled the brothels and favored their keepers, so they avoided working there, preferring to discreetly ply their trade on the streets or by frequenting cafés. Whether in France, Brussels, Russia, Poland, or Italy, the vast majority of sex workers escaped the system. By the end of the century in France and Belgium, independent prostitutes seriously undermined the brothels, which had to resort to outré sexual services to survive.[48]

Prostitutes created their own rules and rituals, establishing territory on streetcorners and helping each other out in brothels. They took control of the streets, harassing the respectable men and women who passed by, and bribing police constables to turn a blind eye. Many women who were identified as prostitutes tried to avoid having sex; instead, they urged their customers to drink themselves blind, and when they passed out, stole their wallets. In the port towns of England, prostitutes tended to be lively and rebellious, unwilling to submit themselves to the onerous constraints of domestic service or the tedium of needlework. For them, prostitution could bring liberty, however problematic. But for other women, prostitution was a painful necessity.[49]

In France, authorities observed that some prostitutes began sexual relationships with each other. They shared beds, looked out for each other, and quarreled in jealous rages. In fact, the French police forbade prostitutes from sharing beds with each other in brothels. According to early nineteenth-century social investigator A.-J.-B. Parent-Duchatelet, when a prostitute seduced a new recruit in a brothel, she would buy a bottle of champagne for herself and her mistress to be displayed at the next meal. Imprisoned prostitutes would also choose an eating partner, or *mangeuse*, to share food and possessions, and, often, a love relationship. One embroideress became involved with a woman called La Marechale, who professed that "if she knew the pleasure that two women could have together, she would abandon her male lover ... and that all men were of no use to her." Upon their release, alleged Duchatelet, these women returned to prostitution and seduced younger women with solicitous care and caresses. Other prostitutes greeted these women with scorn and horror, claimed Duchatelet, although others thought prostitutes accepted lesbians. Duchatelet, unlike some authorities of these times, believed that one could not discern a tribade from external appearance or physical characteristics; they did not adopt masculine voices or bearing. Dr. Michael Ryan, however, found that sex between women was "rare" although not unknown among London prostitutes.[50]

Not all prostitutes were female. The strapping, tall, handsome men of the Brigade of Guards in early nineteenth-century London were notorious for selling sex to gentlemen to supplement their incomes. In Sweden, soldiers would have sex with a gentleman to earn the money to take out their girlfriends on Saturday night. The soldiers themselves would marry and have children later in life.[51]

Same-sex desires

By the early eighteenth century, burgeoning urban economies gave men who wanted sex with other men new ways to meet one another. In the city, men could depend on waged labor, rather than waiting to marry and establish a farm or business. They could slip away from nosy neighbors and find refuge in the relative anonymity of the big city. Large numbers of bachelor, migrant laborers made it seem less unusual for a man to be living with another man, or alone, without a woman.[52] Cities were full of cafés and pubs, new commercialized leisure opportunities where men could find sexual contacts with each other. Some men certainly continued to have casual sex with other men without taking on any kind of sexual identity. But during the eighteenth century two new developments occurred. First, the subcultures of men who had sex with other men began to emerge in the burgeoning cities of Europe, and these subcultures were more developed and more visible. Second, a sodomitical identity was created both by its enemies and its practitioners.

Men who had sex with other men formed networks of sexual exchanges as they traveled along the capitalist circuits of trade. In Stockholm, bachelor workers returned again and again to the same urinal, where they "welcomed newcomers and taught them the manners that were expected of them in the new environment." Men invented signals to communicate their intentions as they sauntered along city streets or strolled in urban parks, eyeing each other with desire. In the Netherlands, men could step on each other's feet, grab an arm, or wave a handkerchief. In eighteenth-century Paris, they placed their hats in a certain way, or struck a tree twice with a cane. Men could get in trouble if they misread an innocent gesture as a proposition. Parisian police informants – called *les mouches* – and London gangs also tried to lure men into making advances in order to arrest or blackmail them.[53]

In the eighteenth century, men caught having sex with other men justified their behavior by declaring that it was pleasurable and natural to them. After William Brown picked up Thomas Newton one night in Moorfields, a notorious cruising ground in London, he allegedly told constables, "I did it because I thought I knew him, and I think there's no Crime in making what use I please of my own Body."[54] Of course, he later denied the accusation, portraying himself as a happily married man. When a Mr. Powell resisted George Duffus's advances, he told him that: "he need not be troubled, or wonder at what he had done to him, for it was what was very common, and he had often practiced it with many others." Powell, however, was outraged, and turned him in to the authorities.[55] Others claimed that sex with men was better than sex with women. An excise officer allegedly told a soldier in the Coldstream Guards, as he reached into his trousers, that "There was a deal more pleasure in a man than in a woman and he wished to sleep with me."[56]

By the eighteenth century, subcultures of men who had sex with each other appeared in northern Europe. The subcultures differed from the networks in that men began to form rituals, take on nicknames, and set themselves apart from the surrounding culture. For instance, in 1726, up to 20 "molly houses" were discovered in London.[57] An informer went to Mother Clap's molly house and found nearly 50 men:

> making Love to one another as they call'd it. Sometimes they'd sit in one another's Laps, use their Hands indecently Dance and make Curtsies and mimick the Language of Women – O Sir! – Pray Sir! – Dear Sir! Lord how can ye serve me so! – Ah ye little dear Toad! Then they'd go by Couples, into a Room on the same Floor to be marry'd as they call'd it. ... When they came out, they used to brag in plain Terms, of what they had been doing.[58]

Initiation rituals cemented together these subcultures. In the London molly houses, "When any Member enter'd into their Society, he was christened by a female Name, and had a Quartern of Geneva thrown in his Face; one was call'd Orange Deb, another Nel Guin , and a third Flying Horse Moll."[59] One group in Dutch Harlem even met at night in a forest to choose a king.[60] In Paris, in 1706 Simon Langlois and a lackey, Emile Bertault (known as La Brie), were "accused of holding gatherings under the guise of a kind of order in which they received all the young lads who wanted to join it and took women's names, got married to each other." Holding a candle, they would kneel and take oaths, kiss "two clusters of fake diamonds in the shape of roses, and swear fidelity to the order."[61] In 1813, a pub in Vere Street, London, kept a room called the Chapel, where marriages "were solemnized with all the mockery of bridesmaids and bridesmen, and the nuptials were frequently consummated by two, three, or four couples, in the same room, and in sight of each other!" as a moralist reported in horrified yet lubricious tones. Effeminate nicknames, however, did not necessarily correspond to dominant or submissive sexual roles or even to a feminine appearance. A pamphleteer on Vere Street commented that: "It is a generally received opinion, and a very natural one, that the prevalency of this passion has for its object effeminate delicate beings only; but this was a mistaken notion ... Fanny Murray, Lucy Cooper, and Kitty Fisher, are now personified by an athletic Bargeman, an Herculean Coalheaver, and a tire Smith; the latter of these monsters has two sons."[62] Rather, men may have used feminine nicknames as a secret code to initiate each other into the subculture.

The subculture did not necessarily follow the pattern of a dominant male using a younger male for sex; instead, they switched roles back and forth. For instance, Martin Mackintosh, who sold oranges, was called Orange Deb. Joseph Sellers, his accuser, was a police informer who passed as Mark Partridge's "husband" to avoid suspicion. Yet Mackintosh propositioned the "husband" Sellers in a molly house, wanting to penetrate him. Sellers testified that "the Prisoner came to me, put his Hands in my Breeches thrust his Tongue into my mouth swore that he'd go 40 Mile to enjoy me and beg'd of me to go backward, and let him." When Sellers refused, Mackintosh offered to take the passive role, saying he would "sit naked" on his lap. Outraged, Partridge ran a redhot poker into Mackintosh's anus.[63] In nineteenth-century Paris, effeminacy was thought to be a mark of belonging to the subculture, rather than an indication of an active or passive sexual role.[64]

The persecution of men who had sex with other men increased dramatically in the eighteenth century. In the 1720s and 1730s, a wave of prosecution of sodomites spread through England and the Netherlands. In the Netherlands, as Theo van der Meer argues, the authorities discovered a sodomitical subculture, rather than imposing a new definition on a disparate group of men. When they found them, the men were tortured to elicit their sexual contacts, revealing a nation-wide network of men and youths and gathering places. Public hysteria then broke out against sodomites, expressed in broadsheets, sermons, and newspapers, as convenient scapegoats for Holland's perceived economic and political decline; sodomy was linked with French influence and effeminacy.[65] In England, the early eighteenth-century Society for the Reformation of Manners initiated this campaign after they discovered the network of molly houses. The Society claimed that this was a foreign sin imported from abroad which would endanger "the Divine Institution of Marriage in Paradise itself, and to the Command of God to encrease and multiply Mankind."[66]

In the eighteenth century, the notion of the "sodomite" once again emerged. This time, he was not just a sinner; moralists, politicians, and newspaper writers saw him as having an exclusive sexual identity, not interested in sex with women, and having a cowardly and effeminate personality. In England, sodomites were known as "womanhaters," and men who frequented the Vere Street pub suppos-edly scornfully referred to their wives as "tommies."[67] As a result, men accused of sodomy, like Martin Mackintosh, would try to defend themselves by asserting that they were fond of their wives. William Brown claimed he had been married for 13 years and "loved the Company of Women better than that of his own Sex" as proof that he was innocent of a charge of sodomy.[68] By the late eighteenth century, French police began to call sodomites "anti-physiques," emulating the Enlighten-ment term, as we have seen in the previous chapter. The "anti-physique" was an identity and an inclination, not just one manifestation of deviant and disorderly lust, such as going to prostitutes. While the police believed that this habit might be acquired in youth, they thought it was almost impossible to eradicate.[69]

After the Vere Street scandal of 1813, moral panics about sodomy were relatively rare through the first half of the nineteenth century. The police preferred to exercise surveillance over men who had sex with other men and prosecute them quietly. In Britain, the New Police of 1828 vastly increased their power to monitor sodomitical behavior, because the earlier constables usually just reacted to public outcries or neighborhood accusations.[70] Now, the police patrolled the streets at night, observing men cruising in dark alleys, and hauled men accused of indecent behavior into crowded magistrates courts alongside prostitutes and drunks. For instance, at least five men a month were prosecuted for attempted sodomy or indecent assault on men in London in 1830.[71] One man even propositioned a police constable on a dark street in Stepney. When the man exposed his privates, the bobby indignantly asked, "Don't you know who I am?" and the man responded, "I know you are an officer but if you turn round a bit I can put this into you in about a minute."[72] Such behavior could earn a large fine or one month in prison.

Police authorities, however, often feared publicizing sodomitical offenses. First, they worried that those who brought accusations of sodomy were trying to blackmail wealthy men. Second, sodomy was quite difficult to prove in court. But most importantly, the police and the authorities did not want to publicize the existence of the homosexual subculture. As historian H.G. Cocks writes, the London police faced the dilemma of trying to use the power of the law against an act they were trying to keep secret and unknown.[73] In Sweden, authorities began to execute sodomites in secret, where executions previously had been public; although they continued to punish sodomy, they declined to include it in their new criminal code.[74] Although the French Napoleonic Code did not punish sodomy, following the Enlightenment idea that it was a religious offense like blasphemy which should not be included in the criminal code, the police continued to punish men who had sex with each other under the code governing misdemeanors and public indecency.[75]

Despite this policing, men continued to seek sex with other men in nineteenth-century cities. Some of them were not part of the subculture, but had sex with other men situationally. French police inspector Canler developed an elaborate taxonomy of the different types of men who sought sex with each other in nineteenth-century Paris: *persilleuses*, lazy and effeminate, luxury-loving working-class men, who sold sex for money, or blackmail; *travailleuses*, working-class, in traditional manly occupations; and *honteuses*, men of all classes who discreetly sought sex, but were ashamed. But other men formed long-term relationships with men of a similar class and age, as historian William Peniston has found, even if they might seek sexual adventures with men from a different social situation. Occasionally, men defended each other from arrest outside the louche cafés of Paris. They continued to mingle at the bohemian cafés and carnival balls of Mardi Gras time, which gave men some license to dress in female finery.[76] By the mid-nineteenth century, Manchester men had formed a network that regularly put on fancy dress balls. As historian Cocks has discovered, to get into such a ball – at the Temperance Hall – one had to whisper the secret password "Sister" to a "man dressed as a nun." Inside, a blind accordionist entertained dozens of masqueraders. At a similar London dance, an older man dressed as a "pastoral shepherdess," while another was seen "committing certain acts while wearing a white dress and veil."[77]

Women who had sex with women escaped much of the persecution inflicted on sodomites, unmarried mothers, and prostitutes. In many countries, sex between women was not illegal, which means we have much less evidence of women acting on their desire for each other. Prosecutions were not unknown, however, especially in Scandinavia and the Germanic states. In the 1790s, a zealous Amsterdam prosecutor went after 11 women for having sex with women. These women, with a couple of exceptions, were mainly poor women on the fringes of society, beggars, perhaps involved in prostitution, in and out of the workhouse. Two of them were discovered at a "bad house," perhaps a brothel, where "a number of women … used to caress and kiss one another and feel each other under their skirts."[78] In a handful of cases, women who lived as "female husbands" were discovered upon injury, death, or conflict. For instance, James Allen was married for 20 years to a woman who thought he was a man; he worked as a sawyer in the London docks. When he died as the result of a work accident, his wife admitted that lately she – and her neighbors – had begun to suspect that he was a "hermaph-rodite", since he had never had sex with her, and their marriage became unhappy. Once her husband's sex was revealed, neighbors "menace[d]" her with threats to "ill-treat her" if she ever appeared in public.[79] Working women may have lived together as factory workers or seamstresses, although it is rare to find expressions of their feelings. But one poem from working-class Paisley, Scotland, testifies to the importance of these feelings:

> I knew her as my schoolmate then
> My glad companion now
> When care first writes, with iron pen
> His name upon my brow.
> Her very smile my heart could move
> To strange wild throbs of joy;
> With Jenny I'd have fallen in love
> If I'd had been a boy.[80]

The Victorian twilight

Buffeted by the traumatic changes of the industrial revolution, working-class people faced intensive regulation by the police and the Poor Law. Authorities tried to define certain types of people – the unmarried mother, the prostitute, the sodomite – as subject to regulation and punishment in the new institutions such as penitentiaries, workhouses, and prisons. With the exception of those in same-sex relationships, women were punished much more harshly than men. The authorities preferred to impose the burden on unmarried mothers rather than fathers, and on prostitutes rather than on their customers. Nonetheless, while these regulatory efforts were onerous, working people sometimes evaded them. They developed alternative cultures, or more often, improvised their own morali-ties, often regarding illicit sex as a twilight moment. Neighbors and families might scold their friends for getting pregnant out-of-wedlock or selling sex, but then forgive and help them. Yet working-class communities were not necessarily tolerant as opposed to rigid governmental institutions. They were also divided by religion and culture. Some working people were very devout and tried to keep up standards of respectability, while others scorned the church. And working-class people often reviled and hated men accused of having sex with other men.

After the mid-nineteenth century, working-class morality started to become closer to middle-class morality. Rates of illegitimacy began to drop in England, France, Ireland, and many areas of Germany, plunging even more sharply after 1880. It is unlikely, however, that state efforts to regulate working-class sexuality had much effect. Rather, working-class cultures restored their ability to regulate sexual behavior as they adjusted their customs to the changing capitalist sexual economy. In many areas, such as England, wages rose after 1850, and the instability which had disrupted so many courtships diminished.[81] Working-class culture became quite sexually puritanical in many areas of Germany and England. Religious institutions revived their influence; for instance, in the Netherlands the Church succeeded in imposing a stricter order of chastity on its parishioners. In rural France, the Catholic Church celebrated virgins in yearly festivals, when priests would crown virginal "rosieres" with roses, and villagers praised them as they processed through the streets.[82] However, in the large cities, many couples continued to cohabit rather than marry.

Middle-class morality

Of course, just because middle-class moralists presented themselves as more sexually pure than the working class did not mean that middle-class people led sexually repressed lives. It was more a matter of keeping up a public reputation and not talking about sex. Since the late eighteenth century, middle-class couples had expected to experience romantic love for their spouses, and a happy sex life was still valued. Some medical advice writers continued to stress that husbands must take care to please their wives sexually. Dr. Auguste Debay argued in 1848 that it was important for men to satisfy their wives in bed with sensitivity and skill. But many other doctors did not think women's sexual pleasure was important or their desire strong. Dr. Alexandre Mayer, "a leading French authority," wrote in 1848 that women only submitted to sexual intercourse out of love for their husbands.[83] Dr. William Acton asserted that most women were not normally troubled with sexual feelings.[84] It became more difficult to obtain sexual information. *Aristotle's Masterpiece* faded out, and its nineteenth-century editions often left out information about the clitoris. Middle-class men could visit Dr. Kahn's seedy museum, which displayed models of the genitals, including the clitoris, but they were all grotesquely diseased; they could read titillating tracts warning them of the terrible dangers of masturbation.[85] Middle-class women were not supposed to have access to sexual knowledge. Historian Anne-Marie Sohn argues that French doctors did not convey explicit sexual information, and even hesitated to give physical examinations to women. Bourgeois people used euphemisms when they spoke of sex, and tried to avoid any mention of it.[86] Furthermore, British authorities cracked down on sexual material in the fourth and fifth decades of the century, suppressing even the mildest racy engraving, such as a girl displaying her ankle.[87]

Of course, middle-class men and women had their own twilight moments and secrets. Friendships between men, or between women, could be more emotionally intense than marriage. Alfred Lord Tennyson, for instance, wrote his famous poem *In Memoriam* out of deep grief at the death of a friend. Respectable social activist Ellice Hopkins wrote to her friend Anne Ridley, "To touch your hand and kiss you would be like long years of pain and sorrow effaced and all things made new."[88] Married ladies often shared beds with their visiting friends, and wrote passionate letters to each other when separated. As literary critic Sharon Marcus points out, these friendships did not necessarily threaten marriages; in fact, they could be seen as strengthening it.[89] Many of these friendships probably did not take a physical expression; rather, emotions of attachment could be articulated in romantic terms, for people did not yet think that romantic heterosexual relationships were the only proper locus for intense bonds.[90]

However, some of these relationships between women were sexual. In her recently decoded diary, Anne Lister, an early nineteenth-century Yorkshire gentlewoman wrote, "I love and only love the fairer sex and thus, beloved by them in turn my heart revolts from any other love but theirs."[91] In her diaries, she noted orgasms with an "x" in the margins of entries. Anne Lister did not face the overt stigma of lesbianism, protected by her wealth and class status, but neighbors remained suspicious of her masculinity and whispered about her close relationship with another woman. Her relationships were twilight moments, to be hidden. The French, however, were much more fearful and aware of the possibility of lesbian relationships between women.[92]

The double standard was very strict in middle-class society. For instance, when Mary Hailey discovered she was pregnant, her sister, the wife of a prosperous farmer, sniffed, "It is impossible for me to notice her again ... she must shift for herself as well as she can."[93] In the Napoleonic Code, adulterous wives could be – and often were – prosecuted by the state, and could even be subjected to two years' imprisonment for taking a lover. Husbands could not be prosecuted for adultery, and only could be divorced if they brought a concubine into the home.[94] In England, husbands could sue their wives' lovers for "criminal conversation," collecting large damages and humiliating their wives – and themselves – with public trials.

Middle-class women were supposed to pretend they did not see the prostitutes who were so apparent on city streets. In Paris, the *grandes horizontales*, wealthy, elite courtesans, dressed in tasteful, yet sensuously elegant gowns and rode in smart carriages along the Bois de Boulogne, discreetly catching the eye of gentlemen ambling by on horseback. In London of the 1860s, well-dressed prostitutes sauntered along the shopping paradise of Regent Street in the afternoon; as a result, gentlemen sometimes mistook respectable female shoppers for professionals. By the 1880s, reformers began to attack the hypocrisy that allowed middle-class men to indulge in prostitutes while keeping middle-class women and girls ignorant of sex. As Russian novelist Leo Tolstoy wrote, "We pretend to these girls that the profligacy which fills half the life of our towns, and even of the villages, does not exist at all ... everybody knows this and pretends not to know."[95] Even as Dr. William Acton obsessively warned against the dangers of female sexual pleasure, male masturbation, and prostitution, he declared that society must "recognize" and openly discuss the problems of prostitution and masturbation in order to drain the "swamp" of social problems.[96] By the third quarter of the nineteenth century, the veil of twilight had begun to lift.

Suggested reading

Adair, Richard. *Courtship, Illegitimacy and Marriage in Early Modern England*. Manchester, 1996.

Bacci, Massimo Livi. *The Population of Europe: A History*. Translated by Cynthia De Nardi Ipsen and Carl Ipsen. Oxford, 2000.

Benabou, Erica-Marie. *La Prostitution et la Police des Moeurs au XVIIIème Siècle*. Paris, 1987.

Blaikie, Andrew. *Illegitimacy, Sex, and Society: Northeast Scotland, 1750–1900*. Oxford, 1993.

Cook, Hera. *The Long Sexual Revolution: English Women, Sex, and Contraception 1800–1975*. Oxford, 2004.

Cook, Matt. *London and the Culture of Homosexuality, 1885–1914*. Cambridge, 2003.

Corbin, Alain. *Women for Hire: Prostitution and Sexuality in France after 1850*. Cambridge, Mass., 1990.

Fuchs, Rachel G. *Poor and Pregnant in Nineteenth-Century Paris*. New Brunswick, 1992.

Gerard, Kent, and Gert Hekma. *The Pursuit of Sodomy: Male Homosexuality in Renaissance and Enlightenment Europe, Research on Homosexuality; v. 17*. New York, 1989.

Gibson, Mary. *Prostitution and the State in Italy*. 2nd edn. Columbus, Ohio, 1999.

Harsin, Jill. *Policing Prostitution in Nineteenth-Century Paris*. Paris, 1985.

Hitchcock, Tim. *English sexualities, 1700–1800*. New York, 1997.

Hull, Isabel V. *Sexuality, State, and Civil Society in Germany, 1700–1815*. Ithaca, 1996.

Knodel, John. *Demographic Behavior in the Past*. Cambridge, 1988.

Laslett, Peter, Karla Oosterveen, and Richard M. Smith, eds. *Bastardy and Its Comparative History*. Edited by Peter Laslett. Cambridge, Mass, 1980.

Marcus, Sharon. *Between Women: Friendship, Desire, and Marriage in Victorian England*. Princeton, 2007.

Mason, Michael. *The Making of Victorian Sexuality*. Oxford, 1994.

Merrick, Jeffrey. *Homosexuality in Early Modern France: A Documentary Collection*. New York, 2001.

Merrick, Jeffrey, and Bryant T. Ragan. *Homosexuality in Modern France: A Documentary Reader*. New York, 2001.

Oram, Alison, and Annemarie Turnbull. *The Lesbian History Sourcebook*. London, 2001.

Rydstrom, Jens. *Sinners and Citizens: Bestiality and Homosexuality in Sweden, 1880–1950*. Chicago, 2003.

Sohn, Anne-Marie. *Du Premier Baiser à l'Alcôve: La sexualité des Français au Quotidien (1850–1950)*. Paris, 1996.

Sundt, Eilert. *Sexual Customs in Rural Norway*. Translated by Odin W. Anderson. Ames, 1993.

Trumbach, Randolph. *Heterosexuality and the Third Gender in Enlightenment London*. Vol. 1, *Sex and the Gender Revolution*. Chicago, 1998.

Vicinus, Martha. *Intimate Friends: Women who Loved Women, 1778–1928*. Chicago, 2004.

Walkowitz, Judith. *Prostitution in Victorian Society: Women, Class, and State*. Cambridge, 1980.

Chapter 9

Boundaries of the nation, boundaries of the self, 1860–1914

One dark night in a Whitechapel alley, two prostitutes accosted 17-year-old James Hinton, roughly demanding, "Which of us shall you have?" Hinton was profoundly shocked by this crude come-on. As he told the story to Ellice Hopkins years later, "his voice suddenly broke and he buried his face and wept like a child." Why were women forced to degrade themselves in this way? he asked Miss Hopkins. They agreed that prostitution must be stopped. But this was a strange conversation, for Ellice Hopkins was a delicate unmarried Christian lady, and James Hinton was a wild-eyed doctor. He proclaimed that "Sexual passion is a force in nature like the wind and sea, untamable and uncageable. For that very reason it should be like the sun, transfiguring rather than destroying what it permeates."[1]

During the late nineteenth century, men and women like Hinton and Hopkins agreed that Victorian society must rip the veil of twilight away and face up to the reality of sexual suffering. New discourses of sex exploded into the public view, as journalists exposed sexual exploitation and stirred up moral panics. Social purity activists such as Ellice Hopkins spread moral purity pamphlets to young people, arguing that they must have sexual education to remain unpolluted. New experts on sexology penned massive tomes. Hinton was one of the first sex radicals – the reformers, philosophers, artists, feminists and socialists who believed that sexual freedom was essential to creativity. Although the sex radicals were often marginalized, they were still part of the conversation.

These new voices disagreed as to whether sexual desire was a source of pollution or creativity, but they were all profoundly influenced by Charles Darwin. A respectable Victorian patriarch himself, Darwin threw a bomb into complacent religious certainties by asserting that sex and death caused human evolution. Through the struggle for survival, some organisms and animals with beneficial natural variations triumphed over the weaker ones, who died and did not pass on their genetic material. Through sexual selection, female birds and animals chose the male with the loudest song, or the brightest plumage, and mated. Their offspring inherited these characteristics, and passed them on. Sexual desire now had to be seen as a natural force, which humans and animals had in common, and which was essential for evolution. Darwin himself saw human sexual desire as stemming from a lower stage of evolution. When a primitive human male battled over women, he would, "have been guided more by his instinctive passions, and less by foresight or reason." Only in civilized societies did conscience and self-control develop.[2]

For some thinkers, like Hinton, sexual selection laid the groundwork for civilization, because the female's preference for beautiful ornaments and musical songs – as in birds – originated the taste for the beautiful, for music and art. But others speculated that if humans evolved, they could also degenerate if the "unfit" reproduced. Darwinian thought led some social critics to predict that uncontrolled sexual desire would undermine the boundaries of the nation itself.

Sexual desire and national boundaries

During the late nineteenth century, European countries competed with each other for dominance, a contest often seen as a Darwinian struggle for survival. Politicians feared that the upper class would degenerate sexually, and that primitive sexual instincts would incite the working class to revolt. New experts fanned these anxieties. While some were religious, they derived their authority not from scriptures, but from the new disciplines of criminology, psychiatry and sexology. They wanted to use the power of the state to regulate and control the sexual behavior of citizens and others.

French scientists, politicians and moralists particularly feared the national implications of sexual degeneration. As Britain and Germany outstripped France in industrial and military capacity, the rate of growth of the French population was declining. In 1859, B.D. Morel, a French physician and Catholic philosopher, hypothesized that the conditions of modern life degenerated the human organism, for people lived in closely packed, hectic cities, worked with noxious substances, drank too much, and indulged in sexual excesses. Citing the biologist Lamarck, he claimed that such systemic damage – not just syphilis – could be passed on to future generations. Perhaps, he surmised, civilization itself weakened and effeminized the white European race.[3]

If men could not control their sexual desires, they would indulge in sex with unsuitable women, and venereal disease would spread across the class boundaries of society. The medico-forensic psychiatrist Tardieu blamed not only prostitutes, but concubines for this danger; concubines made love with artists, and then they sold sex to men of the most "elevated" ranks of society. Syphilis, Tardieu warned in 1862, "attacks that part of the nation that is its greatest strength and wealth," the upper class, but the infected working class would also become more disorderly. Criminologists also claimed that prostitutes undermined the racial health of the nation because they had regressed to a more primitive stage of evolution.[4]

Authorities also feared that male homosexuality would degenerate French manhood. French forensic psychologists began to define the homosexual not only as someone who committed deviant acts, but as a weak, fetishistic, and degenerate personality. Tardieu insisted that the bodies of male homosexuals showed the physical signs of disordered desire: for instance, he alleged that their penises were tapering or dog-like. Police Commissioner Carlier worried that homosexuality would erase the boundaries of class, for "this passion is so imperious that it leads to monstrous couplings. Master and his servant, thief and magistrate, the boor ... accept each other as if they were from the same class of society." In 1882, he warned that homosexuality endangered the national health, for it was a vice that "degenerates vigorous natures, effeminizes them, ... they lose sentiments most noble of patriotism and family, [and] become useless to society." Carlier alleged that homosexuals belonged to a "freemasonry of vice" which crossed national boundaries, much the same as Jews were seen as possibly disloyal to the nation, owing more allegiance to their own "tribe." As historian Erin Carlston observes, such experts alleged that both homosexuals and Jews concealed their true natures with secret codes, and that their sexual excesses made them effeminate and incapable of serving the nation as soldiers.[5]

Prostitution became a metaphor for working-class disorder. After Germany defeated France in the Franco-Prussian War of 1870, the people of Paris refused to surrender and instead organized themselves into the anarchist-socialist Commune, in which women were notably active. When the French government attacked the Commune, fires raged in Paris. The press hysterically insulted anarcho-socialist women as prostitute *petroleuses*, or incendiaries, and claimed they had set fire to the city. Alexandre Dumas fils (author of *The Three Muske-teers*) warned of "strumpets of the street ... these young, beautiful, farouche, savage, hideous women, a thousand times more ferocious than their men, who will burn your great city." Immediately after the Commune was defeated, the police arrested over 6,000 prostitutes. By controlling prostitution, the new republican government established after the Commune tried to prove that a secular state could exert moral regulation.[6]

France extended its system of regulating prostitutes to its new colonies. In North Africa, French soldiers associated with Muslim North African, Jewish, and Maltese merchants, laborers, and prostitutes. French authorities believed that most indigenous prostitutes were infected with syphilis. So they established luxurious official brothels where European prostitutes serviced Europeans, and confined indigenous prostitutes into guarded alleys.[7]

Several European countries imitated France during the late nineteenth century by establishing systems of police registration and regulation of prostitutes aimed at controlling venereal disease. For Germany and Italy, such police regulation strengthened the project of national unification. For the British government, their Contagious Diseases Acts represented a step in the turn away from laissez-faire liberalism toward a more interventionist state.

Although the British had long resisted the regulationist system, the prevalence of venereal disease among its troops – up to 30 percent in the imperial army – alarmed the authorities. The authorities believed that soldiers and sailors, like indigenous men, were "unruly, undisciplined, childish, unschooled, and excessive." Unless their sexual appetites were slaked by registered prostitutes, they might resort to sex with each other or violent crime. The officials decided to adopt what seemed to be a rational, medical approach to the problem. At first, the army tried the "dangle parade," when doctors would move down a line of naked men, inspecting their penises for sores. But officials feared that this humiliated the men, so they tried to inspect women instead. Through the Contagious Diseases Acts, the state established a system of registration and forcible treatment, in Hong Kong in 1857, then in English and Irish garrison and port towns by 1864.[8]

The movement to abolish regulation of prostitution

In response to these systems, a huge movement demanded the abolition of state regulation of prostitution, as new social actors – female activists and socialists – challenged the regulatory state across Europe. In France, socialist activists criticized the police for harassing working-class women on the streets, especially after two women committed suicide rather than submit to registration. They argued that low wages forced women into prostitution; in turn, these prostitutes tempted working-class husbands and undermined their marriages. The anarchists took a more positive view of prostitution, arguing that prostitutes should form trade unions; they asserted the rights of "unmarried males" and even "virgins" to pleasure."[9] In Britain, working-class men joined Josephine Butler in the mass movement against the Contagious Diseases Acts, for they believed the Acts "endanger the liberty and virtue of their wives and daughters while those of the men of the upper classes are safe." For them, the chief problem was capitalist exploitation. Deliberately invoking the earlier anti-slavery movement, they called themselves "abolitionists." They believed that the government was sanctioning the sexual exploitation of women by regulating prostitution. Female abolitionists, led by Josephine Butler, claimed the problem was not female immorality, but male lust and an overweening state. They defended prostitutes as their outcast sisters and regarded them as individuals who had a right to the integrity of their own bodies. But they also were condescending to the prostitutes and tried to control them.[10]

Abolitionists also attacked what they called "white slavery" fearing that sexual exploitation violated national boundaries. French, Belgian, and Jewish procurers allegedly entrapped young girls in London and enslaved them in Belgian brothels.[11] In 1881, Adeline Tanner testified to a government hearing that she was decoyed from Uxbridge at the age of 17, and forced into a Belgian brothel. However, her hymen was so thick that customers could not penetrate her. She claimed that the brothel owners got the police to put her into hospital, where doctors cut her hymen in front of medical students. She remembered that "the operator seemed to tear and cut away my living flesh, inflicting agonies I can never describe, besides the intolerable shame." But not all the women wanted to be rescued. Alfred Dyer was determined to save the British Louisa Mathild Bond from a Belgian brothel, so he disguised himself as a client to visit her. Once they were in a private parlor, he whipped out waterproofs and boots to cover her tawdry dress, so that she could escape into the streets without being apprehended by the police. But she refused to leave, declaring that she stayed in the brothel of her own free will.[12]

By 1885, journalist W.T. Stead created a moral panic about the "Maiden Tribute of Modern Babylon." In his paper, the *Pall Mall Gazette*, he alleged that he had been able to purchase a 14-year-old virgin for ten pounds in a London slum. The girl was locked in a room, where doctors performed a pelvic exam to certify her virginity. Then, as the paper reported, a gentleman entered the locked room – and the girl screamed. The gentleman was Stead himself – and if he could do this, any man could. Alarmed by the sensational engravings and headlines such as "Five pounds for a virgin warranted pure!" a quarter of a million people, chiefly lady abolitionists and working-class men and women, demonstrated in Hyde Park, carrying placards that proclaimed "Men, War on Vice," and "Protection of Young Girls"; they anxiously denounced the "vicious aristocrats" who allegedly sexually exploited young girls.[13]

This moral panic impelled Parliament to pass the 1885 Criminal Law Amendment Act, which raised the age of consent from 13 to 16 for girls. The Liberal Party leader, Sir William Harcourt, protested that the Act "might have hundreds, aye thousands, of the people of this country thrown into prison simply through yielding to the passions of their nature."[14] Many doctors had long been reluctant to acknowledge that even younger girls could be raped, refusing to take vaginal injuries and discharges as evidence of sexual assault. Instead, they blamed unsanitary conditions, neighborhood immorality, or even mothers trying to extort money from the accused. Nonetheless, the legislation passed. Yet in acting to protect young girls, the Criminal Law Amendment Act also criminalized them. It allowed the police to remove girls from homes suspected of being brothels, and confine them in reformatories. Social reformers feared that the child victims of sexual abuse were so sexually contaminated that they would "corrupt" "normal" children in ordinary schools.[15]

Social purity advocates became increasingly influential in the 1880s and 1890s. They distributed thousands of pamphlets warning against going to prostitutes and especially against masturbation. In groups such as the White Cross League, young men would pledge to abstain from sex. Many social purity advocates saw young girls as passive victims who must be protected by upper-class philanthropists; they had to be shielded by modesty and purity against their own lower impulses.[16] Historian Hera Cook argues that the social purity movement contributed to widespread sexual ignorance and inhibition by the end of the nineteenth century.[17]

Sexuality and British imperialism

As Britain and other European nations seized new colonies in the late nineteenth century, they feared that uncontrolled sex between white men and native women – or between native men and white women – would undermine the fiction of racial purity. When colonized people resisted imperial rule, imperialists spread images of the mythical black rapist to discredit such revolts. For instance, in the wake of the 1857 Mutiny in India, popular novels and newspaper accounts alleged that white women had been raped by rebellious Indian soldiers, although there is no evidence of such sexual violence. European imperialists justified their actions by claiming they were "civilizing" colonized peoples by transforming their supposedly "barbaric" sexual customs.[18]

The British imperial government also worried that venereal disease sapped the strength of white soldiers, so they extended the state regulation of prostitution to the colonies in Southeast Asia and India. As historian Philippa Levine argues, British authorities believed that they were imposing a modern system of hygienic regulation. At first, they aimed to ensure that only white prostitutes serviced white troops, and native prostitutes native troops, but this policy proved impossible to enforce, so they focused on the control of venereal disease.[19]

For missionaries and social purity activists, however, the system endangered the empire. Instead of civilizing the colonies, the army sexually exploited native women. As the Rev. J.P. Gledstone declared, "we have provided for the gratification of their lusts at the cost of our moral influence among a subject race." These activists pointed out that native soldiers were much less likely to be infected by venereal disease; they argued that the colonial Contagious Diseases Acts stemmed from, and encouraged, blatant racism. Alfred Dyer declared that "British soldiers and licensed lust officials" were "drilled into treating Indian women" with "great brutality," which also led them to treat Indian men with "coarseness, brutality and contempt." Indian nationalists also strongly objected to the system, blaming British imperialism for encouraging prostitution.[20]

The same activists – missionaries, female abolitionists, and some Hindu reformers – also wanted to reform some Indian sexual practices. The British banned *sati*, or widow burning, in 1828. After the uprising of 1857, the British government was reluctant to interfere further in sexual customs, but then a coalition of activists began to criticize the practice of infant marriage. Traditionally, elite Bengali Hindus believed that girls had to be married before puberty, and that the husband must have sex with his young wife immediately after her first menstruation, with a ceremony called the *garbhadhan*. Otherwise females might pollute their wombs with illicit sexual desire, endangering their families, their caste, and Hinduism itself. However, some Hindu reformers believed that infant marriage itself damaged the Bengali "race." The *Indian Medical Gazette* opined that the "the legalized love of child-wives in marriage" encouraged "lust for female children outside marriage."[21] British women activists also demanded that girls be spared this premature sex. They claimed to act as protectors of "native females," which gave them a moral legitimacy in the imperial project. All these activists demanded that the government ban the marriage of girls under 14.[22]

The British government hesitated to act; as one official noted, "The State in India ... need not deeply embarrass itself by undertaking to scientifically regulate the time and exact degree of sexual intercourse in millions of bed-chambers." Following this logic, some British officials accepted the right of Hindu husbands to force sex on their young wives; as one judge declared, even if physical injury resulted, it "does not include that element of outrage upon a woman's honor which we associate with the term rape."[23] But in 1890, great publicity ensued when a judge acquitted a 35-year-old man for murdering his wife, the ten-year-old Phulmonee, who died in a welter of blood after he penetrated her. Under pressure from activists and missionaries, the government passed the Age of Consent Act in 1891, which raised the age of consent for girls for sex, and marriage, from ten to twelve. Traditionalist Hindus claimed that the act would destroy the Hindu family; the virginal child bride symbolized the nascent Hindu nation. Even Indian nationalists who wanted to reform Hinduism and disapproved of child marriage resented this crude imperial effort to interfere in very personal and religious customs. Fearing to alienate Hindu traditionalists, the government did not enforce the act very effectively.[24] This was just one of many conflicts between nationalists and imperialists in which sexuality symbolized the anxieties over the boundaries of nation and empire.

The Heinze affair in Germany

The issues of prostitution and the age of consent also divided Germany in the 1890s. The long-standing system of police regulation of prostitution became controversial as socialists and feminists entered the political stage. The socialists had gained a great deal of strength through trade unions and grassroots organizations in Germany. In 1892, the laws against their participation in elections lapsed, and they became a potent political force. Although women were prohibited from participating in electoral politics, they actively engaged in social welfare, confronting the problems of prostitution, unmarried mothers, and the sexual exploitation of children.

The police in German states had long regulated prostitution, but a spectacular murder exposed their inability to control it. In 1891, Gottfriedt Heinze, a pimp, broke into a church, killed the nightwatchman, and left him hanging from a tree. When he was put on trial, the pimp appeared "in the dock with a bottle of champagne" while his "underworld friends" applauded his insolent testimony. Bourgeois ladies thronged to the courtroom, fascinated at this depravity. The publicity triggered off a moral panic, in which pimps were "demonized as folk devils" as historian Richard Evans observes, but the affair also became an excuse for a much wider debate on questions of sexual morality. The Kaiser demanded that the Reichstag pass the Lex Heinze. In its first version the Lex Heinze focused on the problem of prostitution, strengthening existing police powers to prosecute pimps, register prostitutes, and even control brothels themselves.[25]

In response, Christian female social purity advocates denounced the system of police registration as sanctioning prostitution. Instead of punishing prostitutes, they wanted to protect young women from sexual exploitation. Supported by the Catholic party, they advocated a bill that would raise the age of consent for girls from 16 to 18. For Evangelical Christians, the problem went beyond prostitution – what was needed was a wider effort to discipline the self. They encouraged "sittlichkeit," "a set of ethical guidelines designed to regulate public and individual morality" and in this context they particularly emphasized sexual matters. Citing a rise in crime, prostitution, and illegitimacy, they believed Germany was facing a crisis of moral decay – and they saw sex as the problem, purity as the solution. They formed all-male associations, linked with anti-Semitic nationalists, to encourage working people to avoid premarital sex, to marry instead of cohabit, and to avoid prostitution.[26] Eventually, Christian women found their own organizations to rescue girls from prostitution and to inculcate moral values in the working class.[27]

Many socialists were actually quite sexually puritanical themselves, but some of them were influenced by the sex reformers who had begun to speak out against traditional morality. These socialists retorted that raising the age of consent would not help poor girls who had to support themselves from the age of 14 onward – an age of consent of 18 was suitable only for middle-class girls. Further, socialists had long protested against sexual harassment of young female factory workers, but what they needed, they argued, was the right to associate and strike, not a stultifying Puritanism. Socialists blamed the Heinze affair on class exploitation. Heinze and his wife lived in a desperately poor neighborhood with cramped housing, where several families or couples might have to share a dirty, unsanitary room with no privacy; women workers often turned to prostitution to make ends meet, and pimps preyed upon them. The socialist August Bebel claimed that the Catholic Church and the police were actually protecting pimps and prostitutes by supporting the system of regulation.[28]

Conservatives reacted by trying to extend the Lex Heinze to censor depictions of sex in art and theatre, to censor radical speech, and to ban birth control information, although by 1900 they only succeeded on the last point. Conservatives claimed that if the socialists had their way, all wives in Germany would become prostitutes.[29] Some German student groups advocated sexual abstinence to defend the purity of German blood and national strength against Jews.[30] In response, the socialists accused the ruling elite of hypocrisy in a series of sex scandals.[31]

Yet as with all these moral panics, the debate did not map clearly onto conservative versus radical. Those who attacked the regulation of prostitution could be Catholic or liberal, devoted to social change in their own way. In Britain and in Germany, both social purity advocates and sex reformers insisted on speaking out about sex; they attacked the double standard and they wanted to change and reform what they saw as a complacent governmental system complicit in the sexual exploitation of women.[32] But they disagreed on the nature of sexual desire and its relationship to the inner self, as the next section will demonstrate.

Sexual desire: purity or liberation?

During the late nineteenth century, scientists, philosophers, artists and activists fiercely debated the nature of the self. By pointing out that humans are animals, Darwin undermined the idea that reason controls human destiny, and since sexual desire was seen as biologistic and animalistic, it became a particularly important issue in these debates. Some scientists argued that the self was determined by hereditary and biological forces which made it either healthy and normal, or degenerate. Other thinkers and activists challenged this determinism. Social purity advocates and socialists argued that it was not biology, but social conditions, that determined sexual behavior, but they disagreed on desire.

Darwin influenced social purity advocates to see the sexual impulses as natural, as emanating from the body. But they also thought that the higher self – the will – should control the lower self – the body – to enhance evolution. Social purity advocates regarded the sexual drive as characteristic of an earlier stage in evolution. As one social purity advocate wrote in 1876, "the defeat of the will degrades the human being beneath the level of a brute." Refuting the notion that sexual desire was "the natural obedience to a true, self-sufficing instinct," this moralist declared that lust is "abnormal, impure, and evil in its personal as in its social consequences."[33] In an advanced state of civilization, this drive would be controlled and devoted to a higher purpose. Emile Laveleye, a French abolitionist, admitted that "this instinct, without doubt, cannot be extirpated; but man, to be moral and free, must discipline it, so that in marriage, it serves the ends of the social order."[34]

During the 1880s and 1890s, some social purity activists even suggested that married couples should restrain their sexual appetites. In his influential novel *The Kreutzer Sonata*, a tale of doomed adulterous love, the Russian author Leo Tolstoy declaimed against sexual passion itself as "horrid, shameful, and painful." Refuting the idea that sex was a "poetic and lofty dwelling in life," he believed that even in marriage, sexual indulgence was "a state of bestiality degrading for a human being."[35] Some doctors refuted the old idea that sex was necessary for health, instead arguing that sexual indulgence sapped a man's vital bodily fluids and harmed his health. Swedish medical men, for instance, declared in 1888 that: "We know of no disease or state of poor health caused by a pure moral life."[36] Social purity feminist activist Edith Ward proclaimed, "In the sight of God immoderate indulgence of the passions is as offensive between" married people as between unmarried people. Ward feared that "many women are but too willing partners in excessive intercourse, and their debasement is as great as that of any wretched prostitute who walks the streets of our seething towns."[37]

Social purity advocates attacked the double standard and insisted that men control their base instincts, not just women. For Ellice Hopkins, the social purity advocate, if men gave in to their sexual desires, they obeyed the "beast" within them, "instead of the beast obeying the man."[38] Hopkins and Ward, like many feminists at that time, believed that women must control sexual desire to protect the boundaries of the autonomous female self. They asserted that females had evolved to a higher level than men, because men did not seem to be able to control their primitive sexual instincts. They insisted that husbands had no right to force their wives into sex. Women had often used abstinence to control how many children they had. But these feminists thought that if men used artificial means of birth control, they were treating their wives like prostitutes. Edith Ward defended married women's "own undoubted right to the custody of their own persons." She also linked a woman's right to control her own body to the strength of the Anglo-Saxon race; the boundaries of both must be protected.[39]

Not all social purity advocates distrusted the sexual drive, but they believed that it should be spiritual. As one moralist pointed out, "impurity is the abuse of a human function, perfectly right and natural in itself, when nominally developed and controlled by reason."[40] For Ellice Hopkins, the "body was a temple of the holy" which should be trusted and respected, but not abused.[41] These feminists also hoped for a higher, more spiritual union of men and women that could transcend earthly bodies.

In contrast, the sex radicals – avant-garde intellectuals, writers, physicians, and social activists – believed that sexual desire was a potent force for human health and creativity. During the 1870s and 1880s, they remained on the margins of society; governments censored their ideas, and even social reform associations blackballed them. And at that time, even the sex radicals believed that couples should be very temperate in their indulgence. Elizabeth Wolstenhome Elmy regarded "physical passion and action as but a phase toward the psychic." She envisioned two lovers lying side by side in a pine wood, communing spiritually in the most intense intimacy, but touching only their hands.[42] Edward Carpenter proclaimed, "How intoxicating indeed, how penetrating – like a most precious wine – is that love which is the sexual transformed by the magic of the will into the emotional and spiritual! And what a loss on the merest grounds of prudence and the economy of pleasure is its unbridled waste along physical channels!"[43] The banned birth control pamphlet, *The Fruits of Philosophy*, advised that a man of "literary pursuits" should only have sex every three or four weeks, and eat a bland vegetarian diet to cool the passions. However, the book also proclaimed that "temperate gratification promotes the secretions, and the appetite for food; calms the restless passions, induces pleasant sleep; awakens social feeling, and adds the zest to life which makes one conscious that life is worth preserving."[44]

In the 1860s and 1870s, James Hinton had become a forerunner to sex radicals by developing the idea that sexual pleasure was essential to human creativity and health. A London physician, he often tried to convince his patients who were social purity activists that sexual passion "was as a god in itself." Drawing upon evolutionary thought, he declared, "What is a simple and uncomplicated function in the ape, the tiger, or the primitive man, may be a supreme expression of the soul in the evolved human being, tending to produce as a result babies, pictures, songs, or word-painting, or only, maybe, a new joy in living, which communicates itself to others by a scattering of forces strengthened by a perfect love union."[45] For him, sexual passion was a fluid, generative force which must burst the bonds of artificial laws. By surrendering to sexual passion, an individual could dissolve the self into the larger divine essence: "God's instrument for casting out self is passion." But he also argued that women must surrender their individual selves to serve men's greater sexual needs. After Hinton's death, his devoted sister-in-law,

Caroline Haddon, kept his ideas alive through a small circle of followers, influencing the future sexologist Havelock Ellis.[46]

Sex radicals found it difficult to reconcile all the different notions about sexual desire in their own lives: sexual desire as dangerous, as spiritual, as healthy. The letters of Havelock Ellis and Olive Schreiner, a South African novelist who emigrated to England, illustrate this tension well. In the 1880s, they met in radical intellectual circles and fell in love, but their affair failed. Schreiner desperately wanted to assert her own individuality, and she refuted Hinton's call for female sexual self-sacrifice. She believed sexual desire could inspire creativity, but also destroy it. She tended to fall passionately in love, but her affairs caused such "agony" that she strove to "to kill and crush all that side of my nature." For her, the body, soul, and creative power were linked. If a man touched a woman without communing with her on a mental level, it was as if he put his fingers into her brain and "snapped the strings." But when she suppressed her desires, she could not write. Havelock Ellis empathized with her struggles, referring to "Love's martyrdom," the difficulty when people try "to crush their physical sexual nature; the physical being taken, of course, as a symbol of the spiritual." Ellis was wracked by sexual desire and compulsively masturbated, despite the bromide of potassium he took to suppress his urges. But he could only experience sexual pleasure by "watching a woman urinate or by urinating in front of her."[47] Ellis devoted his life to the categorization of sexual types – such as homosexuals – as natural variations who should be tolerated by society.[48] But even as Ellis and others campaigned for homosexual rights, men who desired other men faced even greater hostility.

Male homosexuality

In the last quarter of the nineteenth century, legal punishments for homosexuality were becoming even more severe. In England, the Labouchère amendment to the Criminal Law Amendment Act of 1885 made indecent acts between men a felony.[49] The newly unified German state passed the notorious paragraph 175 in 1871, outlawing "unnatural fornication" between men. At the same time, men who desired other men began to try to justify their own desires, and some even began to develop the notion of a homosexual identity. Like the heterosexual sex radicals, they saw sexual desire as the wellspring of the self, of nature, and as spiritual fulfillment, but at first they often coded their justifications in a vague language of desire.

The classical tradition inspired many men – and some women. All elite young men were educated in the classics, which inspired Victorian civic ideals of manly comradeship, citizenship and self-sacrifice – and homoerotic desire. Men who wanted other men cruised each other in the Parthenon galleries at the British Museum, with their muscular statues in glistening marble. Some found a homoerotic subtext in Plato's *Symposium*, especially Socrates' idea that the love of youths could be a higher love than that of women, providing a spiritual pathway to the love of ideal beauty, but they were also inspired by Walter Pater's celebration of the wild Dionysian cult of love as sacrifice.[50]

Karl Ulrichs, a German lawyer, used these ideas more openly to develop the identity of "homosexuality," a term that Karl-Maria Kertbeny invented in 1869 to agitate for greater rights for men who had sex with other men. Ulrichs went back to the speech by Pausanias in Plato's *Symposium*, which opposed common, procreative love, which Ulrichs termed Dione, to spiritual love, bestowed by Aphrodite Urania (heavenly Aphrodite). From this source, Ulrichs derived the term "Uranier" or "Urnings" to describe men who were attracted to other men, emphasizing, unlike Pausanias, that the "Uranier has a God-given sex drive" and so the "right to satisfy it." He also saw the Urning as having a divided self, his inner being with a feminine attraction to other men, and his conventionally masculine outer being. Ulrichs also emphasized this femininity because he observed the men in the Frankfurt subculture who took on feminine nicknames and wore female attire to balls. When Ulrichs published these ideas in pamphlets, he lost his government career.[51]

Homosexuality became a hidden source of aesthetic inspiration. For instance, in 1880, a Swedish philosopher named Pontus Wikner defended the "borderline creatures, who with one part of their nature will fall on one side of the border, and with another part on the other side, and are consequently cut in two by the legitimate border." Most people at the time did not catch the allusion to homosexuality, but men who desired other men certainly did. In private, Wikner wrote in his confessions that his nature was to feel a need for men "penetrating the whole body – ennobled by an authentic amorous feeling – for the mutual satisfaction of the sexual drive." Sexual and spiritual desires could also be melded in a homoerotic ecstasy. Wikner also privately admitted that his desire for Christ was tinged with sexual desire, a bodily love for his savior.[52] Anglo-Catholic male intellectuals also developed the concept of "soul-friends" to whom they could direct their erotic and spiritual energy.[53]

Some men argued that intense sexual desire inspired creativity and transcended banal social constraints on the exceptional individual.[54] Edward Carpenter celebrated "homogenic" love as part of his wider socialist vision; he retreated to the countryside with his working-class male lover, wore sandals, and ate vegetarian food. He wanted sex to be a spiritual, natural force elevating the individual in the service of the whole. Carpenter proclaimed that sex should take place in nature, instead of in "stuffy dens of dirty upholstery."[55]

Oscar Wilde and the decadents or aesthetes scorned the sentimental celebration of nature, and instead lauded art as superior. They sought refined, artistic pleasures, luxuriating – as later became notorious – in perfumed rooms kept dark by velvet curtains, illuminated only by flickering gaslight.[56] For these writers, art must transcend nature. In *The Picture of Dorian Gray*, one of Wilde's characters advocates a "new Hedonism, that was to recreate life, and to save it from that harsh, uncomely puritanism."[57] It would transcend the savage animality of simple procreative experience with spiritual, passionate, and sensual aestheticism. By the late 1880s and early 1890s, Oscar Wilde and other intellectuals began to articulate and justify their sexual tastes in a way that was almost, but not quite, open, a gradual lightening of the twilight. They published homoerotic poems in privately published journals, and most daringly, Wilde tried to spread the custom of wearing a green carnation as the secret sexual code of homosexuality.

Wilde's enemies denounced *The Picture of Dorian Gray* and claimed that it barely masked homosexual desire.[58] The novel became evidence of Wilde's immorality in his trials in 1895. He was imprisoned for two years hard labor for sodomy, his dazzling career in shambles and his health ruined. The trial led to much greater consciousness of homosexuality as an identity, mostly but not always in very negative terms.[59] However, two years later Magnus Hirschfeld established the first organized movement for homosexual emancipation, agitating for the repeal of paragraph 175. Hirschfeld was part of the growing movement of sexology.[60]

Sexology and new understandings of the self

During the late nineteenth century, medical men and psychologists initiated a new "scientific" approach to sex which enabled them to claim institutional power, but their ideas varied considerably between European countries. In England, authorities tried to keep sexological works from ordinary people, although they circulated among intellectuals. After Havelock Ellis tried to publish his *Sexual Inversion*, which justified homosexuality, in 1897, his British publisher was put on trial for obscenity and the book suppressed. In Germany, however, sexologists and sex radicals could publish somewhat more freely – for instance, Ellis was able to publish his book there.[61]

Following Darwin, most sexologists regarded heterosexual gratification as natural and essential to human evolution. The sexologists defined the self in physical and biological terms, diagnosing those who expressed certain desires as having distinct personality types often derived from physiology. But when they explored the vagaries of desire, these experts destabilized the very categories of identity that they tried to establish.[62]

By examining the biology of arousal and orgasm, sexologists undermined the connection between sexual desire and procreation. In 1886, Krafft-Ebing wrote that while procreation might be an unconscious motivation for sex, physiological erection derived from the will to immediate pleasure.[63] Studies of the engorgement of the penis and the clitoris also led them to define sexual activity in terms of "tumescence" and "detumescence," rather than just reproduction. In 1897, Albert Moll declared that detumescence – ejaculation or sexual release – was a simple bodily function, like evacuation. He also identified the other seemingly uncontrollable sexual impulse as "contrection," the desire "to touch and kiss another person, usually of the opposite sex." Moll himself drew on Darwin to insist that heterosexual desire was innate and inherited. But his terms provided a way of thinking of sexual desire and acts between any combination of persons, motivated by pleasure, not procreation.[64]

Most sexologists believed that women desired sex less intensely than men, and that they focused their desires on reproduction.[65] But the sexologists admitted that the clitoris was the seat of female sexual pleasure and that it had nothing to do with reproduction. Krafft-Ebing wrote that women's sexual desires were normally lesser than men's, but he also asserted that if women did not have orgasms, they might fall prey to hysteria or neurasthenia.[66] More radical sexologists, such as the Swedish Anton Nystrom in 1904, proclaimed that sexual abstinence could cause chlorosis, "female diseases," "nervousness, cramps, hysterics with tendency to alternate crying and laughing, hilarity and sadness, insomnia, epilepsy, hallucinations, mental disorders etc."[67]

The sexologists also defined deviant personalities such as the sadist, the masochist, the voyeur, the homosexual, and so on. They maintained that people committed these acts because they had degenerate personalities. Krafft-Ebing first relied on case studies of homosexual patients in insane asylums, who not surprisingly seemed imbecilic or degenerate. Initially, scientists tried to discover a biological basis for homosexuality. They discovered that human embryos only started to develop masculine or feminine characteristics in the second or third month. By the 1890s, Krafft-Ebing began to adopt the idea that rudimentary feminine characteristics could survive in the adult male organism, and cause homosexuality. The adult homosexual therefore had characteristics of the opposite sex. The male "urning" or "uranian" sexual personality was characterized by "feminine timidity, frivolity, obstinacy and weakness of character," while his female equivalent was found among "females wearing their hair short, or who dress in the fashion of men, or pursue the sports and pastimes of their male acquaintants."[68] Sexologists tried to find physical evidence of the homosexual body, such as an "enlarged clitoris" in lesbian women. However, they usually did not find any such physical signs, so they resorted to psychosexual explanations.[69]

The sexologists did not simply invent and impose the notion of the homosexual identity on men and women who desired others of the same sex. First, Krafft-Ebing got the terms "urning" and "uranians" from Ulrichs, who himself stressed effeminacy and inversion. Second, Krafft-Ebing observed and responded to the behavior of homosexual men and a few lesbians. As Harry Oosterhuis has discovered, after Krafft-Ebing published *Psychopathia Sexualis*, many homosexual men and a few lesbians began writing to him with their own stories. For instance, Dr X was a respected physician who nearly lost everything when the police caught him having sex with another man in a field. Escaping prosecution, he nonetheless continued to enjoy the subculture. He wrote to Krafft-Ebing that the majority of homosexual men he knew "in no way regret their abnormality" and "would be sorry if the condition were to be changed." Krafft-Ebing incorporated these narratives into later editions and became much more sympathetic to the cause of homosexuality. He even advocated the repeal of paragraph 175, which enabled the persecution of homosexuals. Krafft-Ebing even came around to Havelock Ellis's argument that homosexuals were a benign, even positive natural variation in Darwinian terms, instead of a degenerate personality type. At the same time, some correspondents of Krafft-Ebing, and also of Havelock Ellis, anxiously scrutinized their own family history for evidence of hereditary degeneracy, and described their own personalities as afflicted with neurasthenia. They took up the identity of "homosexual" for their own purposes by trying to claim a more positive image, but the discourse of degeneracy continued to entrap them.[70]

While the sexologists regarded the homosexual as a distinct personality type, they also warned that anyone could become "perverse" – the boundaries between the normal and deviant were not fixed. Perversions were not just caused by a different kind of desire; they also could be caused by an excess of sexual desire, or misdirected sexual desire, according to most of the sexologists.[71] Heterosexuals might be led astray in particular situations of temptation, such as all-male institutions including schools and barracks, where women were not available, or because excessive masturbation or bad influences inflamed the sexual drives. However, these "normal" individuals could not turn into homosexuals without an innate "tainted instinct."[72] Dr. L. Loewenfeld thought that if men who engaged in "homosexual perversity" retained "normal (heterosexual) instincts" they could be cured "either through falling in love with a girl or through psychological treatment."[73]

In the first decade of the twentieth century, sexologists also began to hint that even the most feminine woman might have perverse appetites. Dr. August Forel noted that "in woman a certain sensual desire for caresses, connected more or less with unconscious and ill-defined sexual sensations ... extends to other women, to children, and even to animals, apart from pathologically inverted sexual appetites."[74] Dr. E. Heinrich Kisch feared that girls would teach each other masturbation in boarding schools and become lesbians.[75]

Sigmund Freud took a very different approach than these sexologists. Instead of diagnosing degenerate personality types, Sigmund Freud portrayed the self as divided and conflicted, unable to master the sexual drives which welled up from the unconscious. Freud first thought that repression of sexual desire caused hysteria in the well-brought-up young ladies of bourgeois Vienna. Several of his patients were women frustrated at the constraints of their lives who later became feminist and socialist activists.[76] He then came to a more shocking hypothesis: that the hysterical symptoms of these young women, such as agonizing mental pain and paralysis, were caused by repressed memories of childhood sexual abuse. Historians disagree whether his patients told him their own stories of sexual abuse or he imagined that they had been seduced.[77] Freud himself soon decided that narratives of incest were actually fantasies of repressed desire for the parent – using his own psyche as an example. This led him to a much more profound and original conception of sexual desire. Freud often referred to the sexual drives, sometimes translated as instincts, and especially in his early years mused whether they had a biological basis.[78] But he soon began to define sexual desire as a set of complicated emotions based on sensuality, attachment, anger, and affection, as well as the desire for genital satisfaction. These emotions had their origins in childhood experience. He saw the infant's thumb-sucking, rhythmic rocking, exploration of its own genitals, and oral and anal orientations as expressions of a "polymorphous perversity." On one hand, this could be seen in a Darwinian frame; Freud suggested that this primitive pansexualism resembled that of earlier stages of biological development, of primitive organisms. The child's development to adulthood recapitulated humanity's development through evolution.[79]

On the other hand, these vague emotions did not necessarily produce the heterosexual drive toward intercourse and procreation – so Freud escaped the Darwinian paradigm. In fact, Freud declared in 1915, "the exclusive sexual interest felt by men for women is ... a problem that needs elucidating and is not a self-evident fact based on an attraction that is ultimately of a chemical nature." Casting his eye back to ancient Greece, he differentiated between the sexual instinct (or drive) and the sexual object, criticizing the assumption that they were necessarily the same. In ancient Greece, boys might begin their sexual lives as the sexual objects of older men, as adults desire male youths, and then marry and desire women. He found that "all humans are capable of making a homosexual object choice."[80] The emotions of polymorphous perversity had to be attached to a particular love object, and this happened first through the child's attachment to the mother. But then, boys had to overcome their Oedipal complex to grow up. The path toward heterosexuality was much more convoluted for girls. Freud wrote that girls must give up their original, masculine focus on the clitoris and transfer their sexual focus to the vagina, in order to be heterosexual and identify with their mothers. Freud believed that the clitoris would still serve as the "kindling" for the vaginal flame, and did not refer to the vaginal orgasm, but his followers were much more strict about this theme.[81]

Freud believed that the id, the part of the self dominated by the libido and other drives, provided the energy for the self, but that the ego or self was formed by reconciling the imperious drives to the reality of relationships with other people, the constraints of social life: the ego was like a rider, trying to control a headstrong horse. Freud regarded sexual desire as a flow of water which must be channeled into the right path; if repressed, or dammed, it would explode in the wrong places, causing neuroses. But humans should not simply express their polymorphous perversity. The best they could do, unless blessed with a happy marriage, was to sublimate their sexual drives into cultural creativity or social service.[82]

Sex and creativity: the new morality

Sex radicals, however, believed that sexual desire *should* be expressed, because it was essential for the life force. The philosopher Nietzsche profoundly influenced them, for he boldly refuted Christianity, "with its ressentiment against life at the bottom of its heart, which first made something unclean of sexuality; it threw filth on the origin, on the presupposition of our life." Writing in the 1880s, Nietzsche believed that the Dionysian intoxication of music, dance, and sex, of terror and pity, was as necessary as cool Apollonian rationality. He defined sexual desire as "the triumphant Yes to life beyond all death and change; true life as the overall continuation of life through procreation, through the mysteries of sexuality." The artist, Nietzsche proclaimed, needed "the frenzy of sexual excitement," in order to create, even an orgiastic, violent frenzy. Yet the self was also at the mercy of these larger dark forces. The Dionysian frenzy subsumed the individual into the universal, and the artist needed to exploit the will to power to create a different kind of self that transcended conventional morality.[83]

Inspired by Nietzsche, sex radicals challenged Christian values of monogamy to envision new kinds of relationships motivated by desire rather than obligation. French philosopher Robert Michels depicted marriage as the "tomb of lyric love" while in contrast, "a change in love-relationships is equivalent to a sprinkling with the waters of health, psychical and physiological."[84] In the pages of the 1890s periodical *The Adult*, devoted to the cause of free love, John Badcock Jr. praised "A butterfly," the non-monogamous lover, as superior to the married man, who drudges away like "a worker-bee."[85]

Yet these sex radicals also realized that non-monogamy was complicated by what they saw as men and women's different needs. As Edward Ross Dickinson observes, by focusing on the Darwinian drive, sexologists undermined the male commitment to monogamy. This could lead to fears of a "sex war."[86] Some philosophers depicted women in very negative terms, such as Nietzsche, who regarded woman as "a dangerous, creeping subterranean little beast of prey ... And yet so agreeable!"[87] Furthermore, both Nietzsche and social critic Otto Weininger saw sexual desire as both creative and destructive. Weininger claimed that: "the highest form of eroticism, as much as the lowest form of sexuality, uses the woman not for herself but as a means to an end – to preserve the individuality of the artist." But sex was destructive for men as well. Weininger pointed out that many a man passionately loved and idealized a woman, but found "the thought of physical union with the object of his love is insupportable." He scathingly described women as totally consumed by sex, as immoral, mediocre, phallus worshippers, their faithfulness only a "dog-like" attachment. Weininger attacked homosexuals and Jews as well, although he was himself Jewish and attracted to men. His best-selling book, *Sex and Character* (1906) expressed his own profound suffering in his diagnosis of the sexual crisis between men and women; in fact, he committed suicide soon after its publication.[88]

Despite the misogyny of Nietzsche and Weininger, some feminist sex radicals found elements of their philosophies appealing.[89] These feminists tried to use their sexual desires in their quest for autonomy of the self and split from the social purity feminists who believed the solution to sexual misery was for men to emulate chaste women. Swedish feminist Ellen Key believed that a non-monogamous relationship could make the water of dried-up springs gush forth, drive the sap to rise "in dead boughs, the renewal of life's creative force" – but this was only for exceptional, creative people.[90] Helene Stöcker was inspired by Weininger's idea that each person had some masculinity and femininity in them, in very individual combinations. In a true love relationship, each lover would contribute to the balance of masculinity and femininity, without having recourse to rigid sex roles. She also liked Nietzsche because he denounced the old Christian "life-denying morality through his proud, life affirming morality, that frees people from a bad conscience and heals their love."[91] But after a long relationship with a married man, Stöcker, like many women, found non-monogamy too emotionally painful. She admitted that a woman must be "strong enough not to waste her great and powerful feelings on little meaningless affairs."[92]

A few feminists proposed passionate relationships between women as a solution to the problems of heterosexuality. German feminist Elisabeth Dauthendey lyrically praised the "blissful peace of satisfied longing" enjoyed by two platonic female partners in contrast to the "bitter, bitter pain" of trying to combine spiritually satisfying motherhood and sexual partnership with a man.[93] A small number of lesbian women adopted the sexological idea of inversion to justify their own existence. Anna Rüling declared that "Uranian women," having masculine characteristics, had special talents which served society well. If they were able to engage openly in sexual and spiritual partnerships with other women, they would not be forced into unhappy, frustrated marriages with men, and she ingeniously noted, they would leave so many more men available for their heterosexual sisters.[94] Helene Stöcker, who was heterosexual, protested efforts to criminalize lesbianism in Germany.[95] However, while Ellen Key acknowledged that passionate love between women could be "the customary and beautiful morning glow of love," she insisted this love "always pales after sunrise" as it gives way to true heterosexual satisfaction.[96] Some writers in the *Freewoman*, a journal for feminist sex radicals, were even more hostile to sexual relationships between women. They attacked their social purity suffragette rivals as "withered spinsters" and warned about "unhealthy" attachments between schoolgirls.[97]

Eugenics and birth control

By the turn of the century, feminist sex radicals also had to contend with the increasingly influential ideas of eugenics. Influenced by Darwin, mainstream eugenicists believed that reproduction of the "unfit" must be discouraged and that of the "fit" must be encouraged. They were especially concerned that the poor or "unfit" had too many children, while educated middle-class women were having fewer children. Some of these eugenicists, such as Karl Pearson, were socialists, but they believed that science must control sexual desire in the interests of the state in order to ensure human progress.[98] In contrast, feminist sex radicals believed that women must be able to control reproduction in order to experience personal and sexual emancipation. French feminist Nelly Roussel denounced the idea that women must serve society by giving birth. Instead, women needed to serve the state as citizens, workers, and thinkers. Yet when radicals tried to spread information about birth control, they were harassed by police, arrested, and even put on trial; around the turn of the century governments even redoubled their efforts against birth control.[99]

While social purity feminists objected to eugenics on Christian ethical grounds, some sex radicals tried to adopt eugenics for their own ends.[100] Eugenics enabled many early twentieth-century sex radicals to try to reconcile their belief that sexual desire was necessary to fulfill the self and their wish to serve the wider society and the nation. They believed that, by freeing sexual desire, couples could use their sexual passion to tap into the great life force of the universe and create healthy, vital children. The Swedish reformer Ellen Key celebrated "erotoplastics: the doctrine of love as a consciously formative art, instead of a blind instinct of procreation." Sex reformers argued that if people could choose their partners freely and rationally, instead of marrying for money and property, they could choose on the grounds of eugenic health. Birth control would enable people to have sex without the danger of procreating children they could not support, or children who would be unfit. Many feminists argued that if women were strong, independent, and healthy, not forced into unwilling marriage by brutal husbands, they could also produce better children for the "race."[101]

Racial politics tinged these radical eugenicists, although when they used the word "race" they often meant the human race rather than the white race. Arguing for birth control and sex reform, Grete Meisel-Hess called for a "social veto upon all procreative acts likely to be injurious to the race; the weakly, the diseased, and those deficient in earning power would no longer propagate to excess."[102] Influenced by Nietzsche, Swedish sexologist Anton Nystrom believed that sex contributed to the human race, but only among a higher class of people: "While sexual desire in uncivilized people, or in those possessing only a low degree of culture and in degenerates, is a natural passion, it assumes a different character in people of more advanced culture and true refinement."[103] But Ellen Key criticized "the prejudiced view that the white humanity of Europe is to be taken as the criterion for the morality as well as for the faith of the whole race."[104] She was a minority voice. Far more often, those who advocated eugenics followed social Darwinism and thought in racial terms.

Conclusion

On the eve of World War I, the perception of antagonism between the sexes continued to fester at a time when political polarization, nationalism, and imperialist competition created a foreboding atmosphere. Despite their intellectual importance, sex radicals continued to remain on the fringes of debates. Social purity feminists continued to be influential, as suffragettes agitated for "Votes for Women and Purity for Men," accusing 80 percent of British men of being infected with venereal disease. Imperialist advocates such as Robert Baden-Powell warned against masturbation lest it sap the energies of the virile British race facing restive "natives" and competition from other European countries.[105] The full onslaught of sexual modernity was yet to come.

Suggested reading

Bland, Lucy. *Banishing the Beast: English Feminism and Sexual Morality 1885–1914.* London, 1995.

Bland, Lucy, and Laura Doan, eds. *Sexology in Culture.* London, 1998.

Engelstein, Laura. *The Keys to Happiness: Sex and the Search for Modernity in Fin-de-Siècle Russia.* Ithaca, 1992.

Mason, Michael. *The Making of Victorian Sexuality.* Oxford, 1994.

Mort, Frank. *Dangerous Sexualities: Medico-Moral Politics in England since 1830.* London, 1987.

Mosse, George. *Nationalism and Sexuality.* New York, 1985.

Nye, Robert A. *Masculinity and Male Codes of Honor.* Berkeley, 1998.

Oosterhuis, Harry. *Stepchildren of Nature: Krafft-Ebing, Psychiatry, and the Making of Sexual Identity.* Chicago, 2000.

Rosario, Vernon. *The Erotic Imagination: French Histories of Perversity.* New York, 1997.

Walkowitz, Judith R. *City of Dreadful Delight: Narratives of Sexual Danger in Late-Victorian London.* Chicago, 1992.

Weeks, Jeffrey. *Sex, Politics and Society: The Regulation of Sexuality since 1800.* 2nd edn. London, 1989.

Chapter 10

Managing desire or consuming sex in interwar culture

Prologue: sex, art and war

In 1907, a time when Edwardian ladies were wearing large feathered hats, stiff corsets, and gloves, Picasso painted the *Demoiselles d'Avignon* – five angular, abstract, naked women in a brothel. Unlike the smooth odalisques of academic painting, still and static in their alluring beauty, or even Renoir's pink, fleshy women, these prostitutes are charged with sexual energy, both titillating and threatening. They boldly gaze at the viewer, spreading their legs and thrusting their breasts. But their faces are like African masks, so we see not the allure of a recognizable woman, but what the artist constructed as primitive, raw desire. At the same time, the painting's sharp Cubist angles and planes resemble the metal machines of modern society; the body has become a machine, and women revealed as commodities. The raw sexuality and the artistic innovation of the *Demoiselles* were so shocking that Picasso did not put the painting on public display until 1916.

In the early twentieth century, a new energy began to surge through art and writing – as the poet Apollinaire proclaimed, "Desire is the great force" of life, but it was no longer seen as ethereally spiritual, but as raw and aggressive.[1] Picasso and the surrealists used African masks to represent raw instincts free from the self. Paradoxically, as critic Nancy Nenno observes, artists exploited "primitive" sexuality as ultramodern.[2] Free from artificial, mechanized society, they thought "primitive" peoples could tap into a simple, creative erotic energy. Of course, these artists and writers also fantasized about the primitive or the oriental and failed to take these complex cultures on their own terms.[3]

The futurists proclaimed that erotic desire was the instinctual drive which propelled modern capitalism. This group of Italian and French artists called themselves the "futurists" – they rejected tradition, such as sentimental romantic love. Instead, they enthused about modern war and machines. They celebrated "action-art, that is, energy of will, optimism, aggression, possession, penetration, joy, brutal reality in art."[4] While the futurists were intently masculine, a few women claimed this virility for themselves. Valentine de Saint-Point, the female futurist poet and dancer, declared in 1913: "Lust, like pride, is a virtue that urges one on, a powerful source of energy;" it fuels capitalists, and "kills the weak and exalts the

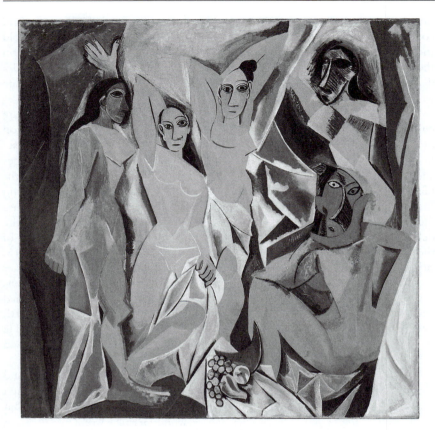

Figure 10.1 *Les Demoiselles d'Avignon* (Paris, June–July 1907). Picasso, Pablo (1881–1973). New York, Museum of Modern Art (MoMA). Oil on canvas, 8' x 7'8" (243.9 x 233.7cm). Acquired through the Lillie P. Bliss Bequest. 331.1939. Digital image © 2008 The Museum of Modern Art, New York/Scala, Florence. © Succession Picasso/DACS London 2007

strong, aiding natural selection," in an orgiastic, militaristic excess.[5] The outbreak of World War I destroyed this grimly utopian vision, but it inspired artists and writers to explore sex and death, intertwined, as primeval instincts. In *Beyond the Pleasure Principle*, Freud wrote that the death instinct was as important as the sexual drive – both were primitive urges of the id, welling up from the unconscious, and difficult to control.[6] Even before the war, German Expressionist artists like George Grosz and Otto Dix drew lurid, disturbing scenes of "Lustmord," or sexual murder, painting mutilated and dismembered female bodies.[7] During the war they witnessed soldiers' bodies exploded and broken on muddy battlefields.

The Great War introduced new technologies, such as the tank and machine gun, which dismembered men's bodies in the millions. Men back on leave sought out the comfort of sex, and some army commanders provided prostitutes and condoms to prevent venereal disease. In Berlin, women desperate for money sold their bodies in streets and cafés to soldiers, as well as to capitalists, who gorged on the profits of the war. Painter Otto Dix portrayed a syphilitic prostitute and a disfigured soldier as capitalism's victims, but he reviled prostitutes for enjoying life while wounded veterans suffered.[8]

Cultural critics also blamed sexual anarchy – especially in commercial leisure culture – for the trauma of defeat on the continent. Sex symbolized the pollution of racial or national boundaries – not a new theme, but one with ominous conse-quences.[9] In Germany, the right attacked the outburst of sexual films, magazines and cabaret to discredit the legitimacy of the republic, and joined with the Cath-olic Center Party to call for censorship. In 1919, the German right-wing "Wilhelm Meister" fulminated that Jews were emasculating the nation with "coffee house music, negro dances, smutty operettas and bordello farces."[10] In Britain, the debate was not so contentious, but a conservative politician blamed the "Cult of the Clitoris" and male homosexuals for undermining the war effort, and in 1915, British authorities banned D.H. Lawrence's rather over-heated novel *The Rainbow*, because it pulsated with "electric" sexual desires and criticized nation-alism.[11] In France, Liberal Paul Bureau declared that "the sexual instinct" had become an "agent of violence, disorder, and anarchy," causing France's low birth rate, sexual debauchery, and alcoholism, and hence its defeat in World War I. He railed against the decadent *cafés chantants*, where nude women danced on stage, and the obscene films and magazines that he claimed flooded the marketplace.[12]

Racial anxieties also intensified when the French employed Senegalese and Moroccan troops and workers, or *tirailleurs*, in the war effort. After the war, when the French used *tirailleurs* in the occupation of the Rhine, Germans claimed that black soldiers might seduce – or even rape – white German women. Titillating pamphlets inspired outrage against those who thrust "barbarians … inspired by Nature with tremendous sexual instincts … into the heart of Europe." although in fact the troops were quite disciplined.[13] Germans also represented the occupation of the Rhine with the image of a bloodthirsty, sexualized, red-capped Marianne, emblem of the French Revolution, like a vampire seizing on German lands. Revo-lutions broke out in Russia and Germany; although social revolution was brutally suppressed in the latter, the fear of it persisted.

Sex and mass culture

In the 1920s, it became apparent that the world had changed, as modernity became starkly visible. Although all these changes had begun decades before the war, in the 1920s popular culture, and people themselves, looked very different: women with their short skirts and bobs, automobiles now everywhere speeding through the streets, interiors with their sharp edges and streamlined curves. Popular culture became more visual – and potentially sexualized – with the new technologies of the movies and mass-produced photographs and newspapers.

Businesses advertised their wares in plate-glass department store windows and magazine pictures.

The modern person existed in a world of mass production and mass culture, working among thousands in an office or assembly line, watching the same film as millions of others, buying the shiny new radios peddled by advertisements. Bodies massed in motions of calisthenics and athletics, as the movies displayed elaborate spectacles of feathered dancers wheeling and twirling in unison. The louche French can-can, where girls revealed ruffled petticoats and soft thighs, moved from the hidden redlight districts of Paris to mainstream music hall stages, and became the precisely machined choreography of the Tiller Girls, a chorus line of smooth bare legs, pointed breasts and bold red lips. In offices and factories, Taylorist experts carefully calibrated workers' movements for utmost efficiency.

Writers and filmmakers were fascinated and inspired by the new mass culture, but it also repelled them. The pulse of the machine, its gaping maw, seemed to resemble the pulse of sex, the push, the pull. As surrealist Georges Bataille declared, "The two primary motions are rotation and sexual movement, whose combination is expressed by the locomotive's wheels and pistons."[14] Writers and filmmakers used the power of sexual images to denounce the distortions of sex in mass culture and the exploitation of humanity under capitalism. Artists and writers complained that popular entertainment drained sex of its erotic power, its raw, instinctive energy, by mass-producing mechanical images of shiny sexual bodies. Cultural critic Siegfried Kracauer declared in 1931 that the Tiller girls, "productions of American 'distraction factories' are no longer individual girls, but indissoluble female units whose movements are mathematical demonstrations." The dancing was like the conveyor belt; it insidiously persuaded workers to accept their own precise mechanized movements on factory assembly lines. The Tiller Girls should exude erotic allure as they flashed their crotches, but they were so impersonal they lacked sexual power. However, because capitalism does not recognize human beings, Kracauer argued, the "dark forces of nature continue to rise up threateningly."[15]

Reformers wanted to manage what they saw as this instinctual energy, to shape it and control it as part of their larger effort to reshape and transform society. These ideas about sex moved from the avant-garde margins to the center of society after the war. New modern sex experts appeared: bureaucrats, social workers, doctors, and psychiatrists whose clinics mushroomed in the early twentieth century. These experts believed that sexual desire must be managed to manipulate populations and prevent degeneration through the new pseudo-science of eugenics. Such reformers came from both the left and the right. Left-wingers wanted to transform poor, downtrodden people into healthy, happy workers – and the sexually satisfied marriage would help in this project. Birth must be managed to produce healthy, fit babies – and that of course required managing sex. New right-wing mass movements argued that the racially "unfit" must be prevented from reproducing. They learned how to manipulate people's behavior through radio and film. Yet reformers found they could not always control and manage

Figure 10.2 The Tiller Girls, from a September 1935 advertisement for stockings. V&A Images, Victoria and Albert Museum

popular culture and leisure. Mass culture was just as powerful a force as sex, if not more so. Mass culture needed citizens to consume, to endlessly desire new commodities, to seek out pleasure in a form of polymorphous perversity escaping the imperatives of reproduction.[16]

The mass culture revolution was also incomplete. While many working-class and middle-class people enjoyed higher wages in the new industries such as vacuum cleaner or radio manufacturing, or as secretaries and sales clerks, others lost their jobs as the old industries faltered. Immediately after the war, inflation in Germany wiped out the savings of millions, and the boom time of the 1920s was followed by the depression. Ordinary people found themselves caught between experts who advised the eugenic management of sex, film fantasies about sex appeal and exotic luxuries, and the reality of overcrowded housing, unemployment, and sexual anxiety.

Popular culture in interwar western Europe: the new woman

During the war, authorities feared that a spike in the number of births outside marriage meant that young women were sexually uncontrollable. During the 1920s, new experts in psychology joined forces with the older matrons of Victorian reformatories to try to discipline wayward girls. In England, they could indefinitely lock up supposedly promiscuous girls or poor unmarried mothers by labeling them as "feeble-minded." Especially in areas such as Liverpool or Limehouse, where several thousand seamen of African or Chinese origin lived, social workers sent white girls to "rescue" homes if they suspected they were in danger of prostituting themselves or taking up with "colored" men.[17] On the Continent, however, some reformers declared that unmarried mothers should be helped instead of punished, since they might have intended to marry soldiers who were killed, and they were producing babies who could replace the population lost in the war. During the war, unmarried mothers sometimes received benefits, in part to prevent abortion and ensure the health of their offspring. But unmarried mothers and their children still did not have equal legal rights, and state officials intruded into their lives and managed their affairs.[18]

Some reformers denounced this attitude toward women as a remnant of what they saw as Victorian sexual repression and hypocrisy. In his silent film, *Diary of a Lost Girl* (1929), G.W. Pabst expored the conflict between hypocritical morality and sexual freedom. The film's heroine, Thymian Henning, played by Louise Brooks with her sleek dark bob, is the innocent daughter of a thriving pharmacist. After she is raped and becomes pregnant, her parents disown her and send her to a reformatory, forcing her to give up the baby. In the reformatory, Louise faces perverse and hypocritical bourgeois discipline. The reformatory evokes both the old Victorian religious institutions, with their uniforms and strict schedules, and the modern world of mechanization. The repressed and repressive matron commands the girls to eat mechanically, all lifting their spoons at the same time. She bangs a gong as the girls do their evening calisthenics. As she bangs the gong faster and faster, and the girls' nubile bodies sway in rhythm, her tight hair loosens and her face convulses in orgasm. Here, Pabst evokes the sexologists' claim that repressed sexuality produced perversion. Thymian escapes, only to end up in a brothel, which is the most free, hedonistic, and friendly place in the movie.

Sexual behavior had started to change before the war. In Germany, more young people had sex before marriage.[19] In France, historian Ann-Marie Sohn has found that around the turn of the century young people had just started to enjoy "le flirt," and French women began using diaphragms, sponges, and douches, and if that failed, resorted to abortion.[20] These trends continued in the 1920s and 1930s. While illegitimacy rates returned to their prewar levels, a survey of British women found that 19 percent of married women born before 1904 had sex before their weddings, while 36 percent of those born between 1904 and 1914 did. Only 8 percent of married women born before 1904 had engaged in "petting" before marriage, but 22 percent of the next generation had petted.[21] Of course, these surveys remain problematic, but they were part of the newer phenomenon of managing sex by surveying samples of several hundred women and do give some indication of change across time. A survey of 500 German women in the late 1920s found that four out of five had sex before marriage, although this was more common in the lower classes.[22] Sohn has found that the French became even more sexually open in the interwar period, as young people enjoyed sex before marriage and men became more skillful at elaborate foreplay. However, she does not attribute these changes to the influence of sexologists, but to the decline in the influence of the Church and the decline in arranged marriages. Women who could earn a living, such as secretaries and teachers, felt they could enjoy premarital sex – as long as they did not allow their pleasure to become public and destroy their reputations.[23] British working-class girls learned from their mothers that sex was dangerous and unpleasant, but then they went to the pictures which glamorized sex appeal.[24]

What cultural critics feared was not the helpless, feeble-minded teenage mother, but the confident New Woman or "garçonne" who enjoyed consumer culture. While the British had already been scandalized by the New Woman of the 1880s, the image of the "New New Woman," or flapper, of the 1920s was much more sexual and pleasure-loving than her earlier, rather earnest predecessor. The idea that female sexuality was bound up in commodity culture was not new – after all, aristo-cratic girls in the Victorian marriage market were expected to show off their décolletés. But the New Woman was a consumer as well as a commodity, a familiar figure in the new mass advertising. She bought lipstick, powder, and rouge, which respectable middle-class women had not widely worn before the war, and wore nude-colored silk hose, instead of Victorian black stockings.[25] Moralists fulminated that if all women wore "paint," they could no longer tell the difference between respectable ladies and prostitutes. They were also outraged that young men and women could advertise for sexual and romantic partners – not just marriage – in the pages of new magazines.[26] The New Woman also adopted masculine styles, wearing tuxedo jackets and shingled short hair, smoking cigarettes, driving cars, and earning money with equal aplomb. By giving up the armor of the corset, long dress and hat, by moving freely, she increased her sexual desirability. Interestingly, until the later 1920s, magazines depicted the short-haired, tuxedo-wearing flapper as attractive to men, with no hint that she might be a lesbian.[27]

Women avidly also consumed the new mass market fiction. These novels were both texts and commodities. As commodities, they sold in the millions, which helped overcome disapproval and censorship. The "Sheik" novels, like Valentino's films, shocked moralists who realized that ordinary women enjoyed these novels for their – not very explicit – soft-core romance; they apparently aroused readers with lurid tales of hard-muscled, handsome, swarthy Arabs abducting white heroines who surrendered to their virile, exotic power.[28]

Novelists also told the story of the New Woman herself. Bohemian radicals celebrated the New Woman's ultramodern individuality, freedom and independence, as she left her husband, took a lover, bore children outside of marriage, or formed a special bond with a woman friend. In a review of these novels, Russian Bolshevik Alexandra Kollontai declared that the New Woman displays self-discipline instead of indulging in emotional rapture: "she does not hide her natural physical drives," thus asserting herself as a person and a woman."[29] Other novelists could assuage readers' moral qualms by punishing the New Woman for her adventures and freedom, but until the end of the tale they could be titillated by the fantasy of the New Woman's sexual escapades and glamorous lifestyle as she took lovers in French resorts and charmed London high society.

Victor Margueritte's *La Garçonne*, (*The Bachelor Girl*) (1922) sold millions of copies, despite a ban by the Catholic church.[30] Margueritte denounced bourgeois sexual hypocrisy but he also felt that the utopian idea of sexual freedom was difficult to put into practice. His heroine, Monique, is an innocent bourgeois girl whose heart is broken by her fiancé, a businessman whom her father wanted her to marry to save his business. Devastated, she becomes an independent woman who pursues a career as a decorator and takes many lovers, often choosing men in traditionally feminine occupations, such as dancers. Monique thinks she can do without love, but she is tormented by longing for a child. At the end of the novel, she discovers she is sterile – the consequence of her sexual freedom.[31]

During the depression of the 1930s, critics feared that the other "New Women" – working women, such as typists and shopgirls – would exchange sex for money to enjoy the new commodity culture. Irmgard Keun, a young working woman herself, expressed her own feelings about the situation. In her novel, *The Artificial Silk Girl* (1932), the heroine Doris feels herself to be a mechanized commodity of sex in the modern city: "I kept walking and walking, the whores were standing at corners plying their trade, and there was a sort of mechanism in me that duplicated precisely their walking and standing still." Doris touchingly longs for those pleasures that are out of reach to her unless she treats her own sex as a commodity:

And you want a few nice clothes, because at least then you're no longer a complete nobody. And you also want a coffee once in a while with music and an elegant peach melba in very elegant goblets, and that's not at all something you can muster alone, again you need the big industrialists for that, and you might as well just start turning tricks.

But she protests

> If a young woman from money marries an old man because of money and nothing else and makes love to him for hours and has this pious look on her face, she's called a German mother and a decent woman. If a young woman without money sleeps with a man with no money because he has smooth skin and she likes him, she's a whore and a bitch. [32]

In these novels, young women might also be lured into perverse pleasures. French moralists often feared that lesbian desire could tempt even feminine women if bourgeois hypocrisy blocked their "normal" heterosexual desires.[33] However, many novelists did not center on the fixed sexual identity of the "lesbian" but portrayed desire for other women as hidden and shadowy, as twisted twilight moments. Innocent young girls might be led astray by a repressed spinster teachers unaware of their own perversity, or sophisticated bohemians all too aware of their own sexual power. For instance, in *La Garçonne*, Monique is seduced by Lady Springfield, who is "Tall and supple, like a dark clinging tropical creeper" and lures her to a lesbian orgy in a brothel. The English translation of *La Garçonne*, *The Bachelor Girl* left out the brothel scene and explicit discussions of Monique's lesbian lovers.[34] The British popular newspaper press regularly reported on women who dressed as men and married other women as odd and amazing, but could not conceive of the concept of the lesbian.[35] Radcliffe Hall's novel *The Well of Loneliness*, however, brought greater visibility to this identity. This notorious book called for tolerance of "invert" females, that is, women who felt themselves to be masculine yet attracted to their own sex. Drawing on sexological writings, Hall clearly articulated a lesbian identity, but her novel was banned in England after 1929, and led to greater suspicion of androgynous women in the 1930s.[36] In Sweden, Margareta Suber's novel *Charlie* (1932) also publicized Freudian and sexological notions of lesbians, but another novel which portrayed explicit erotic sex between women could not be published.[37]

The department store of love: sex management and mass culture

Berliners enjoyed visiting Magnus Hirschfeld's Institute for Sex Research, where they could gawk at thousands of photographs of sexual types and their fetishes and toys: Hirschfeld calculated that there were 43,046,721 possible sexual types.[38] One writer described Hirschfeld's Institute as a "Department Store of Love," a scientific shop "where everyone can purchase their favorite fetish objects and achieve complete satisfaction of their desires."[39] By going to

Hirschfeld's institute, ordinary people exposed themselves to sex reform management, but they also treated it as just another leisure opportunity.

The experts of the sex reform movement wanted to regulate and discipline sexual behavior because they thought the sexually satisfied couple would be better workers and citizens. Instead of admonishing people to take cold showers to distract them from sexual thoughts, as in the older social purity movement, sex manual advisors instructed them on exactly how to have sex. Psychologists and doctors also emphasized the distinction between the "normal" and the "abnormal," which they defined as heterosexual and homosexual. But commercial mass culture may have been more influential in spreading the meaning of sex reform than the experts themselves; and in consuming this mass culture, ordinary people sometimes used the ideas of sex reform in their own way, rather than passively absorbing expert messages.

Between the wars, authorities increasingly followed the sexologists' idea that the homosexual was a distinct inborn personality type. As historian Matt Houlbrook has found, the British police began to link effeminacy and illicit sex between men more firmly, for instance, they arrested young men found with a powder puff as evidence of their perversion. At the same time, authorities continued to be concerned with the "normal" young man whose sexuality was still malleable. Experts feared that the adolescent might become permanently locked in the homosexual stage if he or she was seduced by an "invert." In the early 1930s in London, the police were very concerned that soldiers, especially the Guards, who had a long tradition of prostituting themselves, would become homosexual, so they tried to educate the men about homosexuality and punished them if they succumbed to this temptation.[40] Some doctors in Sweden declared that men who had sex with youths under 20 should be incarcerated in asylums, and others advocated castration, whether physical or chemical.[41]

Greater attention paid to homosexuality could lead to greater persecution. In Britain, prosecutions for male homosexuality increased steadily from prewar levels.[42] Prosecutions also increased in Sweden, especially dramatically in the 1930s.[43] The French could not arrest men just for homosexual acts, but they intensively monitored the sailors who provided sex to other men, and often arrested these men.[44] In Germany the number of prosecutions rose sharply until 1925, and remained high after that, except in Berlin, where the police were more tolerant.[45] Lesbians faced fewer legal obstacles, except in Finland and Austria, where lesbian sex was officially illegal, although rarely prosecuted. In contrast, in England, an effort in 1920–1 to criminalize sexual relations between women failed, as Laura Doan explains, because Members of Parliament did not want to publicize it, assuming very few women could even conceive of lesbianism. But in Sweden, sexual acts between adult women were prosecuted after 1940.[46]

Psychoanalysts tended to argue that homosexuals should be treated with therapy, not punished by the police. Freudian psychoanalysts often thought that homosexuality was sexual development toward adulthood gone wrong, while other physicians believed homosexuality was a hormonal imbalance.[47] Sex hygiene manuals reassured young people that crushes on schoolmates or teachers were normal, but they advised them to outgrow these passions, and avoid masturbation, which might lead to homosexuality. Even many socialists asserted that the frustrations of modern society caused sexual deviations such as homosexuality. But Magnus Hirschfeld continued to lead a growing movement arguing that it was normal for people to have different sexual tastes and personalities, that homosexuals and lesbians should be accepted by society, and that they needed neither treatment nor incarceration.[48]

At the same time, the bohemian avant-garde explored the idea of sexual desire as free flowing, not confined to either sex. Some took on both male and female lovers. The relationship of Virginia Woolf and Vita Sackville-West is well known, but there were many others. For instance, after a fraught relationship with a married man, Hannah Hoch, the Weimar Dada artist, wrote to her sister that the "chapter 'man' is finished for me. The beautiful and the awful endured, explored and exhausted." But when she became involved with Til Brugman, a Dutch artist, she happily wrote, "To be closely connected with another woman for me is something totally new, since it means being taken by the spirit of my own spirit, confronted by a close relative." Brugman's personality was rather controlling, however, and after nine years, Hoch became involved with a younger man.[49] Popular Weimar cabaret singers flaunted a rather stagy decadence, hinting that they had affairs with both boys and girls.[50]

Other women defiantly asserted a self-conscious lesbian identity, melding commercial leisure and politics to create their own subculture. In France, lesbians continued to haunt the alternative bohemian world of erotic culture; the elegant Parisienne could parade along the Champs-Elysées with her poodle, glancing at beautiful women. The working-class lesbian might frequent Susy Solidor's café, where they belted out the lesbian anthem "Ouvre": "open your trembling knees, open your thighs."[51] But lesbian culture reached its apogee in Berlin. The modern Berlin lesbian – perhaps a doctor, a shopgirl, a typist – could entertain friends or live with a lover in her chic apartment, leaf through several lesbian magazines, and saunter out to a different lesbian club each night. Clubs provided a sanctuary from the stresses of straight life: at the Café Dorian Grey, visitors emerged "out of the grey of everyday … into an almost overwhelming colorful world."[52] She might move on to the elegant Maly und Jugel, which offered more privacy: "window panes covered with thick curtains blocked out the street; inside, the decor was a subdued play of garnet red and pearl gray, with light-colored paintings, deep armchairs, and a piano."[53] The magazines and clubs organized expeditions, such as the "Moonlight Steamship Party" when the women cruised to a hotel, where they danced and gambled until early in the morning, bringing back a souvenir photograph of the group. The magazines spread the subculture to the provinces, where they provided a lifeline, a sense of identity, and a way to meet romantic partners for both working-class and middle-class women.[54]

These lesbians reveled in the eroticism of their desire. They insisted that the lesbian periodicals feature bare-breasted "artistic" photos of pretty women on the cover. But they also explored the emotional depths of connections between women. As Ruth Roellig, a lesbian journalist, wrote, "Lesbian love arises from the refinement and depth of emotional experience where all the forces of body and soul become fused, and then unfolded."[55] In the magazines, such as *The Friend*, or *Garçonne*, women also debated the exact nature of lesbian identity. They borrowed the "concept of 'natural variation' from the sexologists to confirm their belief that their desires stemmed from an essential trait rather than an acquired vice."[56]

But were lesbians masculine inverts, as the sexologists claimed? One story took up the idea of the "Mannweib," or masculine woman, by describing the character Olga, who believed she really was a man; she could only feel comfortable in her bachelor digs, with a smoking room and gaming room, austerely decorated with only nude portraits of women to provide warmth. However, some readers challenged the association of masculinity and lesbianism. Feminine women vigorously asserted their place in this culture, boldly refuting the idea that feminine women were superficial, and celebrating the feminine "gamine" character as well as the masculine "bubi," or butch. Many lesbians declared that there was a continuity between masculinity and femininity, rather than a dichotomy of types. For others, the "garçonne" lesbian could be a creation of her times, rather than a biological invert. Interestingly, the lesbian magazines and bars welcomed what we now call male-to-female transgender people, but rejected bisexual women.[57]

These women often faced suspicion and hostility from neighbors and family; conservatives – and even some socialists – reacted with horror at what they perceived as sexual decadence.[58] The German censors repeatedly closed down the lesbian periodicals. In response, lesbians defiantly sang their anthem, "The Lavender Song:"

> We see a world of romance and of pleasure
> All they can see is sheer banality
> Lavender nights are our greatest treasure
> where we can be just who we want to be
>
> Round us all up, send us away
> that's what you'd really like to do
> But we're too strong, proud, unafraid.[59]

Homosexual men also developed even more visible and self-conscious subcultures in capital cities. In London, the young men who hung about Piccadilly flaunted their campness, making up their faces and dressing flamboyantly, enjoying their own style. They described themselves as "queer." But other working-class men, who had sex with these "fairies" for pleasure, or with gentlemen for money, did not necessarily think of themselves as queer, as historian Matt Houlbrook notes.[60] In Berlin, the Cozy Corner, a working-class Berlin bar, "was decorated with photographs of boxers and bicycle racers, and the crowd consisted largely of young laborers who were out of work: they would sit, playing cards and waiting for customers, their shirts open to the navel and sleeves rolled up."[61] But sex also might enable working-class men to join upper-class society. In Stockholm, for instance, middle-class or upper-class men met working-class men while cruising for sex in parks and urinals. If they hit it off, they would invite their sexual partners to elite parties.[62]

Many homosexual men asserted their right to live according to their "nature," not as flaws of nature, but as natural variations. This was true not only of the well-known activists, but of ordinary working-class men as well. For instance, Giovanni Conforti, arrested by the Toulon police, said he was a "young modern man who loved people of two sexes."[63] Men arrested at London West End balls that were put on by a waiter and a barman defended "our love" and declared "we should be free to do as we like." For some British men, sex was the lifting of the twilight veil, a discovery of a new world. After a Mr. Hutton had sex with a man in Belgrave Square, he declared, "It was if a curtain had been drawn back … I could see clearly what had been partially obscured before … this was what … I had been looking for … I knew now … that other people … felt the same way as I did. I was no longer alone."[64]

Men who desired other men formed groups and published periodicals to justify their sexual identity. In France, an unmarried office worker and a postal worker founded the journal *Inversions*, proclaiming:

> We want to cry out to inverts that they are normal and healthy beings, that they have a right to live their lives fully, that they owe nothing to a morality created by heterosexuals – they do not have to standardize their impressions and feelings, to repress their desires, to conquer their passions.[65]

While the censors closed down *Inversions*, the ideas lived on. The German authors of the magazine *Uranos* argued that everyone has elements of inversion (homosexuality) and normality, and that groups of men would invariably contain a homosexual element. The Männerbund movement also contributed to the idea of homoerotic male bonding. It grew out of the prewar Wandervogel movement, which organized young men to go on hiking holidays, where they could exercise in the fresh air and form intense bonds with each other. Their leaders, such as Hans Blüher, openly proclaimed the erotic component of the bonds between older and younger men. Only those who could have orgasm with both men and women were seen as "fully potent." At the same time, the Männerbund movement was anti-Semitic, accusing Jews of being effeminate, promiscuous and corrupt.[66]

Heterosexuality and the challenge of female desire

Heterosexual female pleasure became the most important sign of sexual modernity in the early twentieth century. In the 1920s, sex advisors insisted that women needed sexual pleasure with men in order to have happy marriages. One scholar has insisted that the so-called companionate marriage was just a new way of advising women to submit to their husbands sexually.[67] Indeed, some followers of Freud took to extremes his suggestions that women must shift their erotic focus from the immature, masculine clitoris to the mature vaginal orgasm. Princess Marie Bonaparte, a descendant of Napoleon, argued that "frigidity caused by clitoral fixation can only be cured by a mixture of surgery and psychoanalysis." Bonaparte, who lavished her wealth to encourage psychoanalysis in France, herself underwent surgery to move her clitoris closer to her vagina, so that she could have orgasms during penetration. Unfortunately, the operation failed. Orthodox Freudian analysts blamed women for being "frigid," accusing them of penis envy if they failed to have vaginal orgasms.[68]

In fact, most marriage advice manuals did not take up the theory of the vaginal orgasm until much later in the 1930s, and the idea did not become common outside Freudian circles until the 1940s and 1950s, as historian Hera Cook has found.[69] Instead, radical sex reformers insisted on the role of the clitoris in female sexual pleasure. They blamed a "lack of skill, control, and sympathy on the husband's part" for wives' "sexual anaesthesia."[70] Dr. Theodore van de Velde declared that "the man who neglects the love-play is guilty not only of coarseness, but of positive brutality." The German socialist Max Hodann argued that there was no such thing as frigid women, only incompetent men.[71]

The writers of popular sex manuals were often renegade doctors who witnessed women's sexual frustration, such as the Communist Max Hodann, or van de Velde, whose practice was ruined when he left his wife for a patient. Others were female scientists who had experienced sexual frustration first-hand. Marie Stopes, an unconventional young woman who made her own orange silk dresses, attained a doctorate in botany and a lectureship at University College, London. Her suffragette mother advocated rights for women – and insisted on sexual purity. As a result, Marie Stopes was completely ignorant of sex when she married another scientist, the thin-lipped, pale-haired Dr. Reginald Gates. Gates was impotent, and could not penetrate her, but it took her several years to realize he had not consummated the marriage. British doctor Helena Wright was similarly frustrated by her first experience of marital sex, and complained to her husband, "Peter, I find this a bore." Both Stopes and Wright turned to scientific tomes to discover what was wrong.[72]

These sexual advice writers told husbands they must treat their wives tenderly and spend a long time on foreplay. Marie Stopes was fairly vague about what foreplay actually involved, although she insisted husbands must woo their wives and respect their cycles of desire. Van de Velde was much more explicit: his goal was mutual orgasm, and he presented detailed and technical instructions for attaining it: the man and woman must carefully position their limbs and genitals at precisely the right angles and degrees of thrust to produce the desired result, accelerating or braking their responses – a daunting task much like assembling a piece of Ikea furniture with moving parts.[73]

Long before Masters and Johnson, these writers recognized that a woman's orgasm required clitoral stimulation either externally or through coitus. Van de

Velde advised husbands to delicately stroke the clitoris, "to the accompaniment of kisses and words of love," to prepare their wives for the "supreme act." He even advocated the "genital kiss," or oral sex. Like Marie Bonaparte, van de Velde believed that among many Western European and American women, sometimes the clitoris was too high or too small – what he called "genital infantilism" – to be stimulated in intercourse. But unlike Bonaparte, he believed that sexual practice might enlarge the clitoris, or, failing that, husbands must exercise special skill to bring their wives to orgasm.[74]

Helena Wright discovered that 50 percent of her patients did not experience orgasms with their husbands. After reading van de Velde, she realized that ignorance of the clitoris caused this problem, so she decided to enlighten her patients. Durng physical examinations, the patient would lie naked on a table. With a "light probe," Dr. Wright would first "touch the girl's inner thigh, then her pubic hair and lastly the clitoris." She would get out a mirror and "let the girl see what the small pink object looked like, which gave such a specific reason to touch."[75] Some British husbands who wrote to Marie Stopes for sex advice worried that if they stimulated the clitoris, this would have a "devastating" effect on their wives, ruining their health. But they do not seem to have been influenced by Freud, but rather, by an older fear that clitoral stimulation was really masturbation, with all its wicked consequences. Fortunately, Marie Stopes reassured them that they were still healthy and normal.[76]

The radical sex reformers believed that the West had repressed the art of love and idealized the "orient" as a source of erotic knowledge. Max Hodann proclaimed that "the world of the Orient, the Mohammedan-Arabian world, as well as the Indian and Shintoist, is today still free from this ban against sensuousness which oppresses Europe and America, and prevents the growth of any love culture."[77] In her marriage manual, Helena Wright wrote "there can be nothing impossible about the achievement of a successful sex act, because it is the universal experience of primitive peoples, and of Eastern civilizations" who treated sex as a cultural art and skill.[78] Van de Velde, author of the bestselling *Ideal Marriage*, explored "oriental" sexual manuals for new positions for intercourse.[79]

The sex manual writers thought of sex as spiritual and passionate, but they were shocked by the cruder commercial culture of their time. Hodann attributed the spread of venereal disease to alcohol and "the display of sex which we are constantly running across in the movies, on the dance-floor, and in the burlesques."[80] Grete Meisel-Hess, who came of age in the prewar generation, was repelled by the casual attitude toward sex expressed by young working women, who "were said to regard sex as a fashion, like silk stockings and smoking."[81]

But the writers of sex manuals needed the mass market of commercial publication to overcome censorship. Many publishers rejected Marie Stopes's *Married Love* until 1918, when it became a bestseller. Publishers soon realized that marriage manuals were profitable commodities, like sexy lingerie and movies, so they defied the censors. Reformers could also exploit the popular medium of film to convey their messages. In Britain, Stopes spread knowledge about birth control to the working class through a commercial film, *Maisie's Marriage*. The censors would not allow it to be distributed under the name *Married Love*, but the producers managed to put her name on posters that made it quite clear what the movie was about.[82] Popular magazines also publicized the new thinking beyond those who had read Marie Stopes or van de Velde.[83] In Germany, popular magazines went even further, combining serious discussions of sex reform with erotic photographs and classified ads for fetishes.[84] In the first years of the Weimar Republic, sex reformers also created "enlightenment" films, which combined titillating melodramas with a serious message: the lack of contraception and legal abortion killed women, sexual hypocrisy should end, homosexuals deserved understanding. Conservatives were horrified and mainstream socialists disapproved of them as trashy; the government banned them, but by the early 1930s, sex reformers created new film and stage melodramas about the tragedy of illegal abortion.[85]

An odd combination of capitalism and popular socialism also helped the distribution of contraceptives. The German government had forbidden the advertisement, but not the sale, of contraceptives, but the commodified marketplace of sex enabled evasion of this law. Doctors and chemists were inventing new forms of diaphragms, IUDs (intrauterine devices), and chemical spermicides. Manufacturers worked with lay sex reform leagues – even with Magnus Hirschfeld – to provide condoms, diaphragms, and spermicides. The lay groups, which were membership only, could then distribute them. As historian Atina Grossman has discovered, these largely working-class organizations were linked to "natural healing and lifestyle reform, such as nudism and vegetarianism," with "anti-capitalist and neo-Malthusian rhetoric."[86] Overzealous government officials in some areas tried to confiscate such rubber goods, and even irrigators and other articles not used for birth control, leading manufacturers to complain against state interference in a free market.[87]

In France, as Mary Louise Roberts observes, the law prohibited female methods of contraception and abortion, but the government could not control the spread of condoms. Millions of men had used condoms during the war, encouraged by army officials fearful of venereal disease, and they weren't about to give up the habit.[88] In Britain, the government permitted local government health authorities to dispense birth control advice from 1930, and the Church of England sanctioned birth control for married people in 1930, but both authorities emphasized that contraception should only be used to save a woman's health, not to enable sexual indulgence.[89] German sex reformers took advantage of a 1926 law that allowed the establishment of clinics for eugenic marriage counseling. These clinics were to counsel clients about avoiding marriage – or at least avoiding reproduction – with someone who might have alcoholism, tuberculosis, insanity, epilepsy, or other inherited or acquired characteristics running in his or her family. Their clients, however, rejected eugenic counseling; they demanded contraception and abortion, and, when the sex reformers took over the clinics, they prescribed birth control.[90]

Indeed, family size dropped dramatically between the wars, so couples clearly were doing something to limit births. Although middle-class people had long controlled their fertility, in Germany by the 1930s, the average working-class family size was half what it had been in the previous generation.[91] In one area in South Wales, a sample found that couples had 3.2 children on average, while their parents had had seven children on average. In Britain, women who went out to work could find most information about birth control; chatting in the lunchroom, they learned that they could avoid pregnancy.[92] In more traditional areas where women were less likely to go out to work, they left the knowledge of condoms up to their husbands. Despite the sex reformers' insistence on female desire, many women still felt embarrassed and ashamed to discuss birth control, because that meant talking about sex and perhaps acknowledging their own desires. When one woman heard her workmates talking about "johnnies" – condoms – she was very confused and asked who "Johnny" was.[93]

Many working people may have relied on abstinence as much as the new birth control methods, which were still difficult to obtain and hard to use.[94] To use a diaphragm, a woman had to have a husband who would wait for her to put it in, and a sink to wash the diaphragm and jelly afterwards, in a private room where curious children or neighbors would not interfere. IUDs required a doctor's prescription, and as we now know, could be painful and dangerous. Men could and did buy condoms, which were available from vending machines in pubs by the 1930s, but they were still quite expensive (and not lubricated).[95] Birth control could still be a twilight practice between husbands or wives, something that took place between the sheets in the dark as husbands struggled to withdraw before orgasm, or quickly put on a condom. Of course, many women fell pregnant when their husbands did not withdraw quite soon enough, when the condom broke, when they refused to use birth control, or when they could not afford a diaphragm.

As a result, many women had to find abortionists in the interwar period. Interestingly, English working-class women found it much easier to gossip about another woman's misfortune in falling pregnant and having an abortion than to talk about their own efforts at family planning.[96] In Germany, women whispered the names of abortionists on the street, as they stood on the steps with their aprons, children at their feet, or as they drank in taverns, or gossiped in the stenographers' pool. Sometimes midwives advertised the services of abortionists. Abortionists could even moonlight as fortune-tellers, a practice which no doubt gave them access to desperate clients. Doctors, of course, provided many abortions clandestinely, although they demanded very high fees and sometimes played God, trying to decide which women "deserved" an abortion and which did not.[97]

Abortion was so common that sexological experts started to pressure governments to loosen restrictions on abortion. In France, the Communists protested against the law banning birth control information and abortion in the 1920s, and in 1933 tried to get a bill through the National Assembly allowing abortions for medical or eugenic reasons. French politicians were still too obsessed with the fear of population decline to assent, but French people continued to practice abortion and birth control at high levels.[98] The British government also refused to legalize abortion.[99]

In Germany, both the left and the right became more interested in eugenics as a justification for birth control. Socialist eugenicists wanted to manage people's sex lives, and often disapproved of the more radical claims of sex reformers such as Magnus Hirschfeld. For instance, the German Social Democrat Karl Kautsky did not want to trust poor women with making the decision about whether to have more children; he wanted to have a committee of officials and doctors decide whether abortions would be allowed on a case-by-case basis.[100] These socialist eugenicists, who often preferred to use the term "social hygiene," argued that the environment, poor housing, low wages, and lack of medical care made people unfit to be parents, instead of, or as well as, a degenerate heredity. Although they certainly betrayed racist sentiments themselves, they denounced the more blatant racism and anti-semitism of the right-wing eugenicists. However, until 1933, the eugenic movement failed to push through any of its proposals in Germany, except for marriage counseling, as historian Edward Ross Dickinson observes.[101] In 1926 a coalition government in Weimar Germany, supported by the Democrat and socialist parties, passed a law reducing punishments for abortion, but this could also have been aimed at making it easier to obtain convictions, as Atina Grossmann has noted. A 1928 court case allowed abortions for medical necessity, but these were generally only available to wealthy women in private clinics.[102] Abortion was therefore still very restricted and conditional, and many women still had recourse to illegal abortions.

With this greater access to birth control, and more knowledge, did men and women begin to enjoy sex more or at least have more sex? Experts believed that many women remained sexually unsatisfied in the interwar years, as these changes percolated slowly through the generations. One French study from 1938 found that half of women were not sexually satisfied in marriage, while half regularly or sometimes experienced sexual satisfaction.[103] A German study found that, of the women surveyed, under 40 percent of women born between 1895 and 1907 had had orgasms at any time in their lives, while 78 percent of those born from 1907 to 1916 had.[104] Despite these changes, many British women, especially working-class wives in the 1920s, still found sex to be dangerous and frightening given poor health care, sexual ignorance and lack of birth control.[105] Among the working class living in the vast cities, young people and married couples alike could not experience much sexual pleasure because they lived in overcrowded dirty rooms with no privacy. Instead of the languid foreplay recommended by the sex reformers, young couples resorted to quick knee-tremblers standing up in alleys. Working-class families did not discuss sex, which they regarded as a shameful subject.[106]

This sexual misery dismayed socialist Wilhelm Reich. Like the artists discussed at the beginning of this chapter, Reich saw sexual desire as a form of energy, as electricity that needed to be expressed or it would explode into misery. He rejected the Freudian idea that people must sublimate some of their sexual energy for the good of society. During the 1920s, Reich began to insist that monogamy was unnatural, caused by capitalist sexual relations and the idea that women were property. Reich encouraged young people to have sex before marriage; he told young women to give up their inhibitions and express their desires, and he gave them the birth control technology they needed. In the late 1920s, he helped organize the mass Sex-Pol movement, joining the Communist youth and anarchists who protested against the "sexual disenfranchisement of the poor," and proclaimed sexual rights to be as vital as other human rights, and "sexual pleasure" as one of the "few pleasures left to oppressed people." Like Max Hodann and other sex reformers, Reich and his movement had to contend with the temptations of consumer culture; supposedly girls preferred going out dancing to listening to long speeches at Communist youth meetings.[107] And like other sex radicals, Reich thought that sexual pleasure would turn apathetic workers into revolutionaries and productive citizens. He wanted to manage sex as much as to free it. Reich, and other sex radicals such as Stella Browne, believed that the Soviet Union had solved many of the emotional and practical problems of sex by legalizing abortion and birth control. But were they deluded? Could a new state revolutionize sex?

Suggested reading

Bland, Lucy, and Laura Doan, eds. *Sexology in Culture*. London, 1998.

Cook, Hera. *The Long Sexual Revolution: English Women, Sex, and Contraception 1800–1975*. Oxford, 2004.

Dean, Carolyn. *The Frail Social Body: Pornography, Homosexuality, and Other Fantasies in Interwar France*. Berkeley, 2000.

Doan, Laura. *Fashioning Sapphism: The Origins of Modern English Lesbian Culture*. New York, 2001.

Fisher, Kate. *Birth Control, Sex, and Marriage in Britain, 1918–1960*. Oxford, 2006.

Grossmann, Atina. *Reforming Sex: the German Movement for Birth Control and Abortion Reform, 1920–1950*. New York, 1995.

Houlbrook, Matt. *Queer London: Perils and Pleasures in the Sexual Metropolis, 1918–1957*. Chicago, 2005.

McCormick, Richard W. *Gender and Sexuality in Weimar Modernity: Film, Literature and the "New Objectivity"*. New York, 2001.

Roberts, Mary Louise. *Civilization without Sexes*. Chicago, 1994.

Rydstrom, Jens. *Sinners and Citizens: Bestiality and Homosexuality in Sweden, 1880–1950*. Chicago, 2003.

Tamagne, Florence. *Histoire de l'Homosexualité en Europe*. Paris, 2000.

Usborne, Cornelie. *The Politics of the Body in Weimar Germany: Women's Reproductive Rights and Duties*. Ann Arbor, 1992.

Chapter 11

Sex and the state in the 1930s

Sweden, the Soviet Union, and Nazi Germany

It is not surprising that radicals believed that sex was a revolutionary, creative and "magnetic" force. For instance, Russian Bolshevik Alexandra Kollontai lauded sexual desire as the source of creativity, as "Winged Eros" which would inspire people to make love – and revolt against capitalism.[1] In 1913, the Swedish socialist Dr. Anton Nystrom proclaimed, "Without sexual sensations there would be no poetry and no art, as they all originate from that source."[2] Nystrom was a very handsome, heterosexual man who sympathized with homosexual rights and fought for birth control. But it might seem odd that a Nazi jurist, Rudolf Bechert, echoed Nystrom when he proclaimed, "Without sexual love no poetry, no painting, indeed no music!"[3]

How could the idea of sex as liberating turn out so differently in Sweden, the Soviet Union and Nazi Germany? In Sweden, the new social democratic state allowed birth control and some abortion by 1938. The state wanted its citizens to enjoy a happy, satisfying yet rational sex life, so that they would be good citizens and good consumers. But during the 1930s, the idea of sex as liberating energy took a sinister turn in the Soviet Union and Nazi Germany. Communist authorities advised Soviet citizens that they should satisfy their basic biological need for sex, but once fulfilled, they should use their energy to drive a tractor or turn a lathe.[4] For Nazi leaders, sex was a raw, explosive force, like violence, that should strengthen the fascist state. Hitler encouraged SS men to have sex to produce Aryan sons, just as he urged them to kill for the state. By the late 1930s, both totalitarian states celebrated the male-dominated family and prosecuted homosexuals and abortionists. But neither Stalin nor Hitler was resurrecting the traditional patriarchal family; instead, they wanted the state to manage the sex lives of its citizens.

Were the ideas of sex reform – that the creative power of sex could be channeled and managed to create good citizens – inevitably co-opted into totalitarian rule? Did sex reform lead inexorably to eugenics?[5] During the interwar period, many on both the left and the right believed in eugenics. Anton Nystrom himself asserted that birth control would prevent the large families that bred poverty and disease.[6] The Swedish welfare state also had its darker side when it mandated the sterilization of the unfit. But were the Swedish Social Democrats and other left-wing eugenicists setting a precedent for Nazi racial policies? After all, the Nazis began by sterilizing and castrating the "unfit"; then they proceeded to kill – or "euthanize" the mentally disabled – before they began the mass murder of Jews and others. But many other countries rejected eugenics. European states chose certain styles of managing sex because they chose democracy, communism or fascism. They managed sex like they managed their citizens in general.[7]

The economic crises of the interwar years shaped these choices. The Soviet Union embarked on a crash-course to turn a nation of peasants into an industrial economy, but at great cost in lives. In western Europe, the great crash of 1929 led to a severe depression, which caused unemployment ranging from over 10 percent in Britain to 40 percent in Germany. People were desperate for solutions, and in several countries, the left and the right were polarized. Sometimes authoritarian governments seemed to have the answer.

Nations were competing with each other for dominance, both on the continent and in the colonies, so race became an enormous issue.[8] But several European countries rejected negative eugenic tactics such as sterilization at home, while trying to intervene in sex and race in their colonies. During the early twentieth century, the British, Dutch, and French encouraged women and families to settle in the colonies. Imperialists believed that settlers would modernize the colonies and produce more profits for the mother country. They also hoped settlers would form white families, unlike the old colonial officials who kept native concubines and produced mixed-race children. At the same time, colonized people organized into militant nationalist movements. Imperialist governments became especially anxious about the discontented populations of mixed-race people. As a result, governments instructed their officials to renounce their native concubines and marry white women instead. Controls on marriage and interracial sex, therefore, were seen as preserving white purity and racial domination.[9]

Western imperialist countries also wanted to manage the sexual lives of their colonial subjects. They claimed they were "civilizing primitive people" but of course they wanted to exploit these populations as a labor resource. In Buganda, for instance, British imperialists blamed African "promiscuity" for syphilis, child marriage, and infant mortality, which they feared might weaken the "racial stock." In fact, labor exploitation, imperial wars, and famine were to blame for the declining population. And if colonial officials tried to ban child marriage or other sexual customs, they might offend the local native chiefs who helped them rule. In Kenya, nationalist movements against the British empire protested violently when government officials and missionaries tried to ban clitoridectomy.[10] Furthermore, large-scale intervention in colonial public health would have been very expensive.

The British and French states did not pass negative eugenic policies such as sterilization for their own citizens. In Britain, eugenicists certainly influenced the loosening of laws on birth control. They lobbied for sterilization of mentally disabled people, and some leftists and feminists believed that sterilization would help the poor as a means of birth control, and keep mentally disabled women out of institutions. But in 1935 Members of Parliament defeated sterilization of the "unfit" because the right to reproduce was a right of citizenship; ironically, social workers preferred to institutionalize the mentally disabled.[11] Both the Labour and Conservative Parties opposed overt government involvement in the management of sex, preferring to allow voluntary organizations to organize birth control and venereal disease clinics.[12] The French government, in contrast, was happy to manage marriage and procreation, but it was much more concerned with increasing population than in selecting who could breed. In the late 1930s, the right-wing Alliance Française restricted abortion even more. They demonized the modern woman for indulging in destructive individualism. Alliance Française politicians proclaimed that France could not afford birth control when they were competing with Italy and Germany; French women must produce soldiers. They denounced abortion as "treason against the state," and censored publications seen as attacking the family and "the race."[13] In Britain and France, moreover, consumer culture and civil society could be more powerful than state management of sex.

This chapter will therefore concentrate on Sweden, the Soviet Union, and Nazi Germany. Consumer culture influenced all these three countries but, in contrast, state management became more powerful. Yet they each followed different policies concerning the structure of the state and eugenics. Sweden was a democratic state that passed some eugenic policies; the Soviet Union rejected eugenics but adopted sexual authoritarianism; and Nazi Germany combined eugenics and fascist rule.

The Swedish experiment

At the turn of the century, life in Sweden was harsh, as many poor laborers fled the countryside for the cities – or America. In the countryside, peasants had long passed the long nights by having sex before marriage, and in the cities workers scorned the rituals of the church and engaged in free unions. Since before the First World War, the socialists in Sweden had demanded birth control to prevent poverty. In reaction, conservatives banned the sale and advertisement of birth control in 1910–11. But after the war, some socialist feminists, such as Elise Ottesen-Jensen, began to defy the law and spread birth control information.[14] By the 1920s, almost all Swedish couples tried to control their family size, but they still mainly relied on withdrawal, douching and illegal abortions. By 1930s when the Depression hit, people began to worry that the Swedish population would decline. The birth rate had decreased and people were very reluctant to have children, and in 1930, 44 percent of the population were single. Twenty percent of Swedish women reaching 50 years of age had never married.[15]

Swedes were divided on the solution to the problem. Some right-wing thinkers, and agrarian and nationalist parties feared that foreigners – Finns, Russians and Poles – would contaminate the pure Nordic race.[16] Conservative Christians blamed the decline in the birth rate on consumer society, on "movies, modern literature, and a rationalistic view of life," and, in neighboring Denmark, Copenhagen's mayor said that women would not have children because they would rather "own a car, take a summer trip, go to the movies and dance jazz."[17] The Social Democrats countered that working-class families simply could not afford to have children when husbands were out of work, and families lived crammed into one room and a kitchen. Unemployment benefits would increase population, they argued. Alva Myrdal, a feminist Social Democrat, explained that women did not have children because they could not afford to; after all, married women were fired from their jobs. But the feminists did not have much influence over the Social Democrats.

Alva Myrdal was acutely aware of these problems because her mother was an unhappy woman who feared the pregnancies that left her bed-ridden. Myrdal perceived her mother as sexually repressed, still entrapped in the Victorian world, and unable to support her daughter's education. Myrdal freed herself by escaping with her husband Gunnar Myrdal. She envisioned a different kind of consumerism: not her mother's fussy Victorian parlor with its frilly linens, but new modern houses with clean lines, lots of light, stream-lined functional furniture and colorful, simple glass ornaments and rugs. Part of the "Swedish Modern" movement, the young couple believed that Sweden must modernize using all the expertise of academics such as themselves. Today we best know this as the fashionable mid-century modern style of clean-lined teak furniture, but Swedish modern had a serious political message in the 1930s.

Alva and Gunnar Myrdal came up with a dramatic new solution to the population problem that reconciled left and right: Sweden should provide family allowances to encourage people to have children, but it would also allow birth control to enable couples to plan their families rationally. When their book, *Crisis in Population*, came out in 1934, it instantly caused a huge furor.[18] By presenting themselves as scientific experts in the book as well as in reports prepared for the government, the Myrdals tried to forestall moralistic objections and appeal to conservatives concerned about the birth rate.

Alva Myrdal believed it was a woman's duty to her country and to the human race to procreate – three children was the ideal. She identified birth control with the values of self-control and restraint. Gunnar Myrdal wrote that couples would become better workers, and they would be able to buy furniture and household goods, thus stimulating the Swedish economy.[19] But this was also a way of managing and rationalizing sex, of modernizing it, just as Sweden had been modernized. Alva Myrdal cautioned:

> [while] the sexual urge may carry great possibilities of happiness for individuals ... only if it is to a certain extent exercised according to mores within the society and according to moral norms upheld by the people. Sexual impulses, totally unrestrained by volitional forces, will, on the contrary, become judged by society as hostile to life and happiness.[20]

Some critics feared that rationalizing sex, just as technology had rationalized society, would diminish the natural sex drive and cause neuroses, but the Myrdals argued that this rationalization would enable people to have happier sex lives. The Myrdals blamed Sweden's declining birth rate on the traditional family. As Alva declared, "the family was exalted in literature in the form of idylls; but in the idylls there was the essential falsity of Puritanism." She advised the Swedish government to respect the practice of premarital sex between two young people who could not yet marry. It "violates the honor of the nation" to ban birth control, added Gunnar, when almost everyone used it. Marriage must be celebrated in a new way, not as a patriarchal partnership but as "human relations without inhibitions, the unconditional support of loyalty, the exploration of mutual confidences, and the ecstasy of complete sexual intimacy." Children should be raised with joy and freedom, not harshly repressed.[21]

For Alva Myrdal, women's rights were essential to the proper management of sex. Women had a right and duty to work and combine motherhood, she believed, and the state should help with daycare. Women also needed free time for leisure and recreation, to hike, to go to concerts and the theatre, to discuss intellectual ideas, both to keep their mental and physical health and to be good citizens. But even unmarried mothers should be helped by the state, even accepted, because they were raising children who should become healthy and productive members of society.

Alva Myrdal emphasized that she did not regard the poor who had large families as racially inferior, but disadvantaged by their environment, which the state could help fix. Inherited disabilities were distributed evenly through the different social strata, she argued.[22] The Myrdals repudiated fascist racial ideas and German-type population politics, but they also denounced the Communist idea that the family should be subordinate to the state. Gunnar Myrdal wrote that: "Families ought not to have children in obedience to the state but for their own happiness."[23]

Radios and newspapers covered the book extensively. Although moralists denounced the Myrdals' sexual frankness, and left-wingers repudiated the idea that people should be encouraged to have children, study groups formed all over the country to consider its ideas.[24] "To myrdal" became a euphemism for having sex, and people referred to "Myrdal couches" and "Myrdal sprouts" or offspring. The popular discussion around the Myrdals' proposals also created a consensus around their ideas. Ultimately, the Social Democrats and the agrarian parties, who were in a coalition government, compromised on a plan. For the agrarians, the government provided welfare benefits that would help large families; for the socialists, the government legalized birth control and mandated sex education in schools, and liberalized the abortion laws.[25]

Eugenics influenced the Swedish laws concerning abortion and sterilization. In 1938 the new law also allowed abortion for rape or incest, eugenic reasons – inherited physical or mental disorders – or to save the health of the mother. However, abortion was not allowed on social grounds – having too many children, or being unmarried – and it was totally controlled by the state board of physicians which gave permission to few women.[26] The new law also could be used to justify sterilizations of the Tattare, wandering groups stereotyped as dark, immoral and lazy, although physiologically they could not be distinguished from other Swedes.[27] Sterilization in Sweden was quite widespread, affecting one in 3,000 of the population. Between 1935 and 1940, 822 people – mostly women – were voluntarily sterilized, and between 1941 and 1948, 12,569 were sterilized.[28] Furthermore, the new laws strengthened the hand of experts over the lives of women. Social workers supervised every single mother. Women had to run the gauntlet of experts to get an abortion. And women could be coerced into sterilization. More than race, gender determined who was sterilized – the vast majority of the "mentally deficient" who were sterilized were women, often simply because they were seen as promiscuous.[29]

The Swedish welfare state was deeply flawed by its eugenic sterilization policy, which stigmatized certain types of women and some men as unfit for reproduction and citizenship. Nonetheless, it grew out of the democratic process.[30] The Swedish Social Democrats stemmed from the same socialist roots as Communists, but they insisted on democracy. In contrast, the Bolshevik Communists of the Soviet Union believed in the dictatorship of the proletariat, and wanted a revolution to gain total state control of the economy, politics – and private life.

Sex and the Soviet Union

Fathers ruled with an iron fist in traditional Russian families and, although this had started to change by the turn of the century, it was not fast enough for Russian bohemians and revolutionaries who wanted to destroy the anachronistic, hypocritical structures of tsarist Russia and build a free utopian society.[31] For instance, Alexandra Kollontai, the beautiful daughter of a tsarist general, was brought up in luxury, living in fine homes and dressed in silks. But she repudiated her family to marry a doctor. Accompanying him on his rounds, she saw workers living in squalor, their health ruined by factory work. Kollontai rebelled against her aristocratic upbringing to join the Communist cause; she left her husband, and fell deeply in love with a married fellow comrade. Once the revolution broke out in 1917, she wanted to help transform society. She genuinely believed that sexual rights, employment, and collective childcare would free women and help them make the revolution.

As dedicated Leninists, however, the Communist Bolsheviks believed they must have total power and that all morality must be subordinated to the cause. They wanted to subordinate personal feelings – including love, desire and family life – to the state and the revolution. Monogamy, many Bolsheviks thought, was bourgeois, and meant treating a sexual partner like property. Switching partners could "counteract the formation of coupling relationships that separated lovers from the collective," as historian Orlando Figes notes.[32] In reality, the Soviets instituted sex reform because Russia had degenerated into chaos during the years of revolution and war. The Bolsheviks took power during World War I, and soon faced civil war against the White Russians. Soldiers and revolutionaries rampaged through the countryside, women lost their husbands and lovers, families were separated, and many pregnant women could not find their partners to raise children. Thousands of abandoned children roamed through the countryside and huddled around railway stations, begging – and stealing. As a result, the Bolsheviks legalized abortion in 1920 to prevent fatherless children from being born into this chaos. Legal abortion also saved women's lives, because otherwise women would resort to dangerous substances, such as bleach, to bring on abortion themselves. The Bolsheviks did not think it was practical to abolish marriage, but they made it into a civil contract in 1918 and legalized divorce, leading to a flood of petitions as people sought to escape broken marriages. Women could claim alimony from their former husbands – or lovers – if they had a child.[33]

By the early 1920s, the Bolsheviks had triumphed, so they turned to the task of transforming society into their utopian Communist vision.[34] Alexandra Kollontai criticized the opportunistic, amoral promiscuity she saw among Bolshevik youth. In the early days of the revolution, she remembered, "new relationships were begun for the satisfaction of purely biological needs, both partners treating the affair as incidental and avoiding any commitment that might hinder their work for the revolution." This was wingless eros. But now, it was time for "Winged Eros," an intense spiritual passion that fueled the revolution, for the "person experiencing love acquires the inner qualities necessary to the builders of a new culture – sensitivity, responsiveness, and the desire to help others." She believed that the complex emotions of love glued together society and bound together the collective. Revolutionary love was different from the old, hypocritical bourgeois morality; people did not possess each other, so they could love several different people in different ways. Men respected women as equals, and inquired into their hearts with comradely sensitivity.[35] Some avant-garde Bolshevik writers celebrated sexual desire as a motor of the revolution. These ideas were popular among young people. A Bolshevik girl wrote that: "we want to stand with two firm legs on this wondrous Soviet land and under a May sky with a guy by our side, breathing in the 'scent of grass and flowers.'" But some Bolshevik young men demanded that women satisfy their sexual needs, denouncing them as shriveled up bourgeoises if they refused.

Indeed, the Soviets continued to institute sex reforms. They removed criminal sanctions from homosexuality in 1922 – although homosexuals continued to be harassed – and legalized contraception in 1923. But they were not motivated by Kollontai's spiritual vision, but by the ideology that everything must be subordinated to the task of suddenly transforming this peasant economy into an industrial powerhouse. The Communists built collective housing, childcare, and laundries, not to help women, but to destroy the private family and devote all energies to the collective. Bolshevik officials also subordinated sex to the revolutionary cause. As the functionary Professor Zalkind waspishly noted: "I am very much afraid that with the cult of winged Eros we will build aeroplanes very badly." Instead, he pronounced the "twelve commandments of sex": among them, avoid flirting and sexual deviance, abstain from sex until marriage, and have sex infrequently. Young people must devote their energies to the collective task of building Russia.[36] In a

1925 interview, Lenin said that "lack of restraint in one's sexual life is bourgeois." Trotsky advocated the idea that human beings could rationally control the body, that the body was like a machine.[37]

Yet in order to create a dynamic new economy, the Bolsheviks allowed some capitalist enterprise under the New Economic Policy (NEP) of 1923–27, permitting entrepreneurs to buy and sell commodities and start businesses, meeting consumer demand – and getting rich themselves. The NEP introduced consumer society and modern fashions to Russia. Magazines enticed young factory girls to wear low-cut flapper dresses, pretty shoes, sexy silk stockings and red lipstick.[38] "Boulevard Literature" spread dubious sexual advice, and quack doctors promised to cure venereal disease.[39] But guaranteed employment ended, throwing thousands – especially women – out of work. Many feared that the combination of demand – from the newly rich NEP-men – and supply – unemployed women workers – would increase prostitution. The Bolsheviks denounced the young woman who sold her sexual favors for lipstick or lingerie as a prostitute, the epitome of bourgeois decadence. Kollontai even called these women "doll parasites."[40] As one heroine of fiction proclaimed: "Now counterrevolution hides itself in pretty, painted up eyes and feminine tenderness. My husband got himself one of those, and I got a kick in the ass out the door."[41]

In response, Soviet doctors started a massive campaign of sex education. They advised young people against masturbation and premarital sex, which were seen as using up the energy that could be devoted to steering tractors or turning lathes. Such Bolsheviks hoped that, if sexual images could be cleansed from popular culture, women provided with work so they wouldn't prostitute themselves, and youth properly trained in hygiene, people simply wouldn't be bothered with sexual desire very much, and they could just briskly take care of their needs now and then. As historian Frances Bernstein notes, Soviet physicians admitted that marital sex was healthy, but only in moderation; unlike their western European counterparts, they did not give detailed instructions on how couples could achieve orgasm. And by 1931, even this rather ascetic sex advice literature disappeared, as the Soviet state demanded total focus on public production rather than private life.[42] Although contraception was legalized, doctors remained hesitant to prescribe because they wanted women to bear children for Russia – and in any case there was never enough rubber to make diaphragms and condoms.[43] Once the NEP was over after 1927, the Soviet state devoted its resources to collectivizing agriculture and building heavy industrial machines instead of consumer goods.

Above all, the Bolshevik sexual revolution had not fulfilled its utopian promise for women. Devoting so many resources to heavy industry, the Soviet state did not provide the promised childcare for women, nor did it challenge the sexual division of labor, as Wendy Goldman observes. Women could take different lovers, but, if they became pregnant, they either had to undergo painful abortions or bring up children without resources. The state allowed women to claim alimony from the fathers of their children, whether husbands or lovers, but men easily evaded these demands. A poor peasant or factory worker might not be able to pay for the children of a previous relationship as well as support his current family. Emotionally and practically, sexual revolution was a bad bargain for these women. The throes of collectivization also led to a decline in the birth rate and rise in child abandonment.[44]

The Bolsheviks also tried to reshape the traditional Islamic sexual customs of Azerbaijan, Georgia, and Uzbekistan, now part of the Soviet Union. The Bolsheviks denounced the *bachi*, dancing boys or male prostitutes, who were sold by their parents into brothels, as primitive remnants of the past; they retained the prohibition against sodomy in those areas.[45] In addition, they campaigned against child marriage and the veil. To prevent too-early marriage, the Soviets forced Uzbek girls to strip before doctors to determine if they had reached puberty. Not surprisingly, this deeply insulted some Muslims, who protested violently, and attacked the Uzbek women who had welcomed these changes. By the 1930s, the Soviets ended their effort to reform Islamic customs in Uzbekistan, allowing men to marry young girls and take multiple wives; they wanted to defuse Islamic resistance and unify the state. The Soviets also changed their policy toward the family and allowed Islamic men to return to their traditional patriarchy.[46]

By the mid-1930s, Stalin turned away from the Bolshevik denigration of the family, and began to celebrate Soviet families. Members of the Soviet elite – Communist functionaries, engineers, managers, and other professionals – were even allowed access to consumer goods, and dancing was actually encouraged. Elite wives could stay at home, and the state promised rewards for mothers of large families. Soviet officials denounced men who refused to pay alimony as "sexual hooligans." But the needs of the family were still subordinate to the state. Ordinary wives still had to work, but the state guaranteed their jobs if they became pregnant. Determined to build the Soviet Union into a massive industrial and military power, Stalin knew he needed workers, which meant large families and greater population. So his government severely restricted contraception and outlawed abortion in 1936. Divorce became more difficult. Stalin ruled through terror, controlling every aspect of social life with his secret police. The birth rate increased a little for two years, but soon dropped once again, as women had recourse to illegal abortions.[47]

Stalin intensified the Soviet policy of prying into people's private lives and arbitrarily arresting anyone who resisted – or who was denounced by neighbors. Soviet authorities wanted to distinguish between good, "normal" Soviet comrades who contributed work and children to the state, and the abnormal, who might criticize Stalin or refuse to work in state enterprises. The Soviets stigmatized prostitutes and homosexuals, for example, as "social anomalies" whose unregulated sexual desires threatened the cohesion of the state. Even ordinary citizens had to hold domestic passports and prove they worked at a legitimate job. The police roughly snatched prostitutes from the streets and threw them into labor camps. The Stalinist police also arrested men who continued to cruise on the street. As historian Dan Healey writes, paranoid Stalinist authorities thought that homosexual men were conspiring against the state at their private parties, where intellectuals and sailors might rub shoulders – as well as other body parts. Writer Maxim Gorky denounced homosexuality as "moral degradation and outright seduction of the nation's youth" which sapped Russia's productive energy. The police arrested poets and writers for homosexuality.[48] As critic Gregory Carleton observes, sex disappeared as a topic for discussion and debate in literature. Sex was about the "subjective individual ... it highlighted inquiry and speculation" which was "incompatible with Stalinist culture."[49] Alexandra Kollontai's vision of sexual liberation had been defeated.

Despite this sexual authoritarianism, and Stalin's pernicious anti-Semitism, in the interwar period the Soviet Union did not engage in widespread eugenic policies such as sterilization. To be sure, some Soviet scientists studied eugenics, especially in the 1920s. In 1935, geneticist Hermann Muller excitedly proposed to Stalin that the state artificially inseminate women using the sperm of brilliant men to produce 50,000 geniuses. Stalin rejected this idea; Muller had to flee the country and his fellow scientists were shot. Stalin believed that the Soviet state could reshape human material through revolutionizing the environment and society, rather than through genetics.[50]

The advent of sexual authoritarianism in Germany

By the early 1930s, 40 percent of Germans were out of work, standing disconsolately in long lines for bread, feeling despair – or panic. Political leaders on the left and right clashed in harsh rhetoric, advocating sharply different solutions to the crisis. Along with the larger issues of the economy, democracy, and race, sex became a part of the desperate debate over how to solve Germany's problems. The sex reformers and social democrats we met in the last chapter faced formidable enemies who blamed them for Germany's despair.

The roots of the crisis lay in the years immediately following the Great War. Veterans humiliated by Germany's defeat joined the Freikorps, or paramilitary groups, storming through the streets, attacking Communist rebels, and worshipping ultra-masculine violence. Writers such as Ernst Jünger celebrated the "ecstasy" of soldiers' violence, comparing it to the transcendence of lovers. Hitler appealed to their fears by depicting Jews as procurers, who would "poison the health of the national body" through syphilis. He denounced prostitution as "this Jewification of our spiritual life and mammonization of our mating instinct," thus tapping into people's alienation from fast-paced commodity capitalism.[51] Although the Nazis called themselves "national socialists," they actually hated Communists and socialist Social Democrats. Instead, they demanded an authoritarian, nationalist, racially-based state, and tried to mobilize ordinary people to get it. But in the 1920s, they were still a small minority.

So Hitler appealed to sexual and racial anxieties – as well as much larger political and economic issues – to drive a wedge between center parties and their socialist and democratic allies in the Weimar Republic. The Catholic Center Party, for instance, shared the fear of sexual modernity with the nationalists, although they were not as obsessed with anti-Semitism. The perceived decadence of Weimar culture – the bisexual cabarets, gay clubs, the demand for abortion – frightened many traditional conservatives. But the Catholic Center Party was opposed to eugenics, a central plank in the Nazi party. The Nazis claimed that the "unfit," the mentally or physically disabled, were wasting the nation's resources on welfare, and they also demanded that Germans born of African fathers after the occupation of the Rhine be sterilized so that they would not pollute the nation's blood.[52] In order to stir up support for their cause, the Nazis falsely accused Jews of causing the world financial crisis and unemployment, depicting Jews as wicked capitalists who raped and tortured Aryan women.[53] The Social Democrats and the Communists were too divided to unite against them, and the traditional conservatives were so frightened at the economic and political crisis that Hitler was able to take power.

Immediately on taking power, Hitler appealed to the center and the right by crushing the sex reform movement, closing gay bars and birth control clinics, and disbanding feminist groups. On May 6, 1933, the Nazis directed a gang to trash Magnus Hirschfeld's famous Institute for Sexual Research. They seized his exhibitions, photographs, and books about sexual variety, threw them into the public square, and burned them. The Nazis stigmatized sex reform as a Jewish movement.[54] Hitler projected discomfort about sexual pleasure onto the hated figures of the Jew, the New Woman, and the homosexual, viciously attacking them for polluting Aryanism.

But by this time, thousands of German people had read explicit marriage manuals and learned new pleasures, engaged in sex before marriage and wanted to control the size of their families. They enjoyed the nudist magazines and clubs, which promised healthy eroticism. So the Nazis also exploited sexual modernity itself: they wanted to liberate sex from tradition, and they intended to manage sex in the service of the state. As historian Dagmar Herzog has emphasized, many Nazis were pro-sex. The Nazis regarded the sexual drive as natural, creative, and beneficial, as long as it was directed toward male pleasure and Aryan procreation. To reconcile sexual modernity with hatred for Jews and the Weimar left, the Nazis basically declared that Aryan sex was good, while Jewish, Communist and homosexual sex was evil. For instance, the magazine *Die Schwarze Korps* (The Black Corps) celebrated sex with nude photographs of beautiful women, while ridiculing Christian prohibitions against sex and advocating the killing of the disabled.[55] The Nazis denounced foreign, sexy, "vampish" fashions of blood-red lipstick and pale faces, and celebrated blond, "natural", Aryan beauty. At the same time, the Nazis had to ensure that Germans continued to enjoy consumer culture, as long as it was supposedly purified of French fashion influence. German women thus bought make-up and styles to appear sexy in a natural way.[56] The Nazis tapped into the wider Weimar ideas of "body culture" – popular on both the left and right – which asserted that the body must be free, natural, and healthy, expressed through eurhythmic dancing, exercised through calisthenics, exposed to the fresh air at smoke-free nudist camps, nourished with health food – and pleasured by sex. The strong, Aryan body, Nazis believed, displayed the strength of the state, and banal Nazi art featured nude female Amazons and bare-breasted nursing mothers.[57] The Nazis appropriated the idea of sexual pleasure as a transcendent, creative life-force from the radical sex reformers of the early twentieth century: as we have seen, the Nazi jurist Rudolf Bechert echoed Dr. Anton Nystrom's earlier claim that sex was the origin of art and music. Such an idea derived from the Darwinian notion of sex as essential to the struggle for survival and the evolution of the fittest.

Hitler believed that the Nazi elite could indulge in whatever sexual adventures they wanted, freed from the constraints of bourgeois morality. But the Nazis focused on the sexual pleasure of heterosexual men. While some Nazi sex reformers acknowledged the female orgasm, others advised men to disregard women's needs and seize their own pleasure.[58] One right-wing woman, Dr. Mathilde Ludendorff, the wife of General Erich Ludendorff, believed that Aryan women were not sexually frigid; rather, they had smaller clitorises because this meant they were more evolved than crude non-Western or Southern women; their vaginas lacked sensitivity so they would be able to give birth more easily. One Nazi party activist envisioned vegetarian, polygamous communes where a hundred men could choose from a thousand women for their sexual pleasure, with marriage lasting no more than three months to spread men's sexual energy around.[59] Less radically, Dr. Wollenweber proclaimed, "It is a good thing when a young German man looks his beautiful German girlfriend in the eyes and then makes love to her" – what makes it bad is when there are contraceptives involved.[60]

Fathers of illegitimate children gained more custody rights, but Hitler blocked a proposal to allow the SS to take in illegitimate children against the mother's will. Instead, the Nazis provided single mothers with more welfare benefits in order to deter them from abortion, and to encourage them to give a child to Hitler. They established Lebensborn homes, or maternity hospitals, where SS officers could put their wives – or mistresses – to give birth in safe and comfortable surroundings. Although these homes were rumored to be brothels where SS men could impregnate young girls, there is no evidence of that. However, girls in the various Nazi youth groups were encouraged to bear a child out of wedlock for the cause. If their parents reacted with horror, they could threaten to denounce them to the Reich.[61]

For these Nazis, men needed a sexual outlet, whether within marriage or outside it. Men's virile sexual desires would give them energy for war, and they should demand sexual satisfaction by dominating and exploiting others. The Nazis set up military brothels and brothels in concentration camps to serve soldiers, but also to keep the lines of race clear, so that German soldiers would have sex only with German women. As one woman lamented, "It was nothing personal, one felt like a robot. They did not take notice of us, we were the lowest of the low … Everything was so mechanical and indifferent."[62]

At the same time, Nazis strengthened fathers' authority – as long as they recognized that the state took priority. Nazi films negatively portrayed "New Women" as selfish and encouraged women to assent to their father's choice of marriage partners and give up their freedom. Families could send their daughters to institutions if they were seen as promiscuous – institutions where they might be sterilized or even euthanized as "unfit" and mentally disabled.[63] While men's adventures were treated lightly, women's infidelity was punished.[64]

Above all, the Nazis wanted to control sex and reproduction for racial ends. To preserve the Aryan race, so-called, the Nazis wanted to force Aryan women to have children. Upon seizing power, they immediately restricted birth control information and distribution, repealed the medical necessity clause for abortion, and arrested suspected abortionists and their clients. But the Nazis were not against birth control or abortion because they believed either that having sex for pleasure was immoral, or that life was sacred.[65] Instead, they wanted to prevent "contamination" by the offspring of non-Aryans – and eventually to kill those who were seen as unfit. But they started slowly, to soften up public opinion against the mentally and physically disabled. After all, sterilization had been discussed for years, although the Catholic parties had blocked it. With their new dictatorial powers, in 1933 the Nazis passed a law allowing involuntarily sterilization for the deaf, blind, and mentally ill or disabled. Even alcoholic, poor men who did not support their families could be sterilized as unfit.[66] The Nazis slowly spread propaganda against the disabled in order to justify more and more coercive measures. In 1935, the Nazis re-legalized certain forms of abortion to force the termination of "unfit" pregnancies among prostitutes, the promiscuous, mentally disabled, foreign slave workers, or German women impregnated by Jewish or foreign slave worker men.[67] Eventually, these policies led to euthanasia, or killing, of thousands of people institutionalized as mentally or physically unfit.

In 1935, the Nazis forbade sex and intermarriage between Jews and Aryans, depicting Aryan women as needing protection from lascivious Jews, lest they become corrupted and hypersexual. Fascist writers believed that "a single act of intercourse between a Jew and an Aryan woman is enough to poison her blood forever."[68] Jewish women were seen as racially promiscuous and dangerously seductive. During the war, the Nazis also feared that German women, lonely and sexually frustrated with husbands at the front, might have sexual relationships with French or Polish workers and prisoners of war, and punished such affairs harshly.[69]

Many Nazis and fellow-travellers of the regime, especially the churches, of course, were quite uncomfortable with Nazi sexual indulgence. Parents objected to youth groups that seemed to encourage premarital sex, and some Nazi doctors advised premarital chastity. Hitler and his followers wanted to denigrate the few Christian groups that opposed his policies, so he denounced Christian morality as bourgeois and hypocritical, because people got married for reasons of property and status, instead of race.[70] Under Nazi rule, he proclaimed, "the robust children of a natural emotion will replace the miserable creatures of financial expediency."[71] Hitler wanted to harness this "natural emotion" for the service of the state and the Aryan "race." Members of the SS blamed "oriental Christians" for suppressing "healthy" sexual attitudes. In this case, "oriental" was probably a euphemism for Jewish. Nazi elements also denounced Christian ministers who regarded women as sinners and seductresses.

As historian Julia Roos notes, "Himmler resented the church's 'moralistic' stance on extramarital sex, which he believed was conducive to the spread of male homosexual relations." In 1937, Himmler declared to SS commanders, "One cannot prevent the entire youth from drifting toward homosexuality if at the same time one blocks all the alternatives. This is madness."[72] The Nazis believed that they needed to provide women for German men to deter them from homosexuality.

When historians began looking at the Nazi persecution of homosexuals, they sometimes equated it with the genocide of the Jews. However, more recently historians have painted a more complex picture: the Nazis did persecute homosexuals but they lauded male bonding and thought that some men who had sex with men could be redeemed. Ernst Röhm, the stormtrooper commander, had long been notorious for his sexual relationships with men. Drawing on the ideology of the Männerbund movement of the 1920s, Röhm had celebrated virile male bonding and claimed his right to find pleasure where he wanted. Hitler was well aware of Röhm's tendencies and did not really care about them. But on taking power in 1933, he needed to appeal to conservative Catholic and Protestant voters – and defuse Röhm's anti-capitalist rhetoric. Furthermore, in 1932 the Social Democrat and Communist press had widely publicized Röhm's predilections, trying to discredit the Nazis as perverse. As a result, Hitler ordered Röhm's murder. The Nazis stirred up a moral panic about homosexuality, denouncing it "as a threat to the Volk community, since homosexuals exhibit a tendency to form cliques, seduce the young, and, above all, undermine the natural will to life by propagating an aversion to marriage and the family."[73] They ordered the forcible castration of men accused of sex crimes, whether it be molesting children, or having a homosexual relationship.[74] In 1935, the Nazis strengthened the notorious paragraph 175, which had punished "unnatural" intercourse between men, extending it to cover any sexual contact between men. The Nazis used hatred of homosexuality for political purposes. Just as Jews were regarded as contaminating, homosexuals were described as "filth" who needed to be "cleansed."[75] However, the Nazis did not necessarily believe in homosexuals as a distinct racial type. Rather, they thought that homosexuality was like a contagious disease that could be cured. The military and the SS, needing manpower, were more likely than Himmler to believe that men who had sex with other men only once or twice could be reclaimed. They were determined that the state must steer the "natural" reproductive and sexual instinct into its "proper channel." Until 1936 punishments could still be quite minimal – a few months in prison – if a man had been discreet and was middle-class. After 1936, punishments intensified, but Harry Oosterhuis estimates that only about 10–30 percent of those convicted for homosexuality were sent to the camps, but that still represented from 5,000 to 15,000 men, many of whom died there.[76]

The ambiguities of Nazi attitudes toward sex and women can also be seen in their policies toward lesbians. Once the Nazis had completely defeated feminism, they did not regard lesbians as much of a threat. In 1935, an effort to criminalize lesbianism was rejected because it would be too difficult to distinguish between lesbians and innocent female friends. The Nazis also believed that lesbianism could be a temporary state and that such women could be reclaimed for marriage. However, they also harassed lesbians. The lesbian subculture of bars, magazines and clubs disappeared, and lesbians had to adopt a protective camouflage of more feminine clothing and even false marriages. More visible lesbians could be sent to the concentration camps as "asocial" when Communism or other forms of dissidence brought them to the attention of authorities, or when nosy neighbors denounced them.[77]

The Nazis were able to draw on widespread popular support for their campaigns against homosexuality and interracial sex. In both Germany and Austria, ordinary people denounced men who seemed to fit the homosexual "type" – uninterested in women, quiet, or effeminate. Neighbors harassed and reported mixed couples to the police, although only men could be prosecuted for this offence.[78] The Nazis encouraged female social workers to select for sterilization unwed mothers and others seen as unfit; for the most part, they went along.[79]

Yet the Nazis only partially succeeded in managing the sex lives of German citizens. Restricting contraception and abortion briefly raised the birth rate a little in the 1930s, but it soon fell back to the low level of the 1920s. Frustrated, Dr. Wollenweber blamed the rubber industry, which he blamed for trying to commit "Völkermord" with condoms.[80] An American-style commercial popular entertainment culture persisted, and some teenagers turned the Nazi encouragement to have children out of wedlock for the state into an invitation to sex with multiple partners in teenage clubs and gangs, threatening to denounce their parents if they protested. A few gay clubs discreetly carried on in Berlin, and some homosexual men survived by entering into heterosexual marriages.[81] The churches often protested against Nazi efforts to institutionalize brothels and allow sex outside of marriage, but they eventually bowed to Nazi pressure.

Yet the Nazi effort to shape sexual desire in the service of the state was much more successful than any other example of sex management. They did not continue the efforts of interwar sex reformers, who belonged to the social democratic tradition. The Nazis rejected ideas of citizenship and instead used the state to forcibly implement their sinister ideas, as historian Edward Ross Dickinson points out.[82] By inciting hatred against Jews and homosexuals, yet celebrating Aryan sexual desire, the Nazis assuaged the anxieties of ordinary people confused yet attracted by sexual modernity. Of course, their most vile hatred and lethal government apparatus were focused on exterminating the Jews, resulting in the deaths of over six million. But by linking anxieties about sexual modernity with anti-Semitism, moral panics, the fear that sexual desire could blur racial boundaries and social hierarchies, the Nazis appealed to people's emotions and intensified anti-Semitism. By manipulating ideas of pollution and pleasure, the Nazis used sex in the service of the wider murderous goals of the Holocaust.

Conclusion

In this chapter, we have seen three versions of the modern management of sex. In Sweden, the Myrdals helped to set up a welfare state which tried to create productive citizens by enabling what they saw as sexual health and happiness, yet also rationalizing reproduction. Most Swedes were defined as free individuals with the rights to control their reproduction, but women's choices were limited, and the so-called unfit might be coercively sterilized. The Soviets also started off with the goal of freeing its citizens from the oppression of traditional bourgeois morality, but what happened was sexual alienation and female vulnerability. By default, abortion became a widespread means of birth control. Under the Soviet Union, the interests of the state overrode the interests of the individual, and when the state needed a large population it prohibited birth control and abortion. The Nazis turned the eugenic ideas so widespread among both left and right to murderous extremes, for coercive sterilization and forced abortions – and the prohibition of abortion – were the first steps on the way to the Holocaust; but they also exploited the idea of sexual desire as creative – as long as it served the state.

The influence of eugenics can only partially explain these differences, for the Soviet Union became authoritarian without it. Overall, states instituted sexual authoritarianism because they rejected the democratic process and persuaded, coerced, or even forced their subjects to comply. In democratic states – or even in the Soviet Union before Stalin – sex reform movements did not simply manage people: they responded to the changing needs and desires of ordinary people. The Swedish state had to recognize that working-class people could not be ordered to have more children or marry – premarital sex and birth control were already ingrained habits. Weimar politicians rejected sterilization, and ordinary Germans refused eugenic counseling, until the Nazis crushed representative government and the mass movements.

When the Allies finally defeated the Nazis and tried to rebuild, would the task of sex reform be taken up once again? How could sexual citizenship be reconstructed?

Suggested reading

Adams, Mark B. *The Wellborn Science: Eugenics in Germany, France, Brazil, and Russia*. New York, 1990.

Allen, Ann Taylor. *Feminism and Motherhood in Western Europe 1890–1970*. New York, 2005.

Attwood, Lynne. *Creating the New Soviet Woman: Women's Magazines as Engineers of Female Identity, 1922–53*, University of Birmingham, 1999.

Bleuel, Hans Peter. *Strength through Joy: Sex and Society in Nazi Germany*. Translated by J. Maxell Brownjohn. London, 1973.

Bock, Gisela. "Racism and Sexism in Nazi Germany: Compulsory Sterilization and the State." *Signs* 8, no. 3 (1983): 400–21.

Broberg, Gunnar, and Roll-Hansen, Nils. *Eugenics and the Welfare State: Sterilization Policy in Denmark, Sweden, Norway, and Finland*. East Lansing: Michigan State University Press, 1996.

Carleton, Gregory. *Sexual Revolution in Bolshevik Russia*. Pittsburgh, 2005.

Dickinson, Edward Ross. "Biopolitics, Fascism, Democracy: some Reflections on Our Discourse about 'Modernity'." *Central European History* 37, no. 1 (2004): 1–48.

Giles, Geoffrey J. "Legislating Homophobia in the Third Reich: The Radicalization of Prosecution Against Homosexuality by the Legal Profession." *German History* 23, no. 3 (2005): 339–54.

Goldman, Wendy Z. *Women, the State and Revolution: Soviet Family Policy and Social Life, 1917–1936*. Cambridge, UK, 1993.

Healey, Dan. *Homosexual Desire in Revolutionary Russia: The Regulation of Sexual and Gender Dissent*. Chicago, 2001.

Heineman, Elizabeth. "Sexuality and Nazism: The Doubly Unspeakable?" *Journal of the History of Sexuality* 11, no. 1/2 (2002): 22–66.

Herzog, Dagmar. *Sex After Fascism: Memory and Morality in Twentieth Century Germany*. Princeton, 2005.

Kälvemark, Ann-Sofie. *More Children of Better Quality? Aspects of Swedish population policy in the 1930s*. Stockholm, Sweden, 1980.

Koonz, Claudia. *The Nazi Conscience*. Cambridge, MA, 2003.

Naiman, Eric. *Sex in Public: The Incarnation of Early Soviet Ideology*. Princeton, 1997.

Northrop, Douglas. *Veiled Empire: Gender and Power in Stalinist Central Asia*. Ithaca, 2004.

Chapter 12

The reconstruction of desire and sexual consumerism in postwar Europe

In the novel *Emmanuelle*, men seduce the heroine on airplanes, women make love to her in the jungle, and Thai men penetrate her in orgies. But this familiar soft-core romp follows in the venerable tradition of French philosophical pornography; the author decorates her steamy prose with quotes from Mallarmé, and calls for a sexual utopia to liberate female sexual pleasure. The author called herself Emmanuelle Arsan, but she was really Marayat Rollet-Andriane, the Eurasian wife of a French diplomat. In 1959, the novel had to be published clandestinely, because the Gaullist government prosecuted pornography, fearing it would contaminate the youth. By 1968 the sexual revolution had arrived and the book was finally published openly.[1]

In 1968, Pope Paul VI expressed his horror at sexual liberation and the loosening of laws on birth control and abortion in his encyclical, *Humanae Vitae*. The Pope asserted that marriage was "the wise institution of the Creator to realize in mankind His design of love." Omitting the old notion that sexual desire was evil, the Pope proclaimed that marital sex is: "of the senses and of the spirit at the same time." The Pope insisted that:

> It is not, then, a simple transport of instinct and sentiment, but also, and principally, an *act* of the *free will*, intended to endure and to grow by means of the joys and sorrows of daily life, in such a way that husband and wife become one only heart and one only soul, and together attain their human perfection.[2]

In a stinging response to the Pope, Emmanuelle Arsan rejected his insistence on marriage. Instead, she celebrated an orgiastic vision of sex as: "the return of love to the sources that brought it into being; those of creative intelligence, a freedom that is proud and sure of itself, of artistic imagination and of reason."[3] Unlike the Pope, Arsan imagined that human will could transcend nature with birth control and other technologies. By 1969, Arsan had moved from the avant-garde fringes to join the youth calling for a liberation of all the senses. By 1974, as French censorship vanished, the novel was made into a soft-core porn film, which was wildly popular, and spawned many increasingly trashy offshoots.

Both the Pope and Arsan shared a vision that sexual desire could be a path to a higher, mystical vision of human transcendence – whether in marriage or in an orgy. But postwar European society also generated quite different understandings of sexual desire; increasingly, consumerism defined the sexual self. Could the vision of sexual liberation survive sexual consumerism? Would the Pope or other Christians retain any influence over sexual morality?

Sexual citizenship and postwar boundaries

As Europeans fought against Nazism, secular and spiritual leaders envisioned marriage as a foundation for a society opposed to totalitarianism. Edward Fyfe Griffith, a Jungian Christian psychoanalyst and writer of sex manuals, believed that by "uniting the sex and spiritual life of man into a creative activity. ... We can rebuild broken populations, decrease excess in childbirth, extend the duration of life and encourage the production of only those who are fit and worthy of world citizenship." He defined sexual citizenship as based on mutual responsibility; citizens should lead responsible lives, while the welfare state should support the family, and thus, in turn, protect the state itself.[4]

Many churches, along with peace and social justice activists, tried to find a third way between communism and capitalism; as historian Dagmar Herzog observes, they wanted to repudiate the excesses of consumer society and its perceived lack of authenticity, to find a deeper meaning in life.[5] Indeed, churches were concerned that consumer goods such as fashion and makeup simply hid this true spiritual self. British Christian marriage counselors and clerics had begun to celebrate marital sex as spiritual in the interwar period. In 1930, the Archbishop of Canterbury declared: "We want to liberate the sex impulse from the impression that it is always to be surrounded by negative warnings and restraints, and to place it in its rightful place among the great creative and formative things." Dr. Helena Wright even portrayed the spiritual joys of orgasm in lofty terms: "It is as if there were, hidden among the sensations of the body, a spiritual counterpart, a pleasure of the soul, only attained for a few seconds, bringing with it a dazzling glimpse of the Unity which underlies all nature." In 1960, the influential sex adviser Kenneth Walker wrote that sexual desire has "in its higher manifestations ... close affinities with the creative impulse of the artists and with the religious man's search for the divine."[6]

In postwar Germany, leaders of the Catholic youth movement admonished teenagers "to regard marriage as something sacred ... the crown of life." German Catholic theologian Prof. A.M. Hoffman proclaimed that "joyous completion and fulfillment is an intrinsic purpose of marital union willed by God. It has its natural source in the sexual differences of the couple; it is of divine origin." Theologians repudiated the idea that sexual desire embodied original sin. Instead, they emphasized man's disobedience and lack of control as sinful. German Catholic theologian Dr. R. Geis argued that: "Sexual desire as such is not the consequence of sin, but the fever of lust is, and the seductive fascination of desire."[7]

This vision of sexual citizenship and spiritual marriage was resolutely heterosexual and male-dominated. As historian Robert Moeller observes, German Christian Democratic politicians promoted traditional marriage as the center of society, denouncing women who used birth control and went out to work.[8] Even the British anarchist Alex Comfort, who later became famous for writing *The Joy of Sex*, defined normal sex as a permanent relationship between a man and a woman for the purpose of love and procreation.[9] Fifties British Family Planning Association manuals admonished wives to be proper citizens and proper Christians by saying yes to sex with their husbands.[10]

While the family was seen as a bulwark against communism, Communist countries focused policy toward sex and reproduction toward the needs of the state. Postwar East Germany differed somewhat from its western counterpart by celebrating its "healthy" attitude that sexual pleasure was a normal, necessary part of life. As historian Ingrid Sharp observes, "Sexual fulfillment was a right and a duty for all citizens as one aspect of the 'fully developed Socialist personality'."[11] But Communist moralists still discouraged masturbation and preferred sex to take place in marriage. In an effort to rebuild the population of the Soviet Union after the losses of World War II, the government instructed doctors to report women who sought abortions. In East Germany, legal abortions were not performed from 1950–1965 except in case of severe danger to the women's physical or mental health, rape, or if the pregnant woman was under 16.[12] The most dramatic example of state control over women's fertility came in Romania, where state concern about population led it to ban all abortion and birth control, and women were strictly monitored for pregnancies.[13]

East German Communists denounced homosexuals as capitalist degenerates who distracted the working class from a healthy sex life and procreation.[14] The West German state intensified the prosecution of homosexuals under Paragraph 175, imprisoning more men than had the Nazis.[15] In the west, homosexuality was linked to Communism. An editorial in *The Scotsman* in 1957 warned that:

> Homosexuals, by the nature of their disability, owe their primary allegiance to the homosexual group before any other authority or loyalty in their lives. Hence the connection between perversion and subversion, which is one of world Communism's greatest strengths in this country.[16]

In Sweden in the 1950s "Homosexuality was depicted as a mortal threat to the very core of society ... a public enemy and a threat to the security of the nation."[17] Left-wingers also denounced homosexuality. As late as 1960, a French leftist successfully passed a law proclaiming that the government must classify homosexuality as "'A social scourge' which the welfare state must tackle like tuberculosis, alcoholism, and prostitution."[18] After the Burgess–Maclean homosexual spy case in Britain in the 1950s, the police intensified their prosecution of homosexuals and started prying into the lives of prominent men, such as journalists and intellectuals, arresting them for homosexual behavior even in private.[19]

Yet the British Wolfenden commission of 1954, set up by the government in the wake of the spy case, recommended decriminalization of consenting acts in private. However, it was very influenced by the increasingly prevalent psychiatric interpretation of homosexuality as amenable to treatment. Focusing on acts rather than identities, the commissioners believed that: "The majority of those who are caught in or who indulge in homosexual acts are bisexual." They were very concerned to punish those "predatory" homosexuals who might "infect" young men who could go either way. They also believed that men who had committed homosexual acts might learn to "adjust" to society and control their behavior – perhaps even with the help of estrogen to mute the sex drive, which had been widely if covertly prescribed in Scotland.[20] The Catholic theologian Dr. A. Niedermayer feared that if a young man had sex with another man, even if it was just because he had no other sexual outlet, his orientation might permanently change to homosexuality.[21] Yet some lesbians and homosexual men began to negotiate with psychiatric and religious authorities to argue that they were respectable and well adjusted, and deserved toleration, although in doing so they sometimes repudiated the "pansies" and men who sought rough trade, who did not fit into the respectable image.[22]

Sex advisers mainly concentrated on heterosexuality and female surrender in marriage. Freudian ideas of vaginal orgasm first appeared in popular sex manuals in 1938, and became much more prominent from the end of the 1940s. Griffith, whose works were translated into Swedish, Spanish and German, had discussed clitoral stimulation in his works of the 1940s, but later promoted the superiority of the vaginal orgasm. He advised that: "The woman must relax and flow emotionally towards the husband to achieve a satisfactory orgasm." For Griffith, a clitoral orgasm represented "'What can I get for myself' and not 'what can I give?' which is the nature of the vaginal orgasm. Clitoral values represent self-seeking values rather than the wider feminine values of receptivity and creativity."[23] Griffith was active in the National Marriage Guidance Council and influenced counselors to advise wives to acquiesce to their husband's sexual wishes. These counselors still encountered wives who thought sex was sinful. They encouraged them to experience sexual pleasure, not by asserting their own needs, but by accepting their feminine roles in a happy partnership and meeting their husbands' sexual demands.[24]

Yet many other sex advisors, such as Eustace Chesser – otherwise much influenced by popular psychoanalysis, Kenneth Walker, Rennie Macandrew, and Ernest Parkinson Smith, did not mention the idea of the vaginal orgasm. Based in the commercial marketplace, they tended to plagiarize the prewar bestseller *Ideal Marriage*, by van de Velde, who encouraged foreplay and clitoral stimulation.[25] They celebrated a mutual ideal of marital pleasure predicated on a husband's skill.

Some Catholic writers responded to the new emphasis on female sexual pleasure by trying to reconcile it with traditional Catholic teachings about natural sex for procreation. They advised that devout husbands could stimulate their wives to orgasm with their hands as long as they were open to the possibility of procreation, and if wives came to orgasm before their husbands. But a wife could not be stimulated after her husband came, because that would make non-procreative sex an end in itself.[26] The "rhythm method" of calibrating a safe period had been accepted by the Pope since 1930, when he adjudged that couples could have sex without intending to procreate during the safe period. But the delicate balance of seeking sexual pleasure while restraining penetration for fear of procreation caused agonies for the Catholic laity. According to one British correspondent, "Joan," Catholic wives forced themselves to act like "ice" with their husbands because they feared to bring children into a world of poverty and imminent nuclear destruction. Even if the husband engaged in permissible caresses, their wives might experience "a sick aching weariness ... from too much 'pawing' and an unsatisfied wife might become a 'nervous wreck.'"[27]

Many churchgoers also found that religious advice to young people about sex before marriage no longer made sense. Religiously oriented advisers told young people that they should not feel guilty about their sexual desires, and that sex was not a bad thing in itself. But, using circular logic, they advised against premarital sex because it would lead to guilt feelings, and hence neurosis.[28] Many young men, observes historian Mark Ruff, were: "disillusioned by the fact that marriage frequently failed to meet the standards of excellence and blessedness that the church had promised."[29] In Britain, the religious practices of parents in the 1960s did not influence whether teenagers had premarital sex or not, although the churchgoing of teenagers themselves had a slight effect.[30]

Through the 1950s and 1960s, premarital sex was becoming widely accepted among young people. The American custom of petting became more common, and many even "went all the way." One 1956 survey found that 43 percent of British married women born between 1924–34 had had sex before marriage.[31] In Germany, another survey found that one third of brides had been pregnant at their weddings in the 1950s.[32] By 1967, the vast majority of all Swedes and almost half of the very religious Swedes accepted premarital sex: "One child in 7 in Sweden was born outside of wedlock."[33] People still disapproved of promiscuous sex, however. What appeared to be Scandinavian permissiveness was quite controlled; for instance, in contrast with American teenagers, those Danish teenagers who had sex began to do so later, at around age 19, and were more monogamous.[34]

In response, a few Christian commentators began to suggest that premarital sex might be acceptable in certain circumstances as part of a larger effort to reformulate the faith in the age of the "death of God." In 1966 the British Council of Churches published a report in which a minority of the committee members expressed the view that: "We should leave the individual parties free to decide whether a personal relationship has achieved the intimacy and tenderness of which sexual intercourse is the appropriate expression."[35] In Sweden, Ingmar Strom proposed a confirmation text that asked: "How much would remain of art, literature and music if we ignored all that had, in any way, to do with eroticism?"[36] But in both Britain and Sweden, church authorities slapped down these reformers. Even in liberal Sweden, the Protestant bishops still condemned premarital sex and divorce. But a woman wrote to a Stockholm newspaper asking what single or divorced people should do with their "sexual power": "Can we phone the church and have our sexual power turned off in the same way that we call the electric company when we move?"[37] Historian Callum Brown has argued that the churches' failure to respond to women's changing lives and sexual expectations turned many women away from religion during the 1960s, and started the precipitous decline of Christianity in Europe.[38] Indeed, by 1967 only one third of Swedish young people thought God played a role in their lives, compared to 50 percent of the older generation.[39]

Instead of idealizing marital sexual pleasure as spiritual, some commentators celebrated recreational sex as a temporary pleasure shared by two people that did not have to lead to a permanent relationship. In Britain, the prolific sex manual writer Eustace Chesser, always a barometer of changing attitudes, wrote: "I am not suggesting that we should depersonalize sex but that the false glamour and pseudomystery be stripped off. A physical relationship can be tender and affectionate without the qualities of depth and permanence that are found in a fuller loving relationship."[40] The sociologist Michael Schofield wrote: "if a person chooses to be promiscuous, it often helps a person to develop rewarding mutual relationships and to discover great depths in friends and in oneself."[41] In Sweden, sociologists found that young people had sex out of friendship.[42] Swedish sex education responded to these changes. For instance, Lis Aklund's 1966 advice book *The Way to Maturity* judged a relationship by whether a partner unfolds "in a relationship with me to be a more open, free, and happy person, or does he or she become repressed, unhappy, frightened and insecure."[43]

For this relaxed attitude to spread, contraception was necessary, but in the 1960s the danger of pregnancy still inhibited sexual freedom. Although the pill had been invented, doctors often refused to prescribe it for unmarried women.[44] Sheila Rowbotham recalled that she believed in having sex when she wanted to, but the fear of pregnancy often frustrated her desires. Some young men refused to use condoms, because they seem too inhibiting and artificial, and a male lover accused her of being frigid because she was so afraid of pregnancy.[45] In Britain, single women had to claim they were married or just about to be married to get birth control from family planning clinics in the 1960s.

Women found it difficult to obtain abortions. Even in Sweden, where abortion was legal for sociomedical reasons, in the 1950s a woman had to be " assessed and examined by an obstetrician, a psychiatrist, and a social worker," and then she "had to apply to the National Board of Health and Welfare whose approval might or – usually – might not be granted."[46] In Britain, psychiatrists still used class criteria to determine who would get an abortion: in Aberdeen between 1961, doctors offered curettage abortions to women from the professional classes, for fear that unwanted pregnancy would disrupt their careers or cause emotional distress. But doctors assumed that working-class women could cope with unintended pregnancies – and advised sterilization if necessary.[47] In Britain, abortion was finally legalized in 1967, but the abortion act still required two doctors to certify that a pregnancy would endanger a woman's mental and physical health.

Frustrated, women began to express their expectation that birth control and abortion were their "rights." Rowena Woolf, a family planning activist, noticed that women were more and more determined to get abortions, and would "shop around" from doctor to doctor until they got one, or resort to a neighborhood woman. Working-class women accepted abortion; for instance, when a factory forewoman was put on trial for providing abortions, her female workmates sent her flowers.[48] By the 1960s, Swedish women no longer accepted the idea that they should have to be scrutinized by psychiatrists to decide if they "deserved" abortions. Instead, abortion was seen as a right within the welfare state, predicated on allowing all equal opportunity: as one commentator stated:

> The welfare state cannot with impunity allow – considering its constitutional principles and values – a random fate to mete out to some people the problems and difficulties that accompany an unwanted pregnancy which other people – displaying the same morals, knowledge, behavior, and contraceptive practices – escape.[49]

As a result, Sweden loosened restrictions on abortion, but did not fully legalize it until 1975.[50] In France, feminists had agitated for birth control since the 1950s, but it was only legalized in 1967, and the government delayed implementation of the law for five years. Abortion was not liberalized until 1975, under intense feminist pressure, although the government had basically stopped prosecuting illegal abortions. However, governmental experts still saw birth control and abortion as something that should be managed and regulated by medical and technocratic elites.[51]

Technocrats envisioned that married couples would use birth control as part of their job as consumers; if they had few children, they could save enough to buy the washing machines, refrigerators and cars which fueled the postwar economy, although they also feared women would leave their homes to earn wages to purchase these pleasures. Sexual pleasure, as in the interwar period, was to produce healthy, well-adjusted married citizens. But during the 1950s and especially in the 1960s, sexual consumerism exploded out of the confines of marriage. Even more than in the interwar period, sexual goods became consumer items, starting with sex manuals but quickly expanding to soft-core girlie magazines, sex toys, and even films. A thriving mail order business selling pornography and sex aids apparently served half of Germany's households, estimates historian Elizabeth Heinemann.[52] While couples could use these items to enhance their relationships, they could also contribute to a fantasy life far beyond the confines of marriage. In Britain, magazines such as *Mayfair* transformed pornographic periodicals from grotty, underground rags to glossy sheets with glamorous models. These magazines presented "swinging London" as a "sexual magnet" for "foreign ingénues enraptured by the superior sexual technique of British men," as historian Marcus Collins sardonically notes.[53] In Sweden and Denmark, pornographic films entered the mainstream so rapidly in the 1960s that commentators claimed Swedes soon became bored with them.[54] Despite prosecution, gay bars re-emerged in German cities, as a new style influenced by American bikers and Tom of Finland's drawings of bulgingly muscular men created a new version of male–male desire.[55]

In Britain, the number of teenagers had risen by 20 percent in the postwar period, and young people could earn higher wages in the booming economies of postwar Europe. They were shop assistants, factory workers, mechanics, secretaries, and bank clerks, and they were ready to spend their earnings on music, going out, and cars. Although young people in the 1920s and 1930s had also spent their wages on going dancing and to the cinema, the popular culture they enjoyed was not that different from their parents – both mothers and daughters would swoon over Valentino or Garbo. But in the 1950s and 1960s, teenager culture became distinctive and oppositional. The records, fashions and drugs they bought were not just consumer goods: they expressed their collective rebellious style and personal identity. For instance, the British Teddy boys emulated Elvis Presley with their slicked-back hair, flashy suits, studded leather jackets and drainpipe trousers that revealed their muscular bodies. Teenagers scorned the well-meaning, serious youth workers and church workers who tried to set up clubs for them to contain their energy. Instead, they congregated in commercial venues, such as coffee bars, pubs, and cinemas, because proprietors did not try to police their behavior as long as they spent money. As a social worker found to his horror, teenagers used their cars and mopeds to "drive to the nearby common and indulge in various sexual activities there, behavior which on cold winter nights would be quite unthinkable if not impossible, without the cover of a vehicle."[56]

Young people also rebelled against conventional consumer society. Schofield recognized that: "Most people want more out of life than a routine job, a color television and an automatic washing machine."[57] German radical Reimut Reiche complained that advertising "dictates ... how one goes to bed with somebody"; it instructed consumers to purchase products to keep their attractiveness "at full market value." He demonstrated that popular magazines marketed sexual liberation to young people, but differentiated their targets by class. Downmarket magazines advised working-class young people that a sexual fling before marriage was certainly okay – as long as marriage was the ultimate goal. Magazines directed toward middle-class bohemian consumers casually suggested that if a husband or wife flirted with someone else at a party, their spouses should be "cool" with it in an open marriage. As Reiche pointed out, despite this apparent freedom all the readers of the magazine "are heading in the same direction: towards marriage, in the repressive, monogamous form demanded by the economics of the technocratic society which for the present at any rate remains the absolute norm for all classes."[58]

The civil rights and antiwar movements also inspired young people to see the consumer society and welfare state as repressive, disciplinary institutions. Herbert Marcuse, a guru of the left, pointed out that what seemed to be liberation was just another form of social discipline. Sex becomes just another commodity:

> The sexy office and sales girls, the handsome, virile junior executive and floor walker are highly marketable commodities, and the possession of suitable mistresses – once the prerogative of kings, princes, and lords – facilitates the career of even the less exalted ranks in the business community.

In a technological society, pleasure is managed, and thus "generates submission" to capitalist society.[59]

Swedish sex columnists Inge and Sten Hegeler wanted "good pornography" which was "honest, truthful description," as opposed to "bad pornography" which was "false, hypocritical and twisted."[60] For instance, the famous X-rated movie, *I am Curious (Yellow)*, incited a storm of excitement and censorship when it was distributed in the United States in 1967.[61] But the movie must have frustrated viewers, for the first hour of the film is a critique of the welfare state in Sweden, implicitly comparing it to Stalinist Russia and fascist Spain. Lena, the heroine, is not a glamorous movie star; slightly plump and short, she sports pigtails, floppy hats and a quizzical expression. When she finally beds a handsome young man, the film portrays their sex as "real" and emotional instead of glamorous and pornographic; they awkwardly clutch each other with their underwear around their ankles. After a passionate affair, she discovers that her boyfriend neglected to tell her that he has another girlfriend and a child; even worse, he is both a member of the royal family and a luxury car salesman. In the end, he represents the hypocrisy of consumer society and traditional Sweden.

Figure 12.1   Still from *I am Curious (Yellow)* (1967), directed by Vilgot Sjoman. Ref: IAM006AA. SANDREWS/THE KOBAL COLLECTION

Radicals criticized the consumer society that turned "the art of love into a relationship between things." Even Scandinavian "permissiveness" just produced an artificial, limited form of love: As the Situationist Raoul Vaneigem cried out,

> You have had a bellyful of pleasure mingled with pain: enough of love experienced in an incomplete, deformed or less than genuine way; enough of intercourse by proxy or through intermediary images; enough of melancholy fornication; of meager orgasms; of antiseptic relationships; of passions choked and suppressed and beginning to waste the energy which they would release in a society which favored their harmonization.[62]

Instead of artificial, consumerist sex, radicals wanted to revive the tradition of sexual ecstasy and mysticism as a route to a transcendent consciousness, even social revolution.

The pulsating rhythms of rock and roll, of course, had already infused sensual ecstasy into popular culture. As historian Uta Poiger has found: "one West German commentary in 1956 described rock 'n' roll dancers as 'wild barbarians in ecstasy.'"[63] Most European pop stars had been rather tame, such as the rather proper Cilla Black, with her headband and demure bob, and even the Beatles were rather boyish, even as they excited frenzies in teenaged girls. Then the Rolling Stones burst on the scene, with their raw, aggressive sexual energy, the growling, masculine bass and the pouting yet macho lips of Mick Jagger, and the world was ready to turn from petting to fucking. As Pietro Scaruffi observes, "the sexy singer" became a "shaman" infusing the youth movement with charismatic energy.[64] The working-class German radical man Bommi Baumann mused: "I mean, it's more of a matter of pure feeling with this kind of music. The whole message in rock is fucking or whatever you want to call it, screwing. Period. Make love, not war. It's easier for a worker to grasp or relate to that." Radicals proclaimed that the sexual energy of rock 'n' roll would fuel revolution.[65]

The new radicals wanted sexual energy to transform society, not just to sell cars. They asserted that sex could help free the imagination and society from capitalist fetters, unleashing a world of creativity and harmony.[66] They resurrected Wilhelm Reich's ideas that blocked sexual energy caused neurosis. Unlike the consumerist desire for shiny appearances and sexy women, their desire, they claimed, opened up the human reality of emotions. Sexual desire would not only free up the individual, but revolutionize society. Vaneigem posited an ideal of "total freedom, pleasure without end or future."[67] These radicals believed that sex could become a radical, transformative sacrament. Richard Neville called for the "politics of play," and optimistically proclaimed that: "The new sex helps break-up unhappy families, deconditions us from toil and introduces more of us to one another."[68] For Emmanuelle Arsan and Germaine Greer, even group sex could be a form of communal ecstasy, a sacrament dissolving boundaries between people. In her letter to the Pope, Arsan celebrated an orgiastic vision of sexual love as "the union, the communion, the sympathy, the symbiosis, the fusion of 2, 3, 10 bodies and consciousnesses which make them human."[69] As a writer in *Oz* magazine proclaimed:

> The career counselors build marvelous constructions of seduction and mystery, they
> trans-substantiate symbol money
> into sex
> into power

Instead, the Oz writer declared, students should infiltrate the universities with "dopesellers, sneakthieves, naked dripping seventeen-year-old American girls," producing a university "powered by social magic" with "flesh classrooms."[70] This poem expresses a neat reversal of the Christian sacrament: instead of transubstantiating money into sex, itself a mockery of the Eucharist, they wanted to transubstantiate the drugs and naked American girls into social magic. The student radicals believed that the imagination can "overcome the censorship that controls and ultimately represses the unconscious desires" and that they could transform the "imagination into a productive force against the repressive reality principle."[71]

The celebration of sexual desire helped fuel the student revolts that exploded in the 1960s. In France, students were frustrated at the technocratic government that almost quadrupled the number of students, yet refused to provide jobs for them. The government had founded new universities, but they were sterile, concrete campuses, isolated from the cities. Students were crowded into sex-segregated dormitories, and university authorities forbade female students to receive male visitors, claiming they had to protect them from African and Algerian students. Although this controversy had been simmering since 1962, it really exploded in the miraculous year of 1968.[72] Then, Daniel Cohn-Bendit, the student leader, harnessed student grumbling at dormitory restrictions to the wider social revolution. As he stood in a harsh wind in the bleak cement square of Nanterre University, he proclaimed that:

> the petty hostile regulations are an impertinent infringement of [the students'] personal liberty, that learning is no substitute for the warmth of human companionship. And learning to question these regulations, the student is forced to explore repression in general and the forms it takes in the modern world.[73]

Raoul Vaneigem asked, "Are you ready to smash the reefs of the old world before they wreck your desires? ... Some of us have fallen in love with the pleasure of loving without reserve – passionately enough to offer our love to the magnificent bed of a revolution."[74] As the students occupied the Sorbonne, they scrawled graffiti on the walls, such as:

The more I make love, the more I want to make revolution.
The more I make revolution, the more I want to make love.
I love you!!! Oh, say it with paving stones!!!
I'm coming in the paving stones.
Total orgasm.[75]

The largely male-oriented gay liberation movement, which erupted in the early 1970s, also envisioned sexual ecstasy as a potent force energizing social revolution. French society had long turned a blind eye to the men and women who had same-sex affairs, as long as they kept quiet about it and maintained a proper heterosexual façade.[76] But the new gay liberation movement rejected this tradition, as they sang on May Day 1971:

You'll have to resign yourself to the fact.
We won't wear the pink triangle anymore.
We'll appear in broad daylight,
and long live the revolution.

In Britain, Germany, and Sweden, gay liberation movements tended to be based on the idea of "gay identity." They explored what they saw as a hidden, authentic, inner self, they developed an open sense of identity, and they organized around this identity for greater visibility and more rights, often connected with the wider New Left movement. The French gay liberation movement, however, tended to focus on sexual desire rather than identity. The leader of the movement was Guy Hocquenghem, who had a wild curly hair, and "fabulous red trousers."[77] He theorized a new way of thinking about homosexual desire, following theorists Deleuze and Guattari's idea of desire as a free-flowing force. Deleuze and Guattari describe humans as desiring machines. They repudiate Lacan's idea that desire was a lack. If we think of desire as lack, we want to plug this hole by acquiring objects, trapped by capitalism. Instead, Deleuze and Guattari wanted revolutionary desire to flow through one person to another in "desiring machines" formed of "great gregarious masses." In revolutionary love, possessive love would disappear and "persons give way to decoded flows of desire, two lines of vibration." Desire was once again perceived as an abstract force detached from the person.[78]

Hocquenghem applied these ideas to same-sex desire, refusing the notion of sexual identity, and instead celebrating desire that circulated among men as they had sex in Turkish baths and gay liberation meetings. In the Beaux Arts building where the gay liberation movement met, men smoked "Moroccan hash" and urgently had sex behind sculptures in the hallways," as historian Frederic Martel recounts. Hocquenghem proclaimed: "In truth, the pick up machine is not concerned with names or sexes. ... desire feels no guilt. ... Homosexual love is immensely superior, but precisely because everything is possible at any moment: organs look for each other and plug-in, unaware of the loss of exclusive disjunction."[79] Indeed, as Martel observes, backroom sex created a sacral sense of community: "a swarming mass of men, sighs, bodies in ecstasy, the hunt, potential prey, silence, the glow of burning cigarettes, sweat, sometimes a burst of laughter."[80]

The hope that sex would free the imagination and revolutionize society soon faded as a political agenda. First, many leftists found sexual utopianism to be self-indulgent and distracting from fighting the war in Vietnam and liberating workers from capitalism. Some student occupiers of the Sorbonne tore down gay liberation posters.[81] Second, turning sexual liberation into a concrete utopian program was rather difficult. The radical utopians envisioned sex as a force of the imagination that would transform society, but sex usually involves a relationship between two people that can be complicated. For instance, Vaneigem envisioned a collective utopia where people could freely experience passions – but only after consulting the rather bureaucratic-sounding "harmonization section" of the group.[82]

The authorities certainly tried to repress the May 1968 movement with police force, and they also prosecuted left-wingers for pornography. In France during the 1970s, the police surveilled homosexuals in bars, tried to censor gay magazines, and attempted to close down the gay liberation movement.[83] In England, the police had unsuccessfully tried to prosecute *Oz* magazine and the *Little Red Schoolbook* because they provided sex education to children and advocated "the alternative society." However, the same police turned a blind eye to mainstream pornography – in part because they took payoffs from Soho pornographers. As the *Guardian* reported: "Detective Chief Inspector George Fenwick, then in charge of the "dirty" squad, [secretly told the Home Secretary] that pornography could not be stamped out because it had existed for centuries."[84]

In fact, governments defused demands for sexual freedom by loosening restrictions on pornography. This sexual consumerism, rather than repression, defeated the radical push for sexual revolution. By the early 1970s, the British police followed their Scandinavian counterparts' lead and turned a blind eye to soft-core porn.[85] In Germany, the laws on pornography were modified in 1975, despite Christian Democrat Party objections that this would undermine the family and corrupt youth. Now only hard-core pornography was illegal. Images of nude women spread to bus stops, billboard advertisements, and the front page of mainstream news magazines such as *Die Stern*. In France, the government allowed the open showing of soft-core films such as *Emmanuelle*, which helped to temporarily revive the French film industry; although X-rated movies were confined to special movie houses, they flourished. Sexual images just led to more consumerism, as Emmanuelle Arsan's radical philosophic message was lost in the continual remakes of her film. The idea that sexual desire would lead to revolution was defeated by its own success. After all, left-wing magazines such as *Oz* made money with pictures of nude women that were very similar to those in the more louche mainstream press.

Consumerism also deflated the radical urgency of the French gay liberation movement. The bars of rue de St. Anne, and then the Marais, soon became more attractive than the meetings of the gay liberation organizations. As historian Frederic Martel argues, politics became unfashionable to the "clones" who

cruised the elegant streets of the Marais, with their muscles, tight T-shirts and close-cropped hair.[86] By 1975, French theoretician Michel Foucault pointed out that sexual desires could not simply be "liberated" along with the authentic self. Instead, he demonstrated how psychiatry, medicine, schools, and other authorities constructed discourses of sexual identity which shaped how people understood their sexual selves.[87]

Years before Foucault, however, feminists had pointed out that "natural" sexual desire could not simply be freed, since sexual desire itself was constructed. Verena Stefan, a German feminist, wrote in her bestselling novel, *Shedding*, "The pride I felt about my first bra, my first girdle, my first lipstick! Initiation rites and models moved in on me from all sides."[88] Feminists also rejected sexual liberation's claim that it would reveal women's innermost selves. Leftist women began to realize that left-wing men still treated them as commodities and in fact, that sexual liberation was making matters worse. Indeed, during the student revolution at Nanterre, a radical journalist described female students as "perfumed game," who were "ready for wicked lovemaking, hot grenades unavailable to the CRS [security services]."[89] A man belonging to the German radical collective Kommune1 explained how to initiate a woman into a group: "It is like breaking in a horse. One person has to break it in, and then anyone can ride it. First of all it's love or something like it, and then afterwards it's only pleasure."[90]

Many feminists felt torn between the dream of sex as liberation and the reality of unsatisfactory relationships. They began to realize that women were being treated as stepping stones on the path to sexual revolution. Rowbotham remembered that women still felt caught between the old idea that only love justified sex and the new idea that they should be available to men. She became "uneasy" when she heard "a man at a party talking about a woman's buttocks as if she was meat"; she resented the intellectual men who ignored her despite her achievements. She was "driven by a longing for a sexuality, which was not about possession or being possessed, for forms of relating and loving I could hardly express or even imagine." But she added: "my desire to lose myself in passion locked with a ferocious resolve to hang on to myself."[91]

Feminists pointed out that experts had constructed female sexuality in a way that ignored the biological reality of the clitoris. In 1969 Danish author Mette Ejlersen published the bestselling *I Accuse!*, which reviled doctors for accusing women of being neurotic for not having a vaginal orgasm. Instead, she proclaimed, women should focus on clitoral pleasure as a means to a "really great, intoxicating orgasm." By demanding pleasure, women were also asserting their equality, rights, and needs in the larger world, as individuals, not just as mothers. The American Anne Koedt later quoted this book in her essay "The Myth of the Vaginal Orgasm," which in turn became wildly influential in the United States and Europe.[92]

Some feminists, however, felt uncomfortable with the idea that men simply must learn to stimulate the clitoris in order to prepare women for the all-important heterosexual penetration. As Verena Stefan noted, "a real sense of touch usually gets lost in the myriad of prescribed stimuli and responses."[93] In *The*

Female Eunuch, Germaine Greer proclaimed it was "pompous and deliberate" for a man to make the rounds of the nipple and the clitoris and then "politely let himself into the vagina," a way of lovemaking that "is laborious and inhumanly computerized." She loved penetration and declared that "clitoral orgasm with a full cunt is nicer than a clitoral orgasm with an empty one, as far as I can tell." Greer was a celebrity, a six-foot tall Amazon with flashing eyes and dark curly hair, fearless and demanding of men sexually. In the pages of *Oz* magazine she taunted British men for not satisfying her, mocking the notion that English men were studs attracting continental "birds."[94]

Some feminists believed that women's desire for men was constructed and therefore they could deconstruct it. Their political ideology impelled them to reject men and choose to desire women. As they proclaimed, "any woman can be a lesbian." Heterosexual penetration, they argued, was emblematic of male oppression of women. Verena Stefan dreamily imagined: "The hand on its way to the clitoris of another woman traverses centuries. It can get lost a thousand times. It fights its way through fragments of civilization."[95] In 1975, feminist theorist Luce Irigaray asked "What if the 'commodities' refused to put themselves on the market? Maintaining among themselves an 'other' sort of commerce? Exchanges without identifiable terms, without reckoning, without end … gratuitous pleasures, jouissance without possession."[96] This was a vision of lesbian sexual ecstasy, not only a way of transforming society but, in French theory, undermining the very fixity of language's meaning and the identity of the self. However, the German and British versions of lesbian feminism were more austere. As Sheila Jeffreys, a leader of the movement, asserted, for a feminist to give up men was a moral choice, like a vegetarian giving up meat. Even if a woman enjoyed men, it was her duty to reject them. These separatists even believed that women must avoid penetrating each other so as not to imitate male-dominated, heterosexual forms of love-making. As a result, the idea of sexual ecstasy did not predominate in British and German lesbian feminism.

Many other women asserted a lesbian identity so that they could finally be open about their desires. After having faced hostile families, disapproving employers, and coercive doctors, lesbians could proudly and publicly claim their love and experience intense sexual pleasure. In 1972, a German survey found that two thirds to nine-tenths of lesbians who had had sex with men "described their lesbian experiences as more satisfying, more passionate, exciting, that they were, more partner related, more intimate, more empathetic, more considerate, less aggressive, and more often orgastic."[97] Such lesbians believed that they had been able to discover their innermost authentic sexual self. Today, with the rise of queer theory, it is unfashionable to think of identities as authentic and fixed; instead, queer theory celebrates fluid, unfixed identities – a person might sleep with a man one day and a woman the next. But during the early 1970s, asserting a fixed lesbian – or gay – identity was a radical stance. For decades, psychiatrists and other experts had diagnosed young women who had relationships with each other as going through an adolescent phase, or suffering from a psychiatric illness which could be cured – they would ultimately return to heterosexuality. In the heyday of 1968, bisexuality became fashionable, but lesbianism was seen as rejecting men, and uncool. The lesbian and gay movement was therefore radical for its time in asserting an authentic identity, even if this notion was to be deconstructed later.

Radical feminists also reacted angrily against the onslaught of pornography. They argued that even soft-core films such as *Emmanuelle* portrayed lesbian interludes for male titillation. Even worse, many of these films featured women being violently attacked and degraded. Indeed, historian Marcus Collins has found that 1970s British men's magazines increasingly linked erotic images of violence against women, such as bondage and flogging; their articles denounced women's liberation and claimed that their models were happy to stay at home and service men sexually.[98] In Leeds, a grim northern city in England, some radical feminists actually bombed sex shops, or at least sabotaged them by gluing shut their doors, and picketed soft-core porn in mainstream cinemas. The feminist movement split when other feminists objected to this attack on free speech, and argued that women should be able to explore all their desires, even if they did not fit the romantic, asexual, sanitized version of lesbianism espoused by some of these radical feminists. In the 1980s, some lesbian activists began to experiment with sado-masochism (S-M), arguing that this form of sex play was a way of exploring relationships of power and domination. Highly ritualized, perhaps S-M was a way of transforming the self through pain, another version of desire as transcendence. But some women just wanted access to the sexual supermarket of consumer society; for instance, a female leader of the German Green party, Waltraud Schoppe, said she opposed anti-porn legislation because "she wanted to be able to continue to buy pornos in the supermarket."[99] Sexual shops began to feature items that appealed to women, such as vibrators in ingenious shapes and colors.

More battles over boundaries: the 1980s and 1990s

The utopian promise of the 1960s also ground to a halt as rising oil prices and stalled economies devastated many European countries in the 1970s and 1980s. Struggling to recover, many European countries asserted national identity as important; sexual conflicts once again set off moral panics.

The virulent spread of AIDS in Europe ignited an intense backlash against gay liberation and sexual liberation in general. The press stigmatized gay men as diseased, but it warned that the virus would spread to heterosexuals. The *Sun* tabloid, which daily featured a topless teenager on its page three, declared that:

> the killer plague Aids will spark violence on the streets of Britain. The prospect of bloodshed as terrified citizens make 'reprisal' attacks on homosexuals and drug addicts is now seen as a real threat. Some gays are expected to retaliate by spreading the virus to the rest of the community through 'revenge sex' with bisexuals.[100]

The Chief Constable of Greater Manchester, James Anderton, said that "AIDS was spread by the 'obnoxious practices' of homosexuals and the 'crippled human conditions' of 20th century life."[101] Sir Immanuel Jakobovits maintained in *The Times* in 1986 that:

> Aids is the price we pay for the 'benefits' of the permissive society which, helped by the pill, liberal legislation and more 'enlightened' attitudes, has demolished the last defences of sexual restraint and self-discipline, leading to a collapse of nature's self-defence against degeneracy.[102]

The spread of the virus across national borders also raised fears about sexual boundaries. Swedish politicians referred to AIDS as "the plague of our time" and called for a war to protect public health. Following the more interventionist traditions of Swedish public health, they closed the gay saunas.[103] But the governmental response to AIDS went beyond such public health measures to repress the gay movement itself and punish gay male sexual behavior. In 1987 the formidable Charles Pasqua, French minister of the interior, monitored gay computer networks and publications and tried to censor the French gay press.[104] In Scotland, the police intensified their surveillance and punishment of men who had sex with each other, especially in public places.[105] In Britain, Margaret Thatcher's government celebrated family values and individualism while passing the infamous Clause 28, which prohibited the teaching of any positive images of gays and lesbians in the schools.[106] In Germany, some argued that foreigners should be screened for AIDS – the disease led to a fortress-like mentality.[107] Similarly, the rightwing National Front in France used AIDS to demand restrictions on immigration, albeit unsuccessfully.[108] In Belgium, foreign laborers, especially Africans, were blamed for AIDS.[109]

Gay men, however, mobilized to fight AIDS and to care for each other as their lovers and comrades fell ill and died in tragically staggering numbers. After initial warnings to avoid sex with unknown partners, to avoid anal sex, in fact to avoid much sex at all, gay men began to turn to other means of sexual pleasure, such as mutual masturbation, and to publicize the condom as allowing safer sex. Some sociologists and historians have argued that the campaign against AIDS was more difficult in those places where gay identity was weak. In countries dominated by the Catholic Church, for instance, sociologist Michel Pollack surmised that many men had sex with each other without defining themselves as gay.[110] Thus, they were more difficult to reach with safe sex information targeted at gay men, and they were less likely to have their own self-help groups. In France, the repression of the Catholic Church was not much of a factor, but Pollack and historian Frederic Martel controversially argue that, by focusing on desire more than identity, the gay culture was hampered in its fight against AIDS. Hocquenghem scorned safe sex: "Tobacco causes cancer, we all know that. Have we stopped smoking? Sex causes illness. Must we stop making love?"[111] The link of eros with death, the eroticism of sacrifice and transgression, made it difficult to accept the idea of safe sex.[112] However, some AIDS activists began to reformulate their understandings of sexual identity to reach those who did not define themselves as gay, to address sexual acts rather than identities.

Some activists fought AIDS by arguing that gay men, and lesbians, should form marriage-like unions. If governments legitimized these unions, they would grant homosexuals full citizenship and include them in the boundaries of the nation – in exchange for following the principles of monogamous marriage. Denmark passed the first domestic partnership laws for gay couples in 1989, and Sweden soon followed suit. However, French critics, especially influential Lacanian psychoanalysts, opposed civil unions because they believed they challenged the boundary between men and women – "la différence" – which was seen by some as the foundation for the family, the state, indeed for culture itself. Opponents regarded secular marriage as the "pillar of the republic," and the family as the proper place to bring up children and dispose of property. They preferred erotic extramarital relationships, especially those between people of the same sex, to remain as twilight moments, hidden and private. Nonetheless, civil unions passed in France in 1999.[113]

The fall of the Berlin Wall in 1989 also opened up sexual boundaries between East and West. In the time of glasnost, or openness, people thought they were contributing to democratization by discussing "private" sexual matters publicly, but disillusionment soon set in.[114] During the 1990s, the Russian government allowed more contraceptive information, so that women could use condoms, diaphragms and the pill, rather than having to rely on repeated abortions. However, by 1998, there was a backlash, as anxiety about Russia's declining population spread, and the government withdrew funding for birth control that year.[115] When Russia first opened the economy to capitalism, pornography exploded onto the scene. But after a few years, it lost its shock value. For example, when the Moscow cultural Center Blitz tried to hold a live sex erotic festival, it lost most of its money. As one reporter noted: "ice cream was selling better than pornography."[116] Pornography continues to flourish in the private marketplace, but it no longer functions as an exciting indicator of cultural openness.

As Eastern European countries joined the European Union, they slashed social services, ripping away the safety net for women. Facing unemployment, young Eastern European and Russian women sought a better life in the West. While most worked as nurses, cleaners, factory workers or professionals, some earned money as sex workers. This could be a rational economic decision for some women, but others became embroiled in mafia prostitution rings. For instance, foreigners went to poor rural villages in Romania and bought teenage boys or girls from their families "for as little as a television set or the equivalent of a monthly wage."[117] Although the number of prostitutes had declined a great deal in the postwar period, as fewer young men bought sexual services, the appearance of these new prostitutes – in the context of the problems of drugs and AIDS – caused tensions over boundaries. Although Europeans in general are tolerant of consensual sex, sharp divides persist over the problem of prostitution. Sweden, which despite its reputation for sexual permissiveness allows the government to regulate sexual behavior, in 1998 made it illegal to buy sex, thus punishing the customers of prostitutes. This law, argues Don Kulick, was passed in response to anxiety about Eastern European prostitutes coming into Sweden, and more metaphorically, about the anxiety over the threat to Sweden's borders when it contemplated joining the European Union. However, Yvonne Svanström asserts that the law was passed under pressure by feminists who perceived prostitution as exploitative of women.[118] Similarly, efforts to regulate French prostitutes centered on the "division between the 'good' French prostitutes who did not disturb the peace and 'bad' foreign prostitutes who undercut prices, offer unprotected sex and work indiscreetly, upsetting local residents."[119] Great income differentials between eastern and western Europe insure that the poor provide sexual services to the rich.

Immigration to Europe has also sharpened concern about sexual boundaries. In the postwar period, European nations trying to rebuild, and hungry for labor, encouraged immigration. Countries such as Sweden also took in Iranian and Chilean refugees from persecution. From the 1960s through the 1990s, sociologists assumed that immigrant men from more conservative sexual cultures had to adjust to liberal sexual cultures. One study found that some Iranian female refugees felt inspired by Swedish women to demand their own pleasures. One woman reported: "After learning how Swedish women think about their sexuality, I tried to behave differently ... I don't think that I am a passive object for my partner's sexual desires anymore. I have my own sexual desires and I am proud of it." Some men also changed their views: one Iranian man said he would now rather masturbate than force his wife to have sex, as he used to do. But some men felt frustrated and confused by these changing mores, and marriages broke down.[120] Yet many immigrant men to Sweden found Swedish sexual culture to be very confusing, for the Swedes, despite their vaunted permissiveness, regarded sex in "comradely" terms and did not exhibit eroticism in their everyday life. They found that for the Swedes, sex was like a "disarmed mine." The male immigrants expected that Swedish women would be sexually available, so they were confused when they flirted and then refused them. In turn, some male immigrants complained that Swedish women who used them as exotic sex objects failed to provide an emotional connection.[121]

The influx of Muslim migrants to Europe has also led to new debates about sex as a flashpoint in clashes in culture. Some commentators have argued that the liberal sexual culture of countries such as the Netherlands shocked Muslim immigrants from rural areas of North Africa or Turkey. As journalist Ian Buruma observes: "While many women embrace the liberties of western life, men, faced with rejection and frustration, turn away to a fantasy of tribal honor and religious rectitude. A teenage desire for 'easy' women makes way for disgust and rage."[122] This rage erupted tragically when Mohammed Bouyari stabbed filmmaker Theo van Gogh to death on an Amsterdam street because he made a film with Hirsan Ali about how Islam oppressed women sexually and spiritually. Yet others paint a more complex picture.

In France, as Fadela Amara remembered, second-generation immigrant young people began to adopt French sexual mores in the 1980s and early 1990s as they became involved in SOS-Racisme, an anti-racist youth movement: "While little was said officially in their families, a tacit agreement existed; as long as the young woman did not exhibit herself publicly, she could have a love life." In the 1990s, however, a backlash against immigrants and mass unemployment incited the anger of young men. Young Muslim men witnessed the permissiveness of French culture, with its soft-core porn advertisements, and believed that only Islamic fundamentalism seemed to hold out dignity and answers to them. As a result, complained Amara, they claimed a new right to control the behavior not only of their sisters but of their female neighbors, punishing young women who defied them with gang rape or even murder.[123] Some critics argue, however, that portraying immigrants as conservative and intolerant is a way of defining Europeans as superior and more advanced, and distracting attention away from the widespread discrimination in employment against immigrant youths, police brutality, and substandard housing. Such critics point out that immigrant cultures are not necessarily more intolerant than other parts of European society.[124] In Sweden, a Muslim woman found it "amusing that in Scandinavia, it is okay to be naked, but wearing a headscarf is not."[125] Pope Benedict XVI, after all, has denounced popular media for spreading "sexual perversion," and reaffirmed Catholic opposition to birth control and gay marriage.[126]

Official Christianity, however, has lost most of its influence over European sexual morality. Today, only 15 percent of Europeans attend church once a week, as contrasted with 44 percent of Americans, and only 21 percent of Europeans say religion is "very important" to them, as compared to 59 percent of Americans.[127] Even in Ireland, long a bastion of Catholicism, the scandals about the sexual abuse of children effectively destroyed the faith of many Irish women in their priests by the 1990s.[128] In Eastern Europe, the Catholic Church regained more influence in some countries, especially Poland, and tried to impose stricter rules on abortion. But it often failed in these efforts.[129]

European sexual morality today

Contemporary Europeans have developed a public sense of sexual morality which is quite distinct from that of the United States, although they do not behave all that differently. For the most part, they accept sex education, premarital sex, and see cohabitation as a valid alternative to marriage. European teenagers are much less likely to become pregnant, have abortions, or become infected with venereal disease than American teenagers. For instance, in the 1990s, out of 1,000 15- to 19-year-olds, 7.8 Swedish girls, 10 French, and 28.3 British girls gave birth, contrasted with 54.4 American girls. The abortion rate ranged from 10.2 for France, 17.2 for Sweden, 18.4 for Britain, and 29.2 for American girls that age.[130] And in France and Sweden, half of those teenagers who give birth are married or cohabitating. However, teenagers in Sweden, France, Britain and the United

States have sex at roughly the same age – 17 or 18 – and in roughly the same numbers, around 85 percent. European teenagers are less likely to get pregnant because schools provide sex education and health services dispense contraception to them.[131]

American and European parents approach their children's sex lives in different ways. According to one study, American parents believed that they needed to strictly control their teenagers to prevent them from having sex, but they felt uncomfortable discussing sex with their children; in contrast, Dutch parents talked about sex with their offspring, and allowed them to have their boyfriends or girlfriends sleep over, encouraging them to value commitment and restraint in sexual relationships.[132] German parents accept their offsprings' sex lives and teenagers now see sex as friendly, communicative, rational and "the outcome of an amicable conversation."[133] The abstinence-only sex education movement for teenagers has made very little headway in Europe. In 2007, a Sussex school even prohibited a schoolgirl from wearing a Christian "chastity ring."[134]

Cohabitation is rapidly rivaling marriage in Europe. One study found that French marriage rates are "45 percent below U.S. figures" and 59 percent of all first-born French children were born to unwed parents, most by choice, not chance.[135] In Sweden most couples cohabit before marriage, or have children without marriage. Cohabitation in Sweden and France often resembles marriage, though, in expectations that couples will be faithful and monogamous.[136] Some studies have even found that French and Swedish people were more monogamous and had fewer sexual partners over the course of their lifetime than American and British people, because cohabitation was so strongly associated with monogamy.[137] However, cohabitation was less common in the Netherlands, Great Britain, Germany, and Southern European countries.[138]

In most parts of Europe, the popularity of cohabitation also began to erode some of the differences between heterosexual couples and same-sex couples. In France, heterosexual couples demanded certificates of "concubinage," the legal term for domestic partnership," from their local mayors as an alternative to marriage. Heterosexual couples can now engage in civil unions, just like homosexual couples, but French civil unions only give same-sex couples a second-class status, deprived of full marriage rights over immigration, adoption, inheritance and taxes. However, by 2005 Britain allowed civil unions with all the rights of marriage, and Spain's socialist government defied the Church to allow gay marriages. In fact, most European countries, with the exception of Ireland, Italy, Poland, Greece, and Serbia, allow civil unions, and many municipalities in Italy do.[139]

Conclusion

Have the sex radicals triumphed in their long quest? The sex radicals did succeed in inculcating the idea that sexual pleasure was a right. They pressured governments to provide birth control and abortion services. Yet the idea of sex as creative, spiritual and revolutionary no longer seems central to radical movements. Of course, the idea of sex as transcendent may persist in underground cultures of raves, of the drug ecstasy, S-M, tantric sex, goth subcultures, or anarchists, but it is not prominent in public discourse. Historian Dagmar Herzog has noted the disappearance of "sexual utopias" in German culture, as German young people seem bored with sex.[140] French cultural critics feared that sexual desire has also been domesticated and made "banal."[141] In Norway, notes Anne Sabo, sexuality has lost its "sacredness among youths" and "has come close to the brink of becoming boring."[142] Why is this?

In France, the old tradition of transgressive French eroticism was lost as soft-core images spread on television. Publisher Maurice Girodias, who had often been persecuted for obscenity, complained that by allowing pornography on television, the government robbed eroticism of its subversive power and lulled the people into submission.[143] Since the Church no longer has any influence, sex and pornographic images are not forbidden – but does this mean sex has lost its sacred, transgressive power? Yet religion remains powerful in the United States. Although Americans still get excited about sex scandals which bemuse blasé Europeans, Americans too have lost the vision of sexual utopianism. The decline in the power of the Church, therefore, cannot explain its disappearance.

Instead, it is sexual consumerism which has defeated sexual utopianism. People can now define their sexual selves in terms of their consumer tastes. The 1980s "minitel," and its descendant the internet, allow people to shop for sex on the computer. They can take on new identities daily in these virtual sexual exchanges. The sexual self can be detached from the body. Pornography can encourage the view that women must provide men with new services, such as oral and anal sex; it has been found to stimulate men to go to prostitutes.[144]

Yet is sexual consumerism necessarily such a negative thing? After all, sex manuals spread through the mass market, and the more commercial ones emphasized women's sexual pleasure more than the orthodox Freudian manuals from official sources such as the Marriage Guidance Council. Despite the image of pornography as encouraging women to service men, studies in Britain and France found that sexual practices actually focus more on female sexual pleasure; slightly more men and women experienced cunnilingus than fellatio – although a majority engaged in both practices.[145] But the idea that sexual pleasure is a consumer entitlement has been criticized. Economist Fred Hirsch notes "orgasm as a consumer's right rather rules it out as an ethereal experience."[146] Yet for women, it was difficult to experience the ethereal orgasm unless they could demand sexual pleasure as a right for themselves. As feminists demonstrated, the pursuit of sexual ecstasy as a means to a higher cause, such as social revolution, could often lead to women feeling like stepping stones on the path to transcendence. The idea of sex as utopian and transcendent could be mystical, impractical, and even ridiculously high flown. On one level, sexual desire cannot be liberated, because there is no "authentic" natural desire to be freed; rather, sexual desire is now just constructed in different ways.

Perhaps the utopian vision of sex is no longer part of public debate because we cannot imagine a utopian future for society in general. Yet what have we lost when we can no longer imagine sexual desire as creativity, as fuel for a larger revolutionary vision of transforming society and the self?

Suggested reading

Collins, Marcus. *Modern Love: An Intimate History of Men and Women in Twentieth Century Britain*. London, 2004.

Cook, Hera. *The Long Sexual Revolution: English Women, Sex, and Contraception 1800–1975*. Oxford, 2004.

Eder, Franz, Gert Hekma, and Lesley A. Hall, eds. *Sexual Cultures in Europe: National Cultures*. Manchester, 1999.

Hall, Lesley A. *Sex, Gender and Social Change in Britain since 1880*. London, 2000.

Herzog, Dagmar. *Sex After Fascism: Memory and Morality in Twentieth Century Germany*. Princeton, 2005.

McLaren, Angus. *Twentieth Century Sexuality*. Oxford, 1999.

Spira, Alfred, Nathalie Bajos, and André Bejin. *Les Comportements Sexuels en France. Rapport au Ministre de la Recherche et de l'Espace, Collection des rapports officiels*. Paris, 1993.

Stulhofer, Aleksander, and Theo Sandfort. *Sexuality and Gender in Postcommunist Eastern Europe*. London, 2005.

Wellings, Kaye, Julia Field, Anne Johnson, Jane Wadsworth, and Sally Bradshaw. *Sexual Behaviour in Britain: The National Survey of Sexual Attitudes and Lifestyles*. London, 1994.

Notes

1 Introduction

1 Richard Krafft-Ebing, *Psychopathia Sexualis* 12th edn. (New York, 1965 [1886]), 12.
2 Martha C. Nussbaum, "People as Fictions: Proust and the Ladder of Love," in *Erotikon*, ed. Shadi Bartsch and Thomas Bartscherer, (Chicago, 2005), 235–7.
3 Catherine Cusset, *No Tomorrow: The Ethics of Pleasure in the French Enlightenment* (Charlottesville, 1999), 3.
4 Alexandra A. Kollontai, "Make Way for Winged Eros," in *Selected Writings*, ed. Alix Holt, (London, 1977), 291.
5 Michel Foucault, *The History of Sexuality: An Introduction*, Robert Hurley trans. (New York, 1990), 11.
6 Natalie Angier, "Birds Do It. Bees Do It. People Seek the Keys to It," *New York Times*, 10 April 2007, 10.
7 Thomas W. Laqueur, *Making Sex: Body and Gender from the Greeks to Freud* (Cambridge, MA, 1990).
8 Hera Cook, *The Long Sexual Revolution: English Women, Sex, and Contraception 1800–1975* (Oxford, 2004), 209.
9 J.N. Adams, *The Latin Sexual Vocabulary* (Baltimore, 1982), 123.
10 Sven-Axel Mansson, "Commercial Sexuality," in *Sex in Sweden*, ed. Bo Lewin, (Stockholm, 2000), 267.
11 Judith Butler, *Undoing Gender* (New York, 2004), 15.
12 Sappho, *Poems and Fragments*, Josephine Balmer trans. (London, 1984), 20.
13 Jean-Jacques Rousseau, *The Confessions*, J.M. Cohen trans. (Harmondsworth, 1953 [1781]), 414.
14 Ann Laura Stoler, *Carnal Knowledge and Imperial Power: Race and the Intimate in Colonial Rule* (Berkeley, 2002), 44.
15 Foucault, *History of Sexuality*, 43.
16 David Halperin, *How to Do the History of Male Homosexuality* (Chicago, 2002), 35; Ruth Mazo Karras, "Active/Passive, Acts/Passions: Greek and Roman Sexualities," *American Historical Review* (2000): 1250–65.
17 Bernadette J. Brooten, *Love between Women: Early Christian Responses to Female Homoeroticism* (Chicago, 1996), 176; Michel Foucault, *The Care of the Self*, Robert Hurley trans., 3 vols., vol. 3 (New York, 1988), 22.
18 Mark D. Jordan, *The Invention of Sodomy in Christian Theology* (Chicago, 1997), 45.
19 Georges Vigarello, *A History of Rape: Sexual Violence in France from the 16th to the 20th Centuries* (Cambridge, 2001); Anna Clark, *Women's Silence, Men's Violence: Sexual Assault in England, 1770–1845* (London, 1987).
20 As Judith Butler writes, "Even within the field of intelligible sexuality, one finds that the

binaries that anchor its operations permit for middle zones and hybrid formations." Butler, *Undoing Gender*, 108.

21 For a more academic discussion of this concept, see Anna Clark, "Twilight Moments," *Journal of the History of Sexuality* 14 (2005): 139–160.

22 For critiques of the idea of tolerance, see Michel Foucault, *The Uses of Pleasure*, Robert Hurley trans. (New York, 1990), 191; Wendy Brown, *Regulating Aversion: Tolerance in the Age of Identity and Empire* (Princeton, 2006).

23 This is similar to an "open secret," in Eve Kosofsky Sedgwick's terms. Eve Kosofsky Sedgwick, *Epistemology of the Closet* (Berkeley, 1990), 67.

24 Elizabeth Susan Wahl, *Invisible Relations: Representations of Female Intimacy in the Age of Enlightenment* (Stanford, 1999), 11, quoted in Valerie Traub, *The Renaissance of Lesbianism in Early Modern England* (Cambridge, 2002), 279.

25 Michael Rocke, *Forbidden Friendships: Homosexuality and Male Culture in Renaissance Florence* (New York and Oxford, 1996), 82.

26 Angus McLaren, *Birth Control in Nineteenth-Century England* (New York, 1978), 232.

27 Antonio Vignali, *La Cazzaria: The Book of the Prick*, Ian Moulton trans. (New York, 2003 [1525]), 86.

28 Ellen Ross and Rayna Rapp, "Sex and Society: A Research Note from Social History," *Comparative Studies in Society and History* 23 (1981): 51–72.

29 Anton Blok, *Honour and Violence* (Oxford, 2001), 48. See also Luc Brisson, *Sexual Ambivalence. Androgyny and Hermaphroditism in Graeco-Roman Antiquity*, Janet Lloyd trans. (Berkeley, 2002), 148–9.

30 Robert Darnton, *The Forbidden Best-Sellers of Pre-Revolutionary France* (New York, 1995), 1–30.

31 Lee Edelman, *No Future: Queer Theory and the Death Drive* (Durham, 2004), 113.

32 Mary Douglas, *Purity and Danger* (New York, 1984 [1966]), 54, 126.

33 Stoler, *Carnal Knowledge*, 44.

34 Jock McCulloch, *Black Peril, White Virtue: Sexual Crime in Southern Rhodesia, 1902–1935* (Bloomington, 2000).

35 Stanley Cohen, "Moral Panics and Folk Concepts," *Paedagogica Historica* 35 (1999): 585–91.

36 David Nirenberg, "Conversion, Sex, and Segregation: Jews and Christians in Medieval Spain," *American Historical Review* 107 (2002): 1065–93.

37 Judith Butler, *The Psychic Life of Power* (Stanford, 1997), 147.

38 Butler, *Undoing Gender*, 47.

39 Tim Dean, *Beyond Sexuality* (Chicago, 2000), 164.

40 Ibid., 238.

41 David Lomas, "The Omnipotence of Desire: Surrealism, Psychoanalysis and Hysteria," in *Surrealism: Desire Unbound*, ed. Jennifer Mundy, (Princeton, 2001), 62.

42 Stoler, *Carnal Knowledge*, 44.

43 Ross and Rapp, "Sex and Society: A Research Note from Social History," 51–72.

44 Thomas W. Laqueur, "Sexual Desire and the Market Economy During the Industrial Revolution," in *Discourses of Sexuality from Aristotle to Aids*, ed. Domna C. Stanton, (Ann Arbor, 1992), 205.

45 Jacqueline Darroch, Jennifer J. Frost, and Susheela Singh, *Teenage Sexual and Reproductive Behavior in Developed Countries: Can More Progress Be Made? A Report of the Guttmacher Institute*, (Nw York, 2001), 83.

2 Sex and the city

1 Ross Shepard Kraemer, *Her Share of the Blessings: Women's Religions among Pagans, Jews and Christians in the Graeco-Roman World* (New York, 1992), 39.

2 N.R.E. Fisher, *Hybris: A Study in the Values of Honour and Shame in Ancient Greece* (Warminster, 1992), 120.

3 Froma I. Zeitlin, "Reflections on Erotic Desire in Archaic and Classical Greece," in *Constructions of the Classical Body*, ed. James I. Porter, (Ann Arbor, 1999), 50.

4 James N. Davidson, *Courtesans and Fishcakes: The Consuming Passions of Classical Athens* (New York, 1998).

5 Fisher, *Hybris*, 1–107; Douglas Cairns, "*Hybris*, Dishonour, and Thinking Big," *Journal of Hellenic Studies* 116 (1996): 32; David M. Halperin, "The Democratic Body: Prostitution and Citizenship in Classical Athens," *differences: a Journal of Feminist Cultural Studies* 2 (1990): 7.

6 Andrew Stewart, *Art, Desire and the Body in Ancient Greece* (Cambridge, 1997), 40.

7 The following discussion of girls, women, and marriage relies on Roger Just, *Women in Athenian Law and Life* (London, 1989), 114, 249; Anne-Marie Vérilhac and Claude Vial, *Le Mariage Grec Du VIe Siècle Av. J.-C. À L'époque D'Auguste* (Athens, 1998), 218; Giulia Sissa, *Greek Virginity* (Cambridge, 1990), 76–82; David Cohen, *Law, Sexuality and Society* (Cambridge, 1994), 106; Kraemer, *Her Share of the Blessings*, 23; Stewart, *Art, Desire and the Body*, 122.

8 Peter Bing and Rip Cohen, eds., *Games of Venus: An Anthology of Greek and Roman Erotic Verse from Sappho to Ovid* (New York, 1991), 75–8.

9 Sappho, *Poems and Fragments*, Josephine Balmer trans. (London, 1984), 20; John J. Winkler, "Double Consciousness in Sappho's Lyrics," in *Sexuality and Gender in the Classical World*, ed. Laura McClure, (Oxford, 2002), 39–71; Lauren Hackworth Petersen, "Divided Consciousness and Female Companionship: Reconstructing Female Subjectivity on Greek Vases," *Arethusa* 30 (1997): 35–74.

10 Cohen, *Law, Sexuality and Society*, 106.

11 Kraemer, *Her Share of the Blessings*, 27; Lucia Nixon, "The Cults of Demeter and Kore," in *Women in Antiquity: New Assessments*, ed. Richard Levick, and Barbara Hawley, (London, 1995), 86.

12 Aline Rousselle, *Porneia: Desire and the Body in Antiquity*, Felicia Pheasant trans. (Oxford, 1988); Leslie Dean-Jones, "The Politics of Pleasure: Female Sexual Appetite in the Hippocratic Corpus," *Helios* 19 (1992): 82–3.

13 Aristophanes, *Lysistrata*, Alan H. Sommerstein trans. (Warminster, 1990), 41.

14 Fisher, *Hybris*, 104.

15 Demosthenes, *Private Orations*, A.T. Murray trans. (Cambridge, 1978), 122.

16 Vérilhac and Vial, *Le Mariage Grec Du VIe Siècle*, 56; Alan L. Boegehold, "Perikles' Citizenship Law of 451/0 BC," in *Athenian Identity and Civic Ideology*, ed. Alan L. Boegehold and Adele C. Scafuro, (Baltimore, 1994), 58.

17 Madeleine M. Henry, *Prisoner of History: Aspasia of Miletus and Her Biographical Tradition* (New York, 1995).

18 Jess Miner, "Courtesan, Concubine, Whore: Apollodorus' Deliberate Use of Terms for Prostitutes," *American Journal of Philology* 124 (2003): 19–38; Xenophon, "Symposium," in *Xenophon in Seven Volumes*, (Cambridge, MA, 1979), 9; Davidson, *Courtesans and Fishcakes*, 124; Eva C. Keuls, *The Reign of the Phallus: Sexual Politics in Ancient Athens* (Berkeley, 1985), 176–8.

19 Cynthia Patterson, "The Case against Neaira and the Public Ideology of the Athenian Family," in *Athenian Identity and Civic Ideology*, 208; Demosthenes, *Private Orations*, 88; Debra Hamel, *Trying Neaira: The True Story of a Courtesan's Scandalous Life in Ancient Greece* (New Haven, 2003).

20 Halperin, "The Democratic Body," 11.

21 Stewart, *Art, Desire and the Body*, 165.

22 Ibid., 137; John J. Winkler, "Phallos Politikos: Representing the Body Politic in Athens," *differences* 2 (2000): 36; Keuls, *The Reign of the Phallus*, 388.

23 Davidson argues that this interpretation is not valid, James N. Davidson, "Dover, Foucault, and Greek Homosexuality: Penetration and the Truth About Sex," *Past and Present* 170 (2001): 25. But Marilyn Skinner reviews the evidence and finds that it is. Marilyn B. Skinner, *Sexuality in Greek and Roman Culture* (Malden, MA, 2005), 95.

24 Cairns, "*Hybris,* Dishonour, and Thinking Big," 27.

25 Chris Carey, *Aeschines* (Austin, 2000), 86.

26 Stewart, *Art, Desire and the Body,* 190.

27 Keuls, *The Reign of the Phallus,* 176; Edith Hall, "Ithyphallic Males Behaving Badly," in *Parchments of Gender: Deciphering the Bodies of Antiquity,* ed. Maria Wyke, (Oxford, 1998), 36–7.

28 Davidson, *Courtesans and Fishcakes,* 208.

29 Skinner, *Sexuality in Greek and Roman Culture,* 116. John J. Winkler, "Laying Down the Law: The Oversight of Men's Sexual Behavior in Ancient Athens," in *Before Sexuality: The Construction of Erotic Experience in the Ancient Greek World,* ed. David M. Halperin, John J. Winkler, and Froma I. Zeitlin, (Princeton, 1990), 171–210; Davidson, "Dover, Foucault, and Greek Homosexuality," 20.

30 Carey, *Aeschines,* 50.

31 For Timarchos, see Halperin, "The Democratic Body," 7; Giulia Sissa, "Sexual Body-building: Aeschines against Timarchus," in *Constructions of the Classical Body,* 168; Cohen, *Law, Sexuality and Society,* 72.

32 Carey, *Aeschines,* 56, 43–4.

33 Stewart, *Art, Desire and the Body,* 73; Plato, "Phaedrus," in *The Collected Dialogues of Plato,* ed. Edith Hamilton and Huntington Cairns, (Princeton, 1971), 182 c; Brad Leitao, *The Legend of the Sacred Band* (Chicago, 2002), 158–9.

34 Bing and Cohen, eds., *Games of Venus,* 90.

35 Stewart, *Art, Desire and the Body,* 67.

36 Cohen, *Law, Sexuality and Society,* 167–97; Carey, *Aeschines,* 26–9.

37 Plato, "Symposium," in *The Collected Dialogues of Plato,* ed. Edith Hamilton and Huntington Cairns, (Princeton, 1971), 177–84.

38 Ibid., 189–90.

39 Ibid., 191–2.

40 Plato, "Phaedrus," 525–74, 497.

41 David M. Halperin, "Why Is Diotima a Woman?," in *One Hundred Years of Homosexuality and Other Essays on Greek Love,* ed. David M. Halperin, (New York, 1990), 124; Daniel Boyarin, "What Do We Talk About When We Talk About Platonic Love?," in *Toward a Theology of Eros: Transfiguring Passion at the Limits of Discipline,* ed. Virginia Burrus and Catherine Keller, (New York, 2006), 19.

42 Daniel H. Garrison, *Sexual Culture in Ancient Greece* (Norman, 2000), 238. Simon Goldhill, *Foucault's Virginity: Ancient Erotic Fiction and the History of Sexuality* (Cambridge, 1995).

43 C. Nicolet, *The World of the Citizen in Republican Rome,* P.S. Falla trans. (Berkeley, 1980 [1976]), 22.

44 James A. Arieti, "Rape and Livy's View of Roman History," in *Rape in Antiquity,* ed. Susan Deacy and Karen F. Pierce, (London, 1997), 225.

45 For this paragraph, see Nicolet, *World of the Citizen,* 358; Elaine Fantham, "*Stuprum*: Public Attitudes and Penalties for Sexual Offences in Republican Rome," *Echos du Monde Classique/Classical Views* 35 (1991): 272; Catherine Edwards, *The Politics of Immorality in Ancient Rome* (Cambridge, 1993), 20; Rebecca Langlands, *Sexual Morality in Ancient Rome* (Cambridge, 2006), 58, 283.

46 Jeremy Paterson, "The Idea of Rome," in *The World of Rome,* ed. Peter Jones and Keith Sidwell, (Cambridge, 1997), 11–12; Nicolet, *World of the Citizen,* 321; Jonathan Walters, "Invading the Roman Body: Manliness and Impenetrability in Roman

Thought," in *Roman Sexualities*, ed. Judith P. Hallett and Marilyn B. Skinner, (Princeton, 1997), 37.

47 Catherine Edwards, "Unspeakable Professions: Public Prostitution and Performance in Ancient Rome," in *Roman Sexualities*, ed. Judith P. Hallett and Marilyn B. Skinner, (Princeton, 1997), 67–88; Valerie Hope, "Status and Identity in the Roman World," in *Experiencing Rome: Culture, Identity and Power in the Roman Empire*, ed. Janet Huskinson, (London, 2000), 138.

48 Skinner, *Sexuality in Greek and Roman Culture*, 197. Amy Richlin, *The Garden of Priapus: Sexuality and Aggression in Roman Humor* Revised edn. (New York, 1983), 84.

49 Paterson, "The Idea of Rome," 10; M.I. Finley, "The Silent Women of Rome," in *Sexuality and Gender in the Classical World*, ed. Laura McClure, (Oxford, 2002), 50; Susan Treggiari, *Roman Marriage. Iusti Coniuges from the Time of Cicero to the Time of Ulpian* (Oxford, 1991), 93; Beryl Rawson, "Roman Concubinage and Other Defacto Marriages," *Transactions of the American Philological Association* 104 (1974): 282.

50 Treggiari, *Roman Marriage*, 422–64.

51 Richlin, *The Garden of Priapus*, 8–10; James Rives, "Religion in the Roman Empire," in *Experiencing Rome: Culture, Identity and Power in the Roman Empire*, ed. Janet Huskinson, (London, 2000), 252; James L. Butrica, "Some Myths and Anomalies in the Study of Roman Sexuality," *Journal of Homosexuality* 49 (2005): 250.

52 Ariadne Staples, *From Good Goddess to Vestal Virgins: Sex and Category in Roman Religion* (London, 1998), 142–56; Dominic Montserrat, "Reading Gender in the Roman World," in *Experiencing Rome: Culture, Identity and Power in the Roman Empire*, ed. Janet Huskinson, (London, 2000), 158.

53 For the *galli*, see Staples, *Good Goddess*, 118; Rabun Taylor, "Two Pathic Subcultures in Ancient Rome," *Journal of the History of Sexuality* 7 (1997): 335; Montserrat, "Reading Gender in the Roman World," 158.

54 Staples, *Good Goddess*, 83.

55 Kraemer, *Her Share of the Blessings*, 53; Ross Shepard Kraemer, ed., *Maenads, Martyrs, Matrons, Monastics: A Sourcebook on Women's Religions in the Greco-Roman World* (Philadelphia, 1988), 247, quoting Juvenal and Cicero.

56 Cato quoted in Emiel Eyben, *Restless Youth in Ancient Rome*, Patrick Daly trans. (London, 1993), 232.

57 J.N. Adams, *The Latin Sexual Vocabulary* (Baltimore, 1982), 97–134.

58 Shelley P. Haley, "Lucian's 'Leana and Clonarium': Voyeurism or a Challenge to Assumptions?," in *Among Women*, ed. Nancy Sorkin Rabinowitz and Lisa Auanger, (Austin, 2002), 295. Ovid, however, presented a more poignant picture of female desires in his story of Iphis, in *Metamorphoses*. In this story, Iphis, a woman who is brought up as a boy, becomes betrothed to her female beloved. In agony at her feelings, which she fears to be unnatural, for among animals "A female never fires a female's love"; she prays to the goddess Isis for help, who obliges by turning her into a male on her wedding night. Ovid, *Metamorphoses*, A.D. Melville trans. (Oxford, 1986), 222; Diane T. Pintabone, "Ovid's Iphis and Ianthe: When Girls Won't Be Girls," in *Among Women*, 257.

59 Martial Book 7, No. 67, in J.P. Sullivan and Peter Whigham, eds., *Martial Englished by Diverse Hands* (Berkeley, 1977).

60 John R. Clarke, "Representations of the Cinaedus in Roman Art: Evidence of 'Gay' Subculture?" *Journal of Homosexuality* 49 (2005): 271.

61 John R. Clarke, *Looking at Lovemaking in Roman Art* (Berkeley, 1998), 32.

62 For Roman prostitution, Thomas A.J. McGinn, *Prostitution, Sexuality, and the Law in Ancient Rome* (New York and Oxford, 1998); Thomas A.J. McGinn, *The Economy of Prostitution and the Roman World* (Ann Arbor, 2004); Thomas A.J. McGinn, "Zoning Shame in the Roman City," in *Prostitutes and Courtesans in the Ancient World*, ed. Christopher Faraone and Laura McClure, (Madison, 2005), 171–5.

63 Emma Dench, "Austerity, Excess, Success and Failure in Hellenistic and Early Imperial Italy," in *Parchments of Gender*, ed. Maria Wyke, (Oxford, 1998), 138.

64 Kelly Olson, "Matrona or Whore: Clothing and Definition in Late Antiquity," in *Prostitutes and Courtesans in the Ancient World*, 186–207.

65 Rebecca Flemming, "*Quae Corpore Quastum Facit*: The Sexual Economy of Female Prostitution in the Roman Empire," *Journal of Roman Studies* 89 (1999): 43; Horace, *Satires and Epistles*, Jacob Fuchs trans. (New York, 1977), 5.

66 Taylor, "Two Pathic Subcultures," 357; Beert C. Verstraete, "Slavery and the Social Dynamics of Male Homosexual Relations in Ancient Rome," *Journal of Homosexuality* 5 (1980): 228.

67 Suzanne Dixon, *Reading Roman Women* (London, 2000), 102.

68 Sharon L. James, "A Courtesan's Choreography: Female Liberty and Male Anxiety at the Roman Dinner Party," in *Prostitutes and Courtesans in the Ancient World*, 224–51.

69 Bing and Cohen, eds., *Games of Venus*, 243; Alison Keith, "*Tandem Venit Amor*: A Roman Woman Speaks of Love," in *Roman Sexualities*, 307.

70 Keith, "*Tandem Venit Amor*," 306.

71 Horace, *Satires and Epistles*, 5.

72 Craig A. Williams, *Roman Homosexuality: Ideologies of Masculinity in Classical Antiquity* (New York, 1999), 155.

73 Ellen Oliensis, "The Erotics of *Amicitia*," in *Roman Sexualities*, 155.

74 Catullus, in Bing and Cohen, eds., *Games of Venus*, 210.

75 Brian Arkins, *Sexuality in Catullus* (Hildesheim, 1982), 50–108.

76 Bing and Cohen, eds., *Games of Venus*, 207.

77 Walters, "Invading the Roman Body," 35; Williams, *Roman Homosexuality*, 182–8; Clarke, "Representations of the Cinaedus in Roman Art: Evidence of 'Gay' Subculture?."

78 Bing and Cohen, eds., *Games of Venus*, 235.

79 Taylor, "Two Pathic Subcultures," 366.

80 Fantham, "*Stuprum*," 287; Dench, "Austerity, Excess," 143–4; Janet Huskinson, "Elite Culture and the Identity of Empire," in *Experiencing*, 101; Treggiari, *Roman Marriage*, 60.

81 Williams, *Roman Homosexuality*, 249; Caroline Vout, *Power and Eroticism in Imperial Rome* (Cambridge, UK ; New York, 2007), 13.

82 Goldhill, *Foucault's Virginity*, 123–36; J. Samuel Houser, "*Eros* and *Aphrodisia* in the Works of Dio Chrysostom," and Martha C. Nussbaum, "The Incomplete Feminism of Musonius Rufus: Stoic, Platonist, Roman," both in *The Sleep of Reason*, ed. Martha C. Nussbaum and Juha Sihvola, (Chicago, 2002), 335, 293; Shadi Bartsch, "Eros and the Roman Philosopher," in *Erotikon*, ed. Shadi Bartsch and Thomas Bartscherer, (Chicago, 2005), 79–83.

83 Boyarin, "What Do We Talk About When We Talk About Platonic Love?," 22.

84 Diana M. Swancutt, "Sexing the Pauline Body of Christ," in *Erotikon*, 84, 152–7.

85 Carlin A. Barton, "Savage Miracles: The Redemption of Lost Honor in Roman Society and the Sacrament of the Gladiator and the Martyr," *Representations* 45 (1994): 41–71.

3 Divine desire in Judaisim and early Christianity

1 Ariel and Chana Bloch, ed., *The Song of Songs* (Berkeley, 1995), 45.

2 Carol Meyers, *Discovering Eve: Ancient Israelite Women in Context* (New York, 1988), 52.

3 David Biale, *Eros and the Jews* (New York, 1992), 16. Some scholars have also argued that the story of Ruth was actually written much later, but depicted as written in early times, to justify marriage outside the Hebrew community during a time when prophets

prohibited intermarriage. James. L. Kugel, *How to Read the Bible* (New York, 2007), 403.

4 William G. Dever, *Did God Have a Wife? Archaeology and Folk Religion in Ancient Israel* (Grand Rapids, 2005), 271.

5 Kathy L. Gaca, *The Making of Fornication: Eros, Ethics, and Political Reform in Greek Philosophy and Early Christianity* (Berkeley, 2003), 158.

6 Gale A. Yee, *Poor Banished Children of Eve: Woman as Evil in the Hebrew Bible* (Minneapolis, 2003), 90.

7 Helena Zlotnick, *Dinah's Daughters: Gender and Judaism from the Hebrew Bible to Late Antiquity* (Philadelphia, 2002), 55-106.

8 Bloch, ed., *Song of Songs*, 25.

9 Ross Shepard Kraemer, *Her Share of the Blessings: Women's Religions among Pagans, Jews and Christians in the Graeco-Roman World* (New York, 1992), 113.

10 Grace Jantzen, *Power, Gender, and Christian Mysticism* (Cambridge, 1995), 44; Gaca, *Making of Fornication*, 216.

11 David Winston, "Philo and the Rabbis on Sex and the Body," *Poetics Today* 19 (Spring, 1998): 41–63. Winston differs in emphasis from Boyarin: Daniel Boyarin, *Carnal Israel* (Berkeley, 1993), 39.

12 Halvor Moxnes, *Putting Jesus in His Place: A Radical Vision of Household and Kingdom* (Louisville, 2003), 62.

13 A.E. Harvey, "Eunuchs for the Sake of the Kingdom," *Heythrop Journal* 48 (2007): 1–17; Moxnes, *Putting Jesus in His Place*, 93; Matthew Kuefler, *The Manly Eunuch* (Chicago, 2001), 261.

14 Historians have disagreed on when the negativity about sex began in Christian culture. Since the Reformation, Protestant scholars have downplayed Paul's hostility toward sex and celebration of celibacy, to fit with their own valuation of marriage. They blamed Hellenistic influence and the Church fathers. But many historians today believe that the antagonism toward sexual desire was present in Paul, at the beginning of Christianity. Elizabeth A. Clark, *Reading Renunciation: Asceticism and Scripture in Early Christianity* (Princeton, 1999), 26.

15 John Boswell tried to downplay the significance of these references, but later scholars argue that indeed Paul was making reference to men who had sex with men, both in the active and passive positions, perhaps drawing on the Levitical prohibition of sodomy. John Boswell, *Christianity, Social Tolerance, and Homosexuality: Gay People in Western Europe from the Beginning of the Christian Era to the Fourteenth Century* (Chicago, 1980), 10–50; David F. Wright, "Homosexuals or Prostitutes? The Meaning of Malakoi and Arsenokoitoi (1 Cor. 6:9, 1 Tim. 1:10)," *Vigiliae Christianae* 38 (1984): 125–53.

16 Peter Brown, *The Body and Society: Men, Women, and Sexual Renunciation in Early Christianity* (New York, 1988), 31.

17 Ray Pickett, "Conflicts at Corinth," in *Christian Origins*, ed. Richard A. Horsley, (Minneapolis, 2005), 130.

18 Daniel Boyarin, *A Radical Jew: Paul and the Politics of Identity* (Berkeley, 1994), 172; Kuefler, *The Manly Eunuch*, 256.

19 Anders Nygren, *Agape and Eros*, Philip S. Watson trans. Revised edn. (London, 1982 [1932]), 210.

20 Prudentius, *Peristephanon*, Hymn 14 quoted in Gillian Clark, "Bodies and Blood: Late Antique Debate on Martyrdom, Virginity and Resurrection," in *Changing Bodies, Changing Meanings: Studies in the Human Body in Antiquity*, ed. Dominic Montserrat, (London, 1998), 102.

21 Judith Perkins, "Fictional Narratives and Social Critique," in *Late Ancient Christianity*, ed. Richard A. Horsley, (Minneapolis, 2005), 49-62.

22 "Acts of Paul and Thecla," *The Saint Pachomius Orthodox Library/Internet Medieval Sourcebook*, http://www.fordham.edu/halsall/basis/thecla.html (accessed Apr. 15, 2008); Stephen J. Davis, *The Cult of Saint Thecla: A Tradition of Women's Piety in Late Antiquity* (Oxford, 2001), 21–41; Bart D. Ehrman, *Lost Christianities: The Battles for Scripture and the Faiths We Never Knew* (New York, 2003), 32.

23 Teresa M. Shaw, *The Burden of the Flesh: Fasting and Sexuality in Early Christianity* (Minneapolis, 1998), 183.

24 Brown, *Body and Society*, 84.

25 Shaw, *Burden of the Flesh*, 109.

26 Gunhild Viden, "St. Jerome on Female Chastity: Subjugating the Elements of Desire," *Symbolae Osloenses* 73 (1998): 155.

27 Daniel F. Caner, "The Practice and Prohibition of Self-Castration in Early Christianity," *Vigiliae Christianae* 51 (1997): 411; Kuefler, *The Manly Eunuch*, 269.

28 Athanasius, "Select Works and Letters," *Medieval Sourcebook* (356–62), http://www.fordham.edu/halsall/basis/vita-antony.html (accessed Apr. 15, 2008).

29 Jerome quoted in Joyce E. Salisbury, *Church Fathers, Independent Virgins* (London, 1991), 19. See also Viden, "St. Jerome on Female Chastity," 144.

30 Ross Shepard Kraemer, ed., *Maenads, Martyrs, Matrons, Monastics: A Sourcebook on Women's Religions in the Greco-Roman World* (Philadelphia, 1988), 342.

31 Salisbury, *Church Fathers, Independent Virgins*, 27.

32 Shaw, *Burden of the Flesh*, 231.

33 Tertullian, "On the Apparel of Women," *Early Christian Writings*, http://www.earlychristianwritings.com/text/tertullian27.html (accessed Apr. 15, 2008).

34 Virginia Burrus, "The Heretical Woman as Symbol in Alexander, Athanasius, Ephiphanius, and Jerome," *Harvard Theological Review* 84 (1994): 232.

35 Kuefler, *The Manly Eunuch*, 274.

36 Calvin Roetzel, "Sex and the Single God," in *Text and Artifact in the Religions of Mediterranean Antiquity: Essays in Honour of Peter Richardson*, ed. Michel Robert Desjardins, Peter Richardson, and S.G. Wilson, (Waterloo, Ont., 2000), 242.

37 "Acts of Thomas," in *The Apocryphal New Testament*, ed. M.R. James, (Oxford 1924), 12.

38 Peter Brown, *Augustine of Hippo* (London, 2000), 276; Robert Bradshaw, "Marcion: Portrait of a Heretic" *Earlychurch.org.uk* http://www.earlychurch.org.uk/article_marcion.html (accessed Apr. 15, 2008); Kraemer, ed., *Maenads, Martyrs*, 388.

39 Elaine Pagels, *The Gnostic Gospels* (New York, 1979), 144.

40 Nygren, *Agape and Eros*, 309.

41 Salisbury, *Church Fathers, Independent Virgins*, 47.

42 Clark, *Reading Renunciation*, 216.

43 Jerome, "On Marriage and Virginity, from Letter xxii to Eustochium and from the Treatise against Jovinian," *Internet Medieval Sourcebook*, http://www.fordham.edu/halsall/source/jerome-marriage.html (accessed Apr. 15, 2008); Brown, *Body and Society*, 377.

44 John Oulton, ed., *Alexandrian Christianity: Selected Translations of Clement and Origine* (Philadelphia, 1954), 103.

45 Shaw, *Burden of the Flesh*, 84.

46 Pierre Payer, *The Bridling of Desire: Views of Sex in the Later Middle Ages* (Toronto, 1993), 60.

47 St. Augustine, "On Marriage and Concupiscence," *Internet Medieval Sourcebook*, http://www.fordham.edu/halsall/source/aug-marr.html (accessed Apr. 15, 2008).

48 Brown, *Body and Society*, 307.

49 Gaca, *Making of Fornication*, 255–65.

50 Quoted in Ibid., 265–98; Elaine H. Pagels, *Adam, Eve, and the Serpent* 1st edn. (New York, 1988), 29.

51 Chrysostom discussed in Shaw, *Burden of the Flesh*, 4, 84, 207.
52 Augustine, "On Marriage and Concupiscence."
53 Saint Augustine, *Confessions*, Henry Chadwick trans. (New York, 1991), 24. See also Brown, *Augustine of Hippo*; Peter Burnell, *The Augustinian Person* (Washington, DC, 2005).
54 Augustine, *Confessions*, 24–47.
55 Ibid., 82.
56 Jonathan Dollimore, *Sexual Dissidence* (New York, 1991), 131.
57 Augustine, "On Marriage and Concupiscence," Book 1, ch. 7.
58 Salisbury, *Church Fathers, Independent Virgins*, 45.
59 Augustine, quoted in Brown, *Body and Society*, 426.
60 David Tracy, "The Divided Consciousness of Augustine on Eros," in *Erotikon: Essays on Eros, Ancient and Modern*, ed. Shadi Bartsch and Thomas Bartscherer, (Chicago, 2005), 100.
61 Nygren, *Agape and Eros*, 461–5.

4 Medieval fantasies of desire, sacred and profane

1 Monica Furlong, *Visions and Longings: Medieval Women Mystics* (Boston, 1996), 109.
2 Meg Bogin, *The Woman Troubadours* (London, 1976), 38.
3 James A. Brundage, *Law, Sex and Society in Medieval Europe* (Chicago, 1987), 581.
4 Peter Brown, *The Body and Society: Men, Women, and Sexual Renunciation in Early Christianity* (New York, 1988), 408; R.I. Moore, "Property, Marriage, and the Eleventh-Century Revolution: A Context for Early Medieval Communism," in *Medieval Purity and Piety*, ed. Michael Frassetto, (New York, 1998), 191. Of course, priests continued to take concubines despite prohibitions.
5 Pierre J. Payer, *Sex and the Penitentials: The Development of a Sexual Code 550–1150* (Toronto, 1984), 40; Pierre Payer, *The Bridling of Desire: Views of Sex in the Later Middle Ages* (Toronto, 1993), 78; Ruth Mazo Karras, *Sexuality in Medieval Europe: Doing Unto Others* (London and New York, 2005), 64.
6 Michel Rouche, "The Early Middle Ages in the West," in *A History of Private Life: From Pagan Rome to Byzantium*, ed. Philippe Ariès, George Duby, and Paul Veyne, (Cambridge, MA, 1987), 478.
7 Jeffrey Richards, *Sex, Dissidence and Damnation* (New York, 1991), 21.
8 Malcolm Barber, *The Cathars* (Harlow, 2000), 84; René Nelli, *La Vie Quotidienne Des Cathares Du Languedoc Au XIIIe Siècle* (Paris, 1983), 70.
9 Stephen D. Moore, "The Song of Songs in the History of Sexuality," *Church History* 69 (2000): 330; Glenn Burger and Steven F. Kruger, eds., *Queering the Middle Ages* (Minneapolis, 2001).
10 Karma Lochrie, *Heterosyncrasies: Female Sexuality When Normal Wasn't* (Minneapolis, 2005), xv.
11 John Boswell, *Christianity, Social Tolerance, and Homosexuality: Gay People in Western Europe from the Beginning of the Christian Era to the Fourteenth Century* (Chicago, 1980), 240.
12 Madelain Farah, "Preface," in *Marriage and Sexuality in Islam: A Translation of Al-Ghazali's Book on the Etiquette of Marriage from the Ihya*, ed. Madelain Farah, (Salt Lake City, 1984), 26.
13 J. C. Burgel, "Love, Lust and Longing: Eroticism in Early Islam as Reflected in Literary Sources," in *Society and the Sexes in Medieval Islam*, ed. A.L. al-Sayyid Marsot, (Malibu, 1979), 94.
14 Khaled El-Rouayheb, *Before Homosexuality in the Arab-Islamic World, 1500–1800* (Chicago, 2005), 47.

15 Ibn Hazm, *The Ring of the Dove*, A.J. Arberry trans. (London, *c.* 994–1064). http://www.muslimphilosophy.com/hazm/dove/ringdove.html (accessed Apr. 15, 2008).

16 Annemarie Schimmel, "Eros in Sufi Literature and Life," in *Society and the Sexes in Medieval Islam*, ed. A.L. al-Sayyid Marsot, (Malibu, 1979), 132.

17 Lourdes Alvarez, "The Mystical Language of Daily Life: Vernacular Sufi Poetry and the Songs of Abu Al-Hasan Al-Shushtari," *Exemplaria: A Journal of Theory in Medieval and Renaissance Studies* 17 (2005): 26.

18 Koltun-Fromm, "Sexuality and Holiness: Semitic Christian and Jewish Conceptualizations of Sexual Behavior," *Vigiliae Christianae* 54 (2000): 375–95.

19 David Biale, *Eros and the Jews* (New York, 1992), 44.

20 Gershon Winkler, *Sacred Secrets: The Sanctity of Sex in Jewish Law and Lore* (Northvale, NJ, 1988), 22.

21 Biale, *Eros and the Jews*, 103–12; Daniel Boyarin, *Carnal Israel* (Berkeley, 1993), 52.

22 Yom Tov Assis, "Sexual Behavior in Mediaeval Hispano-Jewish Society," in *Jewish History: Essays in Honour of Chimen Abramsky*, ed. Ada Rapoport-Alpert and Steven J. Zipperstein, (London, 1988), 27; Bogin, *Woman Troubadours*, 45.

23 Norman Roth, "'Fawn of My Delights': Boy-Love in Hebrew and Arabic Verse," in *Sex in the Middle Ages*, ed. Joyce Salisbury, (New York, 1991), 37.

24 C. Stephen Jaeger, *Ennobling Love: In Search of a Lost Sensibility* (Philadelphia, 1999), 26.

25 Guiraut Riquier, 1254, quoted in Michael Routledge, "The Later Troubadours," in *The Troubadours: An Introduction*, ed. Simon Gaunt and Sarah Kay, (Cambridge, 1999), 109.

26 Sarah Kay, "Desire and Subjectivity," in *The Troubadours: An Introduction*, 226.

27 Linda Paterson, *The World of the Troubadours: Medieval Occitan Society, c.1100–c.1300* (Cambridge, 1993), 37.

28 James A. Schultz, *Courtly Love, the Love of Courtliness, and the History of Sexuality* (Chicago, 2006), 54–5.

29 John W. Baldwin, *The Language of Sex: Five Voices from Northern France* (Chicago, 1994), 65.

30 Ibid., 65, 135.

31 Quoted in Grace Jantzen, *Power, Gender, and Christian Mysticism* (Cambridge, 1995), 133.

32 Nancy F. Partner, "Did Mystics Have Sex?," in *Desire and Discipline: Sex and Sexuality in the Premodern West*, ed. Jacqueline Murray and Konrad Eisenbichler, (Toronto, 1996), 307; Amy Hollywood, *Sensible Ecstasy: Mysticism, Sexual Difference, and the Demands of History* (Chicago, 2002).

33 Bernard of Clairvaux, "Commentary on the Song of Songs by St. Bernard of Clairvaux," *Glorify his Name* (1135 and 1153), http://glorifyhisname.com/sys-tmpl/b1/. Sermon 2. (accessed Apr. 18, 2008).

34 Boswell, *Christianity, Social Tolerance, and Homosexuality*, 220; Jaeger, *Ennobling Love*, 113.

35 Boswell, *Christianity, Social Tolerance, and Homosexuality*, 220–4.

36 Susan Schibanoff, "Hildegarde of Bingen and Richardis of Stade: The Discourse of Desire," in *Same Sex Love and Desire among Women in the Middle Ages*, ed. Francesca Canadé Sautman and Pamela Sheingorn, (New York, 2001), 59.

37 Stanzic poem 12 in Marieke van Baest, ed., *The Poetry of Hadewijch* (Leuven, 1998), 103.

38 Furlong, *Visions and Longings*, 114.

39 Ibid., 105.

40 Ibid., 114.

41 Sarah Beckwith, "Passionate Regulation: Enclosure, Ascesis, and the Feminist Imaginary," *South Atlantic Quarterly* 93 (1994): 114.

42 Carolyn Bynum, *Fragmentation and Redemption: Essays on Gender and the Human Body in Medieval Religion* (New York, 1991), 178–9.

43 van Baest, ed., *The Poetry of Hadewijch*, 155.

44 For a useful discussion, see Sarah Salih, "When Is a Bosom Not a Bosom? Problems with Erotic Mysticism," in *Medieval Virginities*, ed. Anke Bernau, Ruth Evans, and Sarah Salih, (Toronto, 2003), 14–32.

45 Clairvaux, "Commentary on the Song of Songs," Sermon 4.4.

46 Richard Kearney, "The Shulammite's Song: Divine Eros, Ascending and Descending," in *Toward a Theology of Eros: Transfiguring Passion at the Limits of Discipline*, ed. Virginia Burrus and Catherine Keller, (New York, 2006), 324.

47 Clairvaux, "Commentary on the Song of Songs," Sermon 84.

48 Salih, "When Is a Bosom Not a Bosom?" 29; C. Stephen Jaeger, "The Loves of Christina of Markyate," and Kathryn Kelsey Staples and Ruth Mazo Karras, "Christina's Tempting," in *Christina of Markyate*, ed. Samuel Fanous and Henrietta Leyser, (London, 2004), 99–115 and 185–96.

49 Walter Simons, *Cities of Ladies: Beguine Communities in the Medieval Low Countries, 1200–1565* (Philadelphia, 2000), 70; Amy Hollywood, "Sexual Desire, Divine Desire; or, Queering the Beguines," in *Toward a Theology of Eros*.

50 Simons, *Cities of Ladies*, 120; Richards, *Sex, Dissidence and Damnation*, 61.

51 Joan Cadden, *Meanings of Sex Differences in the Middle Ages: Medicine, Science, and Culture* (Cambridge, 1995), 143–274.

52 Lochrie, *Heterosyncrasies*, 85–7; Baldwin, *Language of Sex*, 231.

53 Carlo Ginzburg, *The Night Battles: Witchcraft and Agrarian Cults in the Sixteenth and Seventeenth Centuries*, John and Anne Tedeschi trans. (Baltimore, 1983), 24.

54 Peter Biller, "Confessors' Manuals and the Avoiding of Offspring," in *Handling Sin: Confession in the Middle Ages*, ed. Peter Biller, (York, 1998), 166–84.

55 Kevin Robbins, "Magical Emasculation, Popular Anticlericalism, and the Limits of the Reformation in Western France Circa 1590," *Journal of Social History* 31 (1997): 61–83.

56 Walter Stephens, *Demon Lovers: Witchcraft, Sex, and the Crisis of Belief* (Chicago, 2002), 32–57.

57 Mikhail Bakhtin, *Rabelais and His World*, Helene Iswolsky trans. (Bloomington, 1984), 338.

58 Geoffrey Chaucer, *The Canterbury Tales*, Nevill Coghill trans. (Harmondsworth, 1977 [1957]), 280.

59 "The Four Wishes of Saint Martin," in Robert Harrison, *Gallic Salt: Eighteen Fabliaux Translated from the Old French* (Berkeley, 1974), 187.

60 Francois Rabelais, *Five Books of the Lives, Heroic Deeds and Sayings of Gargantua and His Son Pantagruel*, Sir Thomas Urquhart and Peter Antony Motteux trans. (London, 1970 [1659]), 34.

61 Lyndal Roper, *Oedipus and the Devil: Witchcraft, Sexuality and Religion in Early Modern Europe* (London, 1994), 156.

62 Gautier le Leu, "The Widow," in *Fabliaux: Ribald Tales from the Old French*, Robert Hellman and Richard O'Gorman trans. (New York, 1965), 148.

63 Rabelais, *Gargantua and Pantagruel*, 393; Linda Hults, "Baldung and the Witches of Freiburg: The Evidence of Images," *Journal of Interdisciplinary History* 18 (1987): 264; Susan Broomhill, "Rabelais, the Pursuit of Knowledge, and Early Modern Gynaecology," *Limina* 4 (1998): 25–34.

64 Dafydd Johnston, "Erotica and Satire in Medieval Welsh Poetry," in *Obscenity: Social Control and Artistic Creation in the European Middle Ages*, ed. Jan M. Ziolkowski, (Leiden, 1998), 70.

65 Chaucer, *The Canterbury Tales*, 293.

66 Ruth Mazo Karras, *Sexuality in Medieval Europe* (London, 2005), 4.

67 R. Howard Bloch, "Obscenity in the Fabliaux," in *Obscenity: Social Control and Artistic Creation in the Middle Ages*, ed. Jan M. Ziolkowski, (Leiden, 1998), 301.
68 Gautier le Leu, "The Widow," in *Fabliaux*, 154.
69 R.I. Moore, *The Formation of a Persecuting Society* (Oxford, 1987); Richards, *Sex, Dissidence and Damnation*.

5 From twilight moments to moral panics

1 Michael Goodich, *Other Middle Ages: Witnesses at the Margins of Medieval Society* (Philadelphia, 1998), 143; Francesca Canadé Sautman, "'Just Like a Woman:' Queer History, Womanizing the Body, and the Boys in Arnaud's Band," in *Queering the Middle Ages*, ed. Glenn Burger and Steven F. Kruger, (Minneapolis, 2001), 168–79.
2 Pierre J. Payer, *Sex and the Penitentials: The Development of a Sexual Code 550–1150* (Toronto, 1984), 40; Pierre Payer, *The Bridling of Desire: Views of Sex in the Later Middle Ages* (Toronto, 1993), 78; John W. Baldwin, *The Language of Sex: Five Voices from Northern France* (Chicago, 1994), 177.
3 Rob Meens, "The Frequency and Nature of Early Medieval Penance," in *Handling Sin: Confession in the Middle Ages*, ed. Peter Biller and A. J. Minnis, (York, 1998), 48; L.R. Poos, "Sex, Lies, and the Church Courts of Pre-Reformation England," *Journal of Interdisciplinary History* 25 (1995).
4 Peter Biller, "Introduction," in *Handling Sin*, 6.
5 Payer, *The Bridling of Desire*, 85–121; James A. Brundage, *Law, Sex and Society in Medieval Europe* (Chicago, 1987), 581.
6 Poos, "Sex, Lies, and the Church Courts of Pre-Reformation England," 585–607.
7 David Nirenberg, *Communities of Violence: Persecution of Minorities in the Middle Ages* (Princeton, 1996), 9.
8 Ibid., 142; David Nirenberg, "Conversion, Sex, and Segregation: Jews and Christians in Medieval Spain," *American Historical Review* 107 (2002): 1065–70.
9 Mark D. Meyerson, "Prostitution of Muslim Women in the Kingdom of Valencia: Religious and Sexual Discrimination in a Medieval Plural Society," in *The Medieval Mediterranean: Cross-Cultural Contacts*, ed. Marilyn J. Chiat and Kathryn L. Reyerson, (St. Cloud, 1988), 89.
10 Nirenberg, *Communities of Violence*, 140.
11 Heath Dillard, *Daughters of the Reconquest: Women in Castilian Town Society, 1100–1300* (Cambridge, 1984).
12 Kenneth Baxter Wolf, "Muhammad as Antichrist in Ninth-Century Spain," in *Christians, Muslims, and Jews in Medieval and Early Modern Spain: Interaction and Cultural Change*, ed. Mark D. Meyerson and Edward D. English, (Notre Dame, 1999), 10; Roy Rosenstein, "The Voice and the Voiceless in the Cancioneiros: The Muslim, the Jew, and the Sexual Heretic as Exclusus Amator," *La Corónica: A Journal of Medieval Spanish Language and Literature* 26 (1998): 69.
13 Nirenberg, *Communities of Violence*, 145.
14 Maryanne Kowalski, "Singlewomen in Medieval and Early Modern Europe: The Demographic Perspective," in *Singlewomen in the European Past, 1250–1800*, ed. Judith M. Bennett and Amy M. Froide, (Philadelphia, 1999), 50.
15 Judith M. Bennett, "Writing Fornication: Medieval Leyrwrite and Its Historians," *Transactions of the Royal Historical Society* 13 (2003): 144.
16 R. H Helmholz, "Harboring Sexual Offenders: Ecclesiastical Courts and Controlling Misbehavior," *Journal of British Studies* 37:3 (1998): 602.
17 John K. Brackett, "The Florentine Onestà and the Control over Prostitution, 1403–1680," *Sixteenth Century Journal* 24 (1993): 274; Eukene Lacarra Lanz, "Changing Boundaries of Licit and Illicit Unions: Concubinage and Prostitution," in *Marriage and Sexuality in Medieval and Early Modern Iberia*, ed. Eukene Lacarra Lanz, (New

York, 2002), 162; Carol Lansing, "Concubines, Lovers, Prostitutes: Infamy and Female Identity in Medieval Bologna," in *Beyond Florence: The Contours of Medieval and Early Modern Italy*, ed. Paula Findlen, Michelle M. Fontaine, and Duane J. Oshein, (Stanford, 2003), 95.

18 Brundage, *Law, Sex and Society in Medieval Europe*, 44.

19 Linda Paterson, *The World of the Troubadours: Medieval Occitan Society, c.1100–c.1300* (Cambridge, 1993), 178; Lansing, "Concubines, Lovers, Prostitutes," 89; Leah Otis, *Prostitutes in Medieval Society: The Case of Languedoc* (Chicago, 1985), 24; Jacques Rossiaud, *Medieval Prostitution*, Lydia Cochrane trans. (Oxford, 1988), 55.

20 Otis, *Prostitutes in Medieval Society*, 23; Mary Elizabeth Perry, *Gender and Disorder in Early Modern Seville* (Princeton, 1990), 47.

21 Lyndal Roper, *Oedipus and the Devil: Witchcraft, Sexuality and Religion in Early Modern Europe* (London, 1994), 152.

22 Geoffrey Chaucer, *The Canterbury Tales*, Nevill Coghill trans. (Harmondsworth, 1977), 262.

23 Rossiaud, *Medieval Prostitution*, 82.

24 Otis, *Prostitutes in Medieval Society*, 124.

25 Brackett, "The Florentine Onestà and the Control over Prostitution, 1403–1680," 280.

26 Ruth Mazo Karras, *Common Women: Prostitution and Sexuality in Medieval England* (New York, 1996), 58–9.

27 Brackett, "The Florentine Onestà and the Control over Prostitution, 1403–1680," 276.

28 Elisabeth Pavan, "Police Des Moeurs, Societé Et Politique À Venise À La Fin Du Moyen Age," *Revue Historique [France]* 264 (1980): 244.

29 Eukene Lacarra Lanz, "Legal and Clandestine Prostitution in Medieval Spain," *Bulletin of Hispanic Studies (Liverpool)* 79 (2002): 272.

30 Guido Ruggiero, "Marriage, Love, Sex, and Renaissance Civic Morality," in *Sexuality and Gender in Early Modern Europe*, ed. James Grantham Turner, (Cambridge, 1993), 11.

31 Rossiaud, *Medieval Prostitution*, 12.

32 Pavan, "Police Des Moeurs," 259.

33 Payer, *Sex and the Penitentials*, 136–140; James A. Schultz, *Courtly Love, the Love of Courtliness, and the History of Sexuality* (Chicago, 2006), 54–5; Brundage, *Law, Sex and Society in Medieval Europe*, 213, 313.

34 Here I differ from the interpretation of John Boswell that the early Church was more tolerant of sodomy. See John Boswell, *Christianity, Social Tolerance, and Homosexuality: Gay People in Western Europe from the Beginning of the Christian Era to the Fourteenth Century* (Chicago, 1980); for critiques, see Gregory S. Hutcheson, "The Sodomitic Moor: Queerness in the Narrative of *Reconquista*," in *Queering the Middle Ages*, 106; Marc Boone, "State Power and Illicit Sexuality: The Persecution of Sodomy in Late Medieval Bruges," *Journal of Medieval History* 22 (1996): 138; Louis Crompton, *Homosexuality and Civilization* (Cambridge, MA, 2003), 160.

35 For a good critique of the acts/identities distinction see Sarah Salih, "Sexual Identities: A Medieval Perspective," in *Sodomy in Early Modern Europe*, ed. Tom Betteridge, (Manchester, 2002), 121–30.

36 Peter Damian, *Book of Gomorrah: An Eleventh-Century Treatise against Clerical Homosexual Practices*, Pierre J. Payer trans. (Waterloo, 1982), 59–64.

37 Mark D. Jordan, *The Invention of Sodomy in Christian Theology* (Chicago, 1997), 156.

38 Helmut Puff, *Sodomy in Reformation Germany and Switzerland 1400–1600* (Chicago, 2003), 13.

39 Ibid., 110.

40 Alan Bray, *The Friend* (Chicago, 2003), 154; C. Stephen Jaeger, *Ennobling Love: In Search of a Lost Sensibility* (Philadelphia, 1999), 136; Armando Maggi, "On Kissing and Sighing: Renaissance Homoerotic Love from Ficino's *De Amore* and *Sopra Lo Amore* to Cesare Trevisiani's *L'impresa* (1569)," *Journal of Homosexuality* 49 (2005): 321–4; Katherine B. Crawford, "Marsilio Ficino, Neoplatonism, and the Problem of Sex," *Renaissance and Reformation* 28 (2004): 11–13.

41 Cynthia Herrup, *A House in Gross Disorder: Sex, Law, and the 2nd Earl of Castlehaven* (New York, 1999), 34.

42 Crompton, *Homosexuality and Civilization*, 246.

43 Carol Lansing, "Gender and Civic Authority: Sexual Control in a Medieval Italian Town," *Journal of Social History* 31 (1997): 39.

44 Franco Mormando, *The Preacher's Demons : Bernardino of Siena and the Social Underworld of Early Renaissance Italy* (Chicago, 1999), 122.

45 The subsequent discussion is from Michael Rocke, *Forbidden Friendships: Homosexuality and Male Culture in Renaissance Florence* (New York and Oxford, 1996), 150–89.

46 Pavan, "Police Des Moeurs," 282.

47 Crompton, *Homosexuality and Civilization*, 267.

48 Ruggiero, *The Boundaries of Eros: Sex Crime and Sexuality in Renaissance Venice*, 119.

49 Pavan, "Police Des Moeurs," 265.

50 Rocke, *Forbidden Friendships*, 200–20.

51 N.S. Davidson, "Sodomy in Early Modern Venice," in *Sodomy in Early Modern Europe*, 72; Crompton, *Homosexuality and Civilization*, 200.

52 Antonio Vignali, *La Cazzaria: The Book of the Prick*, Ian Moulton trans. (New York, 2003), 85–114.

53 Davidson, "Sodomy in Early Modern Venice," 74.

54 Puff, *Sodomy in Reformation Germany and Switzerland 1400–1600*, 49.

55 Lyndal Roper, *The Holy Household: Women and Morals, in Reformation Augsburg* (Oxford, 1989), 255.

56 Luther quoted in Puff, *Sodomy in Reformation Germany and Switzerland 1400–1600*, 131–42.

57 Alan Bray, *Homosexuality in Renaissance England* (1982), 32.

58 Herrup, *House in Gross Disorder*, 59.

59 Puff, *Sodomy in Reformation Germany and Switzerland 1400–1600*, 74.

60 Mary Laven, *Virgins of Venice: Broken Vows and Cloistered Lives in the Renaissance Convent* (London, 2002), 193.

61 Perry, *Gender and Disorder in Early Modern Seville*, 71.

62 Helmut Puff, "Female Sodomy: The Trial of Katherina Hetzeldorfer (1477)," *Journal of Medieval and Early Modern Studies* 30 (2000): 46.

63 Valerie Traub, *The Renaissance of Lesbianism in Early Modern England* (Cambridge, 2002), 6.

64 E. William Monter, *Frontiers of Heresy: The Spanish Inquisition from the Basque Lands to Sicily* (Cambridge, 1990), 281.

65 Catalina de Erauso, *Lieutenant Nun: Memoir of a Basque Transvestite in the New World*, Michele Stepto and Gabriel Stepto trans. (Boston, 1996).

66 Roper, *Holy Household*, 109.

67 Thomas A. Fudge, "Incest and Lust in Luther's Marriage Theology and Morality in Reformation Polemics," *Sixteenth Century Journal* 34 (2003): 321–8.

68 "Wider den falsch genannten geistlichen Stand" (1522) quoted in Joel F. Harrington, *Reordering Marriage and Society in Reformation Germany* (1995), 63.

69 Martin Luther, "The Estate of Marriage," in *Luther on Women: A Sourcebook*, ed. Susan C. Karant-Nunn and Merry E. Weisner-Hanks, (Cambridge, 2003), 100.

70 Martin Luther, "Lectures on Genesis" and "Sermon on the Sixth Commandment," in *Luther on Women*, 162, 147–8, 152.

71 Roper, *Oedipus and the Devil*, 41; Roper, *Holy Household*, 68.
72 Charlene Black Villaseñor, "Love and Marriage in the Spanish Empire: Depictions of Holy Matrimony and Gender Discourses in the Seventeenth Century," *Sixteenth Century Journal* 32 (2001): 662.
73 Merry Weisner, *Christianity and Sexuality in the Early Modern World* (London, 2000), 105.
74 Helen Rawlings, *The Spanish Inquisition* (Malden, MA, 2006), 124.
75 For sodomy and the Inquisition, see Monter, *Frontiers of Heresy: The Spanish Inquisition from the Basque Lands to Sicily*, 288; Cristian Berco, "Social Control and Its Limits: Local Sexual Economies and Inquisitors During Spain's Golden Age," *Sixteenth Century Journal* 36 (2005): 243; Federico Garza Carvajal, *Butterflies Will Burn: Prosecuting Sodomites in Early Modern Spain and Mexico* (Austin, 2003), 77; Perry, *Gender and Disorder in Early Modern Seville*, 71.
76 Mary Elizabeth Perry, "Deviant Insiders: Legalized Prostitutes and a Consciousness of Women in Early Modern Seville," *Comparative Studies in Society and History* 27 (1985): 138–58.
77 James R. Farr, *Authority and Sexuality in Early Modern Burgundy* (New York, 1995), 139.
78 Ruth Mazo Karras, "Prostitution and the Question of Sexual Identity in Medieval Europe," *Journal of Women's History* 11 (1999): 139–77.
79 Bray, *The Friend*, 212; Traub, *The Renaissance of Lesbianism in Early Modern England*, 257.
80 Carvajal, *Butterflies Will Burn*, 178.

6 The age of exploration

1 For different translations and interpretations of this song either as a political metaphor or as a personal narrative, see Kay A. Read and Jane Rosenthal, "The Chalcan Woman's Song: Sex as a Political Metaphor in Fifteenth-Century Mexico," *Americas: A Quarterly Review of Inter-American Cultural History* 62 (2006): 325; Camilla Townsend, "'What in the World Have You Done to Me, My Lover? Sex, Servitude among the Pre-Conquest Nahuas as Seen in the *Cantares Mexicanos*," *Americas: A Quarterly Review of Inter-American Cultural History* 62 (2006): 357.
2 Camilla Townsend, *Malintzin's Choices: An Indian Woman in the Conquest of Mexico* (Albuquerque, 2006), 10–37.
3 For more on sexual conquest in South America, see James Hoke Sweet, "Recreating Africa: Race, Religion, and Sexuality in the African–Portuguese World, 1441–1770" (Ph.D., City University of New York, 1999); Ruth Trocolli, "Colonization and Women's Production: The Timucua of Florida," in *Exploring Gender through Archeology*, ed. Cheryl Claassen, (Boone, 1992); Michael J. Horswell, "An Andean Theory of Same-Sex Sexuality," in *Infamous Desire: Male Homosexuality in Colonial Latin America*, ed. Pete Sigal, (Chicago, 2003); Ann Twinam, *Public Lives, Private Secrets: Gender, Honor, Sexuality and Illegitimacy in Colonial Spanish America* (Stanford, 1999); Irene Silverblatt, *Moon, Sun and Witches: Gender Ideologies and Class in Inca and Colonial Peru* (Princeton, 1987); Raymond E. Hauser, "The Berdache and the Illinois Indian Tribe During the Last Half of the Seventeenth Century," *Ethnohistory* 37 (1990); Albert Hurtado, "Sexuality in California's Franciscan Missions: Cultural Perceptions and Historical Realities," in *Sexualities in History: A Reader*, ed. Kim Phillips and Barry Reay, (New York, 2002).
   For this theme in other areas, see Kirsten Fischer, *Suspect Relations: Sex, Race, and Resistance in Colonial North America* (Ithaca, 2002); Jennifer M. Spear, "'They Need Wives:' Métissage and the Regulation of Sexuality in Colonial Louisiana," in *Sex, Love, Race: Crossing Boundaries in North American History*, ed. Martha Hodes, (New York,

1999); Ann Stoler, "Sexual Affronts and Racial Frontiers: European Identities and the Cultural Politics of Exclusion in Colonial Southeast Asia," *Comparative Studies in Society and History* 34 (1992): 514–51.

4 James Krippner-Martínez, *Rereading the Conquest: Power, Politics, and the History of Early Colonial Michoacán, Mexico, 1521–1565* (University Park, PA, 2001). For an example of a controversy around this issue, see Ramon Gutierrez, *When the Corn Mothers Went Away: Marriage, Sexuality and Power in New Mexico 1500–1846* (Stanford, 1991); University of New Mexico Native American Studies Center, "Commentaries: When Jesus Came, the Corn Mothers Went Away: Marriage, Sex and Power in New Mexico, 1500–1846," *American Indian Culture and Research Journal* 17 (1993): 141–77.

5 Patricia Seed, *To Love, Honor, and Obey in Colonial Mexico: Conflicts over Marriage Choice, 1574–1821* (Stanford, 1988), 62.

6 Mary Elizabeth Perry, *The Handless Maiden: Moriscos and the Politics of Religion in Early Modern Spain* (Princeton, 2005), 48.

7 E. William Monter, *Frontiers of Heresy: The Spanish Inquisition from the Basque Lands to Sicily* (Cambridge, 1990), 279.

8 Friar Diego de Landa, *Yucatan before and after the Conquest*, William Gates trans. (New York, 1978), 159.

9 Bernal Diaz del Castillo, *The Discovery and Conquest of Mexico*, A.P. Maudslay trans. (New York, 1996 [1632]), 79–105.

10 To avoid confusion, I will use Aztec to refer to the empire based in Tenochtitlan, Mexica and Nahua to refer to the wider culture of the Aztecs and their allies and subsidiaries.

11 Diaz del Castillo, *The Discovery and Conquest of Mexico*, 90, 153; Pedro Carrasco, "Indian-Spanish Marriages in the First Century of the Colony," in *Indian Women of Early Mexico*, ed. Susan Schroeder, Stephanie Wood, and Robert Haskett, (Norman, 1997), 94.

12 Bartolomé de las Casas, *History of the Indies*, Andrée Collard trans. (New York, 1971), 149.

13 Susan Socolow, *The Women of Colonial Latin America* (Cambridge, 2000), 36; Carrasco, "Indian-Spanish Marriages in the First Century of the Colony," 88.

14 Inga Clendinnen, "Yucatec Maya Women and the Spanish," *Journal of Social History* 15 (1982): 431; Matthew Restall, "'He Wished It in Vain': Subordination and Resistance among Maya Women in Post-Conquest Yucatan," *Ethnohistory* 42 (1995): 577; Diaz del Castillo, *The Discovery and Conquest of Mexico*, 333.

15 Gutierrez, *When the Corn Mothers Went Away*, 152.

16 Inga Clendinnen, "Disciplining the Indians: Franciscan Ideology and Missionary Violence in Sixteenth-Century Yucatan," *Past and Present* 94 (1982): 29.

17 Quotes from Lewis Hanke, *All Mankind Is One: A Study of the Disputation between Bartolomé De Las Casas and Juan Giné De Supulveda in 1550 on the Intellectual and Religious Capacity of the American Indians* (De Kalb, 1974), 84. And also see Anthony Pagden, *The Lords of All the World: Ideologies of Empire in Spain, Britain and France 1500–1800* (New Haven, 1995); Krippner-Martínez, *Rereading the Conquest*, 10–20.

18 Hanke, *All Mankind is One*, 95.

19 Quoted in Richard C. Trexler, *Sex and Conquest: Gender Violence, Political Order, and the European Conquest of the Americas* (Ithaca, 1995), 5.

20 Clendinnen, "Disciplining the Indians," 36–42.

21 Laura A. Lewis, "The 'Weakness' of Women and the Feminization of the Indian in Colonial Mexico," *Colonial Latin American Review* 5 (1996): 31.

22 Louise Burckhart, *The Slippery Earth: Nahua-Christian Moral Dialogue in Sixteenth-Century Mexico* (Tucson, 1989), 18.

23 Alfredo López Austin, *Tamoanchan, Tlalocan: Places of Mist*, Bernard Ortiz de Montellano and Thelma Ortiz de Montellano trans. (Niwot, CO, 1997), 136.

24 Inga Clendinnen, *Aztecs: An Interpretation* (Cambridge, 1991), 179.

25 David Carrasco, *City of Sacrifice* (Boston, 1999), 190.

26 This description is from Clendinnen, *Aztecs*, 201–3.

27 Matthew G. Looper, "Women-Men (and Men-Women): Classic Maya Rulers and the Third Gender," in *Ancient Maya Women*, ed. Tracy Ardren, (Walnut Creek, 2002), 191.

28 Pete Sigal, *From Moon Goddesses to Virgins: The Colonization of Yucatecan Maya Sexual Desire* (Austin, 2000), 151, 202.

29 Landa, *Yucatan*, 47.

30 Sigal, *From Moon Goddesses to Virgins*, 202–10.

31 Pete Sigal, "The *Cuiloni*, the *Patlache*, and the Abominable Sin: Homosexualities in Early Colonial Nahua Society," *Hispanic American Historical Review* 85 (2005): 587.

32 This paragraph is from the ideas of Burckhart, *Slippery Earth*, 100.

33 Carrasco, *City of Sacrifice*, 179.

34 Rebecca Overmyer-Velázquez, "Christian Morality Revealed in New Spain: The Inimical Nahua Woman in Book Ten of the *Florentine Codex*," *Journal of Women's History* 10 (1998): 16.

35 Cecelia F. Klein, "Teocuitlatl, 'Divine Excrement': The Significance Of 'Holy Shit' In Ancient Mexico," *Art Journal* 52 (1993): 20–7.

36 Sigal, "The *Cuiloni*, the *Patlache*, and the Abominable Sin," 570.

37 Susan Kellogg, "From Parallel and Equivalent to Separate but Unequal: Tenocha Mexica Women, 1500–1700," in *Indian Women of Early Mexico*, ed. Susan Schroeder, Stephanie Wood, and Robert Haskett, (Norman, 1997), 130.

38 Burckhart, *Slippery Earth*, 64.

39 Ibid., 133, 50.

40 Pete Sigal, "Gendered Power, the Hybrid Self, and Homosexual Desire in Late Colonial Yucatan," in *Infamous Desire: Male Homosexuality in Colonial Latin America*, ed. Pete Sigal, (Chicago, 2003), 121.

41 Matthew Restall, *The Maya World: Yucatec Culture and Society, 1550–1850* (Stanford, CA, 1997), 146.

42 Sigal, *From Moon Goddesses to Virgins*, 112.

43 Pete Sigal, "Queer Nahuatl: Sahagún's Faggots and Sodomites, Lesbians and Hermaphrodites," *Ethnohistory* 54 (2007): 22.

44 Trexler, *Sex and Conquest*, 88.

45 Ibid., 114; Hauser, "The Berdache and the Illinois Indian Tribe During the Last Half of the Seventeenth Century," 45–65; Hurtado, "Sexuality in California's Franciscan Missions," 167; Harriet Whitehead, "The Bow and the Burden Strap: A New Look at Institutionalized Homosexuality in Native North America," in *The Lesbian and Gay Studies Reader*, ed. Henry Abelove, Michèle Aina Barale, and David M. Halperin, (New York, 1993), 498–527; Walter L. Williams, *The Spirit and the Flesh: Sexual Diversity in American Indian Culture* (Boston, 1986).

46 Burckhart, *Slippery Earth*, 150.

47 Landa, *Yucatan*, 41.

48 Ibid.

49 Clendinnen, "Yucatec Maya Women and the Spanish," 430.

50 Susan Kellogg, "The Social Organization of Households among the Tenochca Mexica before and after Conquest," in *Prehispanic Domestic Units in Western Mesoamerica: Studies of the Household, Compound, and Residence*, ed. Robert S. Santley and Kenneth G. Hirth, (Boca Raton, 1993), 221.

51 James Lockhart, *The Nahuas after the Conquest: A Social and Cultural History of the Indians of Central Mexico, Sixteenth through Eighteenth Centuries* (Stanford, CA, 1992), 253.

52 Sigal, *From Moon Goddesses to Virgins*, 109–14.

53 J. Jorge Klor de Alva, "Sin and Confession among the Colonial Nahuas" (paper presented at the La ciudad y el campo en la historia de Mexico: memoria de la VIII Reunion de Historiadores Mexicanos y Norteamericanos, Oaxaca, Mexico, 1985), 97–8.

54 Restall, "He Wished It in Vain," 584.

55 Geoffrey Spurling, "Honor, Sexuality and the Catholic Church," in *The Faces of Honor: Sex, Shame, and Violence in Colonial Latin America*, ed. Lyman L. Johnson and Sonya Lipsett-Rivera, (Albuquerque, NM, 1998), 57.

56 John F.I.V. Chuchiak, "The Sins of the Fathers: Franciscan Friars, Parish Priests, and the Sexual Conquest of the Yucatec Maya, 1548–1808," *Ethnohistory* 54 (2007): 100.

57 Thomas Calvo, "The Warmth of the Hearth: Seventeenth-Century Guadalajara Families," in *Sexuality and Marriage in Colonial Latin America*, ed. Asuncion Lavrin, (Lincoln, 1989), 293–6.

58 Twinam, *Public Lives, Private Secrets*, 63.

59 Robert McCaa, "Marriageways in Mexico and Spain, 1500-1900," *Continuity and Change* 9 (1994): 11–43.

60 Susan M. Deeds, "Double Jeopardy: Indian Women in Jesuit Missions of Nueva Vizcaya," in *Indian Women of Early Mexico*, ed. Susan Schroeder, Stephanie Wood, and Robert Haskett, (Norman, 1997), 262.

61 Amos Megged, "The Social Significance of Benevolent and Malevolent Gifts among Single Caste Women in Mid-Seventeenth Century New Spain," *Journal of Family History* 24 (1999): 420–40; Lewis, "The 'Weakness' of Women," 23.

62 Richard Boyer, "Honor among Plebeians: *Male Sangre* and Social Reputation," in *The Faces of Honor*, 162.

63 Seed, *To Love, Honor, and Obey in Colonial Mexico*, 96.

64 Twinam, *Public Lives, Private Secrets*, 43.

65 Susan Kellogg, "Depicting *Mestizaje*: Gendered Images of Ethnorace in Colonial Mexican Texts," *Journal of Women's History* 12 (2000): 73.

66 Spear, "'They Need Wives:' Métissage and the Regulation of Sexuality in Colonial Louisiana," 35–59.

67 Pamela Cheek, *Sexual Antipodes: Enlightenment Globalization and the Placing of Sex* (Stanford, 2003), 6.

7 Enlightening desire

1 Robert Darnton, *The Forbidden Best-Sellers of Pre-Revolutionary France* (New York, 1995), 266.

2 Jonathan Irvine Israel, *Enlightenment Contested: Philosophy, Modernity, and the Emancipation of Man, 1670–1752* (Oxford, 2006), 11.

3 Darnton, *Forbidden Best-Sellers*, 1–20.

4 Julie Peakman, *Mighty Lewd Books: The Development of Pornography in Eighteenth-Century England* (London, 2003), 17; Wijnand Mijnhardt, "Politics and Pornography in the Seventeenth- and Eighteenth-Century Dutch Republic," in *The Invention of Pornography*, ed. Lynn Hunt, (New York, 1993), 285.

5 This interpretation differs somewhat from Thomas Laqueur who sees the Galenic model as dominant and then replaced in the eighteenth century by the "two-sex model". However, historians have criticized this interpretation and emphasized the long debate between the two models. See Thomas W. Laqueur, *Making Sex: Body and Gender from the Greeks to Freud* (Cambridge, MA, 1990); Katherine Park and Robert

Nye, "Making Sex: Body and Gender from the Greeks to Freud (Book Review)," *New Republic* 1991, 53–8; Michael Stolberg, "A Woman Down to Her Bones: The Anatomy of Sexual Difference in the Sixteenth and Early Seventeenth Centuries," *Isis* 94 (2003): 274–303.

6 Kathleen Wellman, "Physicians and Philosophes: Physiology and Sexual Morality in the French Enlightenment," *Eighteenth-Century Studies* 35 (2002): 269.

7 Laqueur, *Making Sex*, 164.

8 Roy Porter and Leslie Hall, *The Facts of Life: The Creation of Sexual Knowledges in Britain, 1650–1950* (New Haven, 1995), 82.

9 *Aristotle's Compleat Masterpiece. In Three Parts. Displaying the Secrets of Nature in the Generation of Man*, (London, 1733), 22. For more on *Aristotle's Masterpiece*, see Mary Fissell, "Hairy Women and Naked Truths: Gender and the Politics of Knowledge in *Aristotle's Masterpiece*", *William and Mary Quarterly* 60 (2003): 43–74.

10 Levinus Lemnius, *The Secret Miracles of Nature: In Four Books. Learnedly and Moderately Treating of Generation, and the Parts Thereof; the Soul, and Its Immortality; of Plants and Living Creatures; of Diseases, Their Symptoms and Cures, and Many Other Rarities Not Treated of by Any Author Extent* (London, 1658), 9; Jane Sharp, *The Midwives Book. Or the Whole Art of Midwifry, Discovered. Directing Childbearing Women How to Behave Themselves in Their Conception, Breeding, Bearing, and Nursing of Children* (London, 1671), 33.

11 *Aristotle's Masterpiece Compleated, in Two Parts* (London, 1698), 77; *Aristotle's Compleat Masterpiece* (1733), 9; *The Whole of Aristotle's Compleat Masterpiece, in Three Parts: Displaying the Secrets of Nature in the Generation of Man*, 54th edn. (London, 1793), 9.

12 Nicholas de Venette, *Tableau De L'amour Conjugal, Ou La Génération De L'homme* New edn. (Amsterdam, 1745?), 19.

13 Lemnius, *The Secret Miracles of Nature*, 8.

14 *Aristotle's Compleat Masterpiece* (1733), 2.

15 Venette, *Tableau De L'amour Conjugal*, 31.

16 *Aristotle's Compleat Masterpiece* (1793), 18.

17 *Aristotle's Masterpiece* (1698), 106; *Aristotle's Works: Containing the Master-Piece, Directions for Midwives, and Counsel and Advice to Child-Bearing Women, with Various Useful Remedies*, (London, nd [1850s onward?]), 46.

18 Lemnius, *The Secret Miracles of Nature*, 9; Sharp, *Midwives Book*, 40; *Aristotle's Compleat Masterpiece* (1733), 9.

19 *Aristotle's Masterpiece* (1698), 96.

20 Sharp, *Midwives Book*, 47.

21 Nicholas de Venette, *Tableau De L'amour Conjugal*, 328.

22 Helena Whitbread, ed., *No Priest but Love: The Journals of Anne Lister from 1824–1826* (Otley, W. Yorks, 1992), 49.

23 Sharp, *Midwives Book*, 45, 18.

24 *L'Ecole Des Filles, Où La Philosophie Des Dames*, (Paris, 1969 [1655]), 128.

25 Nicholas de Venette, *Conjugal Love Reveal'd; in the Nightly Pleasures of the Marriage Bed, and the Advantages of That Happy State, in an Essay Concerning Humane Generation, Done from the French of Monsieur Venette, by a Physician* 7th edn. (London), 110.

26 Laura Gowing, *Common Bodies: Women, Touch, and Power in the Seventeenth Century* (New Haven, 2003), 104.

27 Thomas W. Laqueur, *Solitary Sex: A Cultural History of Masturbation* (New York, 2003), 60.

28 Denis Diderot, *Rameau's Nephew and D'Alembert's Dream*, Leonard Tancock trans. (Harmondsworth, 1966), 228–9.

29 Denis Diderot, "Jouissance," *Encyclopédie* 8 (1751): 889, http://colet.uchicago.edu/cgi-bin/getobject_?a.63:131:0./projects/artflb/databases/artfl/encyclopedie/

IMAGE/ (accessed Apr. 15, 2008); Denis Diderot, "Jouissance," *The Encyclopedia of Diderot and d'Alembert Collaborative Translation Project.* http://hdl.handle.net/2027/spo.did2222.0000.225 (accessed Apr. 15, 2008).

30 Denis Diderot, "Supplement to Bougainville's Voyage, or a Dialogue between A and B on the Difficulties of Attaching Moral Ideas to Certain Physical Acts That Carry No Such Implications," in *The Libertine Reader,* ed. Michel Feher, (New York, 1997), 91.

31 D. G. Charlton, *New Images of the Natural in France* (Cambridge, 1984), 4; Michel Hénaff, "Supplement to Diderot's Dream," in *The Libertine Reader,* 62.

32 Catherine Cusser, *No Tomorrow: The Ethics of Pleasure in the French Enlightenment* (Charlottesville, 1999), 4.

33 Jonathan Israel, *Radical Enlightenment* (Oxford, 2001), 709.

34 Marquis Donatien-Alphonse de Sade, "Philosophy in the Bedroom," in *The Complete Justine, Philosophy in the Bedroom, and Other Writings,* ed. Richard Seaver and Austryn Wainhouse, (New York, 1965), 300.

35 Julien Offay de La Mettrie, "Machine Man," in *Machine Man and Other Writings,* ed. Ann Thomson, (Cambridge, 1996), 29; Israel, *Enlightenment Contested,* 806.

36 Baron d'Holbach, *The System of Nature,* H.D. Robinson trans. (Kitchener, 2001 [1773]), 162.

37 Ian Moulton, *Before Pornography: Erotic Writing in Early Modern England* (New York, 2000), 151–2.

38 Israel, *Radical Enlightenment,* 586–7.

39 Darnton, *Forbidden Best-Sellers,* 256.

40 Stephen Haliczer, *Sexuality in the Confessional: A Sacrament Profaned* (New York, 1996), 14–20.

41 Darnton, *Forbidden Best-Sellers,* 294; Margaret C. Jacob, "The Materialist World of Pornography," in *The Invention of Pornography,* ed. Lynn Hunt, (Cambridge, MA, 1993), 192.

42 James Grantham Turner, *Schooling Sex: Libertine Literature and Erotic Education in Italy, France, and England 1534–1685* (New York, 2003), 193.

43 Darnton, *Forbidden Best-Sellers,* 275.

44 For withdrawal and population, see Jacqueline Hecht, "From 'Be Fruitful and Multiply' to Family Planning: The Enlightenment Transition," *Eighteenth-Century Studies* 32 (1999): 536–51; Christine Théré, "Women and Birth Control in Eighteenth-Century France," *Eighteenth-Century Studies* 32 (1999): 552–64.

45 *The Present State of Betty-Land,* (London, 1684), 121–2.

46 Peakman, *Mighty Lewd Books;* Turner, *Schooling Sex,* 193.

47 Elizabeth Susan Wahl, *Invisible Relations: Representations of Female Intimacy in the Age of Enlightenment* (Stanford, 1999), 241.

48 *The Present State of Betty-Land,* 148.

49 Nicolas Chorier, *The Dialogues of Luisa Sigea* (Paris, 1890 [1660]), 22–5.

50 Darnton, *Forbidden Best-Sellers,* 266–7; Cusser, *No Tomorrow,* 104.

51 Chorier, *Dialogues,* 23.

52 Ibid., 85; Diderot, *Rameau's Nephew and D'Alembert's Dream,* 230.

53 Boyer de d'Argens, *Thérèse Philosophe* (Paris, 1992), 125.

54 Sade, "Philosophy in the Bedroom," 237.

55 Diderot, *Rameau's Nephew and D'alembert's Dream,* 230.

56 Montesquieu, Spirit of the Laws, excerpted in Jeffrey Merrick, *Homosexuality in Early Modern France: A Documentary Collection* (New York, 2001), 154.

57 Bryant T. Ragan, "The Enlightenment Confronts Homosexuality," in *Homosexuality in Modern France,* ed. Jeffrey Merrick and Bryant T. Ragan, (Oxford, 1996), 21.

58 Julien Offay de La Mettrie, "Anti-Seneca," in *Machine Man and Other Writings,* ed. Ann Thomson, (Cambridge, 1996), 136; Israel, *Radical Enlightenment,* 708.

59 Sade, "Justine," in *The Complete Justine,* 599.

60 Theo Van der Meer, "Sodomy and the Pursuit of the Third Sex in the Early Modern Period," in *Third Sex, Third Gender*, ed. Gilbert Herdt, (New York, 1994), 200–1.

61 Helena Whitbread, ed., *I Know My Own Heart: The Diaries of Anne Lister* (London, 1988), 297.

62 Jean-Jacques Rousseau, *The Confessions*, J.M. Cohen trans. (Harmondsworth, 1953 [1781]), 28.

63 Margaret Ogrodnick, *Instinct and Intimacy: Political Philosophy and Autobiography in Rousseau* (Toronto, 1999), 53.

64 Jean-Jacques Rousseau, "A Discourse on a Subject Proposed by the Academy of Dijon; What Is the Origin of Inequality among Men, and Is It Authorised by Natural Law?," *Constitution Society* (1754), http://www.constitution.org/jjr/ineq.htm (accessed Apr. 15, 2008).

65 Israel, *Radical Enlightenment*, 719.

66 Charles Taylor, *Sources of the Self* (Cambridge, MA, 1989), 370–5.

67 Ogrodnick, *Instinct and Intimacy*, 53.

68 Mary Seidman Trouille, *Sexual Politics in the Enlightenment: Women Writers Read Rousseau* (Albany, 1997), 21.

69 Michel Feher, "Introduction," in *The Libertine Reader*, 19.

70 Choderlos de Laclos, "On the Education of Women," in *The Libertine Reader*, 56.

71 Choderlos de Laclos, "Dangerous Liaisons," in *The Libertine Reader*, 1078.

72 Isabelle de Charrière to Constant d'Hermenches, Nov. 8–9, 1764, in Isabelle de Charrière, *There Are No Letters Like Yours: The Correspondence of Isabelle de Charrière and Constant d'Hermenches*, Janet Whatley and Malcolm Whatley trans. (Lincoln, 2000), 212.

73 de Charrière to d'Hermenches, 7 Oct. 1766; d'Hermenches to de Charrière, 27 Oct. 1767 Ibid., 339, 383.

74 de Charrière to d'Hermenches, 30 Aug. 1764 Ibid., 161.

75 Olivier Blanc, *Les Libertines: Plaisir Et Liberté Au Temps Des Lumières* (Paris, 1997), 166.

76 Charles-Louis Baron de Montesquieu, *Persian Letters*, C.J. Betts trans. (Harmondsworth, 1973), 197, 71.

77 For more on this theme see Anna Clark, *Scandal: The Sexual Politics of the British Constitution* (Princeton, 2004), 19–53.

78 "The Private Life of Marie Antoinette" (1793) in Merrick, *Homosexuality in Early Modern France*, 214.

79 Lynn Hunt, *The Family Romance of the French Revolution* (Berkeley, 1992), 103.

80 Hecht, "From 'Be Fruitful and Multiply' to Family Planning," 536–51.

81 Susanne Desan, "The Politics of Intimacy: Marriage and Citizenship in the French Enlightenment," in *Women, Gender and Enlightenment*, ed. Sarah Knott and Barbara Taylor, (Basingstoke, 2005), 630–48; Hunt, *The Family Romance of the French Revolution*, 151–73.

82 Isabel V. Hull, *Sexuality, State, and Civil Society in Germany, 1700–1815* (Ithaca, 1996), 144, 410.

83 Vivien Jones, "Advice and Enlightenment: Mary Wollstonecraft and Sex Education," in *Women, Gender and Enlightenment*, ed. Sarah Knott and Barbara Taylor, (Basingstoke, 2005), 149; Barbara Taylor, "Feminists Versus Gallants: Sexual Manners and Morals in Enlightenment Britain," in *Women, Gender and Enlightenment*, 30–52.

84 Sade, "Philosophy in the Bedroom," 213–5.

85 Thomas Malthus, *First Essay on Population, 1798* (London, 1921), 128.

8 In the Victorian twilight

1 London Metropolitan Archives, Foundling Hospital, 1815, unnumbered. Name changed.

2 R. Holloway, *The Phoenix of Sodom* (London, 1813), 12.

3 Patrick Colquhoun, *A Treatise on the Police and Crimes of the Metropolis* (London, 1806), 360.

4 Michel Foucault, *The History of Sexuality: An Introduction*, Robert Hurley trans. (New York, 1990), 106.

5 Peter Laslett, "The Bastardy-Prone Subculture," in *Bastardy and Its Comparative History*, ed. Peter Laslett, Karla Osterveen, and Richard M. Smith, (Cambridge, MA, 1980), 217.

6 Massimo Livi Bacci, *The Population of Europe: A History*, Cynthia De Nardi Ipsen and Carl Ipsen trans. (Oxford, 2000), 10; John Knodel, *Demographic Behavior in the Past* (Cambridge, 1988), 124; J. Knodel, "Law, Marriage and Illegitimacy in Nineteenth-Century Germany," *Population Studies* 20 (1967): 282; Michael Mitterauer, *The European Family: Patriarchy to Partnership from the Middle Ages to the Present*, Karla Oosterveen and Manfred Horzinger trans. (Chicago, 1982 [1977]), 123.

7 Isabel V. Hull, *Sexuality, State, and Civil Society in Germany, 1700–1815* (Ithaca, 1996), 269–81.

8 Rachel G. Fuchs, *Poor and Pregnant in Nineteenth-Century Paris* (New Brunswick, 1992), 30.

9 Anna Clark, *The Struggle for the Breeches: Gender and the Making of the British Working Class* (Berkeley, 1995), 179–96.

10 Andreas Gestrich, "After Dark: Girls' Leisure, Work, and Sexuality in Eighteenth- and Nineteenth-Century Rural Southwest Germany," in *Secret Gardens, Satanic Mills: Placing Girls in European History, 1750–1960*, ed. Mary Jo Maynes, Brigitte Soland, and Christine Benninghaus, (Bloomington, 2005), 56; Eilert Sundt, *Sexual Customs in Rural Norway*, Odin W. Anderson trans. (Ames, 1993 [1857]), 54; Jean-Louis Flandrin, *Sex in the Western World: The Development of Attitudes and Behavior*, Sue Collins trans. (Chur, 1991), 275; Tim Hitchcock, "Sociability and Misogyny in the Life of John Cannon," in *English Masculinities*, ed. Tim Hitchcock and Michèle Cohen, (Harlow, 1999), 25–43.

11 Alain Lottin, "Naissances Illegitimes Et Filles-Mère à Lille Au XVIIIe Siecle," *Revue d'Histoire Moderne et Contemporaine [France]* 17 (1970): 304; Kevin McQuillan, *Culture, Religion, and Demographic Behavior: Catholics and Lutherans in Alsace, 1750–1870* (Montreal, 1999), 81; Andrew Blaikie, *Illegitimacy, Sex, and Society: Northeast Scotland, 1750–1900* (1993), 190.

12 Ann-Sofie Kalvemark, "Illegitimacy and Marriage in Three Swedish Parishes in the Nineteenth Century," in *Bastardy and Its Comparative History*, 330; Barry Reay, "Sexuality in Nineteenth-Century England: The Social Context of Illegitimacy in Rural Kent," *Rural History [Great Britain]* 1 (1990): 221; Jan Kok, "The Moral Nation: Illegitimacy and Bridal Pregnancy in the Netherlands from 1600 to the Present," *Economic and Social History in the Netherlands [Netherlands]* 2 (1990): 10; Margareta R. Matovic, "Illegitimacy and Marriage in Stockholm in the Nineteenth Century," in *Bastardy and Its Comparative History*, 336.

13 Hull, *Sexuality, State, and Civil Society*, 121.

14 Anders Brandstrom, "Illegitimacy and Lone-Parenthood in XIXth Century Sweden," *Annales de Démographie Historique [France]* 2 (1998): 95.

15 Kok, "The Moral Nation," 21.

16 Mary Gibson, *Prostitution and the State in Italy* 2nd edn. (Columbus, OH, 1999), 82–102.

17 Clark, *Struggle for the Breeches*, 92–118.

18 Erica-Marie Benabou, *La Prostitution Et La Police Des Moeurs Au XVIIIème Siècle* (Paris, 1987), 40.

19 Fuchs, *Poor and Pregnant*, 36, 101.

20 Matovic, "Illegitimacy and Marriage in Stockholm in the Nineteenth Century," 336; Mitterauer, *The European Family*, 132.

21 Kok, "The Moral Nation," 7–35; Lenard R. Berlanstein, "Illegitimacy, Concubinage, and Proletarianization in a French Town, 1760–1914," *Journal of Family History* 5 (1980): 209.

22 John Gillis, "Servants, Sexual Relations, and the Risks of Illegitimacy in London, 1801–1900," *Feminist Studies* 5 (1979): 142–73.

23 Mitterauer, *The European Family*, 127; W. R. Lee, "Bastardy and the Socio-Economic Structure of South Germany," *Journal of Interdisciplinary History* 7 (1977): 403–25; Knodel, *Demographic Behavior in the Past*, 223.

24 Andrew Blaikie, "Scottish Illegitimacy: Social Adjustment or Moral Economy?," *Journal of Interdisciplinary History* 29 (1998): 226.

25 Brandstrom, "Illegitimacy and Lone-Parenthood in XIXth Century Sweden," 110; Jorg Baten and John E. Murray, "Bastardy in South Germany Revisited: An Anthropometric Synthesis," *Journal of Interdisciplinary History* 28 (1997): 47–56.

26 Anna Clark, *Women's Silence, Men's Violence: Sexual Assault in England, 1770–1845* (London, 1987). Shani d'Cruze found a similar percentage in affiliation cases. Shani d'Cruze, *Crimes of Outrage: Sex, Violence and Victorian Working Women* (De Kalb, 1998), 110–120.

27 Randolph Trumbach, *Heterosexuality and the Third Gender in Enlightenment London*, vol. 1 (Chicago, 1998), 322; Reay, "Sexuality in Nineteenth-Century England," 238.

28 Anne-Marie Sohn, *Du Premier Baiser À l'Alcôve: La Sexualité Des Français Au Quotidien (1850–1950)* (Paris, 1996), 250.

29 Clark, *Women's Silence, Men's Violence*, 30.

30 Clark, *Struggle for the Breeches*, 60–61.

31 While it may be thought that these women would claim rape in order to make themselves look more respectable, Foundling Hospital officials were unlikely to believe a woman who said she had been raped by a stranger. Some of these women were assaulted by their fellow servants, who surprised them as they worked alone in the house. Despite the stereotype of the immoral factory workers, servants were more vulnerable to sexual assault than factory workers, who labored among large numbers of women. Clark, *Women's Silence, Men's Violence*, 81.

32 London Metropolitan Archives, London Foundling Hospital, 1831, n. 2. Name changed.

33 Richard J. Evans, "Prostitution, State and Society in Imperial Germany," *Past and Present [Great Britain]* 70 (1976): 117; Barbara Alpern Engel, "St. Petersburg Prostitutes in the Late Nineteenth Century: A Personal and Social Profile," *Russian Review* 48 (1989): 24–9.

34 Benabou, *La Prostitution*, 309–11.

35 London, Guildhall Library, Printed Old Bailey Sessions Papers, 1796, vol. 1, p. 40; see also Clark, *Struggle for the Breeches*, 61.

36 Carine Steverlynck, "La Traite Des Blanches Et La Prostitution Enfantine En Belgique," *Paedagogica Historica [Belgium]* 29 (1993): 790; Jolanta Sikorska-Kulesza and Agnieszka Kreczmar, transl., "Prostitution in Congress Poland," *Acta Poloniae Historica [Poland]* 83 (2001): 130–31; Judith Walkowitz, *Prostitution in Victorian Society: Women, Class, and State* (Cambridge, 1980), 16; Engel, "St. Petersburg Prostitutes," 41; Jill Harsin, *Policing Prostitution in Nineteenth-Century Paris* (Paris, 1985), 207; Gibson, *Prostitution in Italy*, 82. Sophie de Schaepdrijver, "Regulated Prostitution in Brussels, 1844–1877: A Policy and Its Implementation," *Historical Social Research [West Germany]* 37 (1986): 89–108.

37 Sikorska-Kulesza and Kreczmar, "Prostitution in Congress Poland," 130; Harsin, *Policing Prostitution*, 207; Clark, *Struggle for the Breeches*, 60.
38 Benabou, *La Prostitution*, 385–96.
39 Clark, *Struggle for the Breeches*, 60.
40 Engel, "St. Petersburg Prostitutes," 41.
41 Trumbach, *Heterosexuality*, 187; Benabou, *La Prostitution*, 239.
42 Harsin, *Policing Prostitution*, 55; Alain Corbin, *Women for Hire: Prostitution and Sexuality in France after 1850* (Cambridge, MA, 1990), 68.
43 London Metropolitan Archive, London Consistory Court depositions, DL/C293, Evens v. Evens, 25 Oct. 1810; Clark, *Struggle for the Breeches*, 56.
44 Trumbach, *Heterosexuality*, 123; Gibson, *Prostitution in Italy*, 140; Engel, "St. Petersburg Prostitutes," 44; Walkowitz, *Prostitution*, 146; Corbin, *Women for Hire*, 32.
45 Corbin, *Women for Hire*, 40.
46 Gibson, *Prostitution in Italy*, 129; Sikorska-Kulesza and Kreczmar, "Prostitution in Congress Poland," 124; Engel, "St. Petersburg Prostitutes," 41.
47 Corbin, *Women for Hire*, 108.
48 Steverlynck, "La Traite Des Blanches Et La Prostitution Enfantine En Belgique," 798.
49 Walkowitz, *Prostitution*, 26.
50 Francesca Canadé Sautman, "Invisible Women: Working-Class Lesbians in France, 1880–1930," in *Homosexuality in Modern France*, ed. Jeffrey Merrick and Bryant T. Ragan, (New York, 1996), 186; Jeffrey Merrick, *Homosexuality in Early Modern France: A Documentary Collection* (New York, 2001), 74; A.-J.-B. Parent-Duchatelet, *De La Prostitution Dans La Ville De Paris*, vol. 2 (Paris, 1857), 159–67, 211; Michael Ryan, *Prostitution in London* (London, 1839), 56, 179.
51 Jeffrey Weeks, *Sex, Politics and Society: The Regulation of Sexuality since 1800* 2nd edn. (London, 1989 [1981]), 109; Jens Rydstrom, *Sinners and Citizens: Bestiality and Homosexuality in Sweden, 1880–1950* (Chicago, 2003), 115; "Trial of Charles Bradbury for Sodomy," *Old Bailey Proceedings Online* (1755), http://www.oldbaileyonline.org/browse.jsp?ref=t177550910-42 (accessed Apr. 18, 2008); Dan Healey, "Masculine Purity And 'Gentlemen's Mischief': Sexual Exchange and Prostitution between Russian Men, 1861–1941," *Slavic Review* 60 (2001): 233–65.
52 John d'Emilio, "Capitalism and Gay Identity," in *The Gender/Sexuality Reader*, ed. Roger N. Lancaster and Micaela di Leonardo, (New York, 1997), 169–78.
53 Rydstrom, *Sinners and Citizens*, 118; Jeffrey Merrick, "'Nocturnal Birds' in the Champs-Elysées: Police and Pederasty in Prerevolutionary Paris," *GLQ* 8 (2002): 425–32; Dirk Jap Noordam, "Sodomy in the Dutch Republic, 1600–1725," in *The Pursuit of Sodomy in Early Modern Europe*, ed. Kent Gerard and Gert Hekma, (New York, 1989), 214; Randolph Trumbach, "London's Sodomites: Homosexual Behavior and Western Culture in the 18th Century," *Journal of Social History* 11: 1–33.
54 "The Trial of William Brown for Assault with Sodomitical Intent," *Old Bailey Proceedings Online* (1726), http://www.oldbaileyonline.org/browse.jsp?ref=t17260711-77 (accessed Apr. 18, 2008).
55 "Trial of George Duffus for Sodomy," *Old Bailey Proceedings Online* (1721), http://www.oldbaileyonline.org/browse.jsp?ref=t17211206-20 (accessed Apr. 18, 2008).
56 London Metropolitan Archives, Mansion House Minute Books, Magistrates Courts, 5 Feb. 1803.
57 Rictor Norton, *Mother Clap's Molly House: The Gay Subculture in England, 1700–1830* (London, 1992), 54–70. The term "molly" was a sexual insult, meaning an effeminate man, often, although not always a sodomite, but it certainly had that meaning in the context of molly house. The word may have come from the Latin *molles*, for soft, which was a term used for effeminate men who took the passive role in sex with other men in ancient Rome. Given the importance of classical literature to the English early modern

elite, they may very well have borrowed it. Alternatively, it simply may have been a female nickname, as in "Molly."

58 "Trial of Margaret Clap for Keeping a Brothel and Procuring," *Old Bailey Proceedings Online* (1726), http://www.oldbaileyonline.org/browse.jsp?ref=t17260711-54 (accessed Apr. 18, 2008).

59 "Trial of Julius Cesar Taylor for Assault with Sodomitical Intent, Procuring, and Keeping a Brothel," *Old Bailey Proceedings Online* (1728), http://www.oldbaileyonline.org/browse.jsp?ref=t17281016-60 (accessed Apr. 18, 2008).

60 Noordam, "Sodomy in the Dutch Republic, 1600–1725," 215.

61 Merrick, *Homosexuality in Early Modern France*, 52.

62 Holloway, *The Phoenix of Sodom*, 12.

63 "Trial of Martin Mackintosh for Assault with Sodomitical Intent," *Old Bailey Proceedings Online* (1726), http://www.oldbaileyonline.org/browse.jsp?ref=t17260711-53 (accessed Apr. 18, 2008).

64 William Anthony Peniston, "Pederasts and Others: A Social History of Male Homosexuals in the Early Years of the French Third Republic" (U. of Rochester, 1997), 251.

65 Theo Van der Meer, "Sodomy and the Pursuit of the Third Sex in the Early Modern Period," in *Third Sex, Third Gender*, ed. Gilbert Herdt, (New York, 1994), 137–212.

66 Richard Smalbroke, "Reformation Necessary to Prevent Our Ruin," in *Homosexuality in Eighteenth-Century England: A Sourcebook*, ed. Rictor Norton (1727). http://www.infopt.demon.co.uk/1727ruin.htm (accessed Apr. 18, 2008).

67 Holloway, *The Phoenix of Sodom*, 12.

68 "The Trial of William Brown for Assault with Sodomitical Intent."

69 Michel Rey, "Police and Sodomy in Eighteenth-Century Paris: From Sin to Disorder," in *The Pursuit of Sodomy in Early Modern Europe*, ed. Kent Gerard and Gert Hekma, (New York, 1989), 135; Jeffrey Merrick, "Sodomitical Inclination in Early Eighteenth-Century Paris," *Eighteenth-Century Studies* 30 (1997): 289–95.

70 H.G. Cocks, *Nameless Offences: Homosexual Desire in the Nineteenth Century* (London, 2003), 69.

71 The National Archives: Public Record Office MEPOE 4/13 Daily Return of Police Offices, 1830.

72 Greater London Record Office MJ/SP Information 14 April 1830.

73 Cocks, *Nameless Offences*, 70.

74 Rydstrom, *Sinners and Citizens*, 118.

75 Michael Sibalis, "The Regulation of Male Homosexuality in Revolutionary and Napoleonic France, 1789–1815," in *Homosexuality in Modern France*, ed. Jeffrey Merrick and Bryant T. Ragan, (New York, 1996), 93.

76 Peniston, "Pederasts and Others," 45.

77 Cocks, *Nameless Offences*, 70.

78 Theo van der Meer, "Tribades on Trial: Female Same-Sex Offenders in Late Eighteenth-Century Amsterdam," in *Forbidden History: The State, Society, and the Regulation of Sexuality in Modern Europe*, ed. John C. Fout, (Chicago, 1991), 198.

79 *Weekly Free Press*, 24 Jan. 1829.

80 Tom Leonard, ed., *Radical Renfew: Poems from the French Revolution to the First World War* (Edinburgh, 1990), 234.

81 Knodel, "Law, Marriage and Illegitimacy," 282; Edward Shorter, J. Knodel, and Etienne Van de Walle, "The Decline of Non-Marital Fertility in Europe, 1880–1940," *Population Studies* 25 (1971): 375–93.

82 Corbin, *Women for Hire*, 492.

83 Peter Gay, *Education of the Senses*, 155; Roy Porter and Leslie Hall, *The Facts of Life: The Creation of Sexual Knowledges in Britain, 1650–1950* (New Haven, 1995), 142.

84 William Acton, *The Functions and Disorders of the Reproductive Organs in Childhood, Youth, Adult Age, and Advanced Life, Considered in Their Physiological, Social, and Moral Relations* 4th edn. (Philadephia, 1867), 144.
85 Dr. Kahn, *Handbook of Dr. Kahn's Museum, 3, Tichborne Street* (London, 1863).
86 Sohn, *Du Premier Baiser À l'Alcôve*, 81.
87 Lynda Nead, *Victorian Babylon: People, Streets and Images in Nineteenth-Century London* (New Haven, 2000), 150–80; Lisa Z. Sigel, *Governing Pleasures: Pornography in Nineteenth-Century England* (New Brunswick, 2002), 59.
88 Sue Morgan, *A Passion for Purity: Ellice Hopkins and the Politics of Gender in the Late Victorian Church* (Bristol, 1999), 49.
89 Sharon Marcus, *Between Women: Friendship, Desire, and Marriage in Victorian England* (Princeton, 2007), 58.
90 Lilian Faderman, *Surpassing the Love of Men: Romantic Friendship and Love between Women from the Renaissance to the Present* (New York, 1981), 147.
91 Helena Whitbread, ed., *I Know My Own Heart: The Diaries of Anne Lister* (London, 1988), 297.
92 Sohn, *Du Premier Baiser À L'alcôve*, 52.
93 London Metropolitan Archives, London Foundling Hospital, 1822, petition no. 89.
94 Patricia Mainardi, *Husbands, Wives, and Lovers: Marriage and Its Discontents in Nineteenth Century France* (New Haven, 2003), 17.
95 Leo Tolstoy, *The Kreutzer Sonata*, Louise and Aylmer Maude trans. (New York, 1997 [1899]), 100.
96 William Acton, *Prostitution* 2nd edn. (New York, 1968 [1869]), 144.

9 Boundaries of the nation, boundaries of the self

1 Mrs. Havelock Ellis, *James Hinton: A Sketch* (London, 1918), 103.
2 Charles Darwin, *The Descent of Man, and Selection in Relation to Sex*, 2 vols., vol. 1 (London, 1871), 235–320; Charles Darwin, *The Descent of Man, and Selection in Relation to Sex*, 2 vols., vol. 2 (London, 1871), 383.
3 Daniel Pick, *Faces of Degeneration: A European Disorder, c. 1848–1914* (Cambridge, 1989), 43; Robert A. Nye, *Masculinity and Male Codes of Honor* (Berkeley, 1998 [1993]), 74.
4 Ambrose Tardieu, *Dictionnaire D'hygiène Publique*, 4 vols., vol. 3 (Paris, 1862), 415–40; Alain Corbin, *Women for Hire: Prostitution and Sexuality in France after 1850* (Cambridge, MA, 1990), 301.
5 For Tardieu, see Nye, *Masculinity and Male Codes of Honor*, 107; William Anthony Peniston, "Pederasts, Prostitutes, and Pickpockets in Paris of the 1870s," *Journal of Homosexuality* 41 (2001): 169–87; F. Carlier, *Les Deux Prostitutions* (Paris, 1887), 280, 306; Erin G. Carlston, "Secret Dossiers: Sexuality, Race, and Treason in Proust and the Dreyfus Affair," *Modern Fiction Studies* 48 (2002): 939.
6 Dumas, quoted in Leslie Choquette, "Degenerate or Degendered? Images of Prostitution and Homosexuality in the French Third Republic," *Historical Reflections* 23 (1997): 217.
7 Christelle Taraud, *La Prostitution Coloniale: Algérie, Tunisie, Maroc (1830–1962)* (Paris, 2003), 22.
8 Judith Walkowitz, *Prostitution in Victorian Society: Women, Class, and State* (Cambridge, 1980); Philippa Levine, *Prostitution, Race, and Politics: Policing Venereal Disease in the British Empire* (New York, 2003), 40.
9 Corbin, *Women for Hire*, 44.
10 For discussions of the movement in this and subsequent paragraphs, see Josephine Butler, *A Doomed Iniquity: An Authoritative Condemnation of State Regulation of Vice from France, Germany and Belgium* (London, 1896), 2–11; Anne Summers, "Which

Women? What Europe? Josephine Butler and the International Abolitionist Federation," *History Workshop Journal* 62 (2005): 215–31; Walkowitz, *Prostitution*, 176.

11 Judith Walkowitz, *City of Dreadful Delight: Narratives of Sexual Danger in Late Victorian London* (Chicago, 1992), 106; Sophie de Schaepdrijver, "Regulated Prostitution in Brussels, 1844–1877: A Policy and Its Implementation," *Historical Social Research [West Germany]* 37 (1986): 94; Carine Steverlynck, "La Traite Des Blanches Et La Prostitution Enfantine En Belgique," *Paedagogica Historica [Belgium]* 29 (1993): 798; Louise A. Jackson, *Child Sexual Assault in Victorian England* (London, 2000), 132.

12 Great Britain Foreign Office, *Correspondence Respecting Immoral Traffic in English Girls* (London, 1881), 26–31.

13 Judith R. Walkowitz, *City of Dreadful Delight*, 81–121.

14 Hansard Parliamentary Debates, vol. 300, cols. 899–900 quoted in "Editorial," *Sentinel: Organ of the Social Purity Movement*, January 1888, 2.

15 Jackson, *Child Sexual Assault*, 79.

16 Lucy Bland, *Banishing the Beast: English Feminism and Sexual Morality 1885–1914* (London, 1995), 57.

17 Hera Cook, *The Long Sexual Revolution: English Women, Sex, and Contraception 1800–1975* (Oxford, 2004), 100.

18 Ann Laura Stoler, *Carnal Knowledge and Imperial Power: Race and the Intimate in Colonial Rule* (Berkeley, 2002), 33; Jenny Sharpe, *Allegories of Empire: The Figure of Woman in the Colonial Text* (Minneapolis, 1993), 57–84; Norman Etherington, "Natal's Black Rape Scare," *Journal of Southern African Studies* 15 (1988): 36–53.

19 Levine, *Prostitution, Race, and Politics*, 87.

20 Rev. J.P. Gledstone, *The Indian Cantonments Scandal* (London, 1893), 4; Alfred S. Dyer, "Repentance or Retribution?" *Sentinel*, April 1888, 47; Joseph Edmondson, *Understood but Not Expressed: A Review of Certain Regulations Existing (in the Alleged "Interest of the Public Health") on the Continent of Europe and in Some British Colonies* (London, 1889), 32; Biswanath Joardar, *Prostitution in Nineteenth- and Early Twentieth-Century Calcutta* (New Delhi, 1985), 52.

21 Proposed Legislation to Amend Sec. 375 of the Indian Penal Code, 1890 [Excerpts from public meetings, memorials, and newspapers]. British Library, India Office, L/PJ/6/288 f. 1866.

22 Antoinette M. Burton, *Burdens of History: British Feminists, Indian Women, and Imperial Culture, 1865–1915* (Chapel Hill, 1994), 127–69.

23 Papers Relating to the "Age of Consent Bill." 1891. British Library, India Office, L/PJ/6/298 Judicial and Public Annual Files. Legislative Department. No. 48.

24 Mrinalini Sinha, *Colonial Masculinity: The "Manly Englishman" and the "Effeminate Bengali" in the Late Nineteenth Century* (Manchester; New York, 1995), 136; Tanika Sarkar, *Hindu Wife, Hindu Nation* (Bloomington, 2001), 230.

25 Sources for the Lex Heinze affair discussed in the next paragraphs include: Richard J. Evans, "Prostitution, State and Society in Imperial Germany," *Past and Present [Great Britain]* 70 (1976): 120–124; Carl H. Werner, "Die Lex Heinze Und Ihre Geschichte [the Lex Heinze and Its History]" (Dissertation, Albert Ludwigs Universität, 1935), 3; Gary Stark, "Pornography, Society and the Law in Imperial Germany," *Central European History* 14 (1981): 212; R.J.V. Lenman, "Art, Society and the Law in Wilhelmine Germany. The Lex Heinze," *Oxford German Studies* 8 (1973): 86–113; Richard J. Evans, *Tales from the German Underworld: Crime and Punishment in the Nineteenth Century* (New Haven, 1998), 186. Thanks to Jennifer Illuzi for taking notes on German sources.

26 Henry Darcy, "The 'Lex Heinze': An Inquiry into the Moral and Social Trends of Germany at the End of the 19th Century" (Ph.D., State University of New York at Buffalo, 1976), 83.

27 Nancy R. Reagin, "'A True Woman Can Take Care of Herself': The Debate over Prostitution in Hanover, 1906," *Central European History* 24 (1991): 361.
28 Alex Hall, *Scandal, Sensation and Social Democracy* (Cambridge, 1977), 147.
29 Ibid., 146.
30 Konrad H. Jarausch, "Students, Sex and Politics in Imperial Germany," *Journal of Contemporary History* 17 (1982): 296.
31 Hall, *Scandal, Sensation and Social Democracy:* 13–40.
32 Edward Ross Dickinson, "Dominion of the Spirit over the Flesh: Religion, Gender and Sexual Morality in the German Women's Movement before World War I," *Gender & History [Great Britain]* 17 (2005): 394; Michael Mason, *The Making of Victorian Sexuality* (Oxford, 1994), 267; Lesley A. Hall, "'Hauling Down the Double Standard': Feminism, Social Purity and Sexual Science in Late Nineteenth-Century Britain," *Gender & History [Great Britain]* 16 (2004): 36–56.
33 *The Hour before the Dawn. An Appeal to Men* (London, 1876), 71.
34 *Troisième Congrès International. Compte Rendu Officiel Des Travaux Du Congrès De La Fédération Britannique Continentale Et Générale Pour L'abolition De La Prostitution Spécialement Envisagée Comme Institution Légale Ou Tolérée* (Neuchatel, 1883), 11.
35 "Lesson of the 'Kreutzer Sonata'", in Leo Tolstoy, *The Kreutzer Sonata*, Louise and Aylmer Maude trans. (New York, 1997 [1899]), 164; Laura Engelstein, *The Keys to Happiness: Sex and the Search for Modernity in Fin-De-Siècle Russia* (Ithaca, 1992), 220.
36 Dr. Anton Nystrom, *The Natural Laws of Sexual Life: Medical-Sociological Researches*, Carl Sandzen trans. 3rd Swedish edn. (St. Louis, 1913 [1904]), 120.
37 Bland, *Banishing the Beast*, 13; Edith Ward, *The Vital Question: An Address on Social Purity to All English-Speaking Women* (London, 1892), 10.
38 Sue Morgan, *A Passion for Purity: Ellice Hopkins and the Politics of Gender in the Late Victorian Church* (Bristol, 1999), 120.
39 Bland, *Banishing the Beast*, 13; Ward, *The Vital Question*, 10.
40 Letter to the editor, *Pioneer of Social Purity*, 1 Aug. 1887, 63.
41 Morgan, *A Passion for Purity*, 78.
42 Ellis [Elizabeth Wolstenhome Elmy] Ethelmer, *Phases of Love: As It Was, as It Is; as It May Be* (Congleton, 1897), 53.
43 Edward Carpenter, *Love's Coming of Age* (Chicago, 1912 [1896]), 16.
44 Sripati Chandrasekhar, *'A Dirty, Filthy Book': The Writings of Charles Knowlton and Annie Besant on Reproductive Physiology and Birth Control and an Account of the Bradlaugh-Besant Trial* (Berkeley, 1981), 142.
45 Ellis, *James Hinton*, 70–180.
46 Caroline Haddon, *The Larger Life: Studies in Hinton's Ethics* (London, 1886), 191.
47 Olive Schreiner to Havelock Ellis, 7 July 1884, and Havelock Ellis to Olive Schreiner, 8 August 1884, in *'My Other Self': The Letters of Olive Schreiner and Havelock Ellis, 1884–1920*, ed. Yaffa Claire Draznin (New York, 1992), 13, 81.
48 Havelock Ellis, "Sexual Inversion," in *Studies in the Psychology of Sex* (New York, 1936), 317.
49 Matt Cook, *London and the Culture of Homosexuality, 1885–1914* (Cambridge, 2003), 45. Sodomy was no longer punishable by death after 1861, but this actually made it easier to prosecute, and as we have seen in the last chapter, the police prosecuted sex between men intensively but quietly before the Labouchère amendment.
50 Yopie Prins, "Greek Maenads, Victorian Spinsters," in *Victorian Sexual Dissidence*, ed. Richard Dellamora, (Chicago, 1999), 43–81; Alex Potts, "Subjectivity, Civic Ideals and Figures of Ideal Manliness: Representations of Masculinity in Late Victorian British Sculpture," in *Representing Masculinity*, ed. Stefan Dudink, Karen Hagemann, and Anna Clark, (London, 2007), 169–92; Cook, *London and the Culture of Homosexuality*, 32; Neil McKenna, *The Secret Life of Oscar Wilde* (New York, 2005), 88.

51 Yvonne Ivory, "The Urning and His Own: Individualism and the Fin-De-Siècle Invert," *German Studies Review* 26 (2003): 340; Hubert Kennedy, *Ulrichs: The Life and Works of Karl Heinrich Ulrichs: Pioneer of the Modern Gay Movement* (Boston, 1988), 50–63.

52 Jens Rydstrom, *Sinners and Citizens: Bestiality and Homosexuality in Sweden, 1880–1950* (Chicago, 2003), 44.

53 Frederick S. Roden, *Same-Sex Desire in Victorian Religious Culture* (Basingstoke, 2002), 31.

54 Ivory, "The Urning and His Own," 340.

55 Edward Carpenter, *The Intermediate Sex* (London, 1908), 79; Carpenter, *Love's Coming of Age*, 21.

56 Cook, *London and the Culture of Homosexuality*, 56.

57 Oscar Wilde, *The Picture of Dorian Gray* (Harmondsworth, 1985 [1891]), 162.

58 William A. Cohen, *Scandal: The Private Parts of Victorian Fiction* (Durham, 1996), 219; Jonathan Dollimore, *Sexual Dissidence* (New York, 1991), 68; Morris B. Kaplan, *Sodom on the Thames: Sex, Love and Scandal in Wilde's Times* (Ithaca, 2005), 224–51.

59 Nancy Erber, "The French Trials of Oscar Wilde," *Journal of the History of Sexuality* 6 (1996); H. Montgomery Hyde, *The Trials of Oscar Wilde* (New York, 1962); Eduard Bernstein, *Bernstein on Homosexuality*, Angela Clifford trans. (Belfast, 1977); H.G. Cocks, "Naughty Narrative Nineties: Sex, Scandal, and Representation in the *Fin De Siècle*," *Journal of British Studies* 41 (2002): 526–36; Joseph Bristow, "'A Complex Multiform Creature' — Wilde's Sexual Identities," in *The Cambridge Companion to Oscar Wilde*, ed. Peter Raby, (Cambridge, 1997), 195–218.

60 John C. Fout, "Sexual Politics in Wilhelmine Germany: The Male Gender Crisis, Moral Purity, and Homophobia," *Journal of the History of Sexuality* 2 (1992): 328–41.

61 Lucy Bland and Laura Doan, "Introduction," in *Sexology in Culture*, ed. Lucy Bland and Laura Doan, (London, 1998), 3; Ellis, "Sexual Inversion," 356.

62 French sexology was quite distinct and continued to fuse sexual desire and reproduction. See Nye, *Masculinity and Male Codes of Honor*, 171; Vernon Rosario, *The Erotic Imagination: French Histories of Perversity* (New York, 1997).

63 Richard Krafft-Ebing, *Psychopathia Sexualis* 12th edn. (New York, 1965 [1886]), 44–9; August Forel, *The Sexual Question*, C. F. Marshall trans. (New York, 1908 [1905]), 55–8; E. Heinrich Kisch, *The Sexual Life of Woman in Its Physiological, Pathological and Hygienic Aspects*, M. Eden Paul trans. (New York, 1910 [1904]), 180; Dr. L. Loewenfeld, *On Conjugal Happiness. Experiences and Reflections of a Medical Man*, Ronald E.S. Krohn trans. 3rd edn. (London, 1913 [1912]), 164. For an interesting discussion of the sexologists' differentiation between emotion and instinct, see Suzanne Raitt, "Sex, Love, and the Homosexual Body," in *Sexology in Culture*, 150–63.

64 Albert Moll, *Libido Sexualis*, David Berger trans. (New York, 1933 [1897]), 28, 314.

65 Loewenfeld, *On Conjugal Happiness*, 43; Edward Ross Dickinson, "'A Dark, Impenetrable Wall of Complete Incomprehension': The Impossibility of Heterosexual Love in Imperial Germany," *Central European History* 40 (2007): 470–2.

66 Harry Oosterhuis, *Stepchildren of Nature: Krafft-Ebing, Psychiatry, and the Making of Sexual Identity* (Chicago, 2000), 70.

67 Nystrom, *The Natural Laws of Sexual Life*, 149; Paolo Mantegazza, *The Physiology of Love* (New York, 1894), 201.

68 Krafft-Ebing, *Psychopathia Sexualis*, 31, 324; Joseph Bristow, "Symond's History, Ellis's Heredity: Sexual Inversion," in *Sexology in Culture*, 94; Oosterhuis, *Stepchildren of Nature*, 66.

69 Laura Engelstein, "Lesbian Vignettes: A Russian Triptych from the 1890s," *Signs* 15 (1990): 820.

70 Oosterhuis, *Stepchildren of Nature*, 177; Krafft-Ebing, *Psychopathia Sexualis*, 321; Ellis, "Sexual Inversion," 70–90.

71 Forel, *Sexual Question*, 245.
72 Krafft-Ebing, *Psychopathia Sexualis*, 286, 248.
73 Loewenfeld, *On Conjugal Happiness*, 44.
74 Forel, *Sexual Question*, 95.
75 Kisch, *The Sexual Life of Woman*, 105.
76 Edith Kurzweil, "Freudians and Feminists in Fin-De-Siècle Vienna," *Partisan Review* 66 (1999): 580–7.
77 David H. Gleaves and Elsa Hernandez, "Recent Reformulations of Freud's Development and Abandonment of His Seduction Theory: Historical/Scientific Clarification or a Continued Assault on Truth?," *History of Psychology* 2 (1999): 32–54; Allen Esterson, "Jeffrey Masson and Freud's Seduction Theory: A New Fable Based on Old Myths," *History of the Human Sciences* 11 (1998): 1–21.
78 Sigmund Freud, "Instincts and Their Vicissitudes," in *On Metapsychology: The Theory of Psychoanalysis*, ed. Angela Richards, (Harmondsworth, 1991), 122; Arnold I. Davidson, *The Emergence of Sexuality and the Formation of Concepts* (Cambridge, MA, 2001), 66–93. For a more biological interpretation, Frank Sulloway, *Freud, Biologist of the Mind* 2nd edn. (Cambridge, MA, 1992 [1979]), 159. For an account that shows Freud moving away from a hormonal approach, see Lisa Appignanesi and John Forrester, *Freud's Women* (New York, 1992), 400.
79 Sulloway, *Freud, Biologist of the Mind*, 259.
80 Sigmund Freud, *On Sexuality: Three Essays on the Theory of Sexuality*, James Strachey trans. (Harmondsworth, 1997 [1905]), 57.
81 Ibid., 143, 376; Appignanesi and Forrester, *Freud's Women*, 426.
82 Sigmund Freud, "Beyond the Pleasure Principle," in *On Metapsychology*, 279; Freud, *On Sexuality*, 85.
83 Friedrich Nietzsche, "Human, All-Too-Human," in *The Portable Nietzsche*, ed. Walter Kaufmann, (New York, 1959), 560; Friedrich Nietzsche, *The Birth of Tragedy*, Walter Kaufman trans. (New York, 1967 [1886]), 266, 128; Havelock Ellis, *Affirmations* 2nd edn. (London, 1915 [1897]), 63; Robert B. Pippin, "The Erotic Nietzsche: Philosophers without Philosophy," in *Erotikon: Essays on Eros, Ancient and Modern*, ed. Shadi Bartsch and Thomas Bartscherer, (Chicago, 2005), 172–91.
84 Robert Michels, *Sexual Ethics: A Study of Borderland Questions* (London, 1914), 139–40.
85 John Badcock Jr., "Go to the Butterfly, Thou Slave," *The Adult: A Journal for the Advancement of Freedom in Sexual Relationships* 1 (September, 1897): 10–20. This journal contains many interesting articles on Nietzsche and non-monogamy.
86 Dickinson, "A Dark, Impenetrable Wall of Complete Incomprehension," 472.
87 Fredrich Nietzsche, *On the Genealogy of Morals and Ecce Homo* (New York, 1967), 266.
88 Otto Weininger, *Sex and Character* (New York, 2003 [1906]), 239; Chandak Sengoopta, *Otto Weininger: Sex, Science, and Self in Imperial Vienna* (Chicago, 2000), 141.
89 Carpenter, *The Intermediate Sex*, 1; Judy Greenway, "It's What You Do with It That Counts: Interpretations of Otto Weininger," in *Sexology in Culture*, 27–44.
90 Ellen Key, *Love and Marriage*, Arthur G. Chater trans. (New York, 1911), 39.
91 Helene Stöcker, "Nietzsches Frauenfeindschaft" [Nietzsche's Enmity Towards Women], in *Die Liebe Und Die Frauen*, ed. Helene Stöcker, (Minden in Westf., 1905), 65–74. Thanks to Jennifer Illuzi for notes on these German sources.
92 Helene Stöcker, "Von Mann Und Weib," in *Die Liebe Und Die Frauen*, 109–10.
93 Elisabeth Dauthendey, "Of the New Woman and Her Love: A Book for Mature Minds," in *Lesbians in Germany 1890s–1920s*, ed. Lilian Faderman and Brigitta Eriksson, (Tallahassee, 1990), 44–5; Dorothy Rowe, *Representing Berlin: Sexuality and the City in Imperial and Weimar Germany* (Aldershot, 2003), 103.

94 Anna Rüling, "What Interest Does the Women's Movement Have in the Homosexual Question?," in *Lesbians in Germany*, 89; Christiane Leidinger, "Anna Rüling: A Problematic Foremother of Lesbian Herstory," *Journal of the History of Sexuality* 13 (2004): 477–99.
95 Ann Taylor Allen, *Feminism and Motherhood in Germany, 1800-1914* (New Brunswick, 1991), 170.
96 Key, *Love and Marriage*, 74.
97 Bland, *Banishing the Beast*, 281–9.
98 Carolyn Burdett, "The Hidden Romance of Sexual Science: Eugenics, the Nation and the Making of Modern Feminism," in *Sexology in Culture*, 44–65.
99 Mason, *The Making of Victorian Sexuality*, 63; Ann Taylor Allen, *Feminism and Motherhood in Western Europe 1890–1970* (New York, 2005), 50; Eleonor Accampo, "The Rhetoric of Reproduction and the Reconfiguration of Womanhood in the French Birth Control Movement, 1890–1920," *Journal of Family History* 31 (1996): 357–63; Jean Elisabeth Pedersen, "Regulating Abortion and Birth Control: Gender, Medicine, and Republican Politics in France, 1870–1920," *French Historical Studies* 19 (1995): 673–98; Chandrasekhar, "A Dirty, Filthy Book", 45.
100 Dickinson, "Dominion of the Spirit over the Flesh," 385.
101 George Robb, "The Way of All Flesh: Degeneration, Eugenics, and the Gospel of Free Love," *Journal of the History of Sexuality* 6 (1996): 592; Key, *Love and Marriage*, 147; Edward Ross Dickinson, "Reflections on Feminism and Monism in the Kaiserreich, 1900–1913," *Central European History* 34 (2001): 207–8.
102 Grete Meisel-Hess, *The Sexual Crisis; a Critique of Our Sex Life*, Eden Paul and Cedar Paul trans. (New York, 1917), 328.
103 Nystrom, *The Natural Laws of Sexual Life: Medical-Sociological Researches*, 13.
104 Key, *Love and Marriage*, 147–150.
105 Bland, *Banishing the Beast*, 243, 307; Lesley A. Hall, "Forbidden by God, Despised by Men: Masturbation, Medical Warnings, Moral Panic and Manhood in Great Britain, 1850–1950," *Journal of the History of Sexuality* 2 (1992): 375–87.

10 Managing desire or consuming sex in interwar culture

1 Jennifer Mundy, "Letters of *Desire*," in *Surrealism: Desire Unbound*, ed. Jennifer Mundy, (Princeton, 2001), 11.
2 Nancy Nenno, "Femininity, the Primitive and Modern Urban Spaces: Josephine Baker in Berlin," in *Women in the Metropolis: Gender and Modernity in Weimar Culture*, ed. Katherina von Ankum, (Berkeley, 1997), 155–60.
3 Jody Blake, *Le Tumulte Noir: Modernist Art and Popular Entertainment in Jazz-Age Paris, 1900–1930* (University Park, PA, 1999).
4 Giacomo Balla and Fortunato Depero, "The Futurist Reconstruction of the Universe," (1915) *Futurism, Web page edited by Kim Scarborough*, http://www.unknown.nu/futurism/reconstruction.html (accessed Apr. 15, 2008).
5 Valentine de Saint-Point, "The Futurist Manifesto of Lust," (1913) *Futurism*, http://www.unknown.nu/futurism/lust (accessed Apr. 15, 2008).
6 Frank Sulloway, *Freud, Biologist of the Mind* 2nd edn. (Cambridge, MA, 1992 [1979]), 411.
7 Maria Tatar, *Lustmord: Sexual Murder in Weimar Germany* (Princeton, 1995), 56.
8 Ibid., 75.
9 George Mosse, *Nationalism and Sexuality* (New York, 1985), 42.
10 Paul Wilder Chase, "The Politics of Morality in Weimar Germany: Public Controversy and Parliamentary Debate over Changes in Moral Behavior in the Twenties" (Ph.D., State University of New York at Stonybrook, 1992), 179.

11 Deborah Cohler, "Sapphism and Sedition: Producing Female Homosexuality in Great War Britain," *Journal of the History of Sexuality* 16 (2007): 80; Lucy Bland, "Trial by Sexology? Maud Allen, *Salome*, and the 'Cult of the Clitoris'," in *Sexology in Culture*, ed. Lucy Bland and Laura Doan, (London, 1998), 183–99.

12 Paul Bureau, *Moral Bankruptcy (L'indiscipline Des Moeurs)* (New York, 1930 [1921]), 314.

13 Tyler Stovall, "The Color Line Behind the Lines: Racial Violence in France During the Great War," *American Historical Review* 103 (1998): 262; Carolyn Dean, "Introduction," *Diacritics* 26 (1996): 114; Jean-Yves Le Naour, *Misères Et Tourments De La Chair Durant La Grand Guerre* (Paris, 2002), 402; Keith L. Nelson, "'Black Horror on the Rhine': Race as a Factor in Post-World War I Diplomacy," *Journal of Modern History* 42 (1970): 615–20; Paul Weindling, *Health, Race and German Politics between National Unification and Nazism, 1870–1945* (Cambridge, 1989), 386.

14 Georges Bataille, "The Solar Anus," in *Visions of Excess: Selected Writings, 1927–1939*, ed. Allan Stoekl, (Minneapolis, 1985), 6.

15 Siegfried Kracauer, "The Mass Ornament," *New German Critique.* (1975): 67–73; Patrice Petro, *Joyless Streets: Women and Melodramatic Representation in Weimar Germany* (Princeton, 1989), 65. See also Karl Toepfer, "Nudity and Modernity in German Dance, 1910-30," *Journal of the History of Sexuality* 3 (1992): 93.

16 Lawrence Birken, *Consuming Desire: Sexual Science and the Emergence of a Culture of Abundance* (Ithaca, 1988), 110.

17 Steve Humphries, *A Secret World of Sex* (London, 1988), 64; Pam Cox, *Gender, Justice and Welfare: Bad Girls in Britain, 1900–1950* (Basingstoke, 2003), 118; Laura Tabili, "Women 'of a Very Low Type': Crossing Racial Boundaries in Late Imperial Britain," in *Gender and Class in Modern Europe*, ed. Laura Frader and Sonya Rose, (Ithaca, 1996), 165–90; Lucy Bland, "White Women and Men of Color: Miscegenation Fears in Britain after the Great War," *Gender & History [Great Britain]* 17 (2005): 29–61.

18 Urban Lundberg and Klas Åmark, "Social Rights and Social Security: The Swedish Welfare State, 1900–2000," *Scandinavian Journal of History* 26, no. 3 (2001): 164; Annulla Linders, "Abortion as a Social Problem: The Construction of 'Opposite' Solutions in Sweden and the United States," *Social Problems* 45 (1998): 499; Christl Wickert, *Helene Stöcker, 1869–1943: Frauenrechtlerin, Sexualreformerin Und Pazifistin: Eine Biographie [Helene Stöcker, 1869–1943: Women's Rights Activist, Sexual Reformer and Peace Activist: A Biography]* (Bonn, 1991), 83; Georg Lilienthal, "The Illegitimacy Question in Germany, 1900–1945: Areas of Tension in Social and Population Policy," *Continuity and Change [Great Britain]* 5 (1990): 250–60.

19 Dagmar Herzog, *Sex after Fascism: Memory and Morality in Twentieth Century Germany* (Princeton, 2005), 16; Jans Fleming, "'Sexuelle Krise' Und 'Neue Ethik:' Wahrnehmungen, Debatten Und Perspektiven in Der Deutschen Gesellschaft Der Jahrhundertwende," in *Liebe, Lust Und Leid: Zur Gefühlkultur Um 1900*, ed. Michael Grisko and Helmut Scheuer, (Kassel, 1999), 39; Carola Lipp, "Die Innenseite Der Arbeiterkultur: Sexualität Im Arbeitermilieu Des 19. Und Frühen 20. Jahrhunderts," in *Arbeit, Frömmigkeit Und Eigensinn: Studien Zur Historischen Kulturforschung II*, ed. Richard von Dülmen, (Frankfurt am Main, 1990), 242. Thanks to Jennifer Illuzi for help with these and other translations.

20 Anne-Marie Sohn, *Du Premier Baiser À l'Alcôve: La Sexualité Des Francais Au Quotidien (1850–1950)* (Paris, 1996), 207, 483.

21 Eustace Chesser, *Sexual, Marital, and Family Relationships of the Englishwoman* (London, 1956), 311.

22 Johannes Dück, "Virginität Und Ehe," *Archiv für Bevölkerungswissenschaft und Bevölkerungspolitik* 11 (1941): 305.

23 Sohn, *Du Premier Baiser À l'Alcôve*, 108.

24 Sally Alexander, "The Mysteries and Secrets of Women's Bodies: Sexual Knowledge in the First Half of the Nineteenth Century," in *Modern Times: Reflections on a Century of English Modernity*, ed. Mica Nava and Allen O'Shea, (London, 1996), 161–75.

25 Thanks to Lisa Sigel for this insight about stockings.

26 H.G. Cocks, "'Sporty' Girls and 'Artistic' Boys: Friendship, Illicit Sex and the British 'Companionship' Advertisement, 1913–1928," *Journal of the History of Sexuality* 11 (2002): 457–82; Billie Melman, *Women and the Popular Imagination in the Twenties* (New York, 1988), 18; Matt Houlbrook, "'The Man with the Powder Puff' in Interwar London," *Historical Journal* 50 (2007): 169.

27 Maud Lavin, *Cut with the Kitchen Knife: The Weimar Photomontages of Hannah Hoch* (New Haven, 1993), 198; Laura Doan, *Fashioning Sapphism: The Origins of Modern English Lesbian Culture* (New York, 2001), 106–7.

28 Melman, *Women and the Popular Imagination in the Twenties*, 89.

29 Alexandra A. Kollontai, "The New Woman," in *The Autobiography of a Sexually Emancipated Communist Woman*, ed. Irving Fetscher, (New York, 1971), 93–4.

30 Mary Louise Roberts, *Civilization without Sexes* (Chicago, 1994), 46.

31 Victor Margueritte, *The Bachelor Girl: From the French of La Garçonne*, Hugh Burnaby trans. (New York, 1923), 57.

32 Irmgard Keun, *The Artificial Silk Girl*, Kathie von Ankum trans. (New York, 2002 [1932]), 125. See also Richard W. McCormick, *Gender and Sexuality in Weimar Modernity: Film, Literature and the "New Objectivity"* (New York, 2001), 135.

33 Margueritte, *Bachelor Girl*, 115; Victor Margueritte, *La Garçonne* (Paris, 1923 [1922]), 115.

34 Margueritte, *Bachelor Girl*, 198; Margueritte, *La Garçonne*, 158.

35 Alison Oram, *Her Husband Was a Woman! Women's Gender-Crossing in Modern British Popular Culture* (London, 2007).

36 Doan, *Fashioning Sapphism*, 1–30, 124; Lavin, *Cut with a Kitchen Knife*, 198; Sabine Hake, "In the Mirror of Fashion," in *Women in the Metropolis: Gender and Modernity in Weimar Culture*, ed. Katherina von Ankum, (Berkeley, 1997), 196.

37 Kristina Fjelkestam, "Tale of Transgression: *Charlie* and the Representation of Female Homosexuality in Interwar Sweden," *Nora, Nordic Journal of Women's Studies* 14 (2005): 9.

38 Institute for Sexual Science Online-Exhibition by the Magnus-Hirschfeld Society http://www.hirschfeld.in-berlin.de/institut/en/index1024_2.html (accessed Apr. 15, 2008).

39 Lavin, *Cut with a Kitchen Knife*, 190.

40 Houlbrook, "'The Man with the Powder Puff' in Interwar London," 149; Matt Houlbrook, "Soldier Heroes and Rent Boys: Homosex, Masculinities, and Britishness in the Brigade of Guards, Circa 1900–1960," *Journal of British Studies* 42 (2003): 351–88.

41 Jens Rydstrom, *Sinners and Citizens: Bestiality and Homosexuality in Sweden, 1880–1950* (Chicago, 2003), 171.

42 Matt Houlbrook, *Queer London: Perils and Pleasures in the Sexual Metropolis, 1918–1957* (Chicago, 2005), 273.

43 Rydstrom, *Sinners and Citizens*, 248.

44 Florence Tamagne, *Histoire de l'Homosexualité en Europe* (Paris, 2000), 491.

45 Houlbrook, *Queer London*, 32; Rydstrom, *Sinners and Citizens*, 248; Tamagne, *Histoire de l'Homosexualité en Europe*, 491; Edward Ross Dickinson, "Policing Sex in Germany 1882–1982: A Preliminary Statistical Analysis," *Journal of the History of Sexuality* 16 (2007): 222; Jens Dobler, "Nicht Nur Verfolgung – Auch Erfolge: Zusammenarbeit Zwischen Schwulenbewegung Und Polizei in Der Kaiserzeit Und Der Weimarer Republik [Not Only Persecution: Cooperative Relations between the Homosexual Movement and the Police in Imperial Germany and the Weimar Republic],"

Comparativ [Germany] 9 (1999): 51–3. Stephan Heiss, "München: Polizei Und Schwule Subkulturen 1919–1944 [Munich: Police and Homosexual Subcultures, 1919–1944]," *Comparativ [Germany]* 9 (1999): 65–78.

46 Albert Müller and Christian Fleck, "'Unzucht Wider Die Natur': Gerichtliche Verfolgung Der 'Unzucht Mit Personen Gleichen Geschlechts' in Österreich Von Den 1930er Bis Zu Den 1950er Jahren ['Debauchery Contrary to Nature': Legal Prosecution of 'Fornication with Persons of the Same Sex' in Austria from the 1930s to the 1950s]," *Österreichische Zeitschrift für Geschichtswissenschaften [Austria]* 9 (1998): 419; Antu Sorainen, "Productive Trials: English and Finnish Legislation and Conceptualisations of Same-Sex Sexualities in Course of Trials of Oscar Wilde, Maud Allan, Radclyffe Hall and Herb Grove, from 1885 to 1956," *SQS* 17 (2006), http://www.helsinki.fi/jarj/sqs/SQSSorainen%20Artikkeli.pdf (accessed Apr. 15, 2008); Doan, *Fashioning Sapphism*, 30–57; Jens Rydstrom, "From Sodomy to Homosexuality: Rural Sex and the Inclusion of Lesbians in Criminal Discourse," *Nora, Nordic Journal of Women's Studies* 13 (2005): 30.

47 Chris Waters, "Havelock Ellis, Sigmund Freud, and the State: Discourses of Homosexual Identity in Interwar Britain," in *Sexology in Culture*, 169.

48 Tamagne, *Histoire de l'Homosexualité en Europe*, 344–6; Florence Tamagne, *A History of Homosexuality in Europe: Paris, Berlin, London 1919–1939* (New York, 2004), 20.

49 Lavin, *Cut with a Kitchen Knife*, 188.

50 Alan Lareau, "Lavender Songs: Undermining Gender in Weimar and Beyond," *Popular Music and Society* 28 (2005): 16.

51 Carolyn Dean, *The Frail Social Body: Pornography, Homosexuality, and Other Fantasies in Interwar France* (Berkeley, 2000), 198; Tirza True Latimer, *Women Together/ Women Apart: Portraits of Lesbian Paris* (New Brunswick, 2005), 120.

52 Adele Meyer, ed., *Lila Nächte: Die Damenklubs Im Berlin Der Zwanziger Jahre* (Berlin, 1994), 30.

53 Tamagne, *A History of Homosexuality in Europe*, 47–50.

54 Angeles Espinaco-Virseda, "'I Feel That I Belong to You': Subculture, Die Freundin and Lesbian Identities in Weimar Germany," *Spaces of Identity* 4 (2004), http://www.yorku.ca/soi/_Vol_4_1/_HTML/Espinaco_virseda.html (accessed Apr. 15, 2008); Amy Dawn Young, "'Das Gesprengte Korsett': Gender in Lesbian Periodicals in Berlin, 1924–1933" (Ph.D., University of Nebraska, 2004), 35.

55 Mel Gordon, *Voluptuous Panic: The Erotic World of Weimar Berlin* (Los Angeles, 2000), 112.

56 Young, "Das Gesprengte Korsett," 44.

57 Ibid., 51–3; Katharina Vogel, "Zum Selbstverständnis Lesbischer Frauen in Der Weimarer Republik: Eine Analyse Der Zeitschrift 'Die Freundin,' 1924–1933," in *Eldorado: Homosexuelle Frauen Und Männer in Berlin 1850–1950: Geschichte, Alltag Und Kultur*, ed. e.V. Verein der Freunde eines Schwulen Museum in Berlin, (Berlin, 1992), 164–7. Thanks to Michelle Los for this and other translations.

58 Dean, *The Frail Social Body*, 196. Marie-Jo Bonnet, *Les Relations Amoureuses Entre Les Femmes* (Paris, 1995), 316; Claudia Schoppmann, *Days of Masquerade: Life Stories of Lesbians During the Third Reich* (New York, 1996), 4–6.

59 Lareau, "Lavender Song," 16.

60 Houlbrook, *Queer London*, 6.

61 Tamagne, *A History of Homosexuality in Europe*, 45.

62 Rydstrom, *Sinners and Citizens*, 246.

63 Tamagne, *Histoire de l'Homosexualité en Europe*, 376.

64 Houlbrook, *Queer London*, 44.

65 Tamagne, *A History of Homosexuality in Europe*, 138.

66 Ferdinand Karsch-Haack and René Stelter, eds., *Uranos: Unabhängige Uranische Monatsschrift Für Wissenschaft, Polemik, Belletristik, Kunst* (Hamburg, 2002), 40; Claudia Bruns, "The Politics of Masculinity in the (Homo-)Sexual Discourse (1880 to 1920)," *German History* 23 (2005): 303–31; John Alexander Williams, "Ecstasies of the Young: Sexuality, the Youth Movement, and Moral Panic in Germany on the Eve of the First World War," *Central European History* 34 (2001): 163–90.

67 Sheila Jeffreys, *The Spinster and Her Enemies: Feminism and Sexuality 1880–1930* (London, 1985), 185.

68 Lisa Appignanesi and John Forrester, *Freud's Women* (New York, 1992), 325, 426.

69 Hera Cook, *The Long Sexual Revolution: English Women, Sex, and Contraception 1800–1975* (Oxford, 2004), 209.

70 Stella Browne, "Women and the Race," *Socialist Review* 14 (1917), *Writings of Stella Browne*, ed. Lesley Hall, http://www.lesleyahall.net/womrace.htm#Women%20and%20the%20Race (accessed Apr. 15, 2008).

71 Atina Grossmann, *Reforming Sex: The German Movement for Birth Control and Abortion Reform, 1920–1950* (New York, 1995), 34; Cornelie Usborne, *The Politics of the Body in Weimar Germany: Women's Reproductive Rights and Duties* (Ann Arbor, 1992), 95.

72 Ruth Hall, *Passionate Crusader: The Life of Marie Stopes* (New York, 1977 [Great Britain]); June Rose, *Marie Stopes and the Sexual Revolution* (London, 1992); Barbara Evans, *Freedom to Choose: The Life and Work of Dr. Helena Wright: Pioneer of Contraception* (London, 1984), 151.

73 Theodore H. Van de Velde, *Ideal Marriage: Its Physiology and Technique*, Stella Browne trans. 2d edn. (New York, 1930 [*Volkomen huwelijk*]), 123–79.

74 Ibid.

75 Evans, *Freedom to Choose*, 150–1.

76 Ruth Hall, ed., *Dear Dr. Stopes: Sex in the 1920s* (London, 1978), 144–6.

77 Max Hodann, *Sex Life in Europe: A Biological and Sociological Survey*, J. Gibbs trans. (New York, 1975 [1932]), 12.

78 Helena Wright, *The Sex Factor in Marriage: A Book for Those Who Are or Are About to Be Married* (New York, 1937), 85.

79 Van de Velde, *Ideal Marriage*, 106, 149.

80 Hodann, *Sex Life in Europe*, 156, 220.

81 Usborne, *Politics of the Body*, 88–9.

82 Karen Chow, "Popular Sexual Knowledges and Women's Agency in 1920s England: Marie Stopes's 'Married Love' and E. M. Hull's 'the Sheik'," *Feminist Review* 63 (1999): 67–71.

83 Roy Porter and Leslie Hall, *The Facts of Life: The Creation of Sexual Knowledges in Britain, 1650–1950* (New Haven, 1995), 264.

84 Chase, "Politics of Morality," 278.

85 Weindling, *Health, Race and German Politics*, 380.

86 Grossmann, *Reforming Sex*, 17.

87 Weindling, *Health, Race and German Politics*, 371.

88 Roberts, *Civilization without Sexes*, 96.

89 Porter and Hall, *Facts of Life*, 240.

90 Weindling, *Health, Race and German Politics*, 426; Dr. Kurt Bendix, "Birth Control in Berlin," in *Sexual Reform Congress, 1929: The World League for Sex Reform*, ed. Norman Haire, (London, 1930), 659.

91 Grossmann, *Reforming Sex*, 3.

92 Diana G. Gittins, "Married Life and Birth Control between the Wars," *Oral History* 3 (1975): 54–8.

93 Kate Fisher, "'She Was Quite Satisfied with the Arrangements I Made:' Gender and Birth Control in Britain, 1920–1950," *Past and Present* 169 (2000): 171.

94 Cook, *The Long Sexual Revolution*, 142.
95 Kate Fisher, *Birth Control, Sex, and Marriage in Britain, 1918–1960* (Oxford, 2006), 36.
96 Kate Fisher, "Uncertain Aims and Tacit Negotiation: Birth Control Practices in Britain, 1925–50," *Population and Development Review* 26 (2000): 171.
97 Cornelie Usborne, "Wise Women, Wise Men, and Abortion in the Weimar Republic," in *Gender Relations in German History*, ed. Lynn Abrams and Elizabeth Harvey, (Durham, NC, 1997), 148–50.
98 Ann Taylor Allen, *Feminism and Motherhood in Western Europe 1890–1970* (New York, 2005), 166.
99 Barbara Brookes, *Abortion in England, 1900–1967* (London, 1988), 20–37; Stephen Brooke, "A New World for Women? Abortion Law Reform in Britain During the 1930s," *American Historical Review* 106 (2001): 431–59.
100 Loren R. Graham, "Science and Values: The Eugenics Movement in Germany and Russia in the 1920s," *American Historical Review* 82 (1977): 1140.
101 Edward Ross Dickinson, "Biopolitics, Fascism, Democracy: Some Reflections on Our Discourse About 'Modernity'," *Central European History* 37 (2004): 31–6.
102 Grossmann, *Reforming Sex*, 82.
103 Sohn, *Du Premier Baiser á l'Àlcôve*, 224; Laure Adler, *Secrets d'Àlcôve: Histoire du Couple de 1830 À 1930* (Paris, 1983), 95.
104 Kirsten von Sydow, "Female Sexuality and Historical Time: A Comparison of Sexual Biographies of German Women Born between 1895 and 1936," *Archives of Sexual Behavior* 25 (1996): 479.
105 Alexander, "The Mysteries and Secrets of Women's Bodies," 161–75.
106 Heidi Rosenbaum, *Proletarische Familien: Arbeiterfamilien Und Arbeiterväter Im Frühen 20. Jahrhundert Zwischen Traditioneller, Sozialdemokratischer Und Kleinbürgerlicher Orientierung* (Frankfurt am Main, 1992), 195.
107 Mary Boyd Higgins, "Introduction," in *Wilhelm Reich: Beyond Psychology: Letters and Journals 1934–1939*, ed. Mary Boyd Higgins, (New York, 1994), vii–ix; Elizabeth Ann Danto, *Freud's Free Clinics: Psychoanalysis & Social Justice, 1918–1938* (New York, 2005), 116–18; Grossmann, *Reforming Sex*, 269.

11 Sex and the state in the 1930s

1 Alexandra A. Kollontai, "Make Way for Winged Eros," in *Selected Writings*, ed. Alix Holt, (London, 1977), 286.
2 Dr. Anton Nystrom, *The Natural Laws of Sexual Life: Medical-Sociological Researches*, Carl Sandzen trans. 3rd Swedish edn. (St. Louis, 1913 [1904]), 33.
3 Dagmar Herzog, *Sex after Fascism: Memory and Morality in Twentieth Century Germany* (Princeton, 2005), 30; Nystrom, *The Natural Laws of Sexual Life*, 33.
4 Frances L. Bernstein, *The Dictatorship of Sex: Lifestyle Advice for the Soviet Masses* (DeKalb, IL, 2007), 132.
5 Ann Taylor Allen, *Feminism and Motherhood in Western Europe 1890–1970* (New York, 2005); Edward Ross Dickinson, "Biopolitics, Fascism, Democracy: Some Reflections on Our Discourse About 'Modernity'," *Central European History* 37 (2004): 36; Ann Taylor Allen, "Feminism and Eugenics in Germany and Britain, 1900–1940: A Comparative Perspective," *German Studies Review* 23 (2000): 477–505.
6 Nystrom, *The Natural Laws of Sexual Life*, 255.
7 For reasons of space, this chapter cannot cover Vichy France or fascist Italy, but see Miranda Pollard, *Reign of Virtue: Moralizing Gender in Vichy France* (Chicago, 1998); Michael Sibalis, "Homophobia, Vichy France, and The 'Crime of Homosexuality': The Origins of the Ordinance of 6 August 1942," *GLQ* 8 (2002); Sandro

Bellassai, "The Masculine Mystique: Antimodernism and Virility in Fascist Italy," *Journal of Modern Italian Studies* 10 (Sept. 2005); Lorenzo Benadusi, Ann Pichey, and Alessandro Boccanelli, "Private Life and Public Morals: Fascism and the 'Problem' of Homosexuality," *Totalitarian Movements and Political Religions* 5 (2004); Victoria de Grazia, *How Fascism Ruled Women* (Berkeley, 1992).

8 George Mosse, *Nationalism and Sexuality* (New York, 1985), 151.

9 Ann Laura Stoler, *Carnal Knowledge and Imperial Power: Race and the Intimate in Colonial Rule* (Berkeley, 2002), 33–105; Alice Conklin, *A Mission to Civilize: The Republican Idea of Empire in France and West Africa, 1885–1930* (Stanford, 1997), 169. For parallel developments in German colonies, see Lora Wildenthal, *German Women for Empire, 1881–1945* (Durham, 2001), 81–102.

10 Carol Summers, "Intimate Colonialism: The Imperial Production of Reproduction in Uganda, 1907–1925," *Signs* 16 (1991): 787–807; Lynn M. Thomas, "Imperial Concerns and Women's Affairs: State Efforts to Regulate Clitoridectomy and Eradicate Abortion in Meru, Kenya, c. 1910–1950," *Journal of African History* 39 (1998): 121–45; Susan Pedersen, "National Bodies, Unspeakable Acts: The Sexual Politics of Colonial Policy-Making," *Journal of Modern History* 63 (1991): 649–54.

11 Dorothy Porter, "Eugenics and the Sterilization Debate in Sweden and Britain before World War II," *Scandinavian Journal of History* 24 (1999): 155; Edward J. Larson, "The Rhetoric of Eugenics: Expert Authority and the Mental Deficiency Bill," *British Journal for the History of Science* 24 (1991): 52; Allen, "Feminism and Eugenics in Germany and Britain, 1900–1940: A Comparative Perspective," 477–505.

12 Lesley A. Hall, "No Sex Please We're Socialists: The British Labour Party Closes Its Eyes and Thinks of the Electorate," in *Meetings & Alcôves – the Left and Sexuality in Europe and the United States since 1850*, ed. Jesse Battan, Thomas Bouchet, and Tania Régin, (Dijon, 2004), 65–78.

13 Cheryl A. Koos, "Gender, Anti-Individualism and Nationalism: The Alliance Française and the Pronatalist Backlash against the Femme Moderne, 1933–1940," *French Historical Studies* 19 (1996): 722; Carolyn Dean, *The Frail Social Body: Pornography, Homosexuality, and Other Fantasies in Interwar France* (Berkeley, 2000), 62; Andrés Horacio Reggiani, "Procreating France," *French Historical Studies* 19 (1996): 731.

14 Ellen Key, *Love and Marriage*, Arthur G. Chater trans. (New York, 1911), 147–50; Doris H. Linder, *Crusader for Sex Education: Elise Ottesen-Jensen (1886–1973) in Scandinavia and on the International Scene* (Lanham, MD, 1996), 282.

15 Alva Myrdal, *Nation and Family: The Swedish Experiment in Democratic Family and Population Policy* (Cambridge, MA, 1968 [1941]), 39.

16 Gunnar Broberg and Mattias Tyden, "Eugenics in Sweden: Efficient Care," in *Eugenics and the Welfare State: Sterilization Policy in Denmark, Sweden, Norway, and Finland*, ed. Gunnar Broberg and Nils Roll-Hansen, (East Lansing, 1996), 78; H. Lundborg, "The More Important Racial Elements That Form a Part of the Present Swedish Nation," in *The Swedish Nation in Word and Picture*, ed. H. Lundborg and J. Rundstrom, (Stockholm, 1921), 25; Dr. Hjalmar Anderson, "The Swedish State-Institute for Race-Biological Investigation," in *The Swedish Nation in Words and Pictures*, ed. H. Lundborg and J. Rundstrom, (Stockholm, 1921), 74.

17 Allan C. Carlson, *The Swedish Experiment in Family Politics: The Myrdals and the Interwar Population Crisis* (New Brunswick, 1990), 17.

18 Ron Eyerman, "Rationalizing Intellectuals: Sweden in the 1930s and 1940s," *Theory and Society* 14 (1985): 786. Alva and Gunnar Myrdal, *Kris i Befolkningsfrågan* (1934) was not published in English.

19 Gunnar Myrdal, "Population Problems and Policies," *American Academy of Political and Social Science, Annals* 197 (1938): 211.

20 Myrdal, *Nation and Family*, 193.

21 Gunnar Myrdal and Andrea Andreen-Svedberg, *Report on the Sex Question by the Swedish Population Commission*, Virginia Clay Hamilton trans. (Baltimore, 1940), 14. Myrdal, *Nation and Family*, 6.
22 Weintraub, *Sterilization in Sweden: Its Law and Practice* (New York, 1951), 364.
23 Myrdal, "Population Problems and Policies," 204; Annulla Linders, "Abortion as a Social Problem: The Construction of 'Opposite' Solutions in Sweden and the United States," *Social Problems* 45 (1998): 497.
24 Carl Gustaf Boethius, "Sex Education in Swedish Schools: The Facts and the Fiction," *Family Planning Perspectives* 17 (1985): 276.
25 Carlson, *The Swedish Experiment in Family Politics*, 187.
26 Linders, "Abortion as a Social Problem," 498–503.
27 Alberto Spektorowski and Elisabet Mizrachi, "Eugenics and the Welfare State in Sweden," *Journal of Contemporary History* 39 (2004): 341; Lundborg, "The More Important Racial Elements That Form a Part of the Present Swedish Nation," 35; Nils Roll-Hansen, "Eugenic Practice and Genetic Science in Scandinavia and Germany," *Scandinavian Journal of History* 26 (2001): 75–82.
28 Weintraub, *Sterilization in Sweden: Its Law and Practice*, 370.
29 Broberg and Tyden, "Eugenics in Sweden: Efficient Care," 118. For eugenics and sterilization in Denmark, J. Leunbach, "Abortion and Sterilization in Denmark," in *Sexual Reform Congress, 1929: World League for Sex Reform*, ed. Norman Haire, (London, 1930); Bent Sigurd Hansen, "Something Rotten in the State of Denmark," in *Eugenics and the Welfare State*, 9–76. For Norway, Siri Haavie, "Sterilization in Norway – a Dark Chapter?," *Eurozine* (2003), http://www.eurozine.com/articles/2003-04-09-haavie-en.html (accessed Apr. 15, 2008); Oyvind Giaever, "Abortion and Eugenics: The Role of Eugenic Arguments in Norwegian Abortion Debates and Legislation, 1920–1978," *Scandinavian Journal of History* 30 (2005): 21–44.
30 Dickinson, "Biopolitics, Fascism, Democracy," 36.
31 Laura Engelstein, *The Keys to Happiness: Sex and the Search for Modernity in Fin-De-Siècle Russia* (Ithaca, 1992), 383.
32 Orlando Figes, *The Whisperers: Private Life in Stalin's Russia* (New York, 2007), 10.
33 Wendy Z. Goldman, *Women, the State and Revolution: Soviet Family Policy and Social Life, 1917–1936* (Cambridge, UK, 1993), 255.
34 Gregory Carleton, *Sexual Revolution in Bolshevik Russia* (Pittsburgh, 2005), 58.
35 Kollontai, "Selected Writings," 277–86.
36 Alix Holt, ed., *Selected Writings of Alexandra Kollontai* (London, 1977), 204–5.
37 Carleton, *Sexual Revolution in Bolshevik Russia*, 63.
38 Anne E. Gorsuch, "Moscow Chic: Silk Stockings and Soviet Youth," in *The Human Tradition in Modern Russia*, ed. William Husband, (Wilmington, DE, 2000), 71.
39 Bernstein, *The Dictatorship of Sex*, 29.
40 Elizabeth A. Wood, "Prostitution Unbound: Representations of Sexual and Political Anxieties in Postrevolutionary Russia," in *Sexuality and the Body in Russian Culture*, ed. Jane T. Costlow, Stephanie Sandler, and Judith Vowles, (Stanford, 1993), 130.
41 Carleton, *Sexual Revolution in Bolshevik Russia*, 187.
42 Bernstein, *The Dictatorship of Sex*, 161–84.
43 Susan Gross Solomon, "The Demographic Argument in Soviet Debates over the Legalization of Abortion in the 1920s," *Cahiers du Monde Russe et Sovietique* 33 (January–March, 1992): 67.
44 Goldman, *Women, the State and Revolution*, 233; Figes, *The Whisperers*, 160.
45 Dan Healey, *Homosexual Desire in Revolutionary Russia: The Regulation of Sexual and Gender Dissent* (Chicago, 2001), 159.
46 Douglas Northrop, *Veiled Empire: Gender and Power in Stalinist Central Asia* (Ithaca, 2004), 253; Shoshana Keller, "Women's Liberation and Islam in Soviet Uzbekistan,

1926–1941," in *Bodies in Contact: Rethinking Colonial Encounters in World History*, ed. Tony Ballantyne and Antoinette Burton, (Durham, 2005), 328.

47 Goldman, *Women, the State and Revolution*, 291, 336; Figes, *The Whisperers*, 160–1.

48 Healey, *Homosexual Desire in Revolutionary Russia*, 188–9.

49 Carleton, *Sexual Revolution in Bolshevik Russia*, 221.

50 Amir Weiner, "Nature, Nurture, and Memory in a Socialist Utopia: Delineating the Soviet Socio-Ethnic Body in the Age of Socialism," *American Historical Review* 104 (1999): 1146–7; Loren R. Graham, "Science and Values: The Eugenics Movement in Germany and Russia in the 1920s," *American Historical Review* 82, no. 5 (1977): 1153; Francine Hirsch, "Race without the Practice of Race Politics," *Slavic Review* 61 (2002): 30–42; Mark B. Adams, *The Wellborn Science: Eugenics in Germany, France, Brazil, and Russia* (New York, 1990).

51 Klaus Theweleit, *Male Fantasies: Male Bodies, Psychoanalyzing the White Terror*, Erica Carter and Chris Turner trans., 2 vols., vol. 2 (Minneapolis, 1989), 184.

52 Paul Wilder Chase, "The Politics of Morality in Weimar Germany: Public Controversy and Parliamentary Debate over Changes in Moral Behavior in the Twenties" (Ph.D., State University of New York at Stonybrook, 1992), 506; Paul Weindling, *Health, Race and German Politics between National Unification and Nazism, 1870–1945* (Cambridge, 1989), 450.

53 Linda Schulte-Sasse, *Entertaining the Third Reich* (Durham, 1996), 73.

54 Gerhard Reinhard Ritter, *Die Geschlechtliche Frage in Der Deutschen Volkserziehung* (Berlin and Cologne, 1936), 33.

55 Herzog, *Sex after Fascism*, 32.

56 Irene Guenther, *Nazi Chic? Fashioning Women in the Third Reich* (Oxford, 2004), 103.

57 Hans Peter Bleuel, *Strength through Joy: Sex and Society in Nazi Germany*, J. Maxell Brownjohn trans. (London, 1973), 58.

58 Herzog, *Sex after Fascism*, 27.

59 Bettina Amm, "Völkische Erotik? Differente Weibliche Und Männliche Sexualvorstellungen Innerhalb Der Völkischen Rechten Zwischen Weimarer Republik Und Nationalsozialismus," in *Gebrochene Kontinuitäten? Zur Rolle Und Bedeutung Des Geschlechterverhältnisses in Der Entwicklung Des Nationalsozialismus*, ed. Ilse Korotin and Barbara Serloth, (Munich, 2000), 73. Thanks to Michelle Los for notes from German.

60 Dr. Wollenweber, "Das Gesundheitsamt Im Kampfe Gegen Den Geburtenschwund," *Öffentliche Gesundheitsamt* 11 (1939–1940): 452.

61 Bleuel, *Strength through Joy*, 168.

62 Julia Roos, "Backlash against Prostitutes' Rights: Origins and Dynamics of Nazi Prostitution Policies," *Journal of the History of Sexuality* 11 (2002): 89–94.

63 Elizabeth Heineman, "Sexuality and Nazism: The Doubly Unspeakable?," *Journal of the History of Sexuality* 11 (2002): 44.

64 Manuela von Papen, "Opportunities and Limitations: The New Woman in Third Reich Cinema," *Women's History Review* 8 (1999): 705.

65 Atina Grossmann, *Reforming Sex: The German Movement for Birth Control and Abortion Reform, 1920–1950* (New York, 1995), 122; Herzog, *Sex after Fascism*, 9–12; Roos, "Backlash against Prostitutes' Rights," 90; Georg Lilienthal, "The Illegitimacy Question in Germany, 1900–1945: Areas of Tension in Social and Population Policy," *Continuity and Change [Great Britain]* 5 (1990): 270.

66 Geoffrey J. Giles, "'The Most Unkindest Cut of All': Castration, Homosexuality and Nazi Justice," *Journal of Contemporary History* 27 (1992): 41.

67 Gisela Bock, "Racism and Sexism in Nazi Germany: Compulsory Sterilization and the State," *Signs* 8 (1983): 400–21.

68 Theweleit, *Male Fantasies*, 12.

69 Patricia Szobar, "Telling Sexual Stories in the Nazi Courts of Law: Race Defilement in Germany, 1933 to 1945," *Journal of the History of Sexuality* 11, 2 (2002), 140.
70 Heineman, "Sexuality and Nazism: The Doubly Unspeakable?" 32.
71 Bleuel, *Strength through Joy*, 31.
72 Roos, "Backlash against Prostitutes' Rights," 90.
73 Stefan Micheler, "Homophobic Propaganda and the Denunciation of Same-Sex-Desiring Men under National Socialism," *Journal of the History of Sexuality* 11 (2002): 95–130.
74 Giles, "'The Most Unkindest Cut of All'," 41–61.
75 Roos, "Backlash against Prostitutes' Rights," 90.
76 Harry Oosterhuis, "Medicine, Male Bonding and Homosexuality in Nazi Germany," *Journal of Contemporary History* 32 (1997): 189–205.
77 Claudia Schoppmann, *Days of Masquerade: Life Stories of Lesbians During the Third Reich* (New York, 1996).
78 Micheler, "Homophobic Propaganda," 105–29; Albert Müller and Christian Fleck, "'Unzucht Wider Die Natur': Gerichtliche Verfolgung Der 'Unzucht Mit Personen Gleichen Geschlechts' in Österreich Von Den 1930er Bis Zu Den 1950er Jahren" ['Debauchery Contrary to Nature': Legal Prosecution of 'Fornication with Persons of the Same Sex' in Austria from the 1930s to the 1950s], *Österreichische Zeitschrift für Geschichtswissenschaften [Austria]* 9 (1998): 412–13.
79 Claudia Koonz, "Ethical Dilemmas and Nazi Eugenics: Single-Issue Dissent in Religious Contexts," *Journal of Modern History* 64 (1992): 8–31.
80 Wollenweber, "Gesundheitsamt," 447.
81 Manfred Herzer, "Hinweise Auf Das Schwule Berlin in Der Nazizeit," in *Eldorado: Homosexuelle Frauen Und Männer in Berlin 1850–1950: Geschichte, Alltag Und Kultur*, ed. e.V. Verein der Freunde eines Schwulen Museum in Berlin, (Berlin, 1992), 46.
82 Dickinson, "Biopolitics, Fascism, Democracy," 31.

12 The reconstruction of desire and sexual consumerism

1 Emmanuelle Arsan, *Emmanuelle*, Lowell Bair trans. (New York, 1971); Richard Ivan Jobs, *Riding the New Wave: Youth and the Rejuvenation of France after the Second World War* (Stanford, 2007), 245.
2 Pope Paul VI, "Humanae Vitae: On the Regulation of Human Births," *Papal Encyclicals* (1968), http://www.papalencyclicals.net/ (accessed Apr. 15, 2008).
3 Emmanuelle Arsan, "An Open Letter to Paul VI on the Pill," in *The Evergreen Review Reader*, ed. Barney Rosset, (New York, 1998), 296.
4 Edward Fyfe Griffith, *Morals and the Melting Pot* (London, 1948), 290; Edward Fyfe Griffith, *Sex and Citizenship* (London 1941), 26.
5 Dagmar Herzog, *Sex after Fascism: Memory and Morality in Twentieth Century Germany* (Princeton, 2005), 103.
6 Helena Wright, *The Sex Factor in Marriage: A Book for Those Who Are or Are About to Be Married* (New York, 1937), 13, 19, 82; Kenneth Walker, *Love, Marriage and the Family* (London, 1960 [1957]), 12.
7 Prof. Dr. A.M. Hoffman, "The Nature of the Marriage Union," in *Sex-Love-Marriage: A Handbook and Guide for Catholics*, ed. Franz Xaver Von Hornstein and A. Faller, (New York, 1964), 173–4; Griffith, *Sex and Citizenship*, 26; Dr. R. Geis, "Ethical Values of Sexuality," in *Sex-Love-Marriage*, 22.
8 Robert G. Moeller, *Protecting Motherhood: Women and the Family in the Politics of Postwar West Germany* (Berkeley, CA, 1993), 134; Herzog, *Sex after Fascism*, 106.
9 Alex Comfort, *Barbarism and Sexual Freedom: Lectures on the Sociology of Sex from the Standpoint of Anarchism* (London, 1948), 19–60.

10 Hera Cook, *The Long Sexual Revolution: English Women, Sex, and Contraception 1800–1975* (Oxford, 2004), 228.

11 Ingrid Sharp, "The Sexual Unification of Germany," *Journal of the History of Sexuality* 13 (2004): 349.

12 K.D. Mehlan, "German Democratic Republic," in *International Handbook on Abortion*, ed. Paul Sachdev, (New York, 1988), 170–89.

13 Chantal Blayo, "Fécondité, Contraception Et Avortement En Europe De L'est," *Population* 25 (1970): 829–32.

14 Gunther Grau, "Return of the Past: The Policy of the SED and the Laws against Homosexuality in Eastern Germany between 1946 and 1968," *Journal of Homosexuality* 37 (1999): 13.

15 Robert G. Moeller, "The Homosexual Man Is a 'Man,' the Homosexual Woman Is a 'Woman': Sex, Society and the Law in Postwar West Germany," *Journal of the History of Sexuality* 4 (1994): 471.

16 Roger Davidson, "The Sexual State: Sexuality and Scottish Governance, 1950–1980," *Journal of the History of Sexuality* 13 (2004): 511.

17 Jens Rydstrom, *Sinners and Citizens: Bestiality and Homosexuality in Sweden, 1880–1950* (Chicago, 2003), 330.

18 Frédéric Martel, *The Pink and the Black: Homosexuals in France since 1968*, Jane Marie Todd trans. (Stanford, 2000), 60.

19 Jeffrey Weeks, *Coming Out: Homosexual Politics in Britain, from the Nineteenth Century to the Present* (London, 1977), 156–67.

20 Committee on Homosexual Offences and Prostitution, *The Wolfenden Report: Report of the Committee on Homosexual Offenses and Prostitution* Authorized American edition; Introduction by Karl Menninger, M.D. ed. (New York, 1963), 28; Davidson, "The Sexual State," 520–1; Matt Houlbrook, *Queer London: Perils and Pleasures in the Sexual Metropolis, 1918–1957* (Chicago, 2005), 252.

21 Dr. A. Niedermeyer, "Anomalies of the Sexual Impulse," in *Sex-Love-Marriage*, 360.

22 Matt Houlbrook and Chris Waters, "*The Heart in Exile*: Detachment and Desire in 1950s London," *History Workshop Journal* 62 (2006): 140; Rebecca Jennings, "'The Most Uninhibited Party They'd Ever Been To:' the Post-War Encounter between Psychiatry and the British Lesbian," *Journal of British Studies* 47, 4 (Oct 2008): forthcoming.

23 Edward Fyfe Griffith, *Marriage and the Unconscious* (London, 1957), 158; Edward Fyfe Griffith, *Modern Marriage* 26th edn. (London, 1963 [1935]), 197.

24 Marcus Collins, *Modern Love: An Intimate History of Men and Women in Twentieth Century Britain* (London, 2004), 96.

25 Eugene Chesser, *Love and the Married Woman* (New York, 1969 [1968]), 34; Kenneth Walker, *Marriage, a Book for the Married and the About to Be Married* (London, 1951), 52; Rennie Macandrew, *Approaching Womanhood; Healthy Sex for Girls* (London, 1947), 52; Ernest Parkinson Smith, *A Handbook of Marriage* (London, 1955), 35.

26 Prof. Dr. J. Zürcher, "The Ethical Significance of Sexual Life in Marriage," in *Sex-Love-Marriage*, 93; Martine Sevegrand, *L'amour En Toutes Lettres: Questions à L'abbé Viollet Sur La Sexualité 1924–1933* (Paris, 1996), 132.

27 John Murray Todd, ed., *Christian Letters on Sex and Marriage* (London, 1955), 39.

28 Eustace Chesser, *Grow up and Live* (Harmondsworth, Middlesex [UK], 1949), 252.

29 Mark Edward Ruff, *The Wayward Flock: Catholic Youth in Postwar West Germany, 1945–1965* (Chapel Hill, 2005), 103.

30 Michael Schofield, *The Sexual Behaviour of Young People* (Boston, 1965), 149.

31 Eustace Chesser, *Sexual, Marital, and Family Relationships of the Englishwoman* (London, 1956), 311.

32 Herzog, *Sex after Fascism*, 126.

33 Hans L. Zetterberg, *Sexual Life in Sweden*, Grahama Fennell trans. (New Brunswick, 2002), 113.
34 Harold T. Christensen and George R. Carpenter, "Value-Behavior Discrepancies Regarding Premarital Coitus in Three Western Cultures," *American Sociological Review* 27 (1962): 66–74. This is not to imply that Sweden, Norway, Denmark and Finland all had the same sexual cultures, quite the contrary.
35 Michael Schofield, *Promiscuity* (London, 1976), 39.
36 Birgitta Linner and Richard Litell, *Sex and Society in Sweden* (New York, 1967), 71.
37 Ibid., 72.
38 Callum Brown, *The Death of Christian Britain* (London, 2000), 175–81.
39 Zetterberg, *Sexual Life in Sweden*, 120.
40 Chesser, *Love and the Married Women*, 53.
41 Schofield, *Promiscuity*, 125.
42 Linner and Litell, *Sex and Society in Sweden*, 9.
43 Discussed in Linner and Litell, *Sex and Society in Sweden*, 145.
44 Nick Thomas, *Protest Movements in 1960s West Germany: A Social History of Dissent and Democracy* (Oxford, 2003), 233.
45 Sheila Rowbotham, *Promise of a Dream: Remembering the Sixties* (New York, 2001), 47.
46 Kajsa Sundstrom-Feigenberg, "Sweden," in *International Handbook on Abortion*, ed. Paul Sachdev, (New York, 1988), 428.
47 Sir Dugald Baird, "Experience at Aberdeen," in *Abortion in Britain: Proceedings of a Conference Held by the Family Planning Association* (London, 1966), 16–19.
48 Rowena Woolf, "Changes," in *Abortion in Britain*, 70.
49 Zetterberg, *Sexual Life in Sweden*, 177.
50 Sundstrom-Feigenberg, "Sweden," 438.
51 Janine Mossuz-Lavau, *Les Lois de l'Amour: Les Politiques de la Sexualité en France de 1950s à nos Jours* (Paris, 1991), 28.
52 Elizabeth D. Heineman, "The Economic Miracle in the Bedroom: Big Business and Sexual Consumption in Reconstruction West Germany," *Journal of Modern History* 78 (2006): 846.
53 Collins, *Modern Love*, 143.
54 Richard F. Tomasson, *Sweden: Prototype of Modern Society* (New York, 1970), 184.
55 Clayton Whisnant, "Hamburg's Gay Scene in an Era of Family Politics, 1945–1969" (Ph.D., University of Texas at Austin, 2001), 213.
56 Schofield, *The Sexual Behaviour of Young People*, 11; David Fowler, *The First Teenagers: The Lifestyle of Young Wage-Earners in Interwar Britain* (London, 1995), 111; Ronald Goldman, *Angry Adolescents* (London, 1969), 109–10; Jobs, *Riding the New Wave*, 221.
57 Schofield, *Promiscuity*, 13.
58 Reimut Reiche, *Sexuality and Class Struggle*, Susan Bennett trans. (London, 1970), 63.
59 Herbert Marcuse, *One-Dimensional Man* (Boston, 1964), 15–17.
60 Inge Hegeler and Sten Hegeler, *The XYZ of Love; Frank Answers to Every Important Question About Sex in Today's World* (New York, 1970), 8.
61 Gary Giddins, "Still Curious," *Criterion Collection*, http://www.criterion.com/asp/release.asp?id=180&eid=283&section=essay&page=3 (accessed Apr. 15, 2008).
62 Raoul Vaneigem, "From Wildcat Strike to Total Self-Management," translated by Paul Sharkey, *Situationist International Anthology* (1974), http://www.cddc.vt.edu/sionline/postsi/ratgeb01.html (accessed Apr. 15, 2008). The Situationists were a group in France who critiqued consumer society through absurdist performance art and political action.
63 Uta G. Poiger, "Rock 'N' Roll, Female Sexuality, and the Cold War Battle over German Identities," *Journal of Modern History* 68 (1996): 592.

64 Pierro Scaruffi, "Rolling Stones," *A History of Rock Music 1951–2000*, http://www.scaruffi.com/vol1/stones.html (accessed Apr. 15, 2008).
65 Michael Baumann, *Terror or Love? Bommi Baumann's Own Story of His Life as a West German Urban Guerrilla*, Helene Ellenbogen and Wayne Parker trans. 1st edn. (New York, 1979), 23.
66 Sabine Von Dirke, *All Power to the Imagination! The West German Counterculture from the Student Movement to the Greens* (Lincoln, 1997), 41.
67 Vaneigem quoted in Mossuz-Lavau, *Les Lois de l'Amour*, 141.
68 Richard Neville, *Play Power* (London, 1970), 278.
69 Arsan, "An Open Letter to Paul VI on the Pill," 297.
70 "Garbage or Nothing," *Oz* 14 (1968), 9–10.
71 Von Dirke, *All Power to the Imagination!* , 41.
72 Arthur Marwick, *The Sixties: Cultural Revolution in Britain, France, Italy, and the United States, c.1958–c.1974* (Oxford, 1998), 558.
73 Daniel Cohn-Bendit and Gabriel Cohn-Bendit, *Obsolete Communism; the Left-Wing Alternative*, Arnold Pomerans trans. 1st edn. (New York, 1968), 29–30.
74 Raoul Vaneigem, *The Revolution of Everyday Life*, Donald Nicholson-Smith trans. (Welcombe, England, 2003 [1967]), 41.
75 These graffiti taken from www.bopsecrets.org (accessed Apr. 15, 2008). Translated by Ken Knabb, March 1999; bopsecrets drew them primarily from Julien Besançon's *Les murs ont la parole* (Tchou, 1968), Walter Lewino's *L'imagination au pouvoir* (Losfeld, 1968), Marc Rohan's *Paris '68* (Impact, 1968), René Viénet's *Enragés et situationnistes dans le mouvement des occupations* (Gallimard, 1968), Maurice Brinton's *Paris: May 1968* (Solidarity, 1968), and Gérard Lambert's *Mai 1968: brûlante nostalgie* (Pied de nez, 1988).
76 For this theme, and the earlier, moderate homosexual rights movement, see Julian A. Jackson, "Sex, Politics, and Morality in France, 1954–1982," *History Workshop Journal* 61 (2006): 80.
77 Martel, *The Pink and the Black*, 30–45.
78 Gilles Deleuze and Félix Guattari, *Anti-Oedipus: Capitalism and Schizophrenia*, Robert Hurley, Mark Seem, and Helen R. Lane trans. (Minneapolis, 1983), 25, 351, 366.
79 Guy Hocquenghem, *Homosexual Desire*, Daniella Dangoor trans. (Durham; London, 1993), 131.
80 Martel, *The Pink and the Black*, 168.
81 Ibid., 16.
82 Vaneigem, "From Wildcat Strike to Total Self-Management," chapter 3.
83 Martel, *The Pink and the Black*, 24, 139.
84 Alan Travis, "Oz Trial Lifted Lid on Porn Squad Bribery " *Guardian*, Nov. 13, 1999.
85 Clarissa Smith, "A Perfectly British Business: Stagnation, Continuities, and Change on the Top Shelf," in *International Exposure: Perspectives on Pornography*, ed. Lisa Z. Sigel, (New Brunswick, 2006), 155.
86 Martel, *The Pink and the Black*, 76. For wider parallels, see Jeffrey Weeks, *Sexuality and Its Discontents* (London, 1985), 221–3.
87 Michel Foucault, *The History of Sexuality: An Introduction*, Robert Hurley trans. (New York, 1990).
88 Verena Stefan, *Shedding and Literally Dreaming*, Johanna Steigleder Moore and Beth E. Weckmueller trans. (New York, 1994), 6.
89 Michael Seidman, *The Imaginary Revolution: Parisian Students and Workers in 1968* (Oxford, 2004), 82.
90 Reiche, *Sexuality and Class Struggle*, 149.
91 Rowbotham, *Promise of a Dream*, 158.
92 Mette Ejlersen, *I Accuse*, Marianne Kold Madsen trans. (London, 1969), 105; Anne Koedt, "The Myth of the Vaginal Orgasm," *Philosophical Snippets, Alan Soble's Web Page* (1970), http://scriptorium.lib.duke.edu/wlm/notes/#myth (accessed Apr. 18, 2008).

93 Stefan, *Shedding*, 55.
94 Germaine Greer, *The Female Eunuch* 1st American edn. (New York, 1971), 305; Germaine Greer, "In Bed with Englishmen," *Oz* 1 (1967), 9–19.
95 Stefan, *Shedding*, 61.
96 Irigarary quoted in Martel, *The Pink and the Black*, 81.
97 Siegrid Schäfer, "Sexual and Social Problems of Lesbians," *Journal of Sex Research* 12 (1976): 259.
98 Collins, *Modern Love*, 161.
99 Heather Macrae, "Morality, Censorship, and Discrimination: Reframing the Pornography Debate in Germany and Europe," *Social Politics* 10 (2003): 327.
100 The *Sun* quoted in Jeremy Seabrook, "Agenda: The Disease Waiting in the Wings," *Guardian*, Dec. 22, 1986.
101 Tom Sharratt, "Preacher Anderton Thunders against the Gays," *Guardian*, Dec. 12, 1986.
102 Sir Immanuel Jakobovits, "Only a Moral Revolution Can Contain This Scourge," *The Times*, Dec. 27, 1986.
103 Signild Vallgårda, "Problematizations and Path Dependency: Hiv/Aids Policies in Denmark and Sweden," *Medical History* 51 (2007): 99–112.
104 Martel, *The Pink and the Black*, 247.
105 Davidson, "The Sexual State," 513.
106 Anna Marie Smith, *New Right Discourse on Race and Sexuality: Britain, 1968–1990* (Cambridge, 1994), 183–220.
107 Gunter Frankenberg, "Germany: The Uneasy Triumph of Pragmatism," in *AIDS in the Industrialized Democracies*, ed. David L. Kirp and Robert Bayer, (New Brunswick, 1992), 116.
108 Monika Steffen, "France: Social Solidarity and Scientific Expertise," in *AIDS in the Industrialized Democracies*, 136.
109 Michael Pollack, *The Second Plague of Europe: AIDS Prevention and Sexual Transmission among Men in Western Europe* (Binghamton, New York, 1994), 16.
110 Ibid., 18.
111 Martel, *The Pink and the Black*, 200–27, 304.
112 Fabienne André Worth, "*Le Sacré Et Le Sida* (Aids): Sexuality and Its Contradictions in France, 1971–1996," *Discourse* 19 (1997): 92–101.
113 Camille Robcis, "How the Symbolic Became French: Kinship and Republicanism in the Pacs Debates," *Discourse* 26 (2004): 110–35; Joan Wallach Scott, *Parité! Sexual Equality and the Crisis of French Universalism* (Chicago, 2005), 108.
114 Valerie Sperling, "Peeking Behind the Celluloid Curtain: Glasnost and Explicit Sex in the Soviet Union," *Journal of Popular Film and Television* 18 (1991): 12.
115 Mikhail Ivanov, "Exploring Russia's Sexual Revolution," *Russian Life* 42 (1999): 10–21.
116 Paul W. Goldschmidt, "Pornography in Russia," in *Consuming Russia*, ed. Adele Marie Barker, (Durham, 1999), 323.
117 Lucian Turcescu and Lavinia Stan, "Religion, Politics and Sexuality in Romania," *Europe-Asia Studies* 57 (2005): 302.
118 Don Kulick, "Sex in the New Europe: The Criminalization of Clients and Swedish Fear of Penetration," *Anthropological Theory* 3 (2003): 205; Yvonne Svanström, "Through the Prism of Prostitution: Conceptions of Women and Sexuality in Sweden at Two Fins-De-Siècle," *Nora, Nordic Journal of Women's Studies* 13 (2005): 50–8.
119 Gill Allwood, "Prostitution Debates in France," *Contemporary Politics* 10 (2004): 152.
120 Ahmadi Nader, "Rocking Sexualities: Iranian Migrants' Views on Sexuality," *Archives of Sexual Behavior* 32 (2003): 231.

121 Sven-Axel Mansson, *Cultural Conflict and the Swedish Sexual Myth: The Male Immigrant's Encounter with Swedish Sexual and Cohabitation Culture* (Westport, CT, 1993), 93–174.

122 Ian Buruma, *Murder in Amsterdam: The Death of Theo Van Gogh and the Limits of Tolerance* (New York, 2006), 200.

123 Fadela Amara and Sylvia Zappi, *Breaking the Silence: French Women's Voices from the Ghetto*, Helen Harden Chenut trans. (Berkeley, 2006 [2003]), 63–182.

124 Thanks to Paola Bacchetta for this insight.

125 Jytte Klausen, *The Islamic Challenge: Politics and Religion in Western Europe* (Oxford ; New York, 2005), 173–188; Bronwyn Winter, "Secularism Aboard the Titanic: Feminists and the Debate over the Hijab in France," *Feminist Studies* 32 (Summer, 2006): 279–98.

126 Pope Benedict XVI, "Deus Caritas Est," *Papal Encyclicals* (2007), http://www.papalenclcyicalsonline.net (accessed Apr. 15, 2008).

127 Peter Ford, "What Place for God in Europe," *Christian Science Monitor*, Sept. 7, 2005.

128 Betty Hilliard, "The Catholic Church and Married Women's Sexuality: Habitus Change in Late 20th Century Ireland," *Irish Journal of Sociology* 12 (2003): 28–48.

129 Marina A. Adler, "Social Change and Declines in Marriage and Fertility in Eastern Germany," *Journal of Marriage and the Family* 59 (February, 1997): 45.

130 Jacqueline Darroch, Jennifer J. Frost, and Susheela Singh, *Teenage Sexual and Reproductive Behavior in Developed Countries: Can More Progress Be Made? A Report of the Guttmacher Institute*, (New York, 2001), 129–34.

131 Susheela Singh, Jacqueline E. Darroch, and Jennifer Frost, "Differences in Teenage Pregnancy Rates among Five Developed Countries: The Role of Sexual Activities and Contraceptive Use," *Family Planning Perspectives* 33 (Nov/Dec 2001): 247.

132 Cas Wouthers, *Sex and Manners: Female Emancipation in the West, 1890–2000* (London, 2004), 144.

133 Gunter Schmidt , Dietrich Klusmann, Uta Zeitzsche, and Carmen Lange, "Changes in Adolescents' Sexuality between 1970 and 1990 in West-Germany," *Archives of Sexual Behavior* 23 (1994): 511.

134 Debbie Andalo, "Chastity Ring Centre of New School Religion Row," *Guardian*, May 14, 2007.

135 Molly Moore, "More Longtime Couples in France Prefer L'amour without Marriage," *Washington Post*, Nov. 6, 2006.

136 Bo Lewin, "Sexual Intercourse and Partners," in *Sex in Sweden*, ed. Bo Lewin, (Stockholm, 2000), 77.

137 John Gagnon, Alain Giami, Stuart Michaels, and Patrick de Colomby, "A Comparative Study of the Couple in the Social Organization of Sexuality in France and the United States," *Journal of Sex Research* 38 (2001): 27.

138 Kathleen Kiernan, "Cohabitation in Western Europe," *Population Trends* 96 (1999): 25–32.

139 http://en.wikipedia.org/wiki/Civil_unions_in_Italy (accessed Apr. 15, 2008).

140 Dagmar Herzog, "The Reception of the Kinsey Reports in Europe," *Sexuality & Culture* 10 (Winter, 2006): 45.

141 Alain Giami, "La Banalité Sexuelle," *Passant* 45–46 (2003), http://www.passant-ordinaire.com/revue/45–46–551.asp (accessed Apr. 18, 2008).

142 Anne G. Sabo, "The Status of Sexuality, Pornography, and Morality in Norway Today," *Nora, Nordic Journal of Women's Studies* 13 (2005): 38.

143 John Phillips, "Old Wine in New Bottles? Literary Pornography in Twentieth-Century France," in *International Exposure: Perspectives on Modern European Pornography 1800–2000*, ed. Lisa Z. Sigel, (New Brunswick, 2005), 130.

144 Christina Rogala and Tanja Tyden, "Does Pornography Influence Young Women's Sexual Behaviour?," *Women's Health Issues* 13 (2003): 39–43; Sven-Axel Mansson, "Commercial Sexuality," in *Sex in Sweden*, 267; Bente Træen, Line M Eek-Jensen, and Hein Stigum, "Sex Customers in Norway 2002," *Electronic Journal of Human Sexuality* 8 (2005), http://www.ejhs.org/volume8/Sex_Norway.htm (accessed Apr. 15, 2008).

145 Kaye Wellings, Julia Field, Anne Johnson, Jane Wadsworth, and Sally Bradshaw, *Sexual Behaviour in Britain: The National Survey of Sexual Attitudes and Lifestyles* (New York; London, 1994), 157–67; Alfred Spira, Nathalie Bajos, and André Bejin, *Les Comportements Sexuels en France. Rapport au Ministre de la Recherche et de l'Espace* (Paris, 1993), 128; Lewin, "Sexual Intercourse and Partners," 92.

146 Fred Hirsch, *Social Limits to Growth* (Cambridge, 1976), 101.

Index

Her Husband was a Woman!

Women's Gender-Crossing in Modern British Popular Culture

Alison Oram

'Astonishing' reports of women masquerading as men frequently appear in the mass media from the turn of the twentieth century to the 1960s.

Alison Oram's pioneering study of women's gender-crossing explores the popular press to analyse how women's cross-gender behaviour and same-sex desires were presented to ordinary working-class and lower middle-class people. It breaks new ground in focusing on the representation of female sexualities within the broad sweep of popular culture rather than in fiction and professional literature.

Her Husband was a Woman! surveys these engaging stories of cross-dressing in mass-circulation newspapers and places them in the wider context of variety theatre, fairgrounds and other popular entertainment. Oram catalogues the changing perception of female cross-dressing and its relationship to contemporary ways of writing about gender and desire in the popular press. In the early twentieth century cross-dressing women were not condemned by the press for being socially transgressive, but celebrated for their trickster joking and success in performing masculinity. While there may have been earlier 'knowingness', it was not until after the Second World War that cross-dressing was explicitly linked to lesbianism or transsexuality in popular culture.

Illustrated with newspaper cuttings and postcards, *Her Husband was a Woman!* is an essential resource for students and researchers, revising assumptions about the history of modern gender and sexual identities, especially lesbianism and transgender.

ISBN13: 978-0-415-40006-0 (hbk)
ISBN13: 978-0-415-40007-7 (pbk)

Images of Ancient Greek Pederasty

Boys Were Their Gods

Andrew Lear

Greek pederasty, or paiderastia – the social custom of erotic relations between adult men and adolescent boys – was a central characteristic of Greek culture. Both Greeks and non-Greeks saw it, along with the gymnasium with its intimate connection to pederasty, as markers of Greek identity. It is an important theme in Greek literature, from poetry to comedy to philosophy – and in Greek art as well. In Athenian vase-painting, in particular – the painted scenes that decorate clay drinking vessels produced in Athens between the 6th and the 4th centuries BC – pederasty is a major theme: indeed, pederastic courtship is one of the mortal activities most commonly depicted.

This lavishly illustrated book brings together, for the first time, all of the different ways in which vase-painting portrays or refers to pederasty, from scenes of courtship, foreplay, and sex, to scenes of Zeus with his boy-love Ganymede, to painted inscriptions praising the beauty of boys. The book shows how painters used the language of vase-painting – what we call 'iconography' – to cast pederasty in an idealizing light, portraying it as part of a world in which beautiful elite males display praiseworthy attitudes, such as moderation, and engage in approved activities, such as hunting, athletics, and the symposium. The book also incorporates a comprehensive catalogue of relevant vase-paintings, compiled by noted archaeologist Keith DeVries. It is the most comprehensive treatment available of an institution that has few modern parallels.

ISBN13: 978-0-415-22367-6 (hbk)
ISBN13: 978-0-415-22368-3 (pbk)

Related titles from Routledge

Gender in World History

2nd edition

Peter N. Stearns

Covering societies from classical times to the twenty-first century, *Gender in World History* is a fascinating exploration of what happens to established ideas about men and women, and their roles, when different cultural systems come into contact. This book breaks new ground to facilitate a consistent approach to gender in a world history context.

This second edition is completely updated, including:

- expanded introductions to each chronological section
- extensive discussion of the contemporary era bringing it right up to date
- new chapters on international influences in the first half of the twentieth century and globalization in the latter part of the twentieth century
- engagement with the recent work done on gender history and theory.

Coming right up to the present day, *Gender in World History* is essential reading for students of world history.

ISBN13: 978-0-415-39588-5 (hbk)
ISBN13: 978-0-415-39589-2 (pbk)
ISBN13: 978-0-203-96989-2 (ebk)

Available at all good bookshops
For ordering and further information please visit:
www.routledge.com

Gender

Journals from Routledge

www.informaworld.com/gender

Australian Feminist Studies

Editor-in-Chief:
Mary Spongberg, *Macquarie University, Australia*

Studies on Women and Gender Abstracts

Editor:
June Purvis, *University of Portsmouth, UK*

International Feminist Journal of Politics

Editors:
Sandra Whitworth, *York University, Canada*
Rekha Pande, *University of Hyderabad, India*
Catherine Eschle, *University of Strathclyde, UK*

Women: a Cultural Review

Isobel Armstrong, *University of London, UK*
Helen Carr, *University of London, UK*
Laura Marcus, *University of Edinburgh, UK*
Alison Mark, *University of London, UK*

Journal of Gender Studies

Editors:
Diane Dubois, *University of Lincoln, UK*
Angela Meah, *Leeds Metropolitan University, UK*
Blu Tirohl, *University of the West of England, UK*

Women & Performance: a journal of feminist theory

Managing Editor:
Jeanne Vaccaro, *New York University, USA*

NORA - Nordic Journal of Feminist and Gender Research

Editors:
Elina Oinas, *Nordic Africa Institute, Sweden*
Tutta Palin, *University of Turku, Finland*

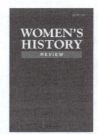

Women's History Review

Editor:
June Purvis, *University of Portsmouth, UK*

For more information about any of these journals visit:
www.informaworld.com/gender

When ordering, please quote:
XL03901A